ACCOUNT OF AN EMBASSY TO THE KINGDOM OF AVA IN THE YEAR 1795

ACCOUNT OF AN EMBASSY TO THE KINGDOM OF AVA IN THE YEAR 1795

SYMES, MICHAEL

GYAN

Published by

Gyan Publishing House
5, Ansari Road
Daryaganj, New Delhi-110002
Phone: 011-47034999, 9811692060
E-mail: books@gyanbooks.com

Distribution Network
gyanbooks.com
India, USA, Canada, UK, Australia, France

ISBN : 978-81-212-3011-7 (PB)

2nd Impression 2020

Printed at: Gyan Press, Delhi.

Account of an Embassy
to the Kingdom of Ava in the Year 1795
Author: Symes, Michael

AN

ACCOUNT

OF AN

EMBASSY

TO THE

KINGDOM OF AVA,

SENT BY

THE GOVERNOR-GENERAL OF INDIA,

IN THE YEAR 1795.

BY MICHAEL SYMES, ESQ.

MAJOR IN HIS MAJESTY'S 76TH REGIMENT.

LONDON:

PRINTED BY W. BULMER AND CO. CLEVELAND-ROW, ST. JAMES'S;
AND SOLD BY MESSRS. G. AND W. NICOL, BOOKSELLERS TO HIS MAJESTY,
PALL-MALL; AND J. WRIGHT, PICCADILLY.

1800.

TO THE

CHAIRMAN,

DEPUTY CHAIRMAN, AND DIRECTORS,

OF THE

HONOURABLE EAST INDIA COMPANY,

THIS

ACCOUNT

OF

AN EMBASSY TO AVA,

IS RESPECTFULLY INSCRIBED,

BY THEIR MOST OBEDIENT,

AND MOST HUMBLE SERVANT,

MICHAEL SYMES.

Welbeck-street,
February 24th, 1800.

PREFACE.

In presenting this Work to the Public, I obey the dictates of a duty incumbent on every person, the incidents of whose life have afforded him an opportunity of visiting countries that are either unknown, or imperfectly described; and by communicating his information, to add somewhat to the stock of general knowledge.

Of the kingdom of Ava, or the Birman Empire, so little is known to the European world, that many persons of liberal education, when the name of the country has been mentioned, were at a loss on what part of the globe to seek for its position; and some were even unacquainted with the existence of such a nation.

This obscurity renders any apology for introducing my Work to the Public, unnecessary; and I have only to lament my own inability to do justice to so important a subject. The military profession, in every part of the world, is unpropitious to literary attainments; but in India, where no repositories of European learning are to be found, and armies are continually moving over a vast region, it can hardly be expected that the soldier and the scholar should be united. It has been my lot to serve in that distant country from an early age, until I attained the meridian of life; and it may perhaps soften criticism, that I aspire not to the ornaments of language, and little aim at a polished structure of style: I have written my own book; my chief object is to be intelligible, and my single claim, to be believed.

The rise and fortunes of Alompra, and the establishment of the present Birman dynasty, supply a short, but highly interesting, period of oriental history; these extraordinary events having happened within the memory of many persons still living, are authenticated by individuals, who themselves bore a part in the transactions: and although their relations are liable to that bias which is inseparable from the human mind, when the passions are engaged, and self-interest is concerned; yet the leading facts are such as do not admit of misrepresentation; to these, therefore, I have confined myself, as closely as perspicuity would allow.

For the account of the disastrous fate of our countrymen at Negrais, and the destruction of the English and French factories, I am chiefly indebted to the repertory of Mr. Dalrymple; a most useful and judicious compilation, which has rescued from oblivion many valuable and curious papers.

The invasion of Ava by the Chinese during the reign of King Shembuan, and the subsequent expedition into the Cassay country, were recounted to me by an old Mussulman soldier who bore arms in both: he could have no inducement to deceive, and the leading circumstances of his narrative were confirmed from other quarters.

The events which took place in the southern countries, in Pegue and Siam, were so generally known, that inquiry need only be made to obtain information.

I am obliged to the kindness of Mr. Dalrymple for the construction of the General Map prefixed to this Work, which has been compiled from the materials collected by Dr. Buchanan, and transmitted to the Court of Directors; it is laid down on a contracted scale, being designed merely to point out the relative situation of the kingdom of Ava, with reference to other countries, and to ascertain its local position on the globe. The materials requisite to give an accurate topographical display of all the parts of so extensive an empire, could not be procured during the short period of our residence; but the ability, and indefatigable industry of Dr. Buchanan have effected much, to which the astronomical labours of Mr. Wood have considerably added. I cannot better do justice to the merits of these gentlemen, than by inserting the words of Mr. Dalrymple in a note on the subject of Ava geography.

"This part of Indian geography has hitherto remained " in inexplicable obscurity, and although much light has " been thrown on the subject in consequence of the Em- " bassy, of which this Work lays an account before the " Public, not only from the astronomical observations by " Ensign Thomas Wood, which do him the greatest credit, " but from the great mass of native geography, which the " assiduous pains of Dr. Buchanan, who accompanied the " Embassy in a medical capacity, have accumulated from " various persons.

"These maps obtained by Dr. Buchanan from the " natives, although they elucidate the geography, cannot " be considered as positive documents for the construc- " tion of an accurate map of these countries, not being " laid down geometrically, nor having even scales af- " fixed; indeed, it is not certain that any of them were " meant to be laid down by an uniform scale; the "wonder is, that there should be any thing like uni-"formity."

The applause of such respectable authority, cannot be enhanced by any encomium of mine. I am, however, happy in having an opportunity to acknowledge the able and friendly assistance which I received from these gentlemen: my thanks are also due to Captain Thomas, commander of the Sea-Horse, for his circumspect and prudent conduct in conciliating the inhabitants of Rangoon, during the time that I was absent at Ummerapoora.

Major Rennell, who never denies the use of his invaluable publications, to those who may require extracts from them, to illustrate their own works, has been so good, as to allow me to copy from his map of Hindostan a part of the Pegue coast, which we had not an opportunity of observing.

The representations of the costume of the country, I am persuaded are as faithful as pencil can delineate: the native painters of India do not possess a genius for fiction, or works of fancy; they cannot invent or even embellish, and they are utterly ignorant of perspective; but they draw figures and trace every line of a picture, with a laborious exactness peculiar to themselves: the Plate of the Kioum, or monastery, page 388, affords a curious specimen of their minute accuracy.

The Plate which represents the introduction of the English gentlemen, page 414, does not include all the objects that were in the original drawing, there not being sufficient room to admit them; it, however, exhibits a just view of the manner, in which the court was assembled. A print cannot convey an adequate idea of the brilliancy of the dresses, and the general effect.

The method of catching wild elephants in Ava, I was assured, is faithfully delineated in the drawing from which the Plate, page 346, was taken. This drawing was copied from a painting on glass, in the possession of the King: it corresponds with the mode practised in Siam, as described in a book, intitled, "A Relation of the Voyage to "Siam, performed by six Jesuits in the year 1685;" in which the following passage occurs: "The huntsmen, who "were mounted on tame elephants, threw their nooses so "exactly in the place where the elephants set their foot, "that they never failed of catching them." This manner of securing these powerful animals, I imagine, is not commonly used in other countries of the East.

Several of the human figures bear a striking resemblance

in feature to the originals, particularly the Sere-dogee, or Secretary of State, page 312, and the man and woman of the Kayn tribe, page 446: the dress and character, in all the figures, are extremely well preserved.

The kindness of Colonel Sir John Murray supplied me with the Code of Arracan Laws, from which the Birman Dherma Sastra is compiled. It should be observed, that all the various law tracts, in use amongst the Hindoos, throughout Hindoostan, in its extensive signification, the region of Hindoos, whether sectaries of Boodh, or of Brahma, are but so many commentaries on the Law of Menu, the great and acknowledged founder of Hindoo jurisprudence, whose original work has been translated with much elegance by the late Sir William Jones.

The account of the city of Pegue, and the stupendous temple of Shoemadoo, has already appeared in the fifth volume of the Asiatic Researches, printed at Calcutta; I did not, however, conceive, that it ought, on that account, to be omitted in a general description of the country. My official transactions are also inserted in the records of the Bengal government.

In the orthography of Birman words I have endeavoured to express, by appropriate letters, the sounds as they struck my own ear. At the same time it is proper to remark, that scarcely any two persons will apply the same English letters to the same Birman words: this variation, which extends to the writing of all Oriental languages, and is not easily to be remedied, greatly discourages the English reader, and diminishes the pleasure of perusing books, on the affairs of India. In the names of places I have in general followed the orthography of Mr. Wood, in his excellent Chart of the Irrawaddy, the great river of Ava.

In the prosecution of this work I have experienced so many acts of friendly attention, that were I to enumerate all the favours conferred on me, I should occupy more room, than the limits of a preface will allow. The patronage of the East-India Company is ever extended to those who can supply useful information on Oriental topics, whilst the encouragement which I received from this munificent body, was rendered doubly gratifying by the politeness of Mr. Inglis, then Chairman, and Mr. Bosanquet, Deputy Chairman, of the Court of Directors. To the spontaneous assistance of men pre-eminently distinguished for science, my book owes its most valuable contents. Sir Joseph Banks selected and described the plants; Mr. Dalrymple, as before mentioned, compiled the General Map; and Mr. Wilkins favoured me with the Shanscrit Alphabet, and pointed out the analogy of the languages. To these gentlemen my acknowledgments are particularly due, whilst, abstracted from a sense of personal obligation, it is a subject of pleasing reflection, that, in England, he who fairly endeavours to communicate beneficial or curious information, can never fail, however he may be a stranger, to obtain the disinterested aid of persons, themselves amongst the most celebrated for learning, and who are the patrons of literature in others. It constitutes a part of the national character, of that native liberality, which may be traced under various shapes, and is manifested in different forms, through every gradation of society, and amidst every class of men, who have the happiness to boast a British birth-right.

I cannot quit the subject without offering my tribute of thanks to my noble friend, Lord Teignmouth, with whom the mission to Ava originated; he selected me to execute the plans which he had formed; and his approbation of my labours, is numbered amongst the most flattering circumstances of my life.

Welbeck-street, MICHAEL SYMES.
February 24th, 1800.

CONTENTS.

CHAPTER VII.

CHAPTER VIII.

CHAPTER IX.

CONTENTS.

ERRATA.

Page 4. line 12. *for* exceed *read* exceeds.

15. — ult. *for* " his thus adherents" *read* " his adherents thus."

16. — 16. *for* Keoummeoum *read* Kioukhoun.

96. — 17. *for* Menderagee *read* Minderagee.

230. — 3. *for* " was" *read* " were."

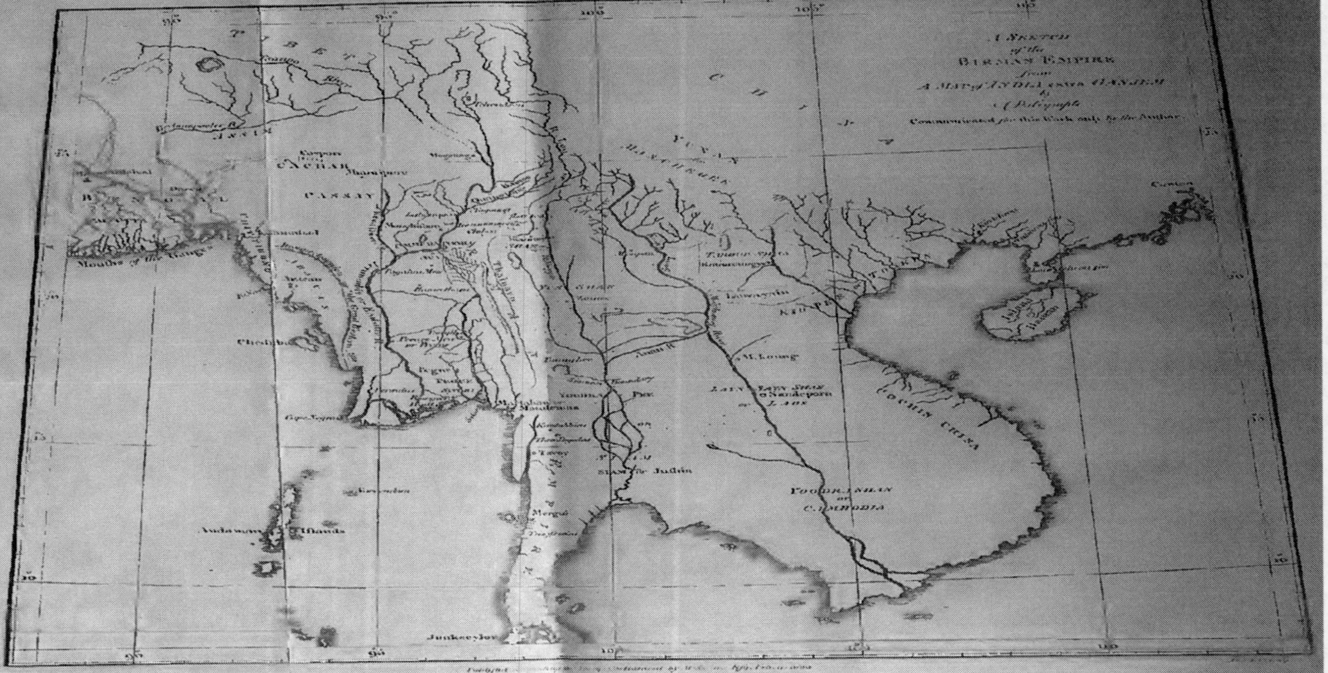
A Sketch
of the
BIRMAN EMPIRE
from
Communicated for this Work only by the Author.
CASSAY
CACHAR
Mouths of the Ganges
Andaman Islands
Junkceylon
Mergui
Tavoy
SIAM
M. Loung
CAMBODIA
COCHIN CHINA
YUNAN
Canton

EMBASSY TO AVA.

THERE are no countries on the habitable globe, where the arts of civilized life are understood, of which we have so limited a knowledge, as of those that lie between the British possessions in India, and the empire of China; concerning India beyond the Ganges, scarcely more was known to the ancients, than that such a country did exist. Undeserved importance is oftentimes attributed to that which is imperfectly known; thus, we find, in the Map of Ptolemy, the terms Aurea Regio, Argentea Regio, and Aurea Chersonesus, bestowed on countries eastward of the Ganges, and on the Peninsula that divides the Bay of Bengal from the Magnus Sinus, or Gulph of Siam. But although no satisfactory information is to be obtained from writers of antiquity, respecting the population, produce, extent, or geographical position of those regions; yet it may be concluded, that even at the remote era, when Ptolemy compiled his chart, the ports of the Eastern Peninsula were the seats of commerce, and resorted to by foreign merchants; as the Author distinguishes places of note, on the sea coast, by the titles Emporia; but with what people trade was carried on, or in what commodities they trafficked, is not any where ascertained.

From this period almost total darkness seems to have obscured India, extra Gangem, from the eyes of Europeans, until the enterprizing genius of Emanuel, at the close of the 15th century, opened a new world, and laid the foundation of general wealth to Europe, on the ruin of the Egyptian trade, and of the state of Venice. Early in the 16th century, the Portuguese made themselves masters of Malacca, and soon acquired influence among the neighbouring maritime states. To the writers of this nation, history is principally indebted for whatever information has been obtained of the eastern countries of India; but their narratives so abound in hyperbole, and they recount such extravagant stories, that credit must be denied to many of their assertions; whilst, at the same time, their writings furnish some accurate traits of the genius and disposition of the people whom they describe. Even the accounts of Mendez de Pinto, the prince of fiction, although an intelligent traveller, will enable his readers to form an estimate of the importance and civilization of nations which, at a later period have, by many, been erroneously considered in a condition bordering on wild barbarity.

From the testimony of Portuguese historians it appears, that in the middle of the 16th century, four powerful states divided amongst them the regions that lie between the south-east province of British India, Yunan in China, and the Eastern Sea; their territories extended from Cassay and Assam,* on the N.W. as far south-eastward as the island of Junkseylon. These nations were known to Europeans by the names of Arracan, Ava, Pegue, and Siam. Arracan, properly Yee-Kein, borders on the S. E. pro-

* There are some petty independent princes whose lands intervene.

vince of British India, and includes the sea coast, with what is called the Broken Islands, as far south as Cape Negrais;* Ava, the name of the ancient capital of the Birmans, has been usually accepted, as the name of the country at large, which is Miamma. This empire is situated eastward of Arracan, from which it is divided by a ridge of lofty mountains, called by the natives Anou-pec-tou-miou, or the great western hilly country. On the N. W. it is separated from the kingdom of Cassay by the river Keen-duem, on the north, it is bounded by mountains and petty independent principalities, that lie contiguous to Assam; on the north-east and east, it touches on China, and North Siam; on the south, its limits have so often varied, that it is difficult to ascertain them with any precision. The city of Prome,† or Pee, seems to be the original and natural boundary of the Birman empire, although conquest has since stretched their dominion several degrees farther south. Pegue, called by the natives Bagoo, is the country southward of Ava, which occupies the sea coast as far as Martaban, properly Mondimaa, Prome was its northern frontier, and Siam adjoined on the east. The kingdom of Siam, or Shaan, comprehended as far south as Junkseylon, east to Cambodia and Laos, and north to Dzemee (probably the Chiamee of Loubere), and Yunan in China This nation calls itself Tai, and is further distinguished by the appellations Tai yay, or great Tai, and Tay-nay, or little Tai; their former capital was named Yoodia,‡ or Yoodra; by De Pinto, Oodia; whence the Siamese are frequently, by the Birmans, denominated Yoodras. These boundaries, however, may be considered rather as the claim of each state, than its

* See Hamilton's new Account of the East Indies.

† It is doubtful whether Prome, of right, belonged to Ava or Pegue; it was claimed by both, and often changed its possessor.

‡ Called Juthea by Europeans.

actual possession: vicissitudes of victory and defeat alternately extended and contracted their dominions.

Pinto, and Faria de Souza, agree that the Birmans, though formerly subject to the king of Pegue, became afterwards masters of Ava, and caused a revolution in Pegue, about the middle of the 16th century. Hamilton, a much more recent author, says, that the kingdom of the Birmans extended from "Maravi," probably Mergui, near Tenasserem, to the province of Yunan in China, about 800 miles from north to south, and 250 from east to west. The Portuguese assisted the Birmans in their wars against the Peguers, and, according to Pinto, performed prodigies of valour. The account of the capture of Martaban,* and the treasures found therein, far exceed the limits of belief.

The Portuguese continued to exercise an influence in the Birman and Pegue countries, and a still greater in Arracan, so long as they maintained an ascendancy over other European nations in the East; but on the seizure of their settlements, and abridgment of their dominions by the Dutch, the consequence that had been deservedly annexed to the Portuguese name, sunk into insignificance; and the Christian settlers degenerated into a contemptible race, distinguished only by their feebleness and vice. During the reign of Louis the XIVth several splendid attempts were made to propagate the doctrines of the church of Rome, and advance the interests of the

* Speaking of the capture of Martaban, Pinto says, "During this siege, they of the city eat 3000 elephants; there were found 6000 pieces of artillery; as for gold, silver, precious stones, and jewels, that were found there, one truly knows not what they were, for those things are ordinarily concealed; wherefore it shall suffice me to say, that so much as the king of Brama had of Chaimbainham's treasure, amounted to an hundred millions of gold." The account of the feast of Tinagoojoo is ludicrously extravagant.

French nation, in the kingdom of Siam. Concerning these expeditions, accounts* of unquestionable fidelity have been published; little, however, is related of Ava and Pegue, with whom, the Abbé Choisy says, " the king of Siam was constantly at war."

In the beginning of the 17th century, both the English and Dutch had obtained settlements in various quarters of the Birman dominions, which were afterwards forfeited by the misconduct of the latter; and Europeans of all nations were banished from Ava. The English, many years subsequent to this expulsion, were reinstated in their factories at Syriam and Ava, where they appear to have traded, rather in the capacity of private merchants, than on the part of the India Company, in whose service they were not regularly enrolled. The Island of Negrais was likewise taken possession of by the English, and a survey made of it by one Weldon, in the year 1687. On this island the government of Fort St. George established a settlement. Little benefit, however, seems to have been derived from the acquisition: the affairs of the India Company, and indeed of the nation, were in too precarious a state in another quarter of Asia, to admit of sparing the supplies of men and money requisite for its effectual support.

The supremacy of the Birmans over the Peguers continued throughout the last, and during the first forty years of the present century, when the Peguers in the provinces of Dalla, Martaban, Tongo, and Prome, revolted; a civil war ensued, which was prosecuted on both sides with savage ferocity. In the year 1744, the British factory at Syriam was destroyed by the contending parties, and the views of commerce were suspended by precautions of personal security. Success long continued doubtful: at length the Peguers,

* Vide Loubere, &c.

by the aid of arms procured from Europeans trading to their ports, and with the assistance of some renegade Dutch and native Portuguese, gained several victories over the Birmans, in the years 1750, and 1751. These advantages they pursued with so much vigour, that, early in the year 1752, the capital of Ava was invested. The Birmans, disheartened by repeated defeats, after a short siege, surrendered at discretion. Dweepdee, the last of a long line of Birman kings, was made prisoner with all his family, except two sons, who effected their escape to the Siamese; from whom they found a friendly reception, and were flattered with assurances of security and succour.

Bonna Della, or Beinga Della, king of Pegue, when he had completed the conquest of Ava, returned to his own country, leaving his brother Apporaza to govern the late capital of the Birman king, whom he carried with him a prisoner to Pegue; enjoining his brother to reduce the refractory, displace suspected persons, and exact an oath of allegiance from such Birmans as should be suffered to retain their former possessions.

Matters at first bore the appearance of tranquillity and submission: the land-holders and principal inhabitants of the country around Ava, acknowledged themselves vassals of the conqueror, and accepted the prescribed oath. Alompra, a Birman of low extraction, then known by the humble name of Aumdzea,* was continued by the conqueror in the chiefship of Monchaboo, at that time an inconsiderable village, about 12 miles from the river, west of Keoum-meoum. This man, who possessed a spirit of enterprize and boldness equal to the most arduous undertakings, at first, like many others, dissembled the reluctance he felt at the imposition of a foreign yoke, and submitted to the necessity of fortune; but, unlike others,

* Signifying huntsman.

he harboured hopes of emancipation, and meditated on the best means of accomplishing his future purpose.

Soon after the Pegue king had reached his capital, he caused a general proclamation to be issued, in terms of insolent triumph, announcing to all nations of the earth, that the Birman king was become his prisoner; that the Birman country, being subdued by the prowess of his arms, was annexed, as a conquered province, to the Pegue monarchy, and that the city of Pegue was in future to be considered as the general metropolis. This proclamation, as might be expected, increased the hatred of the Birmans, and stimulated their desire of revenge. Alompra had at this time, in the town and neighbourhood of Monchaboo, 100 devoted followers, on whose courage and fidelity he could safely rely; he had strengthened and repaired the stockade that surrounded the town,* without awaking any suspicion in the minds of the Peguers, who never dreamt that a person so inconsiderable, would attempt an act of rebellion under the check of a numerous garrison, distant only 15 leagues. Their attention was directed to remoter provinces; and occupied by the fears they entertained, lest the sons of Dweepdee should return in force to recover the possessions of their dethroned father.

Thus, resting in imaginary security, there were not more than 50 Pegue soldiers in Monchaboo, who, on all occasions, treated the Birmans with contemptuous arrogance. Alompra, availing himself of the resentment excited by some particular act of indignity, roused his already well prepared adherents to active resistance, and attacking the Peguers with irresistible violence, put every man of that nation to the sword.

* Almost all towns, and even villages, in the Birman country, are surrounded by a stockade, in like manner as the villages in the Carnatic are inclosed by a bound hedge: the Birmans are very expert in erecting this kind of defence.

Alompra, after this act of open rebellion, still dissembling his real intention, and with a view to gain time, wrote to Apporaza in terms of the utmost humility, expressing much contrition for what had happened, representing it as a sudden gust of intemperate violence, arising from mutual irritation; at the same time, lavishly professing his attachment and fidelity to the Pegue government. These assurances, though they could not be expected to procure an unconditional pardon, yet had the desired effect, of rendering the Pegue governor less alert in preparation to reduce him; and so far was Alompra from being considered in a formidable point of view, that Apporaza, having urgent business at Pegue, left Ava under the government of his nephew, Dotachew, with directions to keep Alompra in strict confinement, as soon as he should be brought from Monchaboo, to which place a force, that was thought equal to the service, had been detached, on hearing of the massacre of the Peguers.

Approaching the fort of Monchaboo, the Peguers expected nothing less than resistance, and had come ill armed and equipped for encountering opposition; but they found the gates of the stockade shut against them, and heard threats of defiance, instead of supplications for clemency. Alompra did not give them leisure to recover from their surprise. At day-break the next morning he sallied forth at the head of his hundred adherents, and attacking the Peguers furiously with spears and swords, routed and pursued them for two miles. After this exploit he returned to his little fortress, and lost no time in preparing for a yet more hazardous contest; he represented to his people, that they must now resolve to conquer or perish; and he invited the Birmans of neighbouring towns to enrol themselves under his standard. Some obeyed the summons, but many were cautious of embracing his yet desperate fortune. In this affair, the number of Peguers defeated by Alompra, is estimated at one thousand.

News of this disaster reaching Dotachew at Ava, he seems to have acted with the most blameable irresolution; undecided what measure to adopt, whether to march in person at the head of his troops, which did not exceed three thousand, wait until a reinforcement should arrive, or retreat to Prome. Whilst he was thus deliberating, reports were daily received of some accession to the force of the adventurer, which, though in part true, were greatly exaggerated by the general consternation that prevailed throughout the city. Alompra had certain intelligence of the state of his interests in every quarter; and determined, by advancing boldly to Ava, to strike a decisive blow, before the fears of the enemy had subsided, and without giving time to recall the numerous detachments of Peguers that were scattered over the neighbouring provinces. The prudence and promptitude of this measure met with all the success it merited; Dotachew, when he heard of Alompra's intention, fled from Ava, whilst the Birmans in that city rose on the few Peguers that either could not, or did not choose to accompany their leader; all of whom they put to death. Alompra, finding that Dotachew had retreated, altered his first resolution of proceeding in person to Ava, and remained at Monchaboo, sending his second son, Shembuan, to take possession of the city, and garrison the fort.

These events appear to have taken place about the autumn of the year 1753: Dotachew did not halt until he reached Pegue. The misfortunes of the Peguers in the remote provinces alarmed Beinga Della, their king, for the safety of his own territories, and particularly for the northern towns and districts of Prome, Keounzeik, Tambouterra, &c. where the Birmans considerably outnumbered the Peguers. A large force was, notwithstanding, collected at Syriam, the command of which was given to Apporaza, who, in the month of January, 1754, sailed up the Irrawaddy, with a numerous fleet of war boats, to reduce the insurgents. At this time both the English and French nations had re-established their factories at Syriam, and, of course, had their separate interests. The French favoured the Peguers, whilst the English leaned to the Birmans; but until the vicinity of their residence again became the seat of war, neither engaged in open hostility: their partialities were manifested by petty assistance lent in secret, and supplies clandestinely conveyed, probably more with a view to private emolument, than from any enlarged political consideration.

When the English last took possession of Negrais, about the year 1751, their affairs were not conducted with prudence. A Mr. Hunter was appointed to the superintendance, who is represented as a man of capacity, but of an unconciliating and perverse disposition; the settlement, under his guidance, continued in a state of unceasing ferment; the Caffre slaves, who had been introduced for the purpose of cultivating the lands, rose upon their masters, and seizing on the boats belonging to the island, effected their escape. When Mr. Hunter died, he was succeeded by the person next in rank, under whose auspices the interests of the infant colony did not improve. In addition to their difficulties, the new settlers became unhealthy; these discouragements, however, did not induce them to evacuate the place, but their exertions were rendered languid by the diminished probability of ultimate success.

The season when Apporaza undertook his expedition to reduce Alompra, was the most unfavourable for making a speedy journey. During the dry months of January, February, March, and April, the waters of the Irrawaddy subside into a stream, that is barely navigable;* frequent shoals and banks of sand, retard boats of burthen, and a northerly wind invariably prevails. These obstructions, whilst they delayed the Peguers, gave opportunity to their enemies to collect the whole of their force, and arrange it in the most advantageous manner, to avert the impending danger.

The progress of Apporaza was uninterrupted until he approached the city of Ava, in the neighbourhood of which small parties of Birmans, from the adjacent banks, molested the boats of the Peguers by desultory attacks; they, however, did not much impede the fleet, which continued to advance. Approaching the fort, a summons was sent from the Pegue general to Shembuan, with a promise to spare his life, provided he immediately surrendered, and threatening exemplary vengeance should he refuse.

The fort of ancient Ava was of sufficient strength to maintain a protracted siege against an enemy inexpert in war, and Apporaza had good reason to suppose that resolution would not be wanting in the besieged. Shembuan replied, that he would defend his post to the last extremity.

In the meanwhile Alompra was unremitting in his preparations to receive the enemy; he had collected a considerable fleet at Keoum-meoum, and his army was recruited to the computed number of ten thousand, whose confidence increased on the approach of danger; whilst, on the contrary, the troops of Apporaza were disheartened by the accounts of the valour and strength of their foes; the Pegue commander, therefore,

* The Ganges, at the same season of the year, experiences a like reduction of its waters. The head of the Hoogly river continues shut for some months, during which, boats, to reach the Ganges from Calcutta, are obliged to navigate through the Sunderbunds, and afterwards surmount the stream with difficulty, owing to the impediments of numerous shallows and sand banks.

judged it more prudent to lead them at once to battle, than to waste time in the operations of a siege, the termination of which seemed precarious and remote.

With this design he left Ava in his rear, and proceeded with his whole force towards Keoum-meoum, where he found Alompra prepared to give him battle; an engagement ensued; the contest was chiefly confined to the fleets, whilst small parties of either army skirmished on shore. The action is said to have been obstinate and bloody: at length the Peguers, on a report being spread that Shembuan had left the fort of Ava, and was advancing to attack their rear, gave way, and fled with precipitation. Numbers were slaughtered in the retreat, and Shembuan issuing from the fort of Ava, completed their overthrow; Alompra pursued the fugitive Peguers as far as the city of Sembew-Ghewn, after which he returned to Monchaboo. Apporaza, with the remains of his army, retired to the province of Pegue.

The power of the Peguers now seemed hastening to its wane; yet, notwithstanding the recent check they had received, fresh preparations were made to prosecute the war. At this time, either real or pretended caution impelled them to a measure, not less repugnant to humanity, than, as the event proved, injurious to their own interests. It was alleged, that a conspiracy had been formed against the Pegue government, by their aged prisoner, the dethroned monarch of the Birmans, which had been discovered when on the point of execution. All the principal men of the Birman nation were supposed to be confederated in the plot; little formality was used to ascertain whether the accusation was true or false. On the 13th of October the Peguers rose, and, having first slain the unhappy monarch, slaughtered indiscriminately several hundred Birmans, sparing neither age nor sex. These sanguinary acts were as cruelly retaliated. The Birmans, though subdued, were still very numerous in the towns and districts of Prome, Keounzeik, Loonzay, and Denoobew. Exasperated at the murder of their monarch, and the fate of their brethren, they flew to arms, and with a barbarity nothing inferior to that which had been exercised by the Peguers, exacted a severe retribution. Prome, Denoobew, Loonzay, &c. changed masters, and their garrisons fell the victims of revenge.

During these transactions, the Birman adventurer was sedulously employed in improving his good fortune. The eldest son of the late deposed and murdered king, hearing that Alompra had raised the standard of revolt, returned to Monchaboo, and with a sect of brave and attached people, called Quois,* that inhabited an eastern province† of the empire, joined the fortunes of the adventurer. This young man, intoxicated by the successes of his party, had the imprudence to assume the distinctions of royalty, and attempt to exercise sovereign sway, as his hereditary right. Such claims, however, were wholly incompatible with the views of the ambitious chief, whose opposition soon convinced the prince, not only of the futility of his hopes, but likewise, that having harboured them, his own person was no longer secure; he therefore secretly withdrew, and again sought an asylum among the Siamese. This step so enraged Alompra, that, under pretence of a conspiracy, he caused near a thousand of the Quois to be put to death.

These events occupied the greater part of the year 1754, which was drawing to a close, when Beinga Della, having made fresh levies, marched from Pegue, accompanied by his brother, to retrieve the late disgraceful

* By some, Yoos. † Called Muddora, east of Ava.

defeats. The king proceeded with all expedition towards Denoobew and Loonzay; the Birmans, on his approach, evacuated those towns and fled. The Peguers advanced to Prome, a city well defended by a solid wall, a deep fosse, and a strong stockade. In this fortress the Birmans prepared to make a resolute defence, and wrote to Alompra, to acquaint him of their situation, entreating him at the same time to come to their aid with all possible dispatch. Beinga Della drove in the straggling Birmans that defended the banks of the river; a general assault followed, which was vigorously repulsed by the besieged; the Peguers then altered the mode of attack into a blockade; and finding that the garrison could only act on the defensive, Beinga Della dispatched part of his fleet and army up the river, as far as Melloon, in order to cut off supplies from the northward, and afford his own people more convenient subsistence.

Alompra, although at this time threatened with an attack from the fugitive prince, and the exasperated Quois, on receiving intelligence of the blockade of Prome, immediately detached Meinlaw Tzezo,* an officer of distinction, with 36 war boats, to the assistance of the garrison. This general, notwithstanding his force was far inferior to that of the enemy, boldly attacked the advanced guard at Melloon, and drove them back to Prome; but finding himself unequal to contend openly against the main body of the Peguers, he threw himself, by a skilful manœuvre, with a considerable supply of men and provisions, into the fort; a few of his boats only falling into the hands of the enemy, whilst the remainder effected their retreat to a place of security.

Forty days are said to have elapsed, without any material advantage on the part of the besiegers. The danger being past that threatened from the

* Grandfather of the present Viceroy of Pegue.

eastward, Alompra had, during this interval, collected the choicest of his troops, and leaving the care of Monchaboo and Ava to his two eldest sons, he proceeded down the river at the head of a formidable fleet, with a rapidity that equally tended to impress the enemy with dread, and inspire his own soldiers with confidence. The attack was not delayed beyond the hour of his arrival; the Peguers were quickly driven from a stockade they had erected on the north side of the fort; but the hottest action took place between the fleets: instead of an ineffectual fire from ill directed musquetry, the boats closed, and the highest personal prowess was evinced on both sides; knives, spears, and swords, were their weapons; after a long and bloody contest, victory declared for the Birmans, whilst the vanquished Peguers sought safety in a precipitate flight.

Alompra, who never failed diligently to improve his advantages, suffered no time to elapse in inaction; proceeding to Loonzay, he found the town evacuated, and, on taking possession, changed its name to Mayah-oun, signifying rapid conquest, by which it is at present known; and such was the terror of his arms, that a body of his troops advanced within a few leagues of Persaim, or Bassien, unmolested by the enemy, who did not attempt even to retard their progress.

The report of this disaster spread general consternation throughout the Pegue dominions; the fugitives that escaped gave such accounts, as the facts, exaggerated by their fears, might be supposed to dictate; a general insurrection of all the Birman subjects subordinate to the Pegue government was apprehended; and certain information of plots and conspiracies proved that these fears were not groundless. The Pegue king, who had retreated to Bassien, left that place by night, and retired to Pegue; his thus adherents, abandoned and terrified, thought of nothing but their own security; every man pursued what he judged the safest track; and so universal was the panic, that on the 17th of February, the town and fort of Persaim were completely deserted, the fugitives having first set fire to several houses, and consumed the public store-rooms, in which was deposited a large quantity of grain.

On the morning of the 23d, an advanced party of the Birman fleet came in sight; shortly after, a body of about 250 men landed, and marched up to a small factory* occupied by the English. These people were well armed, according to the country manner, and not appearing to entertain hostile intentions against any except the Peguers, the English superintendant, Captain Baker, received them with confidence, and, in the character of a peaceable trader, solicited protection for the servants and property of the India Company; his request was granted; neither depredation nor insult were offered to the English. About noon the Birmans departed, having first set fire to what remained of the town, and destroyed part of the stockade; they directed their route back to Keoummeoum, a town situated on the mouth of that branch of the great river that leads to Bassien and Negrais.

From this time until the 12th of March, frequent skirmishes took place between small parties of the Birmans and Peguers, in which the latter were generally worsted; an ineffectual attempt was made to repossess and defend Bassien, by the late Chekey, or Lieutenant, the man who had been second in authority whilst the place was subject to the Pegue government.

The seat of war was now likely to be confined to the mouths of navigable rivers, and the numerous creeks and canals that intersect the lower

* This factory, under the control of the Resident at Negrais, consisted of a few storehouses, erected near the river, for the purpose of facilitating the timber trade.

provinces of Pegue, and communicate between the larger streams; a vessel of burthen, provided with guns, and worked by a few Europeans, became a formidable foe to the open war boats of the natives, though well manned, and conducted with skill and courage. Alompra, who was at this time at Loonzay, or Meyah-oun, formed a right estimation of the advantage to be derived from an alliance with nations so well versed in the arts of maritime war; in order, therefore, to engage the good offices of the English, or at least stipulate for their neutrality, he sent a deputation to Mr. Brooke, Resident at Negrais, and at that time chief of all the English factories.

On the 13th of March, a fleet of twenty-five Birman boats arrived at Bassien, having on board two Birman deputies, accompanied by an Armenian and a Mussulman, as interpreters. These personages brought a letter from Alompra, directed to Mr. Brooke, couched in terms of friendship; but not deeming it prudent to venture with so small a force through the Pegue districts to Negrais, the English superintendant undertook to forward a copy of the letter, whilst the deputies returned to a secure post up the river, at no great distance from Bassien, there to wait an answer, which was expected in four or five days.

At the expiration of the computed time, the schooner, that had been dispatched to Negrais, returned, bringing an order from Mr. Brooke to Captain Baker, to accompany the deputies to Negrais, and to repair thither as speedily as possible: the deputation accordingly left Bassien on the 19th of March, 1755, and reached Negrais on the 22d, at night.

The business of the deputies was not concluded until the 26th; when, having received an answer to Alompra's letter, and their final dismission, they departed, attended by Captain Baker. Approaching Bassien, they were astonished to find the place in the hands of the enemy. A detachment of 3000 Peguers, in 60 war boats, had arrived during their absence; and on the 26th, engaged and captured all the boats that waited to convoy the deputies to their master. Captain Baker finding it impracticable to proceed, conducted the deputies back to Negrais, where they returned on the 3d of April, purposing to wait the occurrence of some more favourable opportunity.

The impediments that had thus prevented the return of the deputies were of short duration. On the 21st of April, 1755, the Peguers received certain intelligence that Alompra had attacked Apporaza, in his camp at Synyangong, and that their countrymen had suffered a total defeat; their own numbers being greatly diminished by desertion, Bassien became no longer a place of safety; they judged it therefore most prudent to withdraw towards Syriam. On the 23d, the ruins of the town, and its vicinity, were completely evacuated, and the navigation of the river again opened to the Birmans.

The retreat of these troops was well timed; several detached parties of Birmans appeared on the subsequent days; and on the 28th, a body of 1000 men arrived at Bassien, a small number by land, the rest by water, with 40 war-boats; they experienced no resistance, and made a few prisoners. A strong convoy was sent down to Negrais to escort the deputies, who now pursued their journey without molestation; they returned on the 3d of June to Bassien, and left it on the 5th, with a letter from the resident at Negrais to Alompra, who had reached Dagon* early in the preceding month.

* Now called Rangoon. Dagon is the name of a celebrated temple, a short distance from the present city.

The victory gained by Alompra at Synyangong, in the end of April, was decisive; the Peguers disheartened, fled to Syriam; and many did not halt until they reached Pegue. Among the latter was Apporaza, who left the defence of Syriam to a relation of the king of Pegue. The fortifications consisted of a feeble rampart, protected by a palisade, and an inconsiderable fosse, almost dry. Light as such obstacles would appear to regular troops, they presented a formidable opposition to the desultory attacks of an undisciplined rabble.

The French and English factories at Syriam were at this time in a state of rivalry, such as might be expected from the spirit of national emulation, and the avidity of traders on a narrow scale; the situation of both became at this juncture highly critical; danger approached, from which they could not hope to be entirely exempt. It was not to be expected that they would be suffered to remain in neutral tranquillity, indifferent spectators of so serious a contest; it therefore became necessary to adopt some decided line of conduct, in order to avoid being considered as a common enemy, whilst the contending powers seemed equally anxious to attach them. In this difficult situation neither the French nor the English seem to have acted with policy or candour; and the imprudence of certain individuals, finally, involved others as well as themselves, in fatal consequences.

Monsieur Bourno, the chief of the French factory, in the interest of the Peguers, but apprehensive of the power, and dreading the success of the Birmans, had recourse to dissimulation, and endeavoured to steer a middle course. Under pretence of occupying a station where he could more effectually aid the Peguers, he embarked on board a French ship, and with two other vessels belonging to his nation, dropped down from Syriam, and moored in the stream of the Rangoon river. Finding, soon after, that Alompra was likely to be victorious, he determined, if possible, to secure an interest in that quarter. With this intent, he quitted his ship, accompanied by two of his countrymen, and proceeded in a boat to Dagon, where Alompra received him with marks of distinction and kindness; but on the second day after the departure of Monsieur Bourno, the officer whom he left in charge of the ship during his absence, in concert with a missionary who had long resided at the factory, either impelled by fear, or prevailed upon by some secret influence, weighed anchor suddenly, and returned to the Peguers at Syriam, without permission from his commander, or even advising him of his intention.

So extraordinary a step surprised Alompra exceedingly; he taxed Bourno with deceit; the Frenchman protested his own innocence, and argued the improbability of his assenting to any such measure, whilst he remained in the Birman camp. He sent an order to his officers to return immediately, an injunction that was disregarded by them, under plea of their commander being a prisoner. He then requested leave from Alompra to go in person, and bring back the ship; to this the king consented, on condition of leaving one of his attendants (Lavine, a youth) as an hostage for his certain return.

From the procedure of Mr. Brooke, resident at Negrais, in his reception of the Birman deputies, and the aid of military stores sent by him to the Birmans, the English, when it became necessary to avow the side they meant to espouse, seem to have declared explicitly for the Birmans; and this principle was adopted not only by the resident at Negrais, but also by the factory at Syriam. The Hunter schooner, belonging to the India Company, the Elizabeth, a country ship, commanded by Captain Swain, and two other vessels, left Syriam in the month of May, and joined the Birmans at Dagon. In the beginning of June, the Company's snow, Arcot, bound to Negrais, commanded by a Captain Jackson, having on board Mr. Whitehill, a gentleman in the service of the East India Company, proceeding to Negrais in an official capacity, put into the Rangoon river, through stress of weather. A boat that had been sent in to fetch a pilot, returned, with an account of the state of affairs; and brought a letter, and an invitation from Alompra to Captain Jackson, to carry his vessel up to Dagon, promising him every aid that the place afforded.

On the 6th of June the Arcot reached Dagon; and Mr. Whitehill went on shore to pay his respects to the Birman king, by whom he was received in a manner that gave no apparent cause for complaint.

After the defeat of the Peguers at Synyangong, and the acquisition of Dagon by Alompra, the English ships sailed from Syriam voluntarily, and came to Dagon to assist the Birmans, in conformity to the evident determination of Mr. Brooke, whose reception of the Birman deputies, together with his subsequent conduct, clearly evinced his friendly intentions towards that nation. Until the arrival of the Arcot, with Mr. Jackson and Mr. Whitehill, no subject of offence seems to have been given to the English by the Birmans.

A short time previous to the arrival of the Arcot, Apporaza returned from Pegue to Syriam, and reassumed the command; he had been made acquainted with the negotiation carrying on between Mr. Brooke at Negrais and the deputies of Alompra; and in order to counteract its effects, commenced a secret correspondence with Captain Jackson. His arguments seem to have strongly influenced that gentleman, and given a decided bias in his favour. Ground of accusation was soon found against the Birmans; personal ill treatment was heavily complained of, which the tenour of Mr. Jackson's dispatches does not satisfactorily establish.

An attempt was shortly after made by the Peguers to surprise the Birman camp, and recover Dagon. Notwithstanding the land forces marched by night, and the fleet advanced with celerity, increased by a rapid tide, they were discovered in time for the Birmans to prepare for their reception. The boats first arriving, were repulsed by a heavy fire from the banks, which were lined with Birman troops. The post of Dagon could only be taken on the side of the land by a resolute assault. The attack of the Peguers was feeble and ineffectual; disheartened by the failure of their fleet, and destitute of able leaders, they soon abandoned their enterprize. An irregular fire of musquetry continued until noon, when the Peguers retreated to Syriam, little loss being sustained on either side.

During this spiritless contest, the English maintained a perfect neutrality, not a shot was discharged from any of the ships; a circumstance that tended to create suspicion in the minds of the Birmans: their distrust, however, seems to have been lulled by assurances of friendship, and probably by the expectation of a supply of cannon and stores from Negrais, which Mr. Brooke had announced his intention of sending, under care of Messrs. Baker and North; whom he meant to depute to the Birman king. Alompra had, a short time before, left Dagon to quell a disturbance in the northern provinces, caused by the Quois and Siamese; who, taking advantage of his absence, had invaded his country, and excited an insurrection of the inhabitants in favour of the fugitive son of the ancient monarch. The sudden appearance of the victorious chief disconcerted his enemies; he soon reduced the disobedient, and obliged the Siamese to retire within their own frontiers.

Previous to his departure from Dagon, Alompra laid the foundation of the town now so well known by the name of Rangoon, or Dzangoon, which signifies victory atchieved. Here stood, in former days, a large and populous city, called in the Pali, or sacred language, Singoun-terra; the site of which Alompra diligently explored, and raised on its ruins the present flourishing sea-port of the Pegue dominions. Dagon, often called Shoe Dagon, or the golden Dagon, is a name peculiar to the temple; a noble edifice, three miles distant from the banks of the river. When Alompra left his camp, he appointed Meinla-Meingoun to command in his absence; an officer of approved reputation and valour.

The clandestine negotiations between the English and Peguers appear to have been renewed after this action; several messages passed, in which a fresh attack on the Birmans was concerted, and the aid of the Company's ships promised to the Peguers, who were thus to be befriended by the whole European force, both French and English. Confiding in their new allies, and assured of victory, the war-boats of the Peguers, during the night, dropped down the Pegue river, and with the French ships moored in the stream of the Irrawaddy,* waiting the return of tide to carry them to Rangoon. Dawn of day discovered them to the Birmans, whose general immediately sent for the English gentlemen, to consult on the best means of defence. At this interview, the Birmans candidly acquainted Mr. Whitehill how ill satisfied they were with the conduct of the English commanders during the late action, and desired a promise of more active assistance on the present occasion: Mr. Whitehill replied, that without the Company's orders, he was not authorized to commence hostilities on

* The name of the great river of Ava. This branch is often called the Rangoon river, to distinguish it from that which leads to Bassien.

any nation; but if the Peguers fired on the English ships, it would be considered as an act of aggression, and resented accordingly. How much it is to be lamented, that such prudent and equitable principles were not better observed; the departure from them affixed a stain on the national honour, which the lapse of more than forty years has not been able to expunge.

The Pegue force was, on this occasion, highly formidable; it consisted of two large French ships, and an armed snow, belonging to the king of Pegue, with 200 Teilee, or war-boats. On the approach of this armament, the Birmans manifested their apprehensions, by repeating their entreaties to the English. Owing to the time of the tide, it was noon before the Pegue boats could advance. When within cannon shot, the French ships came to anchor, and opened their guns, whilst a brisk discharge of musquetry was poured from the Pegue boats on the Birman fleet, that, for the most part, had taken shelter in a creek, and were protected by the fire kept up from a grove of mangoo trees, on the banks of the river, in possession of the Birmans, around which they had raised temporary works, and erected a battery of a few pieces of ship cannon; which, from being ill served, did little execution. At this juncture the English ships Hunter, Arcot, and Elizabeth, commenced a fire on the Birman fleet. Thus assailed by unex pected foes, the Birmans were obliged to abandon their boats, and take shelter in the grove. Had the Peguers improved the critical opportunity, and pursued their advantage with resolution, this action might have retrieved their declining interests, and restored to them possession of the lower provinces. In vain the Europeans persuaded them to attempt the capture of the Birman fleet; too timid to expose themselves to a close discharge of musquetry from the grove, they were contented with the eclat of having compelled the enemy to retreat from their boats: the rest of the day was spent in distant random firing. During the night the English ships removed out of the reach of small arms; two men being killed on board the Arcot. The Peguers kept their situation for some days, during which much irregular skirmishing passed; when having exhausted their ammunition, without advancing their cause, the Peguers thought fit to return to Syriam, accompanied by the English and French ships, leaving the Birmans in possession of the fortified grove, and the lines of the newly projected town.

Apporaza, who held the chief command at Syriam, received the English with every mark of respect; judging this a favourable opportunity to regain the alliance of their nation, he wrote to Mr. Brooke at Negrais, inviting him to come in person to Syriam, and there settle terms of permanent connection. Mr. Brooke, in letters of a friendly tenour, excused himself from personal attendance, and requested that Mr. Whitehill might be suffered to proceed to his station at Negrais, and the Company's ships permitted to pursue their voyage to the same place; whither he ordered the several commanders immediately to repair. The compliance of Apporaza with this request, demonstrated his ardent desire to recover the good will of the English. Mr. Whitehill left Syriam, escorted by 20 armed boats, and proceeding through the rivers, reached Negrais on the 26th of August; the Hunter schooner sailed on the 26th of September following; the Arcot being delayed for some necessary repairs.

Whilst these matters were agitating at Dagon, Mr. Brooke was advancing his negotiations with Alompra; Captain Baker and Lieutenant North were delegated, with presents, and instructions, to conclude a treaty of amity and alliance with the Birman monarch.

It has been already mentioned that Alompra was under the necessity of leaving his post at Dagon about the middle of June, in order to suppress an insurrection of his own subjects, and repel the Siamese: the object of his expedition was attained with little difficulty, and he had the additional satisfaction to learn that his arms had been successful in Cassay, the inhabitants of which, taking advantage of the unsettled state of the empire, had thrown off their dependence. This country is separated from the kingdom of the Birmans on the north-west by the river Keen-duem, which, taking a south-east course, unites its waters with those of the Irrawaddy, a short way above the town of Sembew-ghewn. About the time that Alompra left Ava to relieve Prome, he detached a body of troops across the river, under the command of a distant relation, to chastize the Cassayers: these people had, for ages past, tasted the sweets of independence only at intervals, when the contests of the Birman and Pegue powers left them no leisure to enforce obedience. Thus accustomed to the yoke, though always ready for revolt, they were quickly reduced to submission; the prince, or rajah, who resided at Munnepoora, the capital of Cassay, sued for peace, which was concluded on terms advantageous to the Birmans; and, as is the custom, a young man and young woman, of the kindred of the rajah, were delivered as hostages for the due observance of the compact.

The English deputation proceeded in boats slowly up the river, which, at that season of the year, is swelled by mountain torrents, and the navigation rendered difficult by the rapidity of the stream. A short distance above Prome, they met a detachment, commanded by a Boomien, or general of rank, in its route to Dagon; it consisted of eighty boats, and 4000 troops, to reinforce the army acting against the Peguers. Captain Baker had an interview with the chief, who expressed sanguine hopes of reducing Syriam, and destroying the French ships that had assisted the Peguers

The late extraordinary conduct of the English shipping at Dagon, was no very favourable introduction to the delegates; nor did Captain Baker escape reproach for transactions in which he certainly had no share: to increase his embarrassment, he had the misfortune, the day after he parted with the detachment, to lose his colleague, Lieut. North, who died at Roung-Yooah, of a dysentery and fever. Captain Baker afterwards pursued his voyage, accompanied only by the Birmans. On the 8th of September he reached Ava, lately the metropolis of the empire. Alompra, partial to the scene of his first success, had removed the seat of government to Monchaboo, which he constituted his capital, and fixed on as the place of his future residence. At Ava Captain Baker was civilly entertained by the Governor; on the 12th he reached Keoum-meoum, situated on the west bank of the Irrawaddy, and on the 16th he received a summons to attend "the golden feet."* Leaving his boats, at noon the following day he proceeded by land to the royal presence; his reception was conducted with as much pomp and parade, as a king so recently elevated to his honours, and seated on a throne so imperfectly established, was capable of displaying. During this interview the new monarch, in his conversation, gave a striking instance of that intoxication which usually attends an unexpected and recent rise to power: yet his vain boastings were not accompanied by any mark of personal contempt or indignity to Captain Baker. He vaunted of his victories, and the extent of his empire, in a style of presumptuous vanity, equal to the arrogance of Xerxes; he upbraided our national character in the affair of the shipping at Dagon, alleging that he had treated the English with kindness, which they repaid by perfidiously breaking the promise given to him on his departure from Dagon. To these reproaches Captain Baker

*. A Birman expression used to denote the Imperial presence.

could only reply by expressions of regret; and a solemn declaration, that Mr. Brooke, so far from having authorized, knew nothing of such proceedings. Alompra listened to his assurances with more complacency than could well be expected from a despot, who had waded to a throne through the blood of his enemies.

At a second audience, a few days subsequent to the first, his Majesty dictated a letter, addressed to Mr. Brooke, in which he granted permission to the Company to establish factories at Dagon and Bassien; having determined on the total demolition of Syriam. Captain Baker made a further requisition of the Island of Negrais. Although this desire was not refused, the formal assignment was postponed, owing to a domestic misfortune, which gave the King much uneasiness; but as it was his Majesty's intention shortly to repair to Rangoon, to conduct in person the Pegue war, the completion of the grant was deferred to a future opportunity. Captain Baker, having obtained his dismission, set out for Keoum-meoum, and on the 29th of September embarked to return to Negrais.

Whilst friendship and union were thus likely to be established between the Birmans and the settlement at Negrais, the Peguers hazarded another attempt on the Birman post at Dagon, and were again assisted by the Arcot, and two private English ships, which, it is probable, on this occasion might have acted, in some degree, under compulsatory influence. Three English and one French ship, with 300 armed boats, constituted the Pegue force by water; and 10,000 men marched by land, to attack the heights at Dagon, and the fortified grove. The Birmans, with considerable ingenuity, constructed fire-rafts, consisting of a number of boats fastened together, and filled with combustible materials; these rafts were floated down a strong spring-tide to where the ships lay at anchor, and directed with such skill and effect, as to oblige them to slip their cables, and get under weigh, the French ship narrowly escaping destruction. This manœuvre effectually removed the vessels for that tide, and prevented a co-operation with the land forces, who, thus deprived of the support on which they chiefly depended, made an ineffectual charge on the Birman works: they were easily repulsed, and, with the fleet and army, retreated to Syriam; from whence they never again dared to hazard another enterprize.

The affairs of the Peguers were in this desperate state when Alompra returned victorious from Ava; his presence animated his own army, and spread a heavier cloud over the unfortunate Taliens.* He immediately changed the plan of operation: instead of waiting at Dagon, in fortified posts, the attack of the Peguers, he, in turn, became the assailant, and leaving the great river, boldly advanced his boats to the mouth of the Syriam stream; thereby cutting off all communication with the sea, and the countries to the west of Rangoon. Apporaza about this time retired from Syriam to Pegue, leaving his former station to be maintained by the chief Woon or Woongee, of the Pegue empire. Permission had previously been given to the English ships to depart with the Company's stores. Mons. Bourno, the French Resident, continued at Syriam, where, having moored his vessel close to the factory, he prepared to defend himself. The tide in the Rangoon river rises to an uncommon height; the river of Pegue, or, as it is often called, of Syriam, being fed by the influx of the sea, through the Rangoon river, sinks at low ebb into an inconsiderable stream. The French ship, when the water retired, touched the ground; the Birmans, profiting by her unmanageable state, during the recess of tide, brought gun-boats to bear in such a direction, as to annoy her without

* The Birmans call the Peguers Taliens.

exposing themselves. This judicious mode of attack proved successful; the ship was quickly disabled, and Mons. Bourno finding the post untenable, wrote a letter to Alompra, apologizing for his former conduct, and making fresh overtures of accommodation. The correspondence was either discovered, or suspected by the Peguers, who suddenly removed Mons. Bourno and his adherents into the fort of Syriam, before the purposed negotiation had time to be completed.

Alompra immediately took possession of the evacuated factory and vessel; after which he seemed desirous of attaining his object of Syriam, rather by blockade and famine than by hostile approaches; without attempting to assault the place, he continued in its vicinity, until the month of July, 1756. By such apparent inactivity on the part of the Birmans, the garrison was lulled into fatal security: Alompra, seizing a favourable opportunity, crossed the ditch in the dead of night, carried the outworks without resistance, and soon made himself master of the fort. The commandant, and the greater part of the garrison, favoured by the darkness, escaped to Pegue; many, however, were slain, and all the Europeans were made prisoners.

It has already appeared to have been the determined policy of the French to espouse the cause of the Peguers, and had succours from Pondicherry arrived before the state of things became too desperate, affairs would probably have worn a different aspect, and the Peguers obtained such an addition to their strength, as would have enabled them to conclude a peace on advantageous terms. But assistance in war, to be effectual, must be timely, and unless applied while the scales hang nearly even, often comes too late, and is found, not only to be useless, but even productive of deeper disappointment. In the present case, the French brought those supplies which the Peguers had long buoyed themselves with hopes of, at the unfortunate moment when the communication was cut off, when no relief could be conveyed to them, and all prospect of retrieving their disastrous fortunes had completely vanished.

Mons. Dupliex, Governor of Pondicherry, a man whose comprehensive mind perceived with clearness, whatever could benefit his nation, at this juncture deeply engaged in the important contest that was ultimately to determine the sovereignty of the East, being aware of the consequence of maintaining an influence in Pegue, had, notwithstanding the exigencies of his own situation, equipped two ships, the Galathié and Diligent, vessels of force, well manned and armed, and sent them, with a supply of military stores, to the assistance of the Peguers. Shortly after leaving Pondicherry, they separated; the Galathié had a speedy passage, but owing to a fatal and frequent error of mistaking the mouth of the Sitang river, which is a few miles to the eastward, for that of Rangoon, she did not arrive at the bar until two days after Syriam had fallen into the hands of the Birmans. The boat, sent by the French commander to bring down a pilot, was immediately captured. Alompra being apprized of the circumstance, ordered a pilot, in a country boat, to proceed to the Galathié, and compelled Bourno, who was then under rigorous confinement, to write to the Captain, encouraging him to proceed, and come up to Rangoon, assigning some frivolous excuse for the delay of the Galathié's boat, which he was given to expect would meet him on the way to town. The Captain imprudently became the dupe of this artifice; he weighed, and stood in with a strong flood tide, which in a few hours carried him to Rangoon, where the sudden seizure of his vessel prevented all possibility of retreat; the stores were brought on shore, and the consignments and papers proved that these supplies were meant for the assistance of the Peguers, and directed to Beinga Della, and his brother Apporaza. Alompra became so incensed, that he gave orders for the instant execution of Bourno, Martine, and the Captain and officers of the Galithié. This sanguinary mandate was obeyed with unrelenting promptitude, a few seamen and Lascars alone escaped; and these were preserved, for no other reason than to be rendered of use in the further prosecution of the war, and survived but to experience all the miseries of hopeless bondage.

The Diligent was more fortunate; having separated from her consort, she met with adverse winds, and was obliged to bear away for the Nicobar Islands; this delay prevented her reaching her intended port until six weeks subsequent to the disaster. The caution of the Captain saved him from suffering a similar fate; he got intelligence of the massacre of his countrymen in time to retire, and carried back news of the failure of the expedition, to Pondicherry, whence it was impossible to attempt the extension of further succour to the unhappy Peguers.

The rage of the conqueror was, on this occasion, exhausted on the French. Foreigners of other nations, who had been captured in Syriam, were treated less rigorously; some who incurred his displeasure, and had reason to dread its effects, were dismissed with admonitions, and suffered to depart. Among these were a few English, who had not been able to withdraw from Syriam, before it came into the enemy's possession.

The fall of Syriam seems to have determined the fate of the Peguers; cut off from communication with the western countries of Dalla and Bassien, deprived of the navigation of the Rangoon river and the Irrawaddy, and shut out from all foreign aid, their resources failed, and supplies by water could no longer reach them. The Bago Miop, or Pegue river, extends a very short distance to the north-north-east; the tide alone renders it navigable; where that influence fails, it degenerates into a streamlet which issues from a range of hills about forty miles above the city, remarkable only for their noisome and destructive atmosphere.

Notwithstanding these discouragements, the Peguers prepared to sustain a siege in their capital, which was in a better state of defence than is common in countries, where the science of war is so imperfectly understood. Situated on an extensive plain, Pegue was surrounded with a high and solid wall, flanked by small towers, and strengthened on each face by demi-bastions, equidistant; a broad ditch contained about three feet depth of water; wells or reservoirs supplied the town; the stupendous pagoda of Shoe Madeo, nearly centrical, built on an artificial eminence, and inclosed by a substantial wall of brick, served as a citadel, and afforded an enlarged view of the adjacent country. The extent, however, of the works, the troops necessary to defend them, and the number of inhabitants within the walls, operated to the disadvantage of the besieged, and aggravated the distresses they were shortly to endure.

As soon as the rainy season subsided, and the country, which between Pegue and Syriam is low and swampy, had emerged from the inundations of the monsoon, Alompra ordered his General, Meinla-Meingoung, to advance towards Pegue at the head of a body of troops. A few days after he followed in person with his whole army: in four marches they reached the vicinity of the city, through a country laid waste and depopulated. Circumvallation is a favourite practice of warfare with the Birmans, and famine a weapon on which they repose the greatest reliance. Alompra preferred these to the hazard of a repulse, in an attempt to storm, he invested Pegue with his army, and erected numerous stockades, at once to protect his own troops, and prevent communication with the country. Thus secured by his defences from surprize and sudden attack, fearless of any external enemy, and commanding the navigation of the river, he sat down in the month of January, 1757, to wait the slow, but certain effects of hunger and distress.

The fort of Pegue was occupied by the royal family and the principal nobles of the Talien nation. Among the highest in rank were Apporaza, brother of the king, Chouparea, his son-in-law and nephew, and Talabaan, a general who, on former occasions, had been distinguished by rendering his country signal services, and had raised himself by his valour to the first military honours of the state.

The Birmans, though superior in numbers, persevered in the passive system of reduction, and were not to be allured from the protection of their stockades. Two months thus elapsed in defensive inactivity. The consequences, however, were inevitable; want, and its sure concomitants, discontent and mutiny, began to rage within the walls. On this emergency the King summoned a council of all his family and chieftains: after expatiating on the straits to which they were reduced, and the hopelessness of relief, he declared his intention to sue for peace; and further, to propitiate the conqueror, he proposed sending to him his only unmarried daughter; as by such an act of homage alone he could expect to procure favourable terms. This proposal was listened to with sorrowful acquiescence by all but Talabaan, who is said to have cherished a secret passion for the maiden; for in this country, young women of the highest rank are not, after the manner of India, precluded from the sight and conversation of the other sex. The chief, with haughty indignation, reprobated the disgraceful sacrifice, inveighing against it in the sharpest terms; and concluded with an offer to sally forth at the head of six hundred chosen followers, and either raise the siege, and procure an honourable peace, or perish in the attempt; provided, in the event of success, the King would promise to bestow on him his daughter, as the reward of valour.

Struck with the gallantry of this proposal, the King apparently assented, and the council broke up; but Apporaza and the other chiefs, who long had beheld with jealousy the growing power and increasing fame of Talabaan, remonstrated against the measure, as an act still more derogatory to their monarch, than yielding his daughter as a peace offering to a sovereign potentate. The King, by these persuasions, was prevailed upon to retract the conditions. Talabaan, irritated at his disappointment, took an opportunity of leaving the fort at midnight, and with a few resolute attendants, forced his way in safety through the Birman camp; he afterwards crossed the Setang river, and marched to Mondimaa, or Martaban, where his family resided.

Two days after Talabaan had retired, the Pegue king, in pursuance of his first intention, wrote to Alompra, proposing peace on the terms which he had intimated to his council before the secession of his general. The Birman King readily accepted the offered pacification. A negotiation was opened, which terminated in an agreement, that the Pegue King should govern his country under the stipulation of doing homage to the Birman monarch; that the ancient boundary should be observed; and Prome, or Pee Miou, continue the frontier of the Pegue dominions to the north. A preliminary of these conditions was the surrender of the daughter of the Pegue monarch to the royal victor; Apporaza, her uncle, was appointed to convey her to the Birman camp, where they were received with music, feasting, and every demonstration of joy and amity.

Some days elapsed in festive ceremonies, during which both the besiegers and besieged had frequent and almost uninterrupted intercourse; the guards on both sides relaxed in their vigilance, and small parties of Birmans found their way into the city, whilst the Peguers visited the Birman camp without molestation or inquiry. Alompra, who, it appears, had little intention of adhering to the recent compact, privately introduced bodies of armed men, with directions to secrete themselves within the city, until their services should be required; arms and ammunition were also conveyed and lodged in places of concealment. Matters, however, were not managed with such circumspection as to prevent discovery; Chouparea, the king's nephew, received intimation of the meditated treachery: he instantly ordered the gates of the city to be closed, and having found out the repositories where the weapons were lodged, and detected many Birmans in disguise, he gave directions to put to death every man of that nation who should be found within the walls, and opened a fire upon such part of the Birman camp as was most exposed to the artillery of the fort.

Hostilities now recommenced with exasperated fury; Apporaza with his royal niece were detained in the Birman camp; the uncle under close confinement, whilst the lady was consigned to the guardians of the female apartments. The Peguers having gained no accession to their strength, and added little to their stores, during the short interval of tranquillity, were not in a better condition than before to resist the enemy. The Birmans observed the system of warfare they at first adopted; so that in six weeks, famine had again reduced the garrison to a deplorable state of wretchedness and want; the most loathsome reptiles were eagerly sought after and devoured, and the clamours of the soldiers could no longer be appeased. A few secret hoards of grain were by chance discovered, and many more were suspected to exist; the crowd thronged tumultuously round the quarters of Chouparea, on whom, after the secession of Talabaan, and the imprisonment of Apporaza, the care of defending the fortress entirely devolved. In order to silence and satisfy those whom he could not restrain, he ordered a general search for grain, and granted permission to the soldiers forcibly to enter whatever houses fell under suspicion. This licence was diligently improved, and the house of a near relation of the king was discovered to contain more grain, than either the present situation of affairs or his own wants could justify. The deposit was demanded, and as resolutely refused. The crowd, authorized by the permission of Chouparea, proceeded to take by violence what was not to be obtained by entreaty: a riot ensued, in which some lives were lost, and the prince was at length obliged to abandon his house. Repairing to the royal residence, he uttered violent invectives against Chouparea, whom he accused to the king of harbouring an intention to deprive his sovereign of life, and seize upon the imperial throne; and advised his majesty rather to throw himself on the generosity of the besiegers, and obtain the best terms practicable, than hazard the danger to which his person and kingdom were exposed from the perfidy of a faithless and powerful subject. The king, whose imbecility seems to have equalled his ill fortune, lent an ear to the complaints of a man stimulated by sudden rage, and personal jealousy; the unhappy and distracted monarch resolved to pursue his counsel; but being too timid openly to avow his weakness and suspicion, he sent secret proposals to Alompra to surrender the city to him, stipulating for life alone, and leaving the rest to the discretion of the conqueror. According to the plan agreed on, the Birmans advanced to the gates, which were immediately deserted: the Peguers fled in the utmost panic; many escaped in the confusion; the Pegue king was made prisoner, and the city given up to indiscriminate plunder.

Alompra, having thus triumphed over his natural enemy, and to all appearance, given a final blow to the Peguers, who, with their city, and their sovereign, lost the spirit of resistance, proceeded to bring into subjection the countries to the eastward, including the fertile districts situate between Pegue and the Three Pagodas; which were the ancient boundaries of the Pegue and Siam, or Yoodra territories. Talabaan had fled to Martaban, where his influence was still considerable, and his enterprizing spirit rendered him an enemy not to be despised. This chief, on the approach of Alompra, finding he had not force sufficient to oppose the Birmans, fled into the woods, leaving behind him some of his family, and many persons who were attached to his cause. Alompra seized on these, and, conformably to the barbarous custom of nations of the East, the innocent were condemned to suffer for the guilty: the unfortunate Talabaan was summoned to surrender, and menaces of destruction, in case of refusal, were held out against such of his family and adherents as had fallen into the conqueror's power. The danger to which his dearest connections thus became exposed, suppressed in Talabaan's mind all personal apprehension; he surrendered himself a voluntary prisoner, to preserve those whom he loved more than life. When brought into the royal presence, with unshaken but respectful resolution, he demanded the release of his friends, and his own sentence. Alompra, struck with such an instance of magnanimity, generously forgave him, and ordered the captives to be liberated. He afterwards raised Talabaan to a distinguished station in his own service; the duties of which he executed during the reign of Alompra with strict fidelity, although he was afterwards instrumental in exciting a rebellion against his successor.

The English interests in India were at this time suspended in a doubtful scale; little could be spared from the coast of Coromandel, then the theatre of most important struggles, to aid distant colonies, and support precarious projects; Negrais was in consequence neglected, though not yet abandoned. The Talien or Pegue government, by the surrender of their capital, being now extinct, it became necessary for foreigners to conciliate the new sovereign. Alompra had summoned Mr. Newton,* Resident on the part of the East India Company at Negrais, to attend him at Prome. Mr. Newton deputed Ensign Lyster to the Birman chief, with presents, and instructions to obtain for the Company the settlement of Negrais, with certain immunities and privileges of trade.

In pursuance of his orders, Ensign Lyster left Negrais on the 27th day of June, 1757, and proceeded in the Mary schooner as far as Persaim, or Bassien, where he was detained until the 13th of July, waiting for a person named Antonio, a native descendant of a Portugueze family, who was employed by the Birman government in the capacity of interpreter; and in consequence of that office, possessed some share of power and influence. This man was charged with the provision of boats, and the safe conduct of the deputation. Matters being at length in readiness, Ensign Lyster with his attendants embarked on board four boats, ill equipped against the tempestuous and rainy weather which prevailed at that season of the

* Mr. Brooke had retired; and Captain Howe, who succeeded Mr. Brooke, had died. Mr. Newton was only eventual Resident. A Mr. W. Roberts was intended for that charge. He, however, was killed at the siege of Madras; and from that period Negrais was neglected. Mr. Brooke and Captain Howe had the reputation of being very honourable men.

year. Nearly at the same time, accounts reached Alompra that symptoms of disaffection had again been manifested by the Cassayers, on the west bank of the Keen-Duem. Leaving the command of Rangoon, now considered the capital of the Pegue province, to a general named Namdeoda, with a respectable force to check the Peguers, he departed from Rangoon in the middle of July. On the 23d, Ensign Lyster, who had suffered great inconvenience from the want of a commodious boat, at this stormy season, met the king on his way up the river, and was honoured with an audience on board the royal barge: at which, though from circumstances, little pomp of royalty could be displayed, yet his majesty assumed a lofty tone, boasted of his invincible prowess, and enumerated the royal captives of the Pegue family, who were led prisoners in his train. After asking several questions, he postponed the further discussion of business to a future day, and directed Ensign Lyster to follow him. On the 29th, the king halted at Loonzay, where the English deputy was honoured with a second admission to the royal presence. At this conversation Alompra upbraided Ensign Lyster with the conduct of his countrymen, in giving encouragement and protection to the disaffected Peguers. Having ordered presents of a trivial value to be presented, in return for those brought from Negrais, he referred the deputy to Antonio, and the Birman governor of Persaim, for a ratification and final adjustment of the treaty. Being pressed in point of time, the king departed from Loonzay on the following morning, and left the delegate of the English factory to complete his mission with the Portugueze shawbunder,* and the governor of the province.

* "Intendant of the port." This is a Mussulman term, understood in all the sea-ports of the East. It is called Ackawoon in the Birman language.

After some unnecessary delay, said to be occasioned by the fraud and avarice of the governor of Persaim, or more probably of Antonio the interpreter, an instrument was formally executed, consisting of nine distinct articles. Some valuable commercial immunities were by these ceded to the India Company, the island of Negrais was granted to them in perpetuity, together with a piece of ground opposite to the old town of Persaim, for the purpose of erecting a factory: in return for which, the Company engaged to pay an annual tribute, consisting of ordnance and military stores. A particular clause specified, that aid should be given to the Birmans against the king of Tavoy.*

This agreement, the conduct and completion of which seem to have been influenced by the undignified application of a bribe to the intermediate agents, appears to have received the entire sanction and authority of the King. Negrais, in conformity with the tenor of the compact, was continued in the possession of the English; and on the 22d of August, 1757, Ensign Lyster measured the allotted portion of ground, on which the British colours were hoisted, and three vollies of small arms fired, to solemnize the act of occupancy.

Elated with success, Alompra returned to Monchaboo, now the seat of imperial government. After some months spent in enacting laws, and regulating the internal police of the kingdom, he took up arms against the Cassayers; and proceeding up the Keen-Duem with a fleet of boats, laid waste the western bank, burning villages, and capturing such of the inhabitants as could not save themselves by flight. Having landed his troops,

* Tavoy, now in possession of the Birmans, seems to have once been an independent principality, and was recognised as such by the English, in the year 1753. It probably owed its transitory independence to the wars that raged between the greater powers.

he was preparing to advance to Munnepoora, the capital of Cassay, when information arrived that the Peguers had revolted, and, in their attempts to throw off the yoke, had defeated Namdeoda; and met with such success, as threatened the loss of those territories which his valour had lately acquired. This intelligence induced him to abandon his views to the westward of the Keen-Duem, and return expeditiously to the southern provinces.

It was supposed by the Birmans, and perhaps not without good grounds, that this insurrection of the Peguers, after the departure of Alompra, sprung not less from the instigation of others, than from their own natural desire of emancipation. Crowds of fugitives had fled from the fury of the Birmans, and taken shelter in the Siam country; some had settled on the east borders of the Sitang river; others found an asylum in the province of Martaban; and many wandered, with their families and flocks, over uncultivated plains, and through deep forests, without any fixed abode, or other preference of a place, than as it afforded them protection from their persecutors, and pasturage for their cattle.

The absence of Alompra was deemed a favourable juncture to make the attempt, and the Siamese were not unlikely to encourage the undertaking. The Peguers in the neighbourhood of Dalla and Rangoon rose suddenly, massacred many of the Birmans, and engaging Namdeoda, beat him in a pitched battle. This general after his defeat fled to Henzada, whilst Rangoon, Dalla, and Syriam, again experienced a temporary change of masters.

Nor were the English at Negrais exempt from suspicion of being instrumental in bringing about this insurrection; no acts of publicity, however, have, on any occasion, been established against them: love of gain might have prompted individuals privately to sell arms and ammunition to the

Peguers; and these transactions, if such did take place, were probably represented to the Birman monarch as instances of national perfidy; and the English described as a people hostile to his government, and conspiring to effect its overthrow.

The news of Alompra's approach dissipated this transient gleam of success; Namdeoda, reinforced by troops and supplies from the northward, collected his followers at Henzada, and marched towards Rangoon. The army of the Peguers was encamped a little above the city, and their boats were drawn up to defend the stockade on the side of the river. An irregular, but severe engagement ensued, which terminated in the overthrow of the Peguers: the Birmans again obtained possession of the city of Rangoon; Dalla and Syriam fell in course; and the arrival of Alompra soon after, finally crushed an insurrection, which at first was attended with formidable appearances.

About this time Mr. Whitehill, whose conduct on former occasions had given so much umbrage to the Birman chief, either supposing that the transactions were forgotten, or that he should be able to justify the part he had acted, revisited Rangoon in a small vessel, laden with such commodities as were suited to the market. Whatever might have been the motives of his return, he was mistaken in the consequences. Alompra being apprised of his arrival, ordered the vessel to be seized, and Mr. Whitehill made prisoner. He was sent up in close confinement to Prome, where he met the King returning from Monchaboo: the despot on this occasion displayed unexpected moderation; he spared the life of his prisoner, but compelled him to pay a heavy ransom; his property also was confiscated, together with the vessel that conveyed him. Sometime afterwards he was permitted to depart in a Dutch ship.

The affairs of the British government in India were by no means in such a state of prosperity, as to allow of sending the supplies that were necessary for the effectual support of the settlement of Negrais. Every nerve was on the stretch to maintain, in the Carnatic, the claims of Mahommed Ally, against the French; it was therefore deemed expedient, for the present, to withdraw the settlers from Negrais. Captain Newton was accordingly recalled, and reached Bengal on the 14th of May, 1759, with thirty-five Europeans, and seventy natives; having left a few persons to take care of the teak-timbers, and materials for ship building, that could not conveniently be removed, and to preserve the right of possession, in case it should be determined at any future period to re-establish the settlement.

The tragical catastrophe that followed, presents us with an instance of the sanguinary and cruel disposition that jealousy inspires, when rival interests are to be maintained by the arts of policy and fraud, rather than by open force of arms. The Armenians, the Jews of the East, a description of men subtle, faithless, and indefatigable, whose industry is usually seconded by a competent capacity, beheld with a malignant eye, the progress of European colonies, threatening the annihilation of that influence which they had supported for a long series of years, in the administration both of the Pegue and Birman governments. Amongst these, Coga Pochas, and Coga Gregory, are represented to have been conspicuously active in their efforts to defeat the views, and depreciate the credit of the English; the latter, in particular, who had obtained a considerable office, and carried some weight in the councils of Alompra, especially in what related to strangers, as soon as the affairs of the French were ruined beyond redemption, adopted the policy of attaching to him the few Frenchmen whom Alompra had spared, in order to render them instrumental to the destruction of the English, who were now the favoured nation. Laveene, the youth before-mentioned as left at Dagon by Bourno, an hostage for his fidelity, instead of falling the victim of retaliation, had been kindly treated by the conqueror, who, pleased with his appearance and vivacity, early promoted him to a commission in the guards that attended on his person. The young man is said to have imbibed the strongest prejudices of his nation against the English; and in him, Coga Gregory found an apt instrument to execute his purposes.

Soon after the return of Captain Newton, with his party, the government of Bengal thought proper to send Mr. Southby to Negrais, to take care of the timbers and shipping materials collected there for the use of the Company, and to retain possession of the settlement. The Victoria snow, Alves master, was dispatched on this service, with orders to convey Mr. Southby to Negrais. During her passage, the snow suffered severely from a violent gale of wind; on the 4th of October she anchored in the harbour of Negrais, in a very shattered and distressed condition: happily for her, the Shaftesbury East Indiaman was at this time in the harbour, having put into Negrais for the purpose of procuring a supply of provisions and water.

Mr. Southby disembarked on the evening of his arrival, and next day landed his baggage. Antonio, the interpreter, of whom mention has already been made, came down to Negrais to meet him, and being a man of some official importance, was treated with civility and attention by Mr. Hope, at this time in the temporary charge of the settlement; as well as by Mr. Southby, the new Resident. The pretext for the journey was, to deliver a letter to the English chief, from the King; this letter, however, was a forgery, to give plausibility to the visit, and afford an opportunity of carrying into execution the horrid plot with which he was entrusted.

The address and secrecy with which the intended massacre was concerted, gave no room for taking any precaution. Antonio, who had paid a visit to Mr. Southby on the morning of the 6th, was invited by him to dinner on the same day, at a temporary building belonging to the English. Whilst the entertainment was serving up, the treacherous guest withdrew. At that instant a number of armed Birmans rushed into the room, and put Messrs. Southby and Hope to death: this transaction took place in an upper apartment: Messrs. Robertson and Briggs happened to be below, with eight Europeans of inferior note; a separate attack was made on these by another set of assassins, in which five Europeans were slain; the rest, with Mr. Robertson and Mr. Briggs, shut themselves in a godown, or store-room, where they continued on the defensive until the afternoon, when, receiving a solemn assurance that their lives should be spared, they surrendered, and experienced the utmost brutality of treatment from the murderers. Mr. Briggs being wounded, and unable to move with the alertness required of him, was knocked down, and a period put to his sufferings by having a spear run through his body; the rest were escorted to the water side, where Antonio, who had retired when the massacre commenced, was waiting with a boat to receive them. This fellow had the humanity to unchain the prisoners, and pursued his journey with them to Dagon or Rangoon, where he expected to find the King, and doubtless to receive a reward for the meritorious part he had acted.

A midshipman, of the crew of the Shaftesbury, was about to enter the house when the slaughter commenced, but on hearing the cries of his countrymen, and perceiving the danger, he fled to the water side, wounded by a spear that was cast at him in his retreat. The Shaftesbury's pinnace brought away the midshipman, with several black people belonging to the settlement; the fury of the murderers being indiscriminately levelled against Europeans, and their Indian attendants. The long boat also, that had brought on shore some of Mr. Southby's baggage, was fortunate enough to push off before the Birmans could get possession of her, and letting the ensign fly with the Union downwards, gave intimation to the ship, by that token, of some unexpected mischance.

The Birmans thus becoming masters of the fortified works, and having dispersed or put to death all the settlers, turned the guns of the battery, nine in number, against the Shaftesbury. In the performance of this service, Laveene, the Frenchman, was conspicuously active; indeed, the whole of this diabolic assassination seems to have been executed under his direction: it was afterwards ascertained, that when the English were surprised, and overpowered by the Birmans, this man rushed into the works at the head of a body of banditti, and compleated the slaughter. The precision with which the guns were pointed sufficiently demonstrated, that he who had the management, was not deficient in the art of gunnery. The Shaftesbury returned the fire, but suffered considerably from that of the enemy; the second officer was killed, the running rigging damaged, and nine shots received between wind and water; many of the Birmans are said to have fallen by the fire from the ship: the action continued till dark, and was renewed next morning on the part of the enemy. The Shaftesbury having unmoored in the night, weighed at day light, and dropped down with the ebb to the mouth of the harbour, where, beyond the range of shot, she rode secure: the Victoria snow followed her example.

On the 16th of October, 1759, the Shaftesbury sailed, and the Victoria proceeded to Diamond island to procure water and ballast; whilst they were at this place a small vessel was perceived standing into the harbour of Negrais, Captain Alves humanely sent to warn her of the danger, but before the intelligence could reach her, she had cast anchor within the harbour. It does not however appear, that the Birmans had any intention of doing further mischief; they contended themselves with setting fire to the place, and abandoned it on the night that the vessel arrived. In a few days Captain Alves returned from Diamond island to Negrais: venturing on shore, he was shocked at the sight of the unburied and mangled bodies of his unhappy countrymen. Amongst these he recognized the remains of Messrs. Southby, Hope, and Briggs; the bodies of near 100 natives, who had been attached to the settlement in various capacities, lay scattered around; the boats, buildings, gun-carriages, and every thing combustible, were consumed, except the teak-timbers belonging to the Company, which would not easily take fire, and were too heavy to be removed. Some Birman boats appearing in sight, Captain Alves thought it most prudent to depart; he accordingly weighed anchor, and leaving the shore that had proved so fatal to his friends, prosecuted his voyage to Bengal, where he arrived on the 10th of November, 1759.

After so many proofs of a friendly disposition, the assurances given to Captain Baker, and the compact concluded with Ensign Lyster, it is reasonable to suppose that some acts of hostility, not thoroughly explained, must have been committed, or that very plausible misrepresentations must have been used, to excite the Birman monarch to take such sanguinary revenge. That Gregory, the Armenian, was the principal instigator, is a fact of which no native of the country, who remembers the transaction, entertains the smallest doubt, as well as that Laveene was the agent and instrument of execution. It is said, that the former accused Mr. Hope, who commanded after the departure of Lieutenant Newton, of having supplied the Peguers with provisions, and sold to them four or five hundred musquets; that he had taken pains to instil into his Majesty's mind, a persuasion that the English were a designing and dangerous people; who, having acquired Indian territory, first by fraud, and afterwards by violence, meditated the practice of similar treachery upon them; and only waited a fit opportunity to wrest from him his empire, and enslave his subjects, as they had recently done in the instance of the unsuspecting and abused Mogul. He also added, that the Governor of Negrais prevented vessels from going up to Bassien, by which the royal revenue was defrauded. These arguments, whether groundless or founded, were sufficiently plausible to produce the desired effect; and there is but too much reason to think, that some provocation had been given, though perhaps of a trivial nature, and certainly not sufficient to warrant a step unjustifiable by every law, human and divine.

When Alompra, after returning from the Cassay country, found his presence required in the southern provinces, he left his eldest son, Namdogee Praw, to govern Monchaboo during his absence; and attended by his second son, Shembuan Praw, and the female part of his family, proceeded on his expedition to Tavoy, a sea port on the eastern coast of the gulph of Martaban, which had been wrested from the Siamese by the Birmans. Many Peguers had taken refuge there from the persecution they experienced in the districts of Dalla, Rangoon, Pegue, and Tallowmeou. Encouraged by the first successes of the insurgents, and secretly instigated by the Siamese, the Birman commandant threw off his allegiance, and declared himself independent. Alompra sent a large detachment by land, under Meinla Raja, against Tavoy; also a considerable maritime force to act in concert, commanded by Namdeoda. The previous defeat of the Peguers at Rangoon, had tended to dishearten the rebels. When Meinla Raja had advanced as far as Killegoung, within one day's march of Tavoy, the Commandant came out in a supplicating form to meet him, and surrendered without any stipulation: he was afterwards put to death by order of Alompra.

After the junction of the forces under Meinla Raja and Namdeoda, Alompra sent his women, and the younger part of his family, back to Monchaboo, and accompanied by Shembuan Praw, joined the army at Tavoy. Having now a formidable force collected and embodied, he determined to chastise the Siamese for the encouragement they had given to his rebellious subjects. he accused them of affording protection to delinquents and fugitives, and of secretly abetting the Peguers in all their hostile machinations against his authority. Under this plea, he ordered the fleet to sail to Mergui, a sea port belonging to the Siamese, situated south of Tavoy, whilst the army advanced by land. Mergui, being ill fortified, was easily taken. Leaving a garrison for its defence, the Birmans marched against Tenasserem, a large and populous town, surrounded by a wall and stockade; notwithstanding which it made but a feeble resistance.

These conquests being achieved, Alompra determined to cross the peninsula, and carry the war into the heart of the enemy's country. After a very short halt at Tenasserem, he undertook an expedition against the capital of Siam. The enemy impeded his progress by harrassing his troops, and endeavouring to distress him in his route, without venturing on a decisive action. A month elapsed before he reached the vicinity of the metropolis, which was well prepared to sustain a vigorous siege. Providence, however, interposed; and by abridging the days of the conqueror, in all probability saved the Siamese from total destruction. Two days after the Birman army had erected their stockades, Alompra was taken ill of a disease, which in the event proved mortal; the natives call it Taungnaa, and describe it as a species of scrophula. On the first attack, Alompra foresaw that his end was drawing nigh. He gave orders for an immediate retreat, in the expectation of reaching his capital alive; and of being able to settle the succession, and adjust the affairs of his empire in such a manner, as to avert the calamities of civil discord after his decease. On his return, he did not pursue the route by which he had advanced, but took a direct road by the way of Keintubbien, and the Three Pagodas, which are considered as the boundaries between the Yoodra (or Siam proper), and Birman countries. His intentions, however, were frustrated; the approaches of mortality were too rapid; he grew worse; and death overtook him within two day's march of Martaban, where he expired about the 15th of May, 1760, and carried with him to the grave the regrets of his people, to whom he was justly endeared.

Considering the limited progress that the Birmans had yet made, in arts that refine, and science, that tends to expand the human mind, Alompra, whether viewed in the light of a politician, or soldier, is undoubtedly entitled to respect. The wisdom of his councils secured what his valour had acquired: he was not more eager for conquest, than attentive to the improvement of his territories, and the prosperity of his people; he issued a severe edict against gambling, and prohibited the use of spirituous liquors throughout his dominions; he reformed the Rhooms, or courts of justice; he abridged the power of magistrates, and forbad them to decide at their private houses on criminal causes, or property, where the amount exceeded a specified sum; every process of importance was decided in public, and every decree registered. His reign was short, but vigorous; and had his life been prolonged, it is probable, that his country would at this day have been farther advanced in national refinement, and the liberal arts.

Alompra did not live to complete his fiftieth year: his person exceeded the middle size, strong, and well proportioned; his features were coarse, his complexion dark, and his countenance saturnine: there was a dignity in his deportment that became his high station. In his temper, he is said to have been prone to anger; in revenge, implacable; and in punishing faults, remorseless and severe. The latter part of his character may perhaps have arisen, as much from the necessities of his situation, as from a disposition by nature cruel. He who acquires a throne through an act of individual boldness, is commonly obliged to maintain it by terror: the right of assumption is guarded with more jealousy than that of prescription. If we except the last act of severity towards the English settlers, his conduct on most other occasions, seemed to be marked by moderation and forbearance; even in that one disgraceful instance, he appeared to have been instigated by the persuasions of others, rather than by the dictates of a vindictive mind; and it is manifest, from the expressions of his successor on a public occasion, that it never was his intention to consign the innocent, with the supposed guilty, to the same indiscriminate and sanguinary fate.

Be the private character of Alompra what it may, his heroic actions give him an indisputable claim to no mean rank among the most distinguished personages in the page of history. his firmness emancipated a whole nation from servitude; and, inspired by his bravery, the oppressed, in their turn, subdued their oppressors. Like the deliverer of Sweden, with his gallant band of Dalecarlians, he ſought for that which experience tells us, rouses the human breast above every other stimulant, to deeds of daring valour. Private injuries, personal animosities, commercial emulation, wars of regal policy, are petty provocations, compared to that which animates the resentment of a nation whose liberties are assailed, whose right to govern themselves is wrested from them, and who are forced to bend beneath the tyranny of a foreign yoke.

The decease of an eastern monarch, commonly serves as a beacon to light up the flame of civil discord. The letter of the Birman law immutably vests the right of succession in the heirs male. Laws, however, in all countries, are made subservient to power. Neither the mandates of law, nor the claims of equity, can curb the career of restless ambition. Shembuan, the second son of the late king, who was with the army at the time of his father's demise, endeavoured to influence the troops in his favour. Having gained over a part, he issued a proclamation, declaratory of his right to the throne, on the grounds, that Alompra had nominated him to be his successor, on his death bed. In this step he was premature, and his measures were ill concerted. The ardour of youth seems to have blinded the prince to the dictates of prudence, as well as to the duty and allegiance he owed his elder brother, and lawful sovereign. He soon found that he had been deceived, that his followers were not firm in his interest, and even if they had been sincere, were not sufficiently powerful to support his pretensions; he therefore hastened to repair his error by timely submission, which his brother, through the intercession of their mother, was prevailed on to accept. Shortly after, Shembuan was restored to favour, and no mention is made of his ever attempting a second time to disturb the government of his brother.

Namdogee Praw, although his brother's designs were frustrated, found in a less dignified subject, a still more dangerous competitor. A rebellion that bore a serious aspect, was planned and executed by a person of superior capacity. Meinla Raja, surnamed Nuttoon, a general, high in the good graces of the deceased monarch, commanded the rear of the army that was returning from Siam. Namdogee had always harboured an enmity towards this man, who, sensible that he could expect no protection against the resentment of a vindictive despot, and possessing a considerable share of popularity, determined to contend for empire with his new sovereign. When certain intelligence arrived of the actual decease of Alompra, instead of proceeding to Rangoon, where boats were provided to transport the army up the Irrawaddy, he marched with the utmost expedition, at the head of the division of the army under his command, to Tongho, and took possession of that fort, which is accounted the strongest in the Birman empire. Encouraged by the alacrity with which the soldiers espoused his cause, and anxious to push his rising fortunes, he left a garrison in the fort, and advanced by forced marches towards the capital: as he approached his party strengthened, and the fortifications of Ava were surrendered to him without resistance.

Namdogee Praw was at this time at Monchaboo, making levies to oppose the insurgents. Affairs, however, were not yet in a state of sufficient forwardness to enable him to take the field, as he placed his chief reliance on the arrival of the loyal division of the army that had embarked, and were on the way from Rangoon; but the progress they made against a rapid stream was slow, in comparison to the celerity of a bold adventurer, whose success depended on his expedition and promptitude.

The distance from Rangoon to Monchaboo, by the Irrawaddy, is about 500 miles. In the months of June, July, and August, the river, which, in the hot and dry season, like the Ganges, winds over its sandy bed a slow and sluggish stream, as soon as the mountain torrents fall, swells over the summits of its banks, inundates the adjacent country, and rolls down an impetuous current, unchecked till it approaches the sea, and is repelled by the influence of the flowing tide. Such violence would be insurmountable, and the navigation of the river during this period impracticable, were it not counteracted by the strength of the south-west monsoon. Assisted by this wind, and cautiously keeping within the eddies of the banks, the Birman boats use their sails, and frequently make a more expeditious passage at this, than at any other season of the year.

The division of the army that embarked at Rangoon reached Chagaing, a large fortified town on the west bank of the Irrawaddy, opposite to Ava, shortly after the latter city had fallen into the hands of Nuttoon; whom the breadth of the river, and a want of boats, prevented from taking any effectual measures to oppose the junction of this detachment with the royal standard. Namdogee Praw, when advised of their approach, marched down from Monchaboo with the troops and boats that had been collected. Strengthened by this union, the King's force considerably exceeded that of the rebel general; especially as the numerous fleet that commanded the river, not only secured the safe embarkation, and landing of men and stores, but likewise cut off all supplies by that channel from the enemy. These disadvantages depressed the spirits of Nuttoon's adherents. A party of Namdogee Praw's forces having crossed the river, an irregular action took place, which ended so little in favour of the adventurer, that he threw himself into the fort of Ava; and no longer able to keep the field, prepared to act a defensive part, relying on the arrival of succours from Siam, a quarter to which he had applied with earnest solicitation.

These occurrences occupied little more than two months, from the middle of May, the date of Alompra's decease, to the end of July; about which time the engagement happened that obliged Nuttoon to withdraw from the field, and seek security in the walls of Ava.

Whatever might have been their inclination, the English settlements of India were not, at this juncture, in circumstances to revenge the murder of their servants, and exact retribution for the insult offered to their flag. Perhaps, also, they were not ignorant, that a discussion of the causes might only produce useless explanations: a conjecture that is in some degree corroborated, by there being no steps taken at any subsequent period, when the British superiority in Asia had crushed all rivalry, to vindicate the national honour, and chastize the perpetrators of the cruelty; humanity, however, urged some interference in order to obtain the release of the few survivors, who, on the destruction of Negrais, had been carried into captivity. Policy also rendered it expedient, to avoid an irreconcilable breach with the Birmans, as tending to give the French interests an ascendancy in that quarter, and enable them to gain a firmer footing, in a country whose maritime advantages, and contiguity to our possessions, might afford them opportunities hereafter to disturb our tranquillity, and molest our trade.

Captain Alves, who in the preceeding year had conveyed Mr. Southby to Negrais, and brought back news of the fate of the settlers, was selected to return as the bearer of conciliatory letters, and presents to the Birman monarch, from Mr. Holwell, governor of Bengal, and Mr. Pigot, governor of Madras. These letters appear to have been couched in terms of solicitation, rather than resentment; the liberation of the Englishmen that were carried into confinement, was the principal request; to which a desire was added, that the vessel and property belonging to Mr. Whitehill, confiscated by order of Alompra, should be restored. Mr. Pigott's letter, however, went farther, and intimated expectation that the murderers of the English settlers should be brought to punishment; a requisition that was little attended to, and which the British government of India never manifested any inclination to enforce.

Pursuant to his instructions, Captain Alves sailed from Madras, on the 10th of May, 1760; instead of proceeding direct to Negrais, he shaped his course to the island of Carnicobar, from whence he sent a letter by a Dutch ship to Gregory the Armenian, who held the office of Shawbunder, or *Ackawoon* of Rangoon, acquainting him of his mission, and intreating his good offices with the Birman monarch, to procure the release of the English prisoners; at the same time conciliating him by a present of such articles as he conceived would be most acceptable.

On the 5th of June, Captain Alves reached Diamond Island, but declined entering the harbour of Negrais until he could ascertain the disposition of the natives towards the English, which, after the recent catastrophe, there was room to suspect. His doubts being removed, he sent an officer up to Persaim, with a letter to Antony, the Portuguese superintendant, who on receipt of it came down, as a mark of respect, to meet the English deputy, at a chokey or guard-house, near Negrais. Captain Alves dissembling his knowledge of the part which Antony had acted in the late affair, received his visitor with apparent cordiality, whilst the other took no small pains to convince him that he was guiltless. After a short residence at Persaim, Captain Alves received a very friendly letter from Mungai-Narrataw, a relation of the royal family, and vested with the office of Maywoon, or Viceroy of Pegue, inviting him to Rangoon; desiring him at the same time to bring with him the presents intended for the King. This invitation Captain Alves thought it prudent to accept; and on the 5th of August arrived at Rangoon, where he was received with sufficient politeness by the Viceroy, and made acquainted with the rebellion of Nuttoon, and the deranged state of public affairs at the capital.

Mr. Robertson, and the soldiers who had escaped the massacre at Negrais, were at Rangoon when Captain Alves arrived, and, though under restraint, were by no means treated with harshness. Captain Alves solicited their discharge from the Viceroy; who, though he could not grant the request without special authority from the King, yet consented that Mr. Robertson should accompany Captain Alves back to Persaim; and added, that there was little doubt of procuring a general release. In the course of this communication, the Viceroy gave Captain Alves solemn assurances that Gregory the Armenian, by his misrepresentations and artifice, was the principal instigator of the tragical scene at Negrais; and that Laveene, who was in league with Gregory, was the person to whom the execution of the act had been committed; intimating also that he himself, through the intrigues of these men, had incurred the displeasure of the King, on account of his manifest attachment to the English nation.

Captain Alves continued at Rangoon no longer than was necessary: he left it on the 9th of August, the Maywoon having previously received from him the presents intended for the Birman monarch. An officer belonging to the provincial court accompanied Captain Alves back to Persaim.

Captain Alves expecting to receive a summons to attend the golden feet, was making preparation for his journey, when Gregory the Armenian returned from Monchaboo, whither he had proceeded with all expedition on receipt of the letter which Captain Alves had written from Carnicobar. His zeal on this occasion was prompted by a desire to prevent, if possible, any amicable arrangement; or, in case he should fail in that view, to make himself of personal consequence, from being the ostensible mediator and instrument of reconciliation.

On receiving intelligence of the expected arrival of an authorized agent from the British goverment, Namdogee-Praw directed Gregory to return to Persaim, and dispatched along with him a Birman officer as the bearer of an order to Captain Alves, commanding him to repair to the royal presence. In the translation which Gregory, as interpreter, delivered to Captain Alves, the crafty Armenian introduced passages favourable to himself, attributing the obtainment of any attention, to his intercession: these interpolations were fabricated, as the imperial mandate did not even mention the name of Gregory.

The terms in which the royal order was expressed, encouraged Captain Alves to undertake the journey; he accordingly left Persaim on the 22d of August, accompanied by Antonio the Portuguese, Gregory, and two Birman officers. The unsettled state of the country subjected him to several unpleasant interruptions; his boat, during the course of the voyage, was frequently searched, with the excuse of looking for contraband commodities, and many articles were carried away under various fraudulent pretences.

On the 22d of August, Captain Alves reached Chagaing, at this time the head quarters of the Birman King, who with a numerous army was besieging the rebel general in Ava; on the 23d he was honoured with an audience, to deliver his credentials. The letters from the Governors of Madras and Bengal were translated into the Persian, Portuguese, and Birman languages; and the different versions carefully collated. His majesty expressed his surprize that the Governor of Madras should demand satisfaction for consequences, which the misconduct of their own servants had drawn upon themselves; that the disaster of Mr. Southby, was an accident which could not be foreseen or guarded against: at the same time he used a forcible metaphor, " for," says the Birman King, *" I suppose you have seen that " in this country, in the wet season, there grows so much useless grass, " and weeds in the fields, that in dry weather we are forced to burn them " to clear the ground: it sometimes happens there are salubrious herbs " amongst these noxious weeds, and grass, which, as they cannot easily be " distinguished, are indiscriminately consumed with the others; thus it " happened to be the new Governor's lot." Compensation for Mr. Whitehill's property, that had been confiscated, and restitution of the vessel, were peremptorily refused, for the alleged reason, that Mr. Whitehill and the Governor of Negrais were the aggressors: his majesty was pleased to agree, that the property of the East India Company should be restored. Having given an order for the release of all English subjects that were prisoners in his dominions, he desired that two of the most prudent should remain to take care of the timbers, and reside at Persaim, where he consented to give the Company a grant of as much ground as they might have occasion to occupy, under the stipulation that their chief settlement

* Journal of Captain Alves, recorded in the Bengal Proceedings.

should be at Persaim, and not at Negrais. He assigned as a reason, that at Negrais, they would be exposed to the depredations of the French, or any other nation with whom the English might be at war, without a possibility of his extending that protection to them he wished; but of which they could always have the full benefit at Persaim. In requital for these concessions, his majesty intimated his expectation of a regular supply of arms and ammunition from the English settlements, together with several other products of a useful nature, to all which Captain Alves prudently returned a conditional acquiescence.

During these conferences, explanations took place which created at court, suspicion of the fidelity of Gregory, in his capacity of interpreter: a minute investigation lost him the confidence of his master, and had nearly caused the forfeit of his life. His disgrace was sudden, public, and ignominious.

On the 27th of September, Captain Alves attended in company with the great officers of state, and the principal nobility, to pay his respects at the golden feet, as is the custom on the annual feast of Sandenguit. On this day the King desired Captain Alves to request whatever mark of favour he thought proper, with an assurance that it should be granted to him. The freedom of all the English subjects having been already procured, Captain Alves humanely intreated the emancipation of three Dutchmen, who had been captured by Alompra during his expedition to the Siam country. In compliance with his desire, an order was immediately issued for their release.

The distracted and critical state of public affairs necessarily weakened the hand of power, and diminished the authority of the King. That rigid severity of police, which characterizes the Birman government, became relaxed, and illicit exactions were imposed and levied, by inferior officers, with little dread of punishment. Captain Alves experienced in his own person the inconvenience which an individual, at such a juncture, may expect to suffer. Under frivolous pretences his final dismission was protracted; nor could he procure the promised answers to the letters of the Governor of Bengal and Madras, until he had paid fees to certain officers of government, who took advantage of the times, to extort unauthorized emoluments. After suffering much vexatious imposition, he at length, on the 10th of October, received in form the long expected documents, and on the same evening left Chagaing to proceed to Persaim, accompanied by Antonio. The mandate for liberating the English prisoners was punctually obeyed: there were five in number, two of whom, Messrs. Robertson and Helass, Captain Alves, conformably to the promise made to the Birman King, left at Persaim, to take care of the property belonging to the India Company. On the 1st of November he arrived at Rangoon, where he was received with kindness and hospitality by Mungai-Narrataw, the Viceroy. On the 4th he took leave of his host, and on the 14th got to Persaim, where he again embarked, and sailing from Negrais, reached Calcutta a few days before the expiration of the year.

In the mean while the siege of Ava was carried on with vigour, and the assailants were resolutely resisted. The royal army, computed at 100,000 men, advanced their stockades within fifty yards of the ditch. The batteries, consisting of a few old nine and six pounders, casually procured from shipping at the ports, made little impression on the walls, which were unprovided with artillery, but of an uncommon thickness, being composed of earth and loose stones, supported by a well built face of brick and mortar. The water in the ditch, which during the rains is full, had subsided so low as to become fordable in several places; the besiegers made repeated attempts to carry the place by storm, but were repulsed at every onset. In these attacks many lives were lost. The rebels, knowing that sure destruction awaited those who should be taken, defended themselves obstinately; capitulation was not thought of: whenever the enemy advanced with intent to escalade the works, they poured on them melted lead, boiling petroleum, and hot pitch, whilst a brisk fire of musquetry annoyed them at a distance. The siege was thus protracted for seven months, Nuttoon still cherishing sanguine hopes of succour from the government of Siam.

These expectations were not realized. Supplies from the country failed, and want began to make ravages within the walls, notwithstanding the magazines, which at the commencement of the siege were full, had been husbanded with the utmost economy. Discontent is ever the concomitant of distress. The Governor of Mayah Oun, who had embraced Nuttoon's fortune, deserted from the fort. Flying to Mayah Oun, he collected his adherents, but not being able to resist the royal forces, they set fire to the town, and betook themselves to the woods and jungles, whence they afterwards withdrew to the Eastern provinces, where the authority of the Birman monarch was yet scarcely acknowledged. The rebels had likewise evacuated the fort of Tongho. Towards the end of the year, the garrison in Ava was reduced to the greatest extremity, and their numbers diminished above one half by sickness, famine, and desertion. In this helpless state, without any chance of relief, Nuttoon made his escape from the fort in disguise; but had proceeded only the distance of two days' journey, when he was discovered by some peasants, and brought back in fetters. The fort of Ava fell shortly after the flight of its commandant. Such of his unfortunate adherents as could not effect their escape, were without mercy put to death Nuttoon likewise suffered the doom of a traitor.

The destruction of Nuttoon did not put an end to the disturbances that agitáted the Birman empire. A younger brother of Alompra, uncle to Namdogee-Praw, who had recently been appointed Viceroy of Tongho, aspired to independence, and refused to pay homage to his brother's son. Whilst measures were taking to reduce him, he suddenly detached a body of troops, under a general named Bala-meing-tein, who surprized the fort of Prome; but the Chekey or Lieutenant of Shoe-dong-northa, soon after assembled a respectable force, and compelled Bala-meing-tein to abandon his conquest. Namdogee-Praw raised an army, and, accompanied by his brother Shembuan, marched in person to Tongho to punish the contumacy of his rebellious relation, who, not daring to risk an open action, shut himself within the walls of Tongho. After a siege of three months, the garrison surrendered; several of the ringleaders were punished with death; mercy, however, was extended to the rebellious uncle. The King spared his life, but during the rest of his reign kept him a close prisoner in the fort of Ava.

The appointment of a new Viceroy, and the arrangements necessary to the restoration of good order in these provinces, next occupied the attention of the King. This task being accomplished, he returned with his brother to Monchaboo, from whence he soon after removed the seat of imperial government to the city of Chagaing, the situation of which, equally convenient and salubrious, enjoying a pure air, and surrounded by the most picturesque scenery of nature, had delighted the King during his late residence, whilst directing the operations against Ava. The three succeeding years of his reign were employed in reducing the refractory to obedience, and establishing the royal authority on a firmer basis. Amongst the turbulent was Talabaan, the Pegue chieftain, who had formerly experienced the clemency of Alompra: this man, after he had been received into favour, was sent by the conqueror to the Martaban province, the residence of his family and friends, invested with an office of dignity. So long as that monarch lived, he conducted himself like a dutiful servant; the death of his sovereign, however, cancelled in Talabaan's breast the bonds of duty and gratitude, and though faithful to the father, he took the earliest opportunity to revolt against the son. On this occasion, he seems to have lost his prudence with his principles. His rebellion was feeble, and easily subdued; he was made prisoner, and at last suffered that death which he had before so narrowly escaped. The Peguers at Sitang, a very numerous body, likewise revolted, but were suppressed by the activity of the Viceroy of Pegue, without causing any serious danger to the state. No foreign expedition was undertaken by Namdogee-Praw; indeed the internal state of his empire hardly rendered such a project practicable: his reign was but of short duration, yet he is said to have diligently improved his time, and benefited his country as much as circumstances would admit. He died at his capital about the month of March, 1764, of the same disease that brought his father to the grave, leaving behind him one son named Momien, yet an infant. Of the general character of Namdogee-Praw people speak favourably; bigotry is ascribed to him as his principal failing: he was inflexibly severe on those who transgressed against the tenets of religion, or omitted aught of the respect due to the Rhahaans, its ministers. He punished slight immoralities with the rigour due only to atrocious crimes; slaying animals for the purposes of food, was strictly prohibited, and a second conviction of drunkenness incurred the inevitable penalty of death.

The imbecile minority of the legal heir to the throne gave his uncle Shembuan, who, as the nearest relation, became the natural guardian of the child, an opportunity to undermine the claims and to usurp the right of the son of his deceased brother. Shembuan, on the demise of Namdogee-Praw, assumed the reins of government with a strong hand; nor is it ascertained that he ever acknowledged holding them in trust for the minor. Whatever he might have done on the first assumption of regal power, he soon threw aside all disguise, and was proclaimed and acknowledged lawful sovereign of the Birman and Pegue nations.

Nor would Shembuan, who had thus unjustly deprived a nephew of his birth-right, have scrupled to secure a more firm possession of the throne by imbruing his hands in innocent blood, had not a sister of Alompra humanely interfered, and obtained charge of the child, under a promise that he should be educated in religious obscurity, among the Rhahaans, and never be in a situation to disturb the government of his uncle.

Thus freed from the dread of competition, Shembuan had leisure to follow the bent of his own disposition, which was by nature ardent and ambitious. His first undertaking was against the Siamese; assigning for the rupture the customary excuse, that certain delinquent subjects of the Birman government had received protection from them; likewise that Alompra, his father, had enjoined his children in his last moments to prosecute the war against the Siamese, which he had been prevented by death alone from bringing to a successful issue. Such were the pretences, and perhaps as well founded as pretences for war usually are. Two armies were embodied; one destined to invade North Siam, commanded by a general named Deebedee, the other proceeded to the southward by Sitang and Martaban, under the conduct of Mahanortha; whilst a fleet of small vessels, fitted out for the reduction of the maritime towns, was entrusted to Chedookaminee.

The equipment of these armaments was not completed until the commencement of the year 1765; and their progress, after they were in readiness, was so slow, that nothing of importance could be effected during that year. In the beginning of the next, Deebedee over-ran the province of Zemee, whilst Chedookaminee with the fleet captured Tavoy; which, though it had been reduced by Alompra, was too remote to be retained, and soon reverted to its former possessors. The detachment led by Mahanortha also penetrated to Tavoy by land; and cantoned there during the rains. The forces of Deebedee passed the wet season on the borders of the Yoodra country: these different parties were prepared to act in concert, and attempt the conquest of the Siamese capital.

Whilst matters were thus transacting in the south-east quarter, Shembuan marched in person against the Munipora Cassayers; who, taking advantage of the state of affairs, had thought fit to disclaim the yoke of foreigners, and refused to acknowledge the supremacy of the Birman monarch. This enterprize, however, appears to have been a predatory incursion, rather than an invasion with a view of permanent conquest. The stay Shembuan made in the country did not exceed a month; he returned in obedience to more urgent calls, laden with the booty of the frontier towns, and accompanied by a numerous train of prisoners of every age and sex.

In the beginning of the year 1766, the southern armies commenced their operations against the Siamese. Deebedee entered the Yoodra country by the route of Taunglee and Mainhoot, afterward pursuing a more southerly direction, in order to effect a junction with Mahanortha, who moved from Tavoy in a corresponding time. Their union was resolutely disputed by the Siamese; and Deebedee's division suffered seriously during a march of fifteen days. Notwithstanding this resistance, a junction was effected; after which they advanced against Siam,* the enemy still continuing to harrass them in their march, by irregular attacks and frequent skirmishes. Having at length penetrated as far as the banks of a river,† seven or eight days' journey from the fort, the Siamese tried the fortune of a general action, which terminating unfavourably, their army dispersed; part retreating to Siam, whilst the remainder either concealed themselves in the woods, or sought security in distant provinces. The consequence of this defeat was the immediate investiture of Siam by the Birmans. The fort,‡ by nature strong from its almost insulated situation, is represented to have been well built, according to the Eastern fashion, having a good ditch, protected by a strong rampart faced with masonry, and strengthened by equidistant towers. The artillery on either side was of little use; for though there were a few guns mounted, and some brought against the place, yet they neither contributed to the success of the attack, nor the security of the defence: passive blockade is the favourite system of Birman warfare.

* The city of Siam is frequently called by the Birmans Dwarawuddy, and by the Siamese See-y-thaa. Both these are Pali, or Shanscrit appellations. Most places of note are distinguished by two names, one in the vulgar tongue, which is the most general, the other, a Shanscrit term, seldom used but by the learned, and to be found only in books treating on religion and science; thus Pegue is called Henzawuddy; Arracan, Deniawuddy, &c.

† Probably what is called by the Birmans the Boomagurry Meep.

‡ During the monsoon, the city of Siam is insulated.

The Birman army had been before the city two months, when Mahanortha died. As the officer of highest rank, he held the chief command; which after his decease devolved on Deebedee, who is represented as better qualified for the trust than his predecessor. In a short time after this event, the King of Siam, panic struck and hopeless, secretly withdrew from the fort, in order to avoid falling into the hands of his enemies, and, eluding the Birman outposts, sought refuge among the hills. The Siamese, thus deserted by their leader, offered to capitulate; terms were proposed, and accepted: a heavy mulct was imposed upon the inhabitants, the defences of the city were destroyed, and a Siamese governor appointed, who took an oath of allegiance to the Birman monarchy, and engaged to pay an annual tribute. Deebedee returned with his victorious army to the province of Martaban, enriched by the spoils of Dwarawuddy.

Scarce was the Siamese expedition drawn to a conclusion, when a new danger threatened from an opposite direction. The Chinese government, whose ambition is only exceeded by its pride and arrogance, had planned the subjugation of the Birmans, intending to add the dominion of the Irrawaddy, and the fertile plains of Zomiem,* to their empire; already stretched beyond the limits to which any government can efficiently extend the force of restrictive authority. In the beginning of the year 1767, or 1131 of the Birman æra, the Governor of Quantong sent intimation to Shembuan, that an army of Chinese was advancing from the western frontiers of Yunan, and had already passed the mountains that skirt the Chinese and the Birman empires: this intelligence was scarcely communicated, when it was confirmed by the actual invasion. The Chinese forces, computed at 50,000 men, approached by unremitting marches. Leaving the province

* The name by which the country of Ava is known to the Chinese.

of Bomoo to the west, they penetrated by a town called Gouptoung, between which and Quantong* there is a jee† or mart, where the Chinese and Birmans meet, and barter the commodities of their respective countries: this jee was taken and plundered by the Chinese. Meanwhile Shembuan appointed two separate armies: one, consisting of 10,000 infantry and 2000 cavalry, under the conduct of a general named Amiou-mee, took the direct road leading to Quantong, through the districts of La-be-na-goo, and Tagoung; the other army, of much greater force, was committed to Tengia Boo, a general of high rank and reputation. This latter was directed to make a circuitous march over hills that lay more to the southward, to endeavour, if possible, to get into the rear of the Chinese army, and prevent their retreat. The Governor of Quantong, named Ledougmee, finding that it was not the design of the Chinese leader to waste time by attacking his fort, collected a considerable body of men, and took the field against the invaders. The division of Amiou-mee first met the army near a town called Peengee, where they encamped, within eight miles of the Chinese army; on the following day a partial action took place, in which the Birmans were worsted, and obliged to retreat to the southward of Peengee. The Chinese, animated by this first success, and ignorant of the approach of Tengia Boo, imagined that they should meet no farther impediment until they reached the Birman capital. With

* Quantong, or Canton, signifies a port.

† A similar emporium is established between China and Russia.

"On the boundary of these two empires two small towns were built, almost contiguous, the one inhabited by Russians, the other by Chinese; to these all the marketable productions of their respective countries, are brought by the subjects of each empire.

Robertson's Ind. Note 52.

that persuasion they continued their march, and deviating from the most frequented road, probably for the convenience of forage, pursued another route by the village of Chenghio. Amiou-mee, though repulsed, still kept hovering on the skirts of the Chinese army; which had proceeded only two days farther, to a town called Chiboo, when the division commanded by Tengia Boo suddenly appeared in their rear. Ledougmee, the Governor of Quantong, approached at the same time, with his party: thus inclosed on all sides, a retreat became impracticable, and to advance was desperate. The Tartar cavalry, on whose vigour and activity the Chinese army depended for provision, could no longer venture out, either to procure supplies, or protect convoys. In this situation, the Birmans attacked the enemy with impetuosity, while, on the other hand, the defence made by the Chinese was equally resolute. The conflict had lasted three days, when the Chinese, in an effort of despair, tried to cut their way through the division commanded by Amiou-mee, that occupied the road by which a retreat seemed least difficult. This last attempt proved fatal; Amiou-mee's troops, certain of support, maintained their ground, until the coming up of Tengia Boo, which decided the fortune of the day. The harrassed Chinese now sunk under the pressure of superior numbers; the carnage was dreadful. Birmans, when victorious, are the most unpitying and ferocious monsters on earth. Death, or rigorous slavery, is the certain doom of those they subdue in battle: of the Chinese army, not a man returned to his native country; about 2500 were preserved from the sword; these were conducted in fetters to the capital, where an exclusive quarter in the suburbs of the city was assigned for their residence. They who did not understand any particular handicraft, were employed in making gardens, and in the business of husbandry: mechanics and artificers were compelled to ply their trades according to the royal pleasure, without any other reward for their labour than a bare subsistence. These people, however, were encouraged, as are all strangers, to marry Birman wives, and consider themselves as natives of the country. Compliance with so hospitable and general an invitation, confers even on slaves taken in war certain immunities, from which those who refuse the connexion are by law debarred.

This custom, in which the Birmans follow the example of the wisest and best governed nations of antiquity, is singular amongst the civilized countries of the East; and peculiarly remarkable in a people who believe in the Shaster, and derive their religious tenets from an Hindoo source; who are surrounded also by kingdoms, where women are kept inviolably sacred from the sight and converse of strangers, and where the exclusive system of casts or tribes admits of no proselytes. It is well known, that even the public prostitutes of China are strictly prohibited from having intercourse with other than a Chinese; nor is any foreign woman permitted to enter the territories, or visit the ports of that jealous nation. The Hindoo women of rank are no less inaccessible; and admission into a respectable cast is not attainable by money. To such narrow prejudices the Birmans are superior; with a Lacedemonian liberality, they deny not the comforts of connubial commerce, to men of whatever climate or complexion. They are sensible that the strength of an empire consists in its population; and that a prince is great and powerful, more from the number of his subjects, than from the extent of his territory: hence the politic indulgence that the Birman government grants to every sect freely to exercise its religious rites: they tolerate alike the Pagan and the Jew, the Mussulman or Christian, the disciples of Confucius, or the worshippers of fire; the children of whom, born of a Birman woman, equally become subjects of the state, and are entitled to the same protection and privileges, as if they had sprung from a line of Birman ancestry.

When Shembuan succeeded to the throne, he removed the seat of government from Chagaing, the residence of his brother and immediate predecessor, to Monchaboo, where his father Alompra had kept his court. With this situation also he became discontented; and it is said from certain superstitious reasons, suggested by astrologers, again changed his abode, and made Awa Haung, or ancient Ava, the metropolis of the empire. The city, which had fallen into ruin, was quickly rebuilt; new keoums* and praws† arose; a strong stockade was erected; and the fortifications, which had been neglected since the expulsion of Nuttoon, were put into a respectable state of repair.

The brilliant success that attended the recent irruption of the Birmans into the Siamese country, was productive of no permanent advantages: though beaten, the Siamese were far from being a subjugated people. The inherent enmity that subsists between these two nations, will probably prevent the passive vassalage of one to the other, unless broken by such repeated defeats, as must nearly amount to extirpation. Soon after Deebedee had led his army within the confines of the Birman dominions, the yoke of the conquerors was disclaimed in Dwarawuddy: a man named Pieticksing, a relation of the king, and one who held an official station about his person, had, previous to the capitulation, retired to a town at some distance, attended by his followers. As soon as it was known that the Birmans had withdrawn into their own territories, he returned, at the head of a numerous troop of adherents, by whose aid he easily displaced the

* Monasteries. † Temples. Praw is a term applied to all sacred objects.

new government, and abolished the regulations made by the Birman general. The king, who had pusillanimously abandoned his throne and people, is said to have perished in the woods, but through what means is not clearly ascertained; probably by the dagger of the usurper; who having gained over the populace and conciliated some men of influence, found few obstacles to impede his way to the throne.

Deebedee, who had so eminently distinguished himself, was received on his return to Ava with many flattering demonstrations of applause; his Tsaloe, or cord of nobility, was increased from six to nine strings, and he was farther honoured with the title of Na-ma-boo-dee, or most illustrious commander. The Chinese being vanquished, and the Peguers to appear-pearance so depressed, as to leave no apprehension of disturbance to the state, Deebedee was again detached to punish the contumacious Siamese, and reduce them to vassallage and submission; he left Ava on this service with a fleet of war-boats, early in the monsoon of the year 1771: the troops were debarked at Rangoon, and proceeded from thence by land. On this occasion, the Siamese anticipated the intention of the Birman general, and met him in force on the frontiers, where the opposition he experienced from the enemy, and the difficulty of passing the rivers, which had not yet subsided, were such as to oblige him to retreat; he encamped on the borders of the Sitang river, whence he wrote to Ava to represent the necessity of sending him further reinforcements.

In consequence of this application, Chedookaminee, who had served on the former expedition, received a commission, appointing him Maywoon or Viceroy of Martaban, and of all the possessions belonging to the Birmans southward of Martaban. This officer was ordered to make the levies, necessary for the assistance of Deebedee, within his jurisdiction;

after which he was to join that general, act in concert with him, and, uniting their forces, recommence hostilities against the Siamese.

The southern provinces, over which the authority of Chedookaminee extended, were chiefly inhabited by the families of Taliens, or Peguers, who had either voluntarily left, or were expelled from the ancient city of Pegue, from Dalla, and the districts adjacent; out of these Chedookaminee was obliged to form his new levies. The Peguers, who were then supposed to be sufficiently reconciled to the Birman government, and considered, in many respects, as naturalized subjects of the state, were accordingly required to contribute to the public exigencies, by furnishing men and money, in like proportion as the native Birmans. In fact, the southern countries were not capable of furnishing Birman recruits sufficient for an army; but the confidence reposed in the Peguers was, in this instance, fatally misplaced, and their treachery averted from the Siamese the gathering storm.

Deebedee, probably disgusted by the appointment of Chedookaminee to the Maywoonship of Martaban, obtained permission to retire from the army, and return to the capital: on his departure, Chedookaminee succeeded to the sole command.

Among the troops thus raised, were three popular chieftains of the Talien nation, named Tellakien, Tellasien, and Meenatzi, men of enterprizing, intriguing spirit, and of great influence amongst their people. The Peguers thus collected in a body, and provided with arms, became conscious of their own strength; a sense of which, stimulated by the influence of their chieftains, inspired them with a desire to regain their empire, and retaliate their wrongs on their oppressors. The army was assembled at Martaban when the conspiracy was formed: at the close of the first day's march, the Peguers suddenly rose upon their Birman companions, and commenced an indiscriminate massacre; the officer second in command of the Birman army was slain; and those who escaped the fury of the assassins, fled into the woods. Chedookaminee himself, accompanied by 500 followers, with difficulty effected a retreat to Rangoon; the elated Peguers followed the blow, and pursued the fugitives to the very gates of the city, where their numbers increasing, they formed an encampment, and commenced a regular siege.

Rangoon could not have been attacked at a time, when it was worse prepared for defence; imaginary security had lulled the Birmans into unsuspecting repose. The Maywoon of Pegue, whose residence was in Rangoon, had, a short time before, proceeded on an annual visit of homage to the capital, accompanied by the principal officers of his government; he had also taken with him the greatest part of the troops, in particular those who manned the war-boats; a hardy and ferocious tribe, who usually attend on the governor, or viceroy, on occasions of ceremony. During his absence, a lieutenant or chekey, named Shoe-dong-northa, commanded in the city, and by the gallant defence he made, proved himself no undeserving substitute. News of the revolt quickly spread, and, from its first success, created a general alarm among the Birmans, resident in the adjoining districts. The Meou-gees, or chief men of Henzada, Denoobew, and Padaung, assembled all the force they could collect; and in a spirited manner came down the river in light boats, and threw themselves into Rangoon, which stood in need of such timely succours. The Peguers thrice attempted to storm a strong stockade, that encompassed the walls of the town, and were each time beaten off with serious loss. Intelligence of these events reaching court, the Maywoon, with his train of attendants, and a few additional troops, amounting in the whole to about 3000 men, were ordered to proceed without delay to the relief of Rangoon. The rapid stream of the Irrawaddy quickly transported this detachment to the place of its destination: the Peguers, on their approach, thought it most prudent to raise the seige, and, without making any further attempt to oppose the junction of the reinforcement, retired to the banks of the Saloenmeet. The arrival of the Viceroy of Rangoon, was speedily followed by that of a still more respectable force, under an officer of the highest rank in the empire; Maha-see-soo-ra, one of the Woongees, or chief counsellors of state, was entrusted by the King with the conduct of the southern war, and the restoration of order in the disturbed provinces.

These events did not deter Shembuan from pursuing his favourite scheme of conquest to the westward. The fertile plains and populous towns of Munnipoora, and the Cassay Shaan, attracted his ambition. Early in the year 1774, a formidable force was sent against these places, under the command of three generals of distinction, Moung-wamaa, Captain of the King's guard, Oundaboo, and Kameouza. Part proceeded by water up the Keen-duem, and the remainder by land taking the route of Monchaboo, Kaung-naa, and Naky-oun-mee; the armament by water arrived unexpectedly at a town called Nerting, where the Birmans landing, surprised and carried away 150 women, who were employed in the labours of the harvest. Monadella, the Raja of Nerting, made an ineffectual attempt to rescue the captives: he fell after a gallant struggle, and 250 of his followers lost their lives. The Birmans having ravaged the country, and committed many acts of wanton barbarity, proceeded to join the detachment that advanced by land: when the forces were united, they marched towards Munnipoora, the Raja of which came forth to meet the enemy, and gave them battle at a village called Ampatalla, fourteen miles short of Munnipoora. The conflict was long and obstinate, but fortune in the end favoured the Birmans; the Munnipoora Raja fled from the field of battle to his capital, where confusion and terror prevailed: from thence he withdrew to the Corrun hills, five days journey north-west of Munnipoora, accompanied by his family, and carrying with him his most valuable effects. The city of Munnipoora submitted to the conqueror, who took possession of whatever the inhabitants had not been able to remove or conceal. The spoils, consisting chiefly of merchandize, and vessels of gold and silver, were forwarded to the golden feet, together with 2000 prisoners of both sexes.

Having reduced the Munnipooreans, Oundaboo left to his colleagues, Moung-wamaa and Kameouza, the task of enforcing submission from the Cassay Shaan, and several neighbouring petty states; whilst putting himself at the head of 10,000 men, unincumbered with baggage or artillery, he marched against Chawal, Raja of Cachar, who possessed the independent sovereignty of a rich, though mountainous territory, north-west of Munnipoora. In his progress he overcame Anoupsing, prince of a country called Muggaloo;* thence he is said to have penetrated within the Hamalaya hills, which form a continuation of the lofty Imaus, and seem to be a barrier raised by nature, to protect the mild unwarlike inhabitants of India, from the more hardy natives of the East, who, unrestrained by such impediments, would ages since have spread desolation along the fertile banks of the Burhampooter and the Ganges. Pursuing his conquests,

* Mr. Wood frequently heard of this country whilst he was at Assam, as engineer to a detachment sent thither by Lord Cornwallis.

Oundaboo advanced within three days march of Cospore,* capital of Cachar, passing many rugged mountains and pleasant vallies, embosomed in their range.

Chawal, aware of the storm with which he was threatened, had taken the necessary precautions for his own security; he joined in a defensive league with the lesser rajahs of the hills; who, though waging endless warfare with each other, united in the hour of danger to repel the common enemy. The chief of these was the Prince of Jointy, surnamed the Gossain Raja. Oundaboo, blinded by the ambition of conquest, imprudently pressed forward, until he found himself environed with difficulties he could not hope to surmount, and from which there was now no retreat. To complete his misfortunes, that deadly disease too fatally known to British troops, by the name of the hill fever, had spread its baneful influence through the Birman ranks; famine and pestilence accomplished what the swords of the mountaineers could never have effected. Oundaboo's troops dispersed, and in the defiles of the mountains, and the mazes of the forests, were cut off by the natives in detail, or perished the unresisting victims of a supernatural foe.

The misfortunes of Oundaboo and his army, instead of intimidating the Birmans, excited an insatiable spirit of revenge. Kameouza undertook to exact retribution from the Cachars, for the blood of his slaughtered countrymen; Moungwamaa remained at Munnipoora, with a garrison sufficient to defend the fort, whilst Kameouza marched against Chawal, with a yet greater force than had accompanied the unsuccessful general, whose error afforded an useful lesson to his successor. Instead of the rash and preci-

* Cospore is said to be twenty days journey from Munnipoora by an Hircarra, or messenger.

pitate haste made by his predecessor, this more prudent leader diligently explored his ground, halting wherever subsistence could be collected, with which many of the rich and luxuriant valleys of Cachar abounded: thus continuing a cautious progress, he penetrated as far as the pass of Inchamutty,* two days journey from Cospore, where he was met by a deputation from the Raja to solicit peace. Kameouza prescribed terms, which, though severe and humiliating, were accepted. Chawal consented to pay, besides a sum of money, the abject homage of a maiden of the royal blood to the King of Ava, and to send him a tree with the roots bound in their native clay; thereby indicating, that both person and property were at the disposal of his sovereign pleasure; these acts being considered as the most unequivocal proofs of vassalage; expressing, on one hand, the extreme of submission, and on the other, the most absolute power.

Kameouza, in his return to Munnipoora, chastised a race of mountaineers named Keingee, by whom he had been harrassed in his march, burning several of their villages in the districts of Bodasser and Chaumgaut. Raja Anoupsing likewise made his submission; repossession of Munnipoora was granted to the fugitive prince, on condition of paying an annual tribute, and offering the acknowledgment of a royal virgin, and a tree. Matters being thus adjusted, the Birmans returned to their own country, having lost above 20,000 men, from the commencement to the close of the expedition, by the various casualties of war.

These victories lent only a transitory splendor to the Birman arms, without contributing to the real and permanent advantage of the state; it was impossible to keep possession of the tracts they had over-run, the

* There are passes of the same name in Hindostan.

towns they had stormed, and the countries they had subdued. The Birman nation was far from being populous, in proportion to its widely extended empire. To retain the late acquisition of Pegue, and keep in subjection its discontented and numerous inhabitants, required the utmost vigilance, and occupied all the troops that could with prudence be spared. Oaths of allegiance are considered by eastern vassals, as obligations of conveniency; as mere nugatory forms, to be observed no longer than there is power to punish a breach of them; the conquests therefore, made by the Birmans to the westward, were attended with no other effect, than to add to their native arrogance, and to increase their already inordinate pride.

The Peguers, as before related, having raised the siege of Rangoon, had returned to the Saloenmeet, or the Martaban river, when Maha-see-soo-ra, to whom the management of the southern war was intrusted, arrived at Rangoon, with an additional reinforcement of troops, and several pieces of artillery. Having augmented his strength with the soldiers that accompanied the Maywoon, and drafted part of the garrison, his army amounted to 20,000 men; whilst twenty-four pieces of ordnance rendered him formidable to a foe, casually armed with whatever weapons they could procure.

With this respectable equipment Maha-see-soo-ra took the field, about the end of the year 1774. The enemy were in possession of Martaban, and had collected, from various quarters, a discordant rabble, ill provided with necessaries, and altogether unamenable to control; from whom the Birman commander met with little opposition, in a march rendered tedious by the transportation of heavy guns, and the difficulty of crossing the numerous watercourses that intersect the lower country. On reaching the vicinity of Martaban, overtures of a pacific nature were made by the rebel leaders, which were rejected with contempt and menace: the Peguers in despair shut themselves within the fort, a seige was commenced, and sustained for a considerable time. The Peguers were at length forced to yield. Tellasien and Meenatzi, with several of their adherents, effected an escape to Siam; but Tellakien was not so fortunate; he was captured in the fort, with many others, and being a leader of the rebellion, his fate was reserved for the decision of his sovereign.

Maha-see-soo-ra was preparing to carry the war into the country of the Siamese, when he received intelligence of the intentions of the King to visit Rangoon in person: this circumstance, together with the little probability of being able to advance far, before the season* when the rivers swell, determined him to pass the monsoon in cantonments, at Martaban.

Shembuan having repelled the formidable invasion of one enemy, and carried his victorious arms into the territory of another: having, by prudent conduct, established his throne on the strong foundations of terror and respect, conceived, that his presence would contribute to a more speedy termination of the troubles that agitated the lower provinces, and more effectually destroy the seeds of disaffection among the Peguers, which had so often, at intervals, broke out into open rebellion. The temple of Dagon, called Shoe-Dagon, or the Golden Dagon, an edifice of venerable sanctity, and stupendous size, where Gaudma, the Birman and Pegue object of religious worship, was, from time immemorial, accustomed to receive at an annual festival, the adorations of the devout, had, in the year 1769,

* The rivers in India usually begin to swell before the actual fall of rain in the low countries. This is to be ascribed to the monsoon commencing earlier among the mountains, and to the melting of the snow, with which the tops of the eastern hills are covered, in the hottest season.

suffered much damage from an earthquake; in particular the Tee, or umbrella, which, composed of open iron-work, crowned the spire, had been thrown down by the concussion, and rendered irreparable from the fall. In the Birman empire, a pagoda is not deemed sanctified until it receives the umbrella; and the erection of this last, but most important appendage, is an act of high solemnity. Shembuan, who on this occasion is said to have covered policy with the cloak of religion, caused a new and magnificent Tee to be constructed at Ava, and declared his intention to assist in person at the ceremony of putting it on. For this avowed purpose he left his capital, attended by a numerous train of Birman nobility, whilst, to increase the pride and pageantry of the display, Beinga Della, the unfortunate monarch of Pegue, who had surrendered his sceptre and person to Alompra, was led captive in the procession. An army of 50,000 men composed the body guard: this splendid array, having embarked in boats, sailed down the Irrawaddy, and arrived at Rangoon in the month of October, 1775. Tellakien, the Pegue rebel, who had been sent up the country loaded with irons, met the King at the town of Denoobew, and expiated his treason by a painful death.

Whatever respect the glory of conquest, and the wisdom of a well regulated government, might attach to the reign of Shembuan, it must be wholly obscured by the cruelty exercised on the present occasion towards his royal prisoner, the unhappy King of Pegue; and this too, like a more recent and equally inhuman regicide, in a nation professing Christianity, and enlightened by science, was perpetrated under the mockery of justice. Shembuan, not content with exhibiting to the humbled Peguers their venerable, and yet venerated monarch, bound in fetters, and bowed down with years and anguish, resolved to take away his life; and render the disgrace still deeper, by exposing him as a public malefactor, to suffer under the stroke of the common executioner. In most countries, to the east of Bengal, decapitation is the punishment allotted for common thieves; and he who inflicts the sentence is usually a culprit, who has once been convicted of the crime. To die by such a hand is deemed an ignominy, which the Birmans dread even worse than death itself; but for any subject to spill royal blood, is forbidden by the Birman and Pegue laws, as an act of inexpiable impiety; nevertheless the unfeeling Shembuan, regardless of law, and devoid of humanity, issued orders for his ill fated prisoner to prepare for trial on a charge of high treason.

The process of law, in Birman courts of justice, is conducted with as much formality as in any country on earth. Beinga Della was brought before the judges of the Rhoom, among whom the Maywoon of Pegue* presided. The late King of Pegue was there accused of having been privy to, and instrumental in, exciting the late rebellion. Depositions of several witnesses, supposed to be suborned, were taken; the prisoner denied the charge; but his fate being determined on, his plea availed him nothing. He was found guilty; and the proceedings, according to custom, were laid before the King, who passed sentence of death, and accompanied it with an order for speedy execution.

In conformity to this cruel mandate, on the 7th of the increasing moon, in the month Taboung, the aged victim was led, in public procession, through an insulting populace, to a place called Awa-bock, three miles without the city, where he met his doom with fortitude; and had no dis-

* In the absence of the king, the Maywoon, or viceroy, never attends in person at the Rhoom; he then represents the king; remains in his palace, and receives the report of the judges; to which he applies the law, and finally awards the sentence.

tinction paid him above the meanest criminal, except that all the municipal officers attended in their robes of ceremony, to witness his last moments.

State necessity is sometimes found to be incompatible with individual justice, and on occasions, must be allowed to plead for measures which, abstractedly considered, seem harsh, and bear hard upon particular members of the community; but such necessity, to be admissible, should be made unequivocally evident. Men, whose designs against the public peace cannot be doubted, ought to be restrained by the hand of coercion, even before the commission of any overt act to which the law attaches: the proof of intention, warrants and demands such interference. A despot, who dreads the extinction of his power, and the loss of his crown, will resort to unjustifiable means to remove the object of his jealousy, and anticipate on his enemy the meditated blow; but the circumstances of the present case, appear neither to admit of palliation or excuse: the security of the state was not endangered, and no rivalry could be dreaded. The Pegue King had passed more than twenty years, a contented and inoffensive prisoner: had he been only suspected of encouraging his former subjects, in any one of their several attempts at emancipation, his life would have paid the forfeit of his temerity; but, in the last instance, when bending under the pressure of years and infirmity, there was scarce a possibility of his being accessory to so daring a revolt. On the part of the Birman monarch, it was a wanton and barbarous display of power, designed, perhaps, as a humiliating spectacle to the Peguers, whose attachment to their ancient sovereign bordered on idolatry. It casts a deep shade over a splendid reign, and justly brands the memory of Shembuan with the odious appellation of tyrant.

The execution of many Taliens of rank followed that of the king; all who were suspected of having borne a part in the late rebellion, and all whose influence rendered them formidable, were included in the list of the proscribed. Several fled from persecution; and after the storm blew over, settled in Tongho, or the tributary provinces of Zemee, Sandepoora, and the districts adjacent.

These are amongst the last transactions of Shembuan's life: after duly solemnizing the ceremony of putting on the Tee, he prepared to return to his capital, having given instructions to his general, Maha-see-soo-ra, to prosecute the war against the Siamese.

In the beginning of the year 1776, Shembuan left Rangoon with the same retinue, and in the same pomp which before attended him: during the early stages of his progress, he felt the first symptoms of his mortal illness. Alarmed at the danger, and impatient under his sufferings, he quitted his slow-drawn boat of state, and embarking in a lighter vessel, hastened to his capital, hoping there to find relief; but his days were numbered, and he was doomed shortly to resign his diadem and life to that power, which disregards even the boasted immortality of Birman kings.

Languishing under a slow fever, and distempered with scrofula, Shembuan obtained little benefit from the efficacy of medicine. In order to breathe a freer air, he changed the fort of Ava for the open plains: temporary wooden houses were erected, on the highest banks that overhung the stream, and on spots to which superstition pointed as the site of health. But the skill of astrologers proved fallacious, and no wind that blew wafted alleviation to his pains: after fatiguing himself by frequent removals, he felt it was but an useless aggravation of his sufferings; hopeless of life, he returned to the fort to prepare for the last scene, and settle the affairs of the empire and the succession to the throne.

Shembuan had two sons, Chenguza, and Chelenza, by different mothers; the first, at this time eighteen years of age, was born of the principal queen; the latter, not more than thirteen, the offspring of a favourite concubine. Competition between these brothers was an event scarcely to be dreaded; whilst Momien, the son of Namdogee-Praw, seemed to be too closely immured in monastic privacy, to raise a bar to the succession. Nevertheless Shembuan took every prudent precaution to transmit an undisputed sceptre: he exacted from the nobility a solemn promise of allegiance to his heir, which the respect entertained for the character of the father, inclined few to withhold from the son. Having satisfactorily adjusted his temporal concerns, the monarch yielded up his breath in the city of Ava, about the middle of spring, in the year 1776.

The character of Shembuan is that of an austere, intelligent, and active prince. He reduced the petty sovereigns of several neighbouring provinces, to a state of permanent vassalage, who had before only yielded to desultory conquest: these he compelled, as Chobwas, or tributary princes, to repair in person, or by representatives, at stated periods, to his capital, and pay homage at the Golden feet; among them are numbered the lords of Sandepoora (Cambodia), Zemee, Quantong, Bamoo, and others; together with several less civilized* tribes, inhabiting the western hills, and the mountainous tracts that intersect the country eastward of the river Irrawaddy.

Shembuan was in most points a superstitious observer of the rites and precepts of the Birman religion, which originating, as it indisputably does, from the same source as that of the Hindoos, differs nevertheless from the latter, in many essential tenets. Admitting the sanctity, and reverencing the learning of the Braminical sect, the Birmans, votaries of Buddho Tachor,

* Carreaners, Keins, and Yoos.

altogether deny the supremacy of the Bramin professors over their Rhahaans, or Phonghis. The Birmans, Peguers, and Siamese, as well as all nations whose fundamental principles of religion can be traced to the Hindoo system, and who acknowledge the Shanscrit as their holy text, unite in one benevolent doctrine; the sinfulness of depriving any animal of life, to satisfy a carnivorous appetite. To eat flesh, is not deemed a crime by the Birmans; but he who eats it is not exempt from sin, unless the creature died a natural death, or was slain by accident, or by other hands. This precept of the church, it may be supposed, is not very scrupulously observed; and in many parts of the empire is wholly disregarded, except by the priesthood, who never even prepare their own victuals. Mandates have been issued by viceroys, and proclamations gone forth from the Golden palace, to enjoin obedience to the sacred law; but these were little more than expiatory manifestoes, suggested by remorse, danger, or superstition. It is likewise at times used as an instrument of venal oppression; the greedy retainers of the law being entitled to a certain quota of the fine levied from a convicted delinquent. Shembuan, strongly tinctured with bigotry, often, in the course of his reign, repeated the pious prohibition, with no other effect than causing that to be done in secret, which before the order, little precaution had been used to conceal.

On the demise of Shembuan, it does not appear that any effort was made, either by Momien himself, or the nobles attached to his father, to recover a throne, from which he was most unjustly debarred. Chenguza ascended without opposition, and assumed the government, at a juncture when the flourishing state of public affairs, held out a flattering prospect of an auspicious reign.

But in the succession to sovereignty, it sometimes happens, as in the succession to an estate, that he who comes to the fairest inheritance, does not always prove a benefactor to his realm, and his subjects, or his tenants and demesnes. Numerous errors will, and ought to be forgiven, in the presumptive heir to an high public trust, or an affluent private property; but a radical want of honest principle, a long continued course of base and licentious conduct, never fails in time to alienate the affections of men, whether subjects or tenantry, however inclined they may be to venerate the virtues of the sire, in the person of the son. Even the *jus divinum,* so strenuously inculcated by the Birman articles of political faith, did not, in the end, prove sufficiently strong to protect from violence a throne polluted by the lowest profligacy, and disgraced by an open violation of every moral and religious duty.

With all the advantages arising from his father's memory, and with a government thoroughly established in power, Chenguza commenced his reign: but these distinctions he studied by every means in his power to abuse. His first imprudent act was to recall the army from the southward, which, shortly after the departure of Shembuan, had marched from Martaban under Maha-see-soo-ra, and had commenced operations against the Siamese. This general, Chenguza not only displaced from his military command, but likewise degraded from his high ministerial office of Woon-gee, or chief counsellor of state; a measure that drew on himself much odium; as Maha-see-soo-ra was a person of conciliatory manners, and an officer of approved integrity and valour.

The other parts of Chenguza's conduct, corresponded with this arbitrary outset: and he plunged at once into the most shameless debauchery. Not content with repealing the edicts of his father against the use of spirituous liquors, he exhibited, in his own person, an example of ebriety and dissipation: stimulated by jealousy, he caused his younger brother, Chilenza, to be put to death: he submitted the affairs of his empire to be administered by favourites, and accustomed himself to be absent from his capital, whole months together indulging in rural sports and carousals; and preferring his hunting seats, on the borders of deep forests, to the splendid Piasath* of the royal palace. In the year 1779, his father's younger brother, Terroug-mee,† incurred the suspicion of the tyrant, and fell a victim to his jealousy: Pagahm-mee, another of his uncles, was kept a close prisoner in the fort of Ava, under pretext that he was plotting against the state: his uncle, Minderagee Praw, the present King, resided sometimes at Chagaing, and sometimes at Monchaboo; and though he affected to live in the most inoffensive obscurity, was nevertheless vigilantly watched by the minions of the palace.

Agreeably to the usage of the Birman court, Chenguza had early been betrothed to a relation‡ of his own; this marriage proving unfruitful, he espoused, as his second wife, the daughter of one of the Attawoons§ of the court: a young woman endowed with virtue, beauty, and accomplishments. Although it was generally believed that he was extremely fond of this wife, yet the irritation of an intemperate life, together with a

* Piasath, the regal spire, that distinguishes the dwelling of the monarch, and the temples of the divinity; to none other is it allowed.

† Or possessor of Terroug.

‡ A prince, to be properly qualified to ascend the Birman throne, should be of blood royal both in the male and female line. In order to guard against plebeian contamination, the Birman law admits of incestuous marriages in the royal family: this licence is restricted to them alone.

§ The Attawoon may be called a privy counsellor; there are four, who have access to his majesty at all hours, and are consulted by the king on affairs of importance; they have influence enough, sometimes, to counteract the decisions of the Woon-gees passed in the Lotoo, or high court of judgment, when laid before his majesty for royal approbation.

disposition from nature prone to jealousy, caused them to live on terms of unceasing discord. One day, actuated by an impulse of sudden rage, he accused her of infidelity; and without allowing himself time to judge dispassionately, or suffering the unhappy princess to vindicate herself, he pronounced sentence of immediate death. There are wretches in every nation ready to execute the sanguinary mandates of a cruel tyrant; the trembling and innocent victim was dragged from the palace, and inclosed in a sack of scarlet cloth, richly ornamented: thus confined, she was put on board a boat,* when the sack being suspended between the narrow necks of two earthen jars,† the whole was sunk in the deepest part of the Irrawaddy. The jars filling, carried the body down, and prevented emersion. This diabolical act was perpetrated in open day, before thousands of spectators, amongst whom were many of her friends and relations. Her afflicted father, overwhelmed with anguish and deprived of all his offices, retired in despair to the city of Chagaing.

The universal disgust that a conduct so flagitious could not fail to raise, even in the most depraved society, caused the majority of the nobles, and the great body of the people, anxiously to desire a change. Under such a dominion, no man's life was secure from becoming a sacrifice to the caprice of an intoxicated barbarian, or the personal enmity of some despicable parasite: at such a juncture, the eyes of all were naturally turned to the rightful heir, who had now attained the years of manhood. The retreat chosen for Momien, was the Keoum and Praw of Lo-ga-ther-poo,

* It is expressly forbidden by the Birman law to spill the blood of one of the royal family; drowning is esteemed the most honourable death.

† The jars of Pegue are in general estimation throughout India, being remarkable for their size and excellence.

an inconsiderable distance from the fort of Ava, where, protected by his sacerdotal habit, by the influence of his aunt, and perhaps, above all, by his own want of capacity and personal insignificance, the tyrant had hitherto considered him as an object too contemptible for notice; little imagining that the simple Phonghi, was one day to be, in the hands of others, the instrument of his destruction.

A conspiracy was the result of the discontents of the people, and the misconduct of the prince. The principal actors were Shembuan Minderagee Praw,* the Attawoon before mentioned, and Maha-see-soo-ra, the degraded minister. These personages easily gained the monks over to their side, who, though less willing to meddle in state affairs, than is customary with their order in many countries, yet, being exasperated by the open contempt Chenguza manifested for religion, its rights and ministers, gladly lent their aid to bring about a change, which, by placing Momien, their illustrious disciple, on the throne, promised to advance the interests of the church. Momien was accordingly tutored for the part he was to act, and nothing remained but to embrace a favourable moment to execute the projected revolution.

During Chenguza's reign, military operations seem to have been wholly suspended; whilst the neighbouring nations, the Chinese, the Siamese, and Cassayers, had so recently experienced the power of the Birman arms, that they felt no inclination to stand forth as aggressors. Repeated defeats and severe penal laws, crushed the spirit of revolt among the Peguers, who appeared to acquiesce in their subjugated state. The Anoupectoumeou, or great western mountains, had not in the present dynasty been crossed by an hostile army; the tranquillity of the empire, therefore, during the

* The present monarch, and younger brother of the deceased Shembuan.

six years that Chenguza wore the crown, compensated, in some measure, for the licentiousness that was introduced among the people. Population increased, and tracts of land were cultivated, which under a more warlike prince, would probably have continued an unproductive waste.

After matters were in readiness, the first opportunity of acting occurred in the month of November, 1781. Chenguza had gone to Keoptaloun, a town on the banks of the river, about thirty miles below Ava, to celebrate an high festival. As he never observed any regular times of going out, or returning to the fort, it often happened that he presented himself at the gates when least expected, and at hours when entrance is debarred to the multitude. Momien was secretly furnished with the dress, and equipments of royalty: thus personating Chenguza, and attended by the customary retinue, he appeared at midnight before the gate called Shoedogaa, and demanded admission: at first the wicket only was opened by the guard on duty; who, suspecting treachery from the unusual earnestness of the foremost persons to enter, attempted to close the door, and called out treason: resistance, however, was too late; the centinel was cut down, and the gate thrown open by those who had penetrated through the wicket. The conspirators being reinforced by a number of armed men that lay in ambuscade, proceeded to surround the palace, which was in itself a fortification, being encompassed by a high wall, defended by a parapet, and flanked by small bastions; each gate was further protected by a piece of ordnance. On the first alarm, the Woon-gees and principal officers of state, took refuge within the inclosure of the palace. During the night, the utmost terror and confusion prevailed throughout the city: at day-break, the number of conspirators being augmented, an attack was made on one of the palace gates, which was blown open: the guard, commanded by an Armenian named Gabriel, stood their ground, and poured three discharges from their cannon on the assailants. After a smart conflict, the event which usually decides the fate of battle between Eastern armies, terminated this; Gabriel was killed by the stroke of a spear, and his party fled on the fall of their leader: the ministers of Chenguza were put to death on the spot. As soon as the tumult subsided, Momien was solemnly proclaimed sovereign of the Birman Empire; a new council was sworn, officers of state appointed, and dignities conferred on the most active partizans. The next measure adopted to secure possession of the throne, was to proclaim Chenguza an outlaw, in a manifesto declaratory of Momien's prior claim, and expatiating on the unworthiness of his predecessor. An armed force was likewise detached both by land and water to Keoptaloun, to seize his person: but Chenguza having received timely information, withdrew across the river; and, accompanied by several attendants, effected his escape to Chagaing, where some men of consequence, who were sensible that they had little to hope from the benevolence of the new government, joined his fortunes, and fed him with hopes of being able to recover the sceptre so suddenly wrested from him. These expectations, however, were of short duration; a tyrant dethroned, has no other friends than the companions of his profligacy, and the accomplices of his guilt.

The fort of Chagaing was immediately invested by troops in the interest of the new king. Chenguza at first thought of defending himself; but finding that he was deserted by those on whom he placed his chief reliance, after a resistance of four days, his resolution failed; and he determined on flying to the Cassay country, there to throw himself on the protection of the Munnipoora Raja. This intention he privately communicated to his mother, the widow of Shembuan Praw, who resided in his palace, in the city of Ava. Instead of encouraging her son to persevere in so pusillanimous a resolve, she earnestly dissuaded him from flight; urging, that it was far more glorious to die even by ignoble hands, within the precincts of his own palace, than to preserve life under the ignominious character of a mendicant, fed by strangers, and indebted for a precarious asylum to a petty potentate. Chenguza yielded to his mother's counsel, and preferring death to disgraceful exile, he caused a small boat to be privately prepared, and kept in readiness at the gaut, or landing place: disguising himself in the habit of a private gentleman, and attended only by two menials, he left Chagaing by break of day, and embarking, rowed towards Ava, on the opposite shore. When the boat approached the principal gaut, at the foot of the walls, he was challenged by the centinels on duty: no longer desirous of concealing himself, he called out in a loud voice, that he was "Chenguza Nandaw-yeng Praw;" "Chenguza, lawful lord of the palace." A conduct at once so unexpected and so resolute, struck the guards with astonishment, who, either overawed by his presence, or at a loss how to act, for want of instructions, suffered him to proceed unmolested; the crowd also, that so extraordinary a circumstance had by this time brought together, respectfully made way for him to pass. Scarce had he reached the gate of the outer court of the palace, when he was met by the Attawoon, father of the princess whom he had so inhumanly slain: Chenguza, on perceiving him, exclaimed, "Traitor, I am come to take possession of my right, and "wreak vengeance on mine enemies." The Attawoon instantly snatched a sabre from an attendant officer, and at one stroke cut the unhappy Chenguza through the bowels, and laid him breathless at his feet. No person was found to prevent, or avenge his death; he fell unlamented, as he had lived despised.

Momien, destined to be a wretched tool in the hands of others, was not long suffered to enjoy his unexpected elevation. At the instigation, it is believed, of the partizans of the present king, he caused the Attawoon who had slain Chenguza to be apprehended; and on the accusation of having shed royal blood, contrary to the express letter of the civil and religious law, when it was his duty only to have seized the person of Chenguza, and brought him a prisoner to the king, this ill-fated nobleman was, without remorse, delivered over to the public executioner.

Shembuan Mia Shean Minderagee Praw, the fourth son of the deceased Alompra, had ever carefully concealed under an humble exterior, and apparent love of retirement, ambition that aspired to the possession of the throne; his influence, though less prominent than that of the other confederates, yet contributed above all to the successful accomplishment of the late revolution. An ideot youth, who had passed his life in monastic retirement, could have but few attached to him from personal affection; and the use he made of his early power, did not encourage a hope that the state would derive much benefit from his future administration. Menderagee, therefore, found no difficulty in forming a party sufficiently powerful to crush in its first stage, the government of the young ecclesiastic. It is, however, surmised, and apparently on good grounds, that the whole chain of events had been preconcerted; and that Momien, when urged to take on him the imperial dignity, after he had fulfilled the views of others, was himself marked for destruction: be this as it may, Minderagee met with little to obstruct the execution of his plans. On the first notice that Chagaing was abandoned by Chenguza, he left Monchaboo, and, at the head of 4000 men, took possession of the evacuated fortress: the partizans of Menderagee profess, that it was not his intention to proceed farther, but to do the duty of a good subject, by preserving the fort for his legal sovereign; and add, that a deputation from the principal personages in Ava, intreating him to come and assume the reins of government, which Momien was found unworthy to hold, alone induced him to take the subsequent steps. In compliance with this real or pretended solicitation, he crossed the Irrawaddy, and seized on the ensigns of imperial authority. Momien was of course made prisoner. Deposition and imprisonment, however, did not satisfy the usurper: without assigning any cause, or granting even the form of trial, the unfortunate nephew was, by his uncle's orders, conveyed to the river, and there plunged into the stream, between two jars, conformably to the Birman mode of executing members of the royal family.

The reign of Momien, from the date of his accession to that of his death, included only eleven days. These events happened in the Birman year 1144.* The present King was then forty-three years of age; he had two sons already grown up to man's estate, and a third by a different mother, yet an infant. Minderagee Praw having now past the impetuous season of youth, ascended the throne with all the advantages derivable from experience and example.

The intoxication that so frequently attends on sudden prosperity, seems not to have affected the new monarch: he did not forget or prove ungrateful to those whose fidelity screened him in his days of danger, and afterwards raised him to the summit of his wishes. Although he obtained the sceptre by an act of aggravated murder, yet, after he became securely seated, he punished with moderation, and rewarded with liberality, wisely extending clemency to the servants of his predecessors. Maha-see-

* Anno Domini, 1782.

soo-ra, who had been dismissed and exiled by Chenguza, was recalled, and placed at the head of the King's private council. The chief Woon-gee,* who possessed power in the reign of Alompra, and had proved under every change a faithful servant to the crown, was continued in office. The person who arrested Momien, and superintended his execution, became principal Maywoon † of the city. The present Viceroy ‡ of Pegue, then a very young man, had the district and town of Meedee conferred on him by a royal grant, as a return for the attachment his father had manifested towards the King, when suffering under the jealousy of Chenguza; deriving also an additional claim, from the circumstance of the King's eldest son having been fostered by his mother, which procured him the honorary title of Teekein, or prince. Many others likewise tasted of the imperial bounty; and whilst obnoxious persons received the benefit of an act of oblivion, denunciations of rigour were proclaimed against such as should in future act contumaciously, or dare to disturb the public repose.

Kings, however, have other enemies to guard against, than avowed foes or rival competitors: the wild maniac, or fanatical enthusiast, often under the influence of frenzy, directs the poignard to the breasts of monarchs. The Birman King had but a short time enjoyed the crown, when he had nearly been deprived both of his life and diadem, by a person of

* *Woon ving Miazo.* This nobleman still presides in the assembly of Woons; and although, from years, become incapable of close attention to business, is held in high respect for his long tried probity and private worth.

† There are four Maywoons, each of whom superintends the jurisdiction of a quarter of the city; they represent the king in their respective courts; their decisions, in capital cases, are revised by the Woons in the Lotoo, and afterwards finally determined by the king himself.

‡ This personage is commonly called Meedee Teekein, or Prince of Meedee; spelt by Mr. Wood, Meeayday.

this description. Magoung, a low born man, unconnected, and it is said without the privacy of any person of condition, who had always been remarkable for the regularity of his actions, and a gloomy cast of thought; had influence enough to form a confederacy of 100 men, as visionary and desperate as himself. This troop bound themselves in secrecy and fidelity to each other by an oath: their object was to take away the life of the king; but to answer what end, or whom they designed to elevate, is not ascertained. These desperadoes, headed by Magoung, at daybreak in the morning, made an attack on the palace. The customary guard over the king's dwelling consists of 700 men, who are well appointed, and kept alert on duty. Notwithstanding this, the attempt had nearly succeeded: bearing down the centinels, they penetrated into the interior court, and the king escaped, from the casual circumstance of being in the range of apartments belonging to the women, which he was least accustomed to frequent. His guards, who at first shrunk from the fury of the onset, quickly rallied; their courage and numbers overpowered the assassins; and Magoung, with all his associates, were slain within the precincts of the palace.

Minderagee Praw, whilst he led a recluse and private life, had imbibed much of the superstition that so strongly tinctures every form of religion in the East. The gloomy Islamite,* and tranquil Hindoo,+ are alike bigotted

* The Mussulman and Hindoo, though equally bigotted, yet, in their doctrinal tenets, are curiously contrasted. The Koran enjoins the disciples of Mahommed to make proselytes of the whole world, by the edge of the sword; the Shaster proscribes the whole world, and denies the cord of Hindooism to all mankind. The Mussulmen, 700 years ago, cut the throats of the Hindoos, because they refused to be circumcised: the Indians never invite any man to abjure his faith.

to their faith, and susceptible of the prejudices which ignorance and priest-craft inculcate into minds uninstructed in the benign and enlightened doctrines of Christianity. During his days of leisure, the king had directed much of his attention to astronomical studies, and became a thorough believer in judicial astrology: Bramins, who though inferior in sanctity to the Rhahaans, are nevertheless held in high respect by the Birmans, had for ages been accustomed to migrate from Cassay and Arracan, to Ava, where they always met with a favourable reception, and, on account of their superior knowledge, were appointed professors of science. A college was established, and certain lands appropriated for its support: these doctors composed almanacs, calculated eclipses, and pronounced, from their intercourse with the planets, the propitious or adverse season, to attempt any momentous undertaking. Minderagee Praw had early accustomed himself to reverence this sect; he received from them instructions in his favourite study, and listened to their predictions with implicit credulity. Long before his elevation they had foretold the fortune that awaited him, and the accomplishment of their prediction, confirmed Braminical influence: he appointed a certain number to be his private chaplains, who, on court days, arrayed in white robes, and standing round the throne, chant a solemn benediction in melodious recitative. This ceremony is performed as soon as the king ascends the imperial seat, and before the commencement of public business. Prompted partly by the persuasions of his inspired counsellors, and partly by that desire of change which Birman monarchs superstitiously entertain, Minderagee resolved to withdraw the seat of government from Awa Haung,* and found a new city. The site fixed on for the projected settlement was judicious: about four miles

* Ancient Ava.

north-east of Ava, there is a deep and extensive lake called Tounzemaun, formed by the influx of the river during the monsoon, through a narrow channel, which afterwards expands and displays a body of water a mile and a half broad, and seven or eight miles long. This lake first takes a northerly direction, nearly parallel with the river; it afterwards curves to the south-east, in a lessening sheet, and diminishes to a morass, favourable for the culture of rice. When filled by the periodical rains, the lake, with the river on one side, incloses a dry and healthy peninsula, on which Ummerapoora, the name given to the new city, now stands. Buildings in the Birman country are composed for the most part of wood, and water carriage being here convenient, the old town was speedily demolished, and the present capital rose from its materials; whilst such was the assiduity used in removal, that Ummerapoora became in a short time one of the most flourishing and well built cities of the East; the fort, likewise, which is spacious and regular, is completely fortified after the Asiatic manner. A lofty rampart, protected by a parapet, and strengthened by bastions composed of excellent masonry, is further secured by a deep and broad ditch, faced with brick, and filled with water: the gateways are guarded by cannon, and retrenchments defend the passes of the ditch.

The first year of the reign of Minderagee, was distinguished by the attempt of another petty insurgent, who meditated nothing less than the overthrow of the Birman, and the re-establishment of the Talien monarchy. A fanatic fisherman of Rangoon, named Natchien, a man of mean extraction, availed himself of a prophecy circulated among the vulgar, that a person of his profession was to prove the instrument of deliverance to the Pegue people; and on the faith of this prediction, he induced several Peguers, who lived in the district of Dalla, to enter into his designs, and engage in his support. These desperadoes made an attack upon the municipal officers, when assembled in the Rhoom, or public hall of justice, several of whom they put to the sword; but by the spirited exertions of the Maywoon, the rebellion was crushed before it reached to a height that could endanger the state. Tranquillity and order were speedily restored. On this occasion, upwards of 500 Peguers suffered death by the executioner; which impressed such a lasting terror on the minds of others, that no attempt has since been made by the Peguers, to cast off the Birman yoke.

The new monarch, more ambitious than his nephew, not content with the widely extended dominions which he possessed, meditated yet further acquisitions, in a quarter hitherto untried by any descendant of Alompra. Conquest had already been stretched southward as far as Mergui, on the coast of Tenasserem, comprehending Tavoy, and the several ports on the western shore of the peninsula. Complete subjugation of the Cassayers was scarcely to be expected, as from their hills and fastnesses they could incessantly harrass the invaders, and render the country an unproductive waste. Zemee, Sandapoora,* and many districts of the Yoodra Shaan to the eastward, were tributary and governed by Chobwas, who annually paid homage to the Birman King. The province of Bamoo, the fort of Quantong, and several places of less note, had been taken from the Chinese, as far as the woody mountains that divide the south-west of Manchegee, or Yunan, from the kingdom of Ava. West of Anoupectoumiou lay a country, the fertility of whose soil, and its aptitude for commerce, attracted the avarice of the Birman monarch, whilst the imbecility of its government invited to an easy conquest. The distance from the town of

* The Pali name for Lauchung, or Laos.

Sembeu-Ghewn, on the west bank of the river Irrawaddy, to Merong Chickien, at the eastern foot of the hills, does not exceed forty-five miles; thence the distance over the mountains to Tellakee, on the opposite side, is fifty-six miles, but the road* is so difficult from natural impediments, that an enterprizing people might, with a small force, defend the passes against any numbers. The Birman King, however, was too well acquainted with the supineness of Mahasumda,† Raja of Arracan, and the unwarlike disposition of his subjects, to dread any vigorous opposition; he determined to invade the country, with a view to wrest it from its ancient rulers, and render it an appendage to the Birman crown.

The ancient government of Arracan, according to the most authentic writers, had never been so completely conquered as to acknowledge implicit vassalage to a foreign power: it experienced, in the two last centuries, the usual convulsions to which all states, and those of the eastern world in particular, are liable. The Moguls on the west,‡ and the Peguers on the east, had, at different periods, carried their arms into the heart of the country. The Portugueze,§ sometimes as allies, at others as open enemies, gained an establishment in Arracan, which decayed only

* Since the final conquest of Arracan, the road from Sembeu-Ghewn to Tellakee has been considerably improved; it is nevertheless still a laborious journey, owing to the ruggedness of the way, and the steep mountains over which the traveller must pass.

† Mahasumda is the Shanscrit title given to a long line of Kings of Arracan. Eastern kings, whilst living, are usually denominated by their titles, of which they have many.

‡ The unfortunate Sultan Sujah, brother to Aurungzebe, was, by the king of this country, basely betrayed and put to death, for the sake of his treasure. See Dow's Hindostan.

§ Faria de Souza, on the Portugueze conquests in Asia.

One Sebastian Gonzales, owing to a combination of successful events, made himself master of the island of Cheduba, or Sandiva, which he maintained for some time, as an with the general ruin of their interests in Asia. Arracan, however, though often exhausted, was never wholly consumed; it always rose from its own ashes, a free and independent nation.

The natives of Arracan proper, call their country Yee-Kein; the Hindoos of Bengal, Rossaun; the latter, who have settled in great numbers in Arracan, are denominated, by the original inhabitants, Kulaw Yee-Kein, or unnaturalized Arracaners; the Moguls know it by the Persian name of Rechan. Mogo is a term of religious import, and high sanctity, applied to the priesthood, and the king; whence the inhabitants are often called by Europeans, Mughs: such a number of epithets used indiscriminately, must prove embarrassing to the reader of the few sketches that have been given of this country. Arracan, or Yee-Kein, stretches south-south-east from the river Naff, the boundary that divides it from the territories of the India Company, as far as Cape Negrais, where the ancient Pegue empire commenced. The range of lofty mountains already mentioned, under the name of Anoupectoumiou, nearly encircles it. From the quarter of Bassien and Negrais, Arracan can be invaded only by water, through the many rivers that intersect the country adjacent to the sea. From the side of Chittagong, entrance into Arracan must be effected by a march along the sea beach, which is interrupted by several channels, that chiefly owe their waters to the action of the tide. Arracan thus displays a great space of coast, very disproportionate to its internal extension. A few miles below Tellakee, at the western foot, the river, till then a streamlet that rises in the hills, becomes navigable from the influx of the sea; in two tides a boat reaches the fort of Arracan.

independent principality; his rise was owing to a series of heinous crimes, and his rapid fall is to be ascribed to the same source. Faria.

From the fort to the sea, the river expands into a noble sheet of water, well adapted for trade, and the reception of shipping. Cheduba and Ramree, called by the Birmans Magou Kioun, and Yamgee Kioun,* are extensive and highly cultivated islands, which, with Arracan and Sandowy, form four distinct provinces, and comprehend the whole of the Arracan empire.

The trade of Arracan was never very considerable; it is confined to salt, bees' wax, elephants' teeth, and rice. This latter article is produced in such abundance, that it might be improved, by proper policy, into a lucrative branch of commerce; the soil is luxuriant and well watered, and the contiguous islands are uncommonly fruitful. Possession of Arracan and these islands, became a still more desirable acquisition to the Birmans, as affording protection to their boats, which, navigating in the north-west monsoon through the channel and along the coast, make an annual voyage from Bassien, Rangoon, and Martaban, to Chittagong and Calcutta, where they dispose of the produce of their countries, and in return bring back cloth, and commodities of India.

The invasion of Arracan being finally determined on, the Engee Teekien, or prince royal, with his brothers, the princes of Prome, Tonghò, and Pagahm, in the Birman year 1145† (corresponding to 1783 of the Christian era), in the month Touzelien, left the imperial city, and crossed to Chagaing, now become a place of religious resort from the number of Praws, or temples erected in its neighbourhood; as well as for being the principal manufactory of idols, which, hewn out of an adjacent quarry‡

* These are the vulgar names, they have also Shanscrit appellations.

† The Birman solar year, ending at the vernal equinox, may create an apparent confusion in stating the two eras.

‡ The quarry is at Meengoung, about twelve miles distant.

of fine alabaster, are sculptured here, and afterwards transported to the remotest corners of the empire. At this city, they passed three days in the performance of religious ceremonies; proceeding thence to Pagahm,* in past ages the residence of a long dynasty of kings, and still famed for its numerous temples, they renewed the pious rites; after which they pursued their journey to Kama, whence 5000 men, under the Princes of Tongho and Pagahm, were detached with orders to debark at Maoung (formerly Loonzay), and invade Arracan, by penetrating through the passes of the mountains. When the Engee Teekien and the Prince of Prome reached the city of Prome, the Seree of Shegoo was ordered to fall down the Irrawaddy with a strong fleet of boats, and enter Arracan by the creeks and channels of the Bassien river. The elder princes remained at Prome five days, and then crossed to Podang on the opposite bank, three miles lower down; here they halted fifteen days, in order to give the other detachments, whose routes were more circuitous, time to advance.

At the expiration of the period that was judged necessary for the cooperation of the different detachments, the Engee Teekien ordered the Prince of Prome, at the head of 7000 men, to advance, and attempt the defiles of the hills leading from Podang, whilst he conducted, in person, the main army, keeping three days march in the rear of the front division.

* Pagahm was once a city of no ordinary magnificence and extent; the writer of this memoir, accompanied by the Viceroy of Pegue, ascended one of the pagodas or praws, by a decayed and dangerous flight of steps on the outside; they had from the summit a view of ruins, thickly scattered over the face of the country, as far as the eye could reach. The Viceroy remarked, that to count the number of decayed temples on the plain before us, was among the proverbial impossibilities of the Birmans.

Two generals of reputation accompanied the Engee Teekien, Kioumee Matoung, and Nunda Siekyan: the detachment sent by water, under the Seree, reached its destination before those that went by land could arrive. This officer met with no obstacle until he reached the frontiers of Arracan, where, hearing that the prince of the country was preparing to attack him, he judged it most prudent to halt, and wait the approach of his friends, in order to prevent the Arracaners from concentrating their force against his party.

The way pursued by the junior princes,* was yet more difficult and distant than that by which the prince royal proceeded; probably they were sent only to make a diversion, and distract the attention of the enemy. After a troublesome march of three weeks, the Prince of Prome, with the advanced guard of the main army, reached Loungyat,† two days journey from the fort of Arracan, where, learning the situation of the Seree, he sent a body of 1000 men, under an Ackawoon, to his assistance.

Impatient of delay, and probably desirous of seizing the present opportunity to distinguish himself, the Prince of Prome resolved to assault the fort before his brother should arrive; with this intent he wrote to the Seree, ordering him to advance next day with the fleet, promising to co-operate and support him. In compliance with the Prince's commands, the Seree put his armament in motion; the King of Arracan had by this time collected a fleet of boats, which surpassed, in size, those of the Birmans, although they were inferior in point of numbers. An action took

* The Princes of Tongho and Pagahm were infants at this time; the direction of the armies was intrusted to others. It is a customary thing for Eastern princes to send their sons into the field, at a very tender age.

† The distance is estimated at one hundred and twenty miles.

place about two miles from the fort, which terminated decidedly in favour of the Birmans. The Arracan vessels were for the most part destroyed; those that escaped, spread consternation around: the approach of the Prince of Prome's army, completed the terror of the frighted inhabitants. Mahasumda, in despair, collected his most valuable effects, which he put on board boats, and then embarked himself, accompanied by twenty females of his palace, and thirty attendants, chiefly relations. This party directed their course to an island called Kiounchoppa; but the Prince of Prome, receiving early intelligence of their flight, ordered a detachment of 500 men, in light boats, to pursue the fugitives. The Birmans overtook them within one mile of the island, where Mahasumda being made prisoner, together with all his retinue, was conducted back a captive to his own capital.

When the Engee Teekien reached Loungyat, he was apprized of the success of his brother. The town and fort of Arracan fell after a faint resistance; the booty found is said to have been very considerable, but on nothing was a higher value placed than on an image of Gaudma (the Goutema* of the Hindoos), made of brass, and highly burnished. The figure is about ten feet high, in the customary sitting posture, with the legs crossed and inverted; the left hand resting on the lap, and the right pendant. This image is believed to be the original resemblance of the Reshee, taken from life, and is so highly venerated, that pilgrims have for centuries been accustomed to come from the remotest countries, where the supremacy of Gaudma is acknowledged, to pay their devotions at the feet of his brazen representative. There were also five images of Rakuss, the demon of the Hindoos, of the same metal and of gigantic stature; these were accounted

* Goutema is a name for Boodh, or Budhoo.

of value, being guardians to the sanctuary of the idol. A singular piece* of ordnance was also found, of enormous dimensions, composed of huge bars of iron beaten into form: this ponderous cannon measured thirty feet in length, two feet and a half in diameter at the mouth, and ten inches in the calibre; it was transported to Ummerapoora by water, and deposited in the yard of the royal palace, where it is now preserved as a military trophy; it is mounted on a low carriage supported by six wheels, and is covered from the weather by a wooden pent-house. Gaudma and his infernal guards were, in like manner, conveyed by water to the capital, with much pomp and superstitious parade.

The surrender of Cheduba, Ramree, and the Broken Isles, followed the conquest of Arracan: many of the Mughs,† or subjects of the Great Mogo, preferred flight to servitude, taking refuge in the Dumbuck hills, on the borders of the province of Chittagong, and in the deep forests and jungles that skirt the frontier: where they formed themselves into independent tribes of robbers, that have since created infinite vexation to the Birmans, and to this day commit merciless depredations on the persons and property of their conquerors; many have settled in the districts of Dacca and Chittagong, under the protection of the British flag, whilst others accepted the oath of allegiance, and bowed their necks to slavery, rather than abandon their country, and their household gods.‡

The Princes of Tongho and Pagahm did not reach Arracan until the

* The writer of this memoir, after his first audience, was indulged with a sight of this extraordinary piece of ordnance, and honoured with an introduction to the Arracan Gaudma.

† The ancient inhabitants of Arracan are so called, from being subjects of the Great Mogo.

‡ The sectaries of Budhoo are much attached to their Lares, or domestic gods. A Birman family is never without an idol in some corner of the house, made of wood, alabaster, or silver.

business was decided; although they bore no share in the conquest, they secured a proportion of the booty;* the followers of the Tongho Prince, in particular, are said to have committed the most wanton excesses on the unhappy natives of the country through which they passed.

The arrangements attending their conquest, occupied the princes for some time. Arracan, with its dependencies, was constituted a province of the Birman empire, and a Maywoon, or Viceroy, appointed to govern it. A man named Sholamboo, was first invested with that office, and one thousand Birman soldiers were left to garrison the fort; small parties were likewise distributed in the different towns, and many Birmans, who had obtained grants of lands, came with their families and settled in the country, thereby increasing the security of the state. These matters being adjusted, the princes returned to the Irrawaddy by the same route they had advanced, and embarked at Podang, carrying with them Mahasumda and all his family. This unfortunate monarch was treated at Ummerapoora with much respect; he was allotted a suitable dwelling and establishment, which he did not long enjoy; before the first year of his captivity had elapsed, he died a natural death; after his decease his relations were suffered to sink into obscurity and want. The reduction of Arracan was completed in the short space of a few months.

The more recent actions of the reign of the present emperor† may with greater propriety be circumstantially recounted at some future period; a

* The inhabitants of Tongho are famous for their ferocity and licentiousness; a character well preserved by the numerous followers of the Prince of Tongho, when the writer of this memoir was at the Birman capital.

† *Boa*, or emperor, is a title which the present king of the Birmans has assumed; the sovereign of China is called *Oudee Boa*, or Emperor of Oudee, or China.

brief recital of the principal events, and a concise view of the existing state of the empire, with the reflections which such a view naturally suggests, will enable the reader to form an adequate opinion of the political importance of the nation that has been treated of, and will close the subject of the present Chapter.

The valuable acquisition of Arracan, did not satisfy the lust of conquest that inflamed the emperor; he turned his eyes towards the eastern peninsula, where the rival state of Siam was recovering its former vigour, after enjoying a long respite from hostility

The success of the Birman arms over the Siamese, conducted by King Shembuan, has already been recounted. Although the Birmans could not retain possession of the inland parts of Siam, they nevertheless preserved dominion over the sea coast; all the ports on the western shore of the Peninsula, as far as Mergui, in north lat. 12° 20′, continued subject to them. The island of Junkseylon was the only addition wanting to give them the entire dominion of the western coast, as far as the territories of the Malay Prince of Queedah; by obtaining this island, the Birmans would monopolize the commerce of the Peninsula, and prevent the Siamese from communication with India by any other channel than that of the Gulf of Siam. The trade of Junkseylon is considerable in ivory and tin: it stretches nearly north and south, about fifty or sixty miles: the centre of the island is situated in eight degrees north; it is likewise said to be desirable from the blessings of a luxuriant soil, and a mild climate. To effect this object, eleven ships of burthen were fitted out at Rangoon, destined to convey troops and warlike stores: the Birmans, though expert shipwrights, are indifferent seamen, and altogether ignorant of the science of navigation: the present Shawbunder of Rangoon, descended of a Portugueze family, was appointed to conduct the fleet. The different vessels were commanded by persons of a like description, who had been bred up under the Birman government, and held petty offices in the maritime ports; they, however, were considered in a light little superior to pilots, being under the check and control of the commander of the land forces on board: this fleet reached Mergui in the month of January, 1785.

In support of the troops and squadron sent by sea, a detachment of 8000 men marched in the month of November from Rangoon; this body did not reach Mergui until the 18th of February: on the 7th of March following, the fleet weighed anchor, and the forces by land made in a correspondent movement. The arm of the sea that divides Junkseylon from the main, is in some places very narrow: the Birmans immediately on their arrival, attacked the fort, which is situated on the east side of the island; and were successful, notwithstanding a spirited resistance made by Prawselong, the Siamese governor, who afterwards withdrew from he fort into the interior of the island. The Birmans found here a valuable booty, which they embarked on board a vessel captured in the harbour, belonging to a Mussulman merchant of Masulipatam; but the ship never reached her destined port: meeting with a gale of wind in the Bay of Martaban, she foundered at sea, and every soul perished. The triumph of the Birmans was of short duration; the Siamese governor rallied his forces, and having procured an addition to his strength, became in his turn the assailant, with so good effect, that the Birmans thought fit to retreat to their shipping, which they did not accomplish without a heavy loss: apprehensive of yet greater disasters, they returned to Mergui, whence the fleet sailed for Rangoon, and the troops marched to Martaban, with intent to canton during the rainy season.

The Birman monarch, whose pride was deeply mortified at the ill fortune of his arms at Junkseylon, resolved to repair the disgrace, and invade Siam with such a force as he conceived would be irresistible; and further, to insure success, announced his intention to lead the troops in person. He accordingly left Ummerapoora at the head of 30,000 men, with a train of twenty field pieces, and taking the route of Tongho, reached Martaban in the spring of the year 1786: a detachment was likewise sent to invade north Siam, and another ordered to penetrate on the southern quarter from Tavoy. A fleet was also equipped, consisting of sixteen ships, mostly belonging to traders, which were either hired of the owners, or impressed for the occasion: this armament blocked up the harbour of Junkseylon. Such vigorous preparations inspired the Birmans with sanguine hopes: too much confidence, however, often betrays into error. The Emperor, already anticipating victory, marched from Martaban, and had scarcely entered the Siamese territories, when he was opposed by Pietick-sing, the King of Siam, with a powerful army; a furious engagement ensued, in which the Birmans were completely routed, and their useless cannon* taken by the enemy. The Emperor himself, who narrowly escaped being made prisoner, returned to his capital with precipitation: the fugitives found protection in Martaban; and the other detachments hearing of the misfortune of the main body, likewise retreated. The season for field operations being far advanced, hostilities were for sometime suspended on both sides.

In the commencement of the ensuing year, the Siamese, in considerable force, laid siege to Tavòy; but after a long struggle were compelled to

* Many well informed men among the Birmans, ascribe their defeat to the incumbrance of their cannon, which were old ship guns mounted on low carriages.

retreat and abandon the enterprize. The place was defended by Maha-see-soo-ra, who in the month of April, 1788, was promoted to the Maywoonship, or Viceroyalty of Martaban, which comprehends within its jurisdiction, Tavoy, Mergui, and all the Birman possessions to the southward. Tavoy being a place of great importance, was left with a strong garrison, to the care of an officer named Numeapeou, by some called Miapeou, a man of low extraction, whose father had originally been a merchant of small ware between China and Ava, and having amassed money, obtained influence by a judicious application of his wealth. For some time Miapeou conducted himself with fidelity in his command; but on the decease of Maha-see-soo-ra, in the year 1790, being disappointed of the Viceroyalty of Martaban, which was given to an officer named Meen-la-ze-zo, he entered into an intrigue with the Siamese, and agreed to deliver up the fort to them, on certain stipulations for himself and his adherents; the compact being concluded, possession was given to the enemy, who stationed a strong garrison in it, and as a further protection, encamped a body of troops in its neighbourhood.

Early in the year 1791, Sombee Meengee and Attawoon Mien, officers of high distinction, were ordered to proceed from Ummerapoora by land against the rebel; a fleet of sixty boats sailed about the same time from Rangoon, which were speedily to be followed by three ships, then fitting out at the same port. The boats having arrived before the ships could reach their destination, injudiciously entered the river of Tavoy, and began an attack on the suburbs bordering on the banks. Miapeou, with a party of rebel Birmans and a detachment of Siamese, opposed them, and in light war-boats soon got the better of the unwieldy junks that had crossed the bay. Many of the Birman vessels were destroyed, and those that escaped took refuge in Mergui, where soon after this disaster, the ships also arrived.

The army from Ummerapoora having reached Martaban, halted there during the rainy monsoon. Early in the season for action, the Engee Praw, or Prince royal, left the capital and came down to Rangoon, bringing with him a considerable accession to the southern force; the Assay Woongee, and several officers of distinguished rank, attended in his suite. By the time he had reached Rangoon, the first division, under Sombee Meengee and Attawoon Mein, had proceeded against Tavoy; the prince halted at Rangoon, but sent forward the greatest part of his troops to support the advanced army: the ships also that had put into Mergui, again sailed for Tavoy. On the arrival of the army and shipping, an engagement took place between the Siamese and Birmans, partly on land, and partly at the mouth of the river, the Siamese disputing the entrance in their war-boats; in this contest the Siamese were worsted, and driven with great slaughter into the fort, which the Birmans immediately invested; and having entrenched and stockaded themselves, commenced a formal blockade. No supplies could now reach the besieged, whilst the Birmans, though the adjacent country was unproductive, being masters of the sea, procured subsistence from Arracan and Rangoon, which the provincial officers of those countries transported to the army, in whatever ships they could lay their hands on, pressing indiscriminately the vessels* of all nations, that

* Amongst these were several ships belonging to English traders, the commanders of which forwarded a remonstrance to Lord Cornwallis, and the Supreme Council, complaining of the outrage. It is generally supposed, that the Birman King ordered liberal remuneration to be made to those whose ships were pressed, but that the provincial officers fraudulently withheld his bounty.

happened to be in their ports. The seige was thus protracted for some months, and the place at last fell by treachery. The Birmans, who under Miapeou had originally been instrumental to putting the fort in possession of the Siamese, became discontented, probably through want: a clandestine correspondence commenced between them and the leaders of the besieging army: a proper understanding being established, at a concerted hour of the night, the enemy advanced to storm the outworks of the fort; when the Siamese rose to repel the assault, the Birmans within, whose fidelity was not suspected, fell upon the garrison, which, consisting of 3000 gallant soldiers, were cut to pieces, either by their pretended allies, or avowed foes, who soon gained admission through the means of their perfidious countrymen. Miapeou was not found; he had withdrawn from the fort sometime before, and escaped into the country of the Siamese. The Birmans thus again became masters of the important fortress of Tavoy.

In the mean while affairs at Mergui seemed likely to exhibit a different scene from that which was passing at Tavoy: here, the Birmans acted on the defensive, and the Siamese were the assailants. A brother of the King of Siam had invested the garrison with a strong force, and pressed the siege so closely that the Birmans were reduced to the utmost extremity, and must have surrendered, but for the opportune arrival of six ships and 5000 men, detached to their aid from Tavoy; the besiegers, disheartened by the appearance of these succours, relinquished the enterprise, and retired into the interior of the country.

Subsequent to these events, no action of importance appears to have taken place between the contending powers; the year 1793 opened with overtures for peace on the part of the Siamese; a negociation commenced, which speedily terminated in the ratification of a treaty, highly favourable to the Birman interests. By this compact, the Siamese ceded to the Birmans, the western maritime towns, as far south as Mergui, thus yielding to them entire possession of the coast of Tenasserem, and the two important ports of Mergui and Tavoy; acquisitions of great moment, when considered either in a political or commercial light.

Indisputably pre-eminent among the nations inhabiting the vast peninsula that separates the gulf of Bengal from the Chinese sea; possessed of a territory equal in extent to the German empire; blessed with a salubrious climate, and a soil capable of producing almost every article of luxury, convenience, and commerce, that the East can supply, Miamma, or Birmah, thus happily circumstanced, enjoyed the pleasing prospect of a long exemption from the miseries of war; but unbending pride, and resentment unjustifiably prosecuted, nearly embroiled them in fresh troubles, before they had time to profit by the advantages of peace, and threatened to raise them up a foe far more formidable than the Chinese, Arracaners, Peguers, Siamese, and Cassayers.

The trade of Arracan, which is chiefly carried on with the eastern ports through an inland navigation, when the rivers are swollen by the rains, had suffered repeated interruptions from piratical banditti, who, infesting the Broken Islands, among which the channels wind, that are the usual course of boats, not only committed depredations on private merchants, but had even the hardiness to attack fleets, laden with the royal customs.* These robbers, when the season of the year did not admit of their plundering on the water, sought adventures by land; and, as the Birmans allege, conveyed their booty of goods and cattle across the river Naaf, into the

* Customs are usually received in kind, viz. one-tenth of the commodity.

Chittagong province, where, secure from pursuit, being then under protection of the British flag, they disposed of their spoils to advantage, and lived at ease, until returning want impelled them to renew their predatory inroads.

The river Naaf, which bounds the British and Birman territories, is situated at a considerable distance from the town of Chittagong, the seat of provincial government, and residence of the English magistrate. The banks of this river are covered with deep jungles, interspersed with scanty spots of cultivation, and a few wretched villages, where dwell the poorest class of herdsmen, and the families of roving hunters, whose occupation it is to catch and tame the wild elephants, with which these forests abound. The asylum that such unfrequented places offered to persons concerned in a lawless traffic, rendered it easy to be carried on without the knowledge of the English officers of justice; nor could it possibly reach the notice of the Supreme Board, unless a proper representation was made, either by the individuals that were aggrieved, or by the government of their country. This, however, was a condescension, to which the mighty Emperor of the Birmans, who conceives himself superior to every potentate on earth, would never stoop. To ask redress was beneath his dignity; he proceeded by a more summary course to do himself justice. On its being ascertained that three distinguished leaders of the robbers had sought refuge in the British districts, his Birman Majesty, without communicating his intention, or in any form demanding the fugitives, thought fit to order a body of 5000 men, under an officer of rank, to enter the Company's territories, with positive injunctions to the commander not to return, unless he brought with him the delinquents, dead or alive; further, to support this detachment, an army of 20,000 men were held in readiness at Arracan.

So unexpected an aggression, offered without any previous remonstrance, or the assignment of any plea, left no room for discussing the merits of the case. The Birmans having taken upon themselves to redress their own grievances, it became necessary to convince them that they had mistaken the mode; and what they might readily procure from English justice, they could never extort through fear: to accomplish this purpose, a strong detachment was formed at the presidency, the conduct of which was intrusted to Major General Erskine; the troops proceeded from Calcutta to Chittagong, a battalion of Europeans and artillery by water, and the native sepoys by land.

Seree Nunda Kiozo, the Birman chief, to whom the arduous task of reclaiming the fugitives was assigned, acted with more circumspection and prudence, than the government from which he had received his instructions. After his army had crossed the river, and encamped on the western bank, he dictated a letter to the British judge and magistrate of Chittagong, acquainting him of the reasons for the inroad; that the caption of the delinquents was his sole object, without harbouring any design of hostilities against the English. At the same time he declared, in a style of of peremptory demand, that until they were given up, he would not depart from the Company's territories: in confirmation of this menace, he fortified his camp in the Birman manner, with a stockade, and seemed determined to resist any attempt to oblige him to retire. These matters being reported to government, the Governor General was pleased to order the Magistrate of Chittagong to apprehend the refugees, and keep them in safe custody until further directions.

On the approach of General Erskine, Seree Nunda Kiozo sent a flag of truce, to propose terms of accommodation, stipulating for the surrender of the fugitives, as the basis of the agreement. The General replied, that no proposals could be listened to whilst the Birmans continued on English ground; but as soon as they should withdraw from their fortified camp, and retire within their own frontiers, he would enter upon the subject of their complaints; notifying also, that unless they evacuated the Company's possessions in a limited time, force would be used to compel them. The Birman chief, in a manly confidence of the English character, personally waited on General Erskine, and disclosed to him the nature of his instructions, the enormity of the offenders, and the outrages they had committed. General Erskine, whose moderation and judgment on this occasion cannot be too highly commended, assured him, that it was far from the intention of the British government to screen delinquents, or sanction in their country an asylum for robbers; but as the manner in which the Birman troops had entered the Company's district, was so repugnant to the principles that ought to regulate the conduct of civilized nations, it was impossible for him to recede from his first determination. He gave hopes, notwithstanding, that if the Birmans peaceably retired, the Governor General would institute a regular inquiry into the charges preferred against the prisoners: adding, that instant compliance with the conditions prescribed, was the only ground on which they could expect so great an indulgence. The Birman General, either contented with this intimation, or convinced that opposition would be fruitless, professed his reliance on General Erskine, and agreed to withdraw his troops: the retreat was conducted in the most orderly manner; and so strict was the subordination observed in the Birman army, that not one act of violence was committed either on the person or property of British subjects, during the time their troops continued within the Company's districts. General

Erskine was afterwards empowered, by the Governor General, to investigate the charges against the refugees, when, after a formal and deliberate hearing, their guilt being established on the clearest evidence, they were delivered over to their own laws, by whose sentence, two out of the three underwent capital punishment.

The amicable termination of this difference, afforded favourable opportunity to acquire a more accurate knowledge than had hitherto been obtained, of a people, whose situation, extent of territory, and commercial connections with British India, rendered a liberal intercourse with them highly desirable. The trade between Calcutta, Madras, and Rangoon, had of late years so rapidly increased, as to become an object of national importance, more particularly on account of teak timber, the produce of Ava and Pegue, whence Calcutta and Madras* draw all their supplies of wood for ship building, and for various other purposes. A commerce in one article so essential to us, and, on a general scale, so extensive as to require an annual return of Indian commodities to the amount of £200,000. sterling, was an object well worth cultivating. Representations had, at different times, been made to the Supreme Board by private merchants, and mariners, complaining of injustice and oppression at the port of Rangoon; the recent inroad of the Birmans, which originated partly in pride, and partly in ignorance, would probably not have occurred, had there existed an

* Teak cannot be conveyed from the Malabar to the Coromandel coast, or to Calcutta, unless at an expence so great, as to preclude the attempt. It is said, that this incomparable wood grows in perfection on the banks of the river Godavery; but the impediments of procuring it from that quarter have hitherto been found insurmountable. Several excellent ships, built in the river of Bengal, of Pegue teak, have delivered and received cargoes in the river Thames.

authorized channel of intercourse between the respective governments. To prevent the recurrence of a like misunderstanding; to form a commercial connexion on equitable and fixed principles, and to establish a confidential and authentic correspondence, such as ought to subsist between two great and contiguous nations; Sir John Shore (now Lord Teignmouth) thought proper to send a formal deputation to the Birman court. Nor were these the only ends to be answered by the embassy; the influence, which the natural enemies of Great Britain had acquired in that quarter, was to be combated, and, if possible, overcome; whilst the natives were to be impressed with an adequate sense of the power, the resources, and, above all, the equity of the British character, in such a manner as to convince them that their real interests were connected with a state that neither meditated, nor would suffer encroachment; and sought for nothing beyond an interchange of merchandize, on terms mutually beneficial. The result of this mission, through the various stages of its progress and completion, will be detailed in the subsequent pages; thus far it has realised the expectations of the British government, and gives a flattering promise of national advantage, except it should hereafter be obstructed by impediments, which no penetration can foresee, and against which no human compact can provide.

The Birmans, under their present monarch, are certainly rising fast in the scale of Oriental nations; and, it is to be hoped, that a long respite from foreign wars, will give them leisure to improve their natural advantages. Knowledge increases with commerce; and as they are not shackled by any prejudices of casts, restricted to hereditary occupations, or forbidden from participating with strangers in every social bond, their advancement will, in all probability be rapid. At present, so far from being in a state of intellectual darkness, although they have not explored the depths of science, or reached to excellence in the finer arts, they yet have an undeniable claim to the character of a civilized, and well instructed, people. Their laws are wise, and pregnant with sound morality; their police is better regulated than in most European countries; their natural disposition is friendly, and hospitable to strangers; and their manners rather expressive of manly candour, than courteous dissimulation: the gradations of rank, and the respect due to station, are maintained with a scrupulosity which never relaxes. A knowledge of letters is so widely diffused, that there are no mechanics, few of the peasantry, or even the common watermen (usually the most illiterate class) who cannot read and write in the vulgar tongue. Few, however, are versed in the more erudite volumes of science, which, containing many Shanscrit terms, and often written in the Pali text, are (like the Hindoo Shasters) above the comprehension of the multitude; but the feudal system, which cherishes ignorance, and renders man the property of man, still operates as a check to civilization and improvement. This is a bar which gradually weakens, as their acquaintance with the customs and manners of other nations extends; and unless the rage of civil discord be again excited, or some foreign power impose an alien yoke, the Birmans bid fair to be a prosperous, wealthy, and enlightened people.

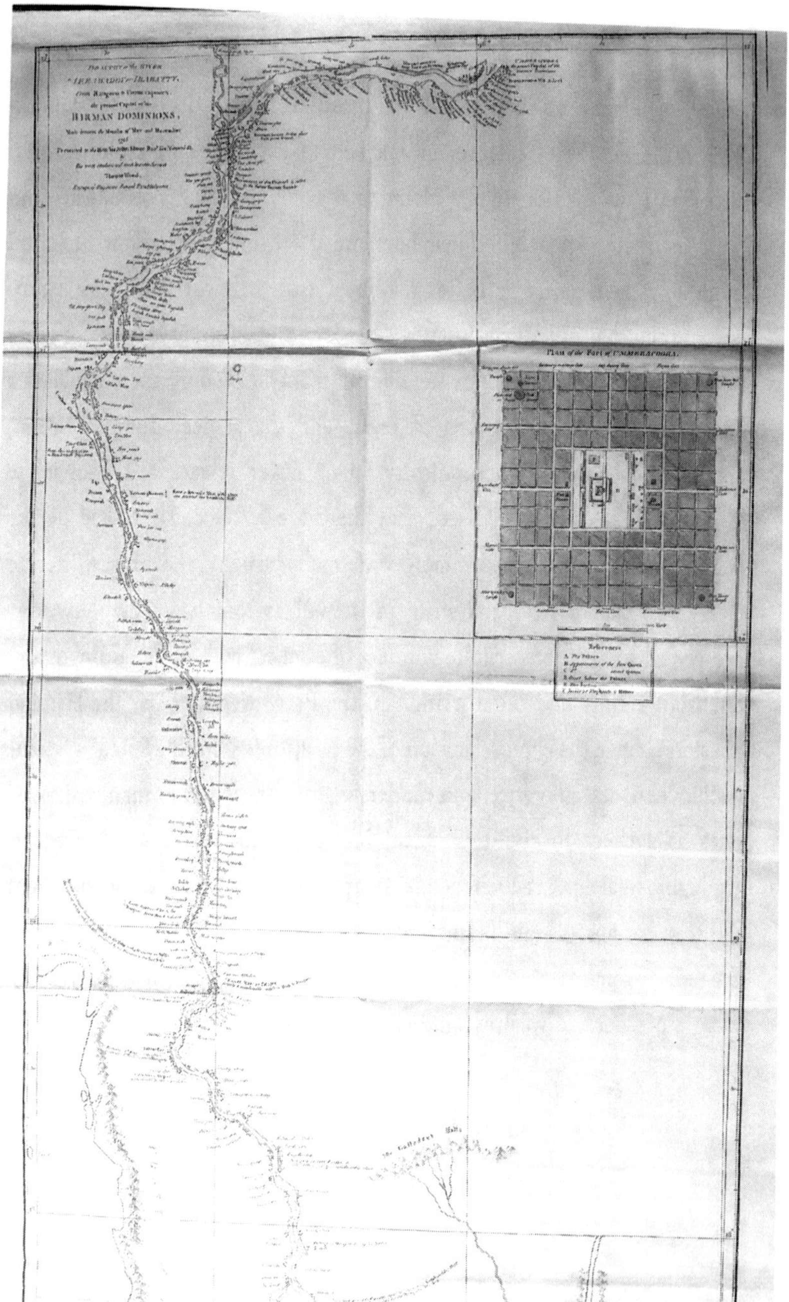
BIRMAN DOMINIONS,
References
A. The Palace
B. Apartments of the first Queen
D. Court before the Palace

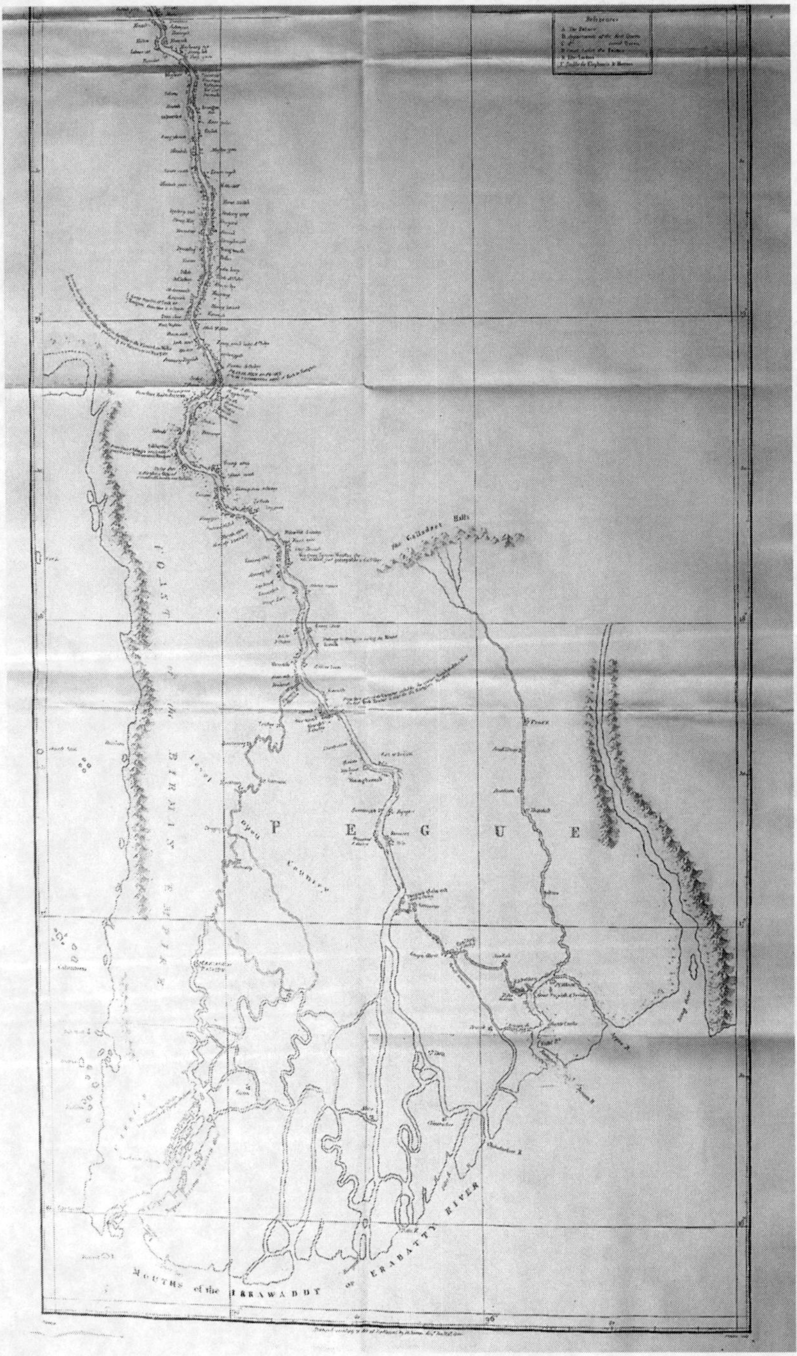

References
the Galladzet Hills
COAST of the BIRMAN EMPIRE
Level open Country
P E G U E
MOUTHS of the IRRAWADDY or ERABATTY RIVER

CHAPTER I.

Embark on board the Sea-Horse—sail from Calcutta—make the Cocoa Islands—touch at Port Cornwallis, in the Great Andaman.—Hospitably received by Captains Ramsay and Stokoe.—Some Account of the Island—imperfectly known to the Ancients—barbarism and wretched State of the Natives.—Singular Account of two young Women.—Frequent scarcity of Food.——Brutal Behaviour of some Bengal Fisherman.—Natural Products of the Island.—Rains excessive.—Colony sickly—causes.—Prepare to depart.

HAVING received my commissions from the Governor General, one appointing me Agent Plenipotentiary, with powers to treat, in the name of the Supreme Government of India, with the Emperor of Ava; the other, vesting in me authority to take cognizance of the conduct of the British subjects, trading to, or residing in, the countries I was destined to visit; on the 21st of February, 1795, I embarked at Calcutta, on board the Sea-Horse, an armed cruizer belonging to the East India Company, Captain Thomas, Commander, attended by Mr. Wood, Assistant and Secretary, and Dr. Buchanan, Surgeon to the mission. A Havildar,* Naick,† and 14 Sepoys, selected from a battalion at the military station of Barracpore, formed an attendant guard; these, with an Hindoo Pundit,‡ for whose company I

* Native serjeant † Native corporal. ‡ Professor of Hindoo learning.

was indebted to the goodness of Sir Robert Chambers, a Moonshee,* and inferior domestics of various descriptions, increased our numbers to more than seventy persons. Light and unfavourable breezes retarded our progress down the river, and before we had got clear, an accident happened that created much concern. An hospital assistant, in the employment of Dr. Buchanan, who had never before been in a ship, arose in the middle of the night, walked leisurely to the gangway, and, insensible to his situation, stepped overboard into a rapid tide, and was heard of no more; this early loss of a good and useful man, impressed a general sentiment of regret upon the whole crew.

On the evening of the 26th, our pilot left us in seven fathom water, having then passed all the dangers of the channel. The wind continuing foul, we anchored for the night; next morning weighed and stood to the south-east with a favouring breeze, which blew without intermission till the 4th of March, when we made the Great and Little Cocoa Islands, so called from being clothed with cocoa-nut trees of unusual luxuriance. These islands are flat, small, and swampy; they are uninhabited, and destitute of good water. We perceived the ruins of a hut on the sea shore, which had been erected by an adventurer, who came thither from Madras to express oil from the cocoa-nut. the scheme did not succeed; some of the party died, and the rest relinquished the project. Steering between the southern Cocoa, and the north end of the Island of Andaman, we opened Port Cornwallis on the east side of the latter. At eleven o'clock on the 5th, we hauled our wind and stood in; at one, our ship came to anchor, a quarter of a mile from the shore. On landing we were received by Captains Ramsay and Stokoe (Colonel Kyd, the Governor, being

* A Mussulman professor of language.

absent) with the kindest hospitality, which was equally extended to the captain and officers of the ship, and continued to every individual belonging to the mission, during the time that we remained their guests.

The settlement in Port Cornwallis is not situated on the principal island, but on a smaller one within the harbour, named by the English, Chatham Island; the utmost length of which does not exceed two miles, and the breadth little more than half a mile: the southern extremity terminates in a narrow neck of land, fordable at low water to the main.

The Andaman Islands are a continuation of the Archipelago, that extends from Cape Negrais to Atchein Head, stretching from 10° 32′ to 13° 40′ north latitude, and from 90° 6′ to 92° 59′ east longitude. What has been considered as the Great Andaman, is the most northern, about one hundred and forty miles in length, and not exceeding twenty broad. A separation, or strait, however, has lately, owing to a fatal accident,* been discovered in this island, which, in fact, divides it into two, and opens a clear passage into the Bay of Bengal. The first settlement of the English was made in the year 1791, near the southern extremity of the island, in a bay on the east side; but it was afterwards removed in 1793, by advice

* In the month of February, 1792, a vessel was freighted from Madras to carry stores to his Majesty's fleet at Andaman; the master being unacquainted with the harbour, sent a small boat, in the afternoon, to explore an opening in the land, that appeared like the entrance; the boat stood in, it fell dark, and she was swept, by a rapid current, through a channel that divided the main island, and opened into the Bay of Bengal. The north-east monsoon prevailed with great violence: unable to work against stream and wind, the boat was borne to leeward, and driven irresistibly into the Indian ocean. Eighteen days afterwards she was picked up by a French ship, near the equinoctial line. The crew consisted of two Europeans and six Lascars; and, shocking to relate, when relieved by the French ship, three of the Lascars had been killed and eaten by their companions.

of Admiral Cornwallis, to the place where it is now established. The original object of the undertaking was to procure a commodious harbour on the east side of the bay, to receive and shelter his Majesty's ships of war, during the continuance of the north-east monsoon; it was also used as a place of reception for convicts, sentenced for transportation from Bengal.

No writer of antiquity has transmitted a distinct account of the Andamans; they were included by Ptolemy, together with the Nicobars and lesser islands, in the general appellation of *insulæ bonæ fortunæ*, and supposed by him to be inhabited by a race of Anthropophagi.* The mild inoffensive Nicobarians have long since been acquitted of the horrid imputation; but the different form, disposition, and habits of the few wretched savages who wander on the shores of the Andamans, may have given ground for a supposition that human flesh has been eaten by them; if so, it probably arose more from the impulse of excessive hunger, than from voluntary choice; a conclusion, that well authenticated instances of the distress they at times endure, appear to authorize.

In the evening we walked round the grounds that had been cleared, making a circuit of little more than a quarter of a mile, partly along the beach, and partly by a path leading through heaps of brushwood, and the trunks of huge trees that had recently been felled. A small garden, diligently tilled, produced but a scanty crop of Indian vegetables. A

* Eusebius Renaudo, in his translation of the account given by two Mahomedan travellers, who journeyed eastward, in the ninth century, says, "beyond these two islands (probably the "Nicobars) lies the sea of Andaman. The people on this coast eat human flesh quite raw; "their complexion is black, their hair frizzled, their countenance and eyes frightful, their "feet are very large, almost a cubit, and they go quite naked."

shallow soil, impregnated with leaves and decayed brushwood, washed down by the mountain streams, proved at first unfavourable to cultivation; the pains, however, which had been bestowed, seemed likely in the end to overcome this discouragement. The situation of the settlement on the side of a hill, rising abruptly from the verge of the sea, although calculated to avoid the unwholesome effects of stagnant waters, was yet at times attended with great inconvenience, owing to the impetuosity of the torrents.

Notwithstanding the colony had been established on its present site little more than sixteen months, the habitations of the commandant and officers, and the huts of the inferior classes, were rendered extremely comfortable. The first constructed of stone and planks, the latter of mats and clay, thatched with leaves of the rattan, or covered with boards. The surgeon had a separate dwelling assigned him, and there was likewise a commodious mess-room. The number of inhabitants altogether was about 700, including a company of sepoys as a guard over the convicts, and a defence to the settlement.

A situation more picturesque, or a view more romantic, than that which Chatham island and Cornwallis harbour present, can scarcely be imagined: land-locked on all sides, nothing is to be seen but an extensive sheet of water, resembling a vast lake, interspersed with small islands, and environed by lofty mountains clothed with impenetrable forests. The scenery of nature, in this sequestered spot, is uncommonly striking and grand.

All that voyagers have related of uncivilized life, seems to fall short of the barbarism of the people of Andaman. The ferocious natives of New Zealand, or the shivering half-animated savages of Terra del Fuego, are in a relative state of refinement, compared to these islanders.* The population of the Great Andaman, and all it dependencies, does not, according to Captain Stokoe, exceed 2,000 or 2,500 souls; these are dispersed in small societies along the coasts, or on the lesser islands within the harbour, never penetrating deeper than the skirts of the forests, which hold out little inducement for them to enter, as they contain no animals to supply them with food. Their sole occupation seems to be that of climbing rocks, or roving along the margin of the sea in quest of a precarious meal of fish, which during the tempestuous season they often seek for in vain.

The Andamaners are not more favoured in the conformation of their bodies, than in the endowments of their mind. In stature, they seldom exceed five feet; their limbs are disproportionably slender, their bellies protuberant, with high shoulders and large heads; and, strange to find in this part of the world, they are a degenerate race of Negroes with woolly†

* Mr. Marsden, in his excellent history of the Island of Sumatra, is of opinion, that the inhabitants of the Batta country, in the northern part of that island, eat human flesh; and the authorities on which he grounds his belief, seem to authenticate the fact: it does not, however, appear, that human flesh was substituted by them in place of ordinary food, but eaten rather as a barbarous ceremony, to indicate revenge on their enemies, or abhorrence of crimes, the only victims being prisoners taken in war, or capital convicts.

† It is a matter of much curiosity to discover the origin of a race of people, so widely differing, not only from all the inhabitants of that vast continent in the bosom of which the Island of Andaman is embayed, but also from the natives of the Nicobar Islands, which are immediately contiguous to it. Hitherto, the inquiries of travellers seem to have produced no satisfactory conclusion: some have supposed that a Portugueze ship, early in the 16th century, laden with slaves from Mosambique, had been cast on these shores, and that the present Andamaners are the descendants of such as escaped drowning. This conjecture is proved to be grossly erroneous, from the account given by the two Mahommedan travellers, long anterior to the navigation of those seas by Europeans. The Arabians, however, who

hair, flat noses, and thick lips; their eyes are small and red, their skin of a deep sooty black, whilst their countenances exhibit the extreme of wretchedness: a horrid mixture of famine and ferocity. They go quite naked, and are insensible of any shame from exposure. Two young women, allured by the temptation of fish, were secured, and brought on board a ship at anchor in the harbour: the captain treated them with great humanity; they soon got rid of all fear of violence, except what might be offered to their chastity, which they guarded with unremitting vigilance: although they had a small apartment allotted to themselves, and had no real cause for apprehension, one always watched whilst the other slept; they suffered clothes to be put on, but took them off again as soon as opportunity offered, and threw them away as useless incumbrances. When their fears were over they became cheerful, chattered with freedom, and were inexpressibly diverted at the sight of their own persons in a mirror; they were fond of singing, sometimes in melancholy recitative, at others in a lively key; and often danced about the deck with great agility, slapping their posteriors with the back of their heel. Wine and spirituous liquors were disagreeable to them; no food seemed so palatable as fish, rice, and sugar. In a few weeks, having recovered strength and become fat, from the more than half-famished state in which they were brought on board, they began to think confinement irksome, and longed to regain

sailed on the Indian Ocean so early as the 7th century, and who not only explored the continent of India as far as the Chinese sea, but likewise gained a knowledge of most of the eastern islands, might, by an accident similar to that which has been ascribed to the Portugueze vessel, have peopled Andaman with its present Negro race. It deserves remark, that on the continent of India extra Gangem, figures of Boodh, or Budhoo, the Gaudma of the Birmans and Siamese, are often seen with the characteristic hair and features of the Negro.

their native freedom. In the middle of the night, when all but the watchman were asleep, they passed in silence through the captain's cabin, jumped out of the stern windows into the sea, and swam to an island half a mile distant, where it was in vain to pursue them, had there been any such intention; but the object was to retain them by kindness, not by compulsion, an attempt that has failed on every trial. Hunger may (and these instances are rare) induce them to put themselves in the power of strangers; but the moment that want is satisfied, nothing short of coercion can prevent them from returning to a way of life, more congenial to their savage nature. The few implements they use are of the rudest texture; a bow from four to five feet long, the string made of the fibre of a tree, or a slip of bamboo, with arrows of reed, headed with fish bone, or wood hardened in the fire, is their principal weapon. Besides this, they carry a spear of heavy wood sharply pointed, and a shield made of bark, to defend themselves from the assaults of their enemies; for even these poor wretches have rights to assert, and dignities to maintain: necessity has taught them an expert management of their arms, on which they rely for subsistence: happily for them, their numerous bays and creeks abound with fish, which they shoot and spear with surprising dexterity. They are said also to use a small hand net, made of the filaments of bark; the fish when caught is put into a wicker basket, which they carry on their backs. Having kindled a fire, they throw the food on the coals, and devour it half broiled. A few diminutive swine are to be found in the skirts of the forests, and among the mangrove thickets in the low grounds; but these are very scarce, and are probably the progeny of a stock left by former navigators. When a native has the good fortune to slay one, he carefully preserves the skull and teeth to ornament his hut. They cross the bays, and go to fish either in canoes formed of a hollow tree, or on rafts of bamboo, which they direct by paddles. Their habitations display little more ingenuity than the dens of wild beasts; four sticks stuck in the ground, are bound together at the top, and fastened tranversely by others, to which branches of trees are suspended; an opening is left on one side, just large enough to admit of entrance: leaves compose their bed. Being much incommoded by insects, their first occupation in a morning is to plaister their bodies all over with mud, which, hardening in the sun, forms an impenetrable armour; they paint their woolly heads with red ochre and water: when thus completely dressed, a more hideous appearance is not to be found in human form.

Their religion is the simple, but genuine homage of nature, to the incomprehensible ruler of the universe, expressed in adoration to the sun, as the primary and most obvious source of good; to the moon as the secondary power; and to the genii of the woods, the waters, and the mountains, as inferior agents. In the spirit of the storms, they confess the influence of a malignant being; and, during the south-west monsoon, when tempests prevail with unusual violence, they deprecate his wrath by wild chorusses, which they chant in small congregations assembled on the beach, or on some rock that overhangs the ocean. Of a future state, it is not known that they have any idea, which possibly arises from our imperfect means of discovering their opinions; it affords, however, satisfactory reflection, to find, among the most ignorant and barbarous of mankind, a confirmation of the great and pleasing truth, that all reasoning existence acknowledges a God. The half humanized Andamaner invokes the luminaries that lend him light; and in that simple and spontaneous praise, he offers up the purest devotion of an unenlightened mind.

Although the principal food of the Andamaners consists of fish, yet they eagerly seize on whatever else presents itself; lizards, guanas, rats, and snakes supply a change of repast. Birds are not numerous, and seldom come within reach; doves, parroquets, and the Indian crow, are the most common: hawks are sometimes seen hovering over the tops of the trees; but they are only temporary visitors from the neighbouring continent: a few aquatic birds frequent the shores; amongst these are the kingfisher, a sort of curlew, and the small sea gull. Within the caverns and recesses of the rocks is found the salangane, or *hirundo nidis edulibus*, described by Monsieur Poivre: this bird, whose nest produces a high price in China, is perfectly black, and resembles a small martin; its nest is thickly glazed with a mucilaginous substance, which the bird collects from the sea blubber, and is said to swallow, and afterwards emit from the stomach; it is prized by the Chinese for its supposed medicinal and restorative qualities.

The vegetable diet of the Andamaners consists of the natural produce of the woods, in which the researches of Europeans find little that is palatable or nutritious; the fruit of the mangrove is principally used, having often been found in their deserted habitations, steeping in an embanked puddle of water. As they have no pot* or vessel that can bear the action of fire, they cannot derive much advantage from such esculent herbs as the forests may contain; indeed their extenuated and diseased figures too plainly indicate the want of wholesome nourishment; unhappily for them, the cocoa nut, which thrives in the utmost luxuriance in

* The fragments of earthen vessels, mentioned by Mr. Colebrooke, were probably brought from the Nicobars, or from the continent, by the boats that often visit the Andamans for the purpose of taking the nests before mentioned.

the neighbouring isles, is not to be found here; they are extremely fond of it; whenever a nut was left in their way by the settlers, it was immediately carried off with much apparent satisfaction. Captain Stokoe, who constantly resided on the island, disappointed in his attempts to establish a social intercourse, endeavoured to alleviate their wants by sending, as often as circumstances would admit, small supplies of victuals to their huts, which were always abandoned on the approach of his people, but resorted to again when they had withdrawn. A party of fishers belonging to the settlement, enticed a woman by the allurement of food, to come so close that she was made prisoner; instead of relieving her hunger, they proceeded to offer violence; the cries of the poor creature brought a numerous troop of savage friends to her assistance, who rushing out of the thickets, attacked and killed two of the yet more savage aggressors. Their bodies* were afterwards found disfigured in a shocking manner. A coasting party one day discovered a man and a boy stretched on the beach, apparently in the last stage of famine; they were conveyed to the settlement: unfortunately every effort of humanity failed to save the man, but the boy recovered, and is now in the service of Colonel Kyd, at Calcutta, where he is much noticed for the striking singularity of his appearance.

The language of the Andamaners has not been discovered to possess the slightest affinity to any that is spoken in India, either continental or islandic. Captain Stokoe informed me, that what he heard was not at all harsh or disagreeable to the ear; their songs are wildly melodious, and their gesticulation, whilst singing, is extremely impassioned. This is one among

* This circumstance rather seems to indicate that they are not cannibals; the bodies of the Bengal fishermen were pierced by sharp weapons, and pounded by stones until every bone was broken; but the flesh was not cut off, or any limb severed.

the many evidences to prove, that poetry is coeval with the language of man.

The only quadrupeds seen on the island, are hogs, rats, and the ichneumon; the guana also, of the lizard tribe, may be reckoned in this class; these proved very destructive to poultry: there are several species of snakes and scorpions. Labourers, whilst clearing away the underwood, were frequently bitten; but in no instance did the bite prove mortal, although the patients commonly fell into violent convulsions; eau de luce and opium were the remedies in most cases administered.

During the prevalence of the north-east monsoon, fish is caught in great abundance, but in the tempestuous season it is difficult to be procured; grey mullet, rock cod, skate, and soles, are among the best; oysters have been found, but in no great quantity. The shores abound in a variety of beautiful shells, gorgonias, madreporas, murex, and cowries,

Specimen of the language of Andaman, from the 4th Vol. of the Asiatic Researches.

Andaman island, or native country, *Mincopie*	To drink, *meengohee.*	Man, *camolan.*
Arrow, *buttohie.*	Ear, *quaka.*	Moon, *tabie.*
Arm, *pilie.*	Earth, *totongnangee.*	Neck, *tohie.*
Black, *cheegheooga.*	To eat, *ingelholiah.*	Nose, *mellee.*
Blood, *cochengohee.*	Eye, *tabay.*	Rain, *oye.*
To beat, *ingotaheya.*	Finger, *momay.*	To sing, *gokobay.*
Belly, *napoy.*	Fire, *mona.*	To sleep, *comoha.*
Bird, *lohay.*	Fish, *nabohee.*	Sky, *madama.*
Boat, *loccay.*	Foot, *gookee.*	Star, *chelobay.*
Bow, *tongie.*	Head, *tabay.*	Sun, *ahay.*
Bone, *geetongay.*	Hot, *booloo.*	Teeth, *mahoy.*
Cold, *choma.*	Knee, *ingolay.*	Water, *migway.*
Door, *tang.*	To laugh, *onkeomai.*	Wind, *tomjamay.*
	Leg, *chigie.*	Wood, *tanghee.*

with many other kinds, of which Captain Stokoe had made a curious and valuable collection.

There are several sorts of trees on the island; the *ficus religiosa,* or banyan tree; the almond tree, the oil tree, that grows to a great height, from which a very useful oil is thus produced. A horizontal incision being made in the trunk, six or eight inches deep, a chip fourteen or fifteen inches long, is cut at right angles, and the surface of the incision being hollowed and filled with live coals, the turpentine, or wood oil, exudes copiously from the top of the wound. The penaigre tree also is found, and is well adapted for the knees of ships; and the iron tree of stupendous size, whose timber almost bids defiance to the axe of the wood-cutter; the red-wood, which makes beautiful furniture, little inferior to fine mahogony. Besides these, there are numberless creepers and rattans which surround the stems of the larger trees, and interwoven with each other, form so thick a hedge, that it is impossible to penetrate far into the forests, unless by the slow and laborious process of cutting a road.

The first settlers in an uninhabited land have not only to contend against natural obstacles, and the want of several necessary comforts of life, but must likewise encounter the effects of an unwholesome atmosphere; no country thoroughly agrees with the human constitution, until it is cleared and cultivated. The new colonists, notwithstanding every possible attention was paid to the preservation of their health, became sickly; they were afflicted, during the four dry months, December, January, February, and March, with the scurvy. This complaint, however, was owing to a change of food, and a want of vegetable diet: as soon as the rains commenced, it mitigated and quickly disappeared, but it gave way to a dreadful successor, the intermittent fever and ague, which baffled all power of medicine. An induration and enlargement of the spleen, a disease well known in India by the name of Boss, was generally its concomitant. The cause of these fevers being local, could not be remedied. Situated in the full sweep of the south-west monsoon, and the clouds being obstructed by high mountains, the island is, for eight months in the year, washed by incessant torrents. According to a meteorological table kept by Captain Stokoe, there appears to have fallen in seven months, 98 inches of water, a quantity far exceeding what I had ever heard of in any other country.

CHAPTER II.

Sail from the Andamans—make the Island of Narcondam.—Arrive at the Mouth of the Rangoon River—delayed for a Pilot—proceed—Precaution of a Custom-house Officer.—A Deputation from Rangoon meets the Sea-Horse—singular Appearance of the Deputies.—Arrive at Rangoon—extraordinary Conduct of the Government.—Uncomfortable Building allotted for our Residence—Restriction imposed on our People.—Commanders and Crews of the Ships in the River prohibited from holding any Intercourse with the Sea-Horse.—Situation unpleasant, and degrading—remonstrate—declare my Intention to withdraw.—Concession on the Part of the Rangoon Government.

HAVING passed five days in this wild sequestered abode, where the novelty of the scene, and friendly attention of our entertainers, Captains Ramsay and Stokoe, would have rendered a longer stay agreeable, we prepared to depart. The Hindoos, whose religion forbids them to drink water drawn by impure hands, had filled their own casks; and the stock of our numerous company was replenished. On the 10th we reimbarked, and stood to sea: next morning at day-light made the island of Narcondam, about twenty leagues east of the Andamans; a barren rock, rising abruptly out of the ocean, uninhabited, and seemingly destitute of vegetation. The wind being foul, we were obliged to tack; and on the following day we had advanced so little to the northward, that Narcondam was still in sight. About noon, we discovered two ships and a schooner, standing to the south-east: they hoisted English colours, and we kept our course. On the 13th the wind veered to the southward, and became fair: on the 16th we found ourselves, by a meridian observation, nearly in the latitude of the roads of Rangoon, but by our reckoning and time-piece too far to the eastward: after steering west some hours, we anchored for the night in five fathoms, and plainly perceived lights on the beach. Next morning we discovered low land, about six miles to the north-west. Here we remained till the 18th, waiting for a pilot, standing off and on with short tacks in the day time, and at anchor during the night. Finding that our signals, by firing guns and hoisting colours in the usual manner, were not answered, Mr. Palmer, the second officer, was sent in the pinnace, with instructions to proceed up the river as far as Rangoon, in case he did not find a pilot sooner. On the ensuing day, the wind being moderate and fair, Captain Thomas ventured to stand in; and steering by land-marks, and sending a boat a-head, crossed the bar without a pilot, at half flood, in four fathoms. At twelve o'clock we entered the Rangoon river; the land on each side appeared low and swampy, and the banks skirted with high reeds and brushwood. Four miles within the extremes we came abreast of a small village, whence a boat rowed towards us: it proved to be a watch boat, stationed at the mouth of the river, to send intelligence of the arrival of vessels to the nearest guard, whence it is forwarded to the Governor of Rangoon. The Birman officer that came on board was a mean looking man, dressed in a shabby cotton jacket, and a piece of faded silk, which, after twice encircling his waist, was passed loosely between his legs and fastened behind, covering the thighs about half way to the knees. This personage, in his own opinion of no insignificant consequence, sat down on a chair* without the smallest ceremony, and called in an authoritative tone for his implements of writing, which were produced by one of three attendants that accompanied him. These, when their master was seated, squatted upon their heels on the deck before his chair, attentive only to his commands, in an attitude and manner very much resembling baboons, although they were well proportioned strong men. The officer inquired, in broken Portugueze, the name of the ship, whence she came, what arms and ammunition were on board, and the name of the commander: being satisfied in these points, he carefully committed them to writing. Hearing that we were not provided with a pilot, he desired the captain to come to an anchor till one could be procured; as, in case of any accident happening, he would be held responsible for permitting us to proceed. Just then, Mr. Palmer in the ship's boat made his appearance. He had been to Rangoon, and brought down a pilot with him: our cautious visitor offered no farther objections, but took his leave with as little ceremony as he had entered.

About two o'clock a small boat from Rangoon met the ship: a man in it hailed our pilot, in the language of Hindostan, and desired him to cast anchor, as it was the intention of the Governor of Rangoon to come down and receive the British deputation in person. We immediately complied with his desire.

The place where we brought to, is twelve miles below Rangoon. The entrance of the river, and the banks on each side, bore a near resemblance

* We were not yet aware that a sitting posture is the most respectful among the Birmans; and on this occasion were inclined to attribute to insolence, what, if it had any meaning, was in fact a mark of deference.

to those of the Ganges; but the navigation is much more commodious. The channel is bold and deep, from six and a half to eight fathoms, uninterrupted by shoals or inequality of soundings. Mr. Wood judged the river at this place to be from three-quarters to a mile in breadth. We continued at anchor till next day, in expectation of the promised visit. About noon the fleet came in sight: it consisted of from twenty to thirty boats; on a nearer approach, only four out of the number seemed to belong to persons of superior condition; these were not unlike, in form, to the drawings of the state canoes of some of the South-Sea Islands: they were long and narrow, with an elevated stern, ornamented with peacocks' feathers, and the tails of Thibet cows; each boat bore a different flag, and had a long, flexible, painted pole, with a gilded ball at the extremity, protruding horizontally from the stern. Three persons, apparently of higher rank, came on board; they meant to be civil, but were perfectly free from restraint, and took possession of chairs without waiting for any invitation, or paying the smallest regard to those who were not seated; whilst their attendants, seemingly as much at ease as their masters, formed a semicircle around them on the deck, in like manner as the servants of our former visitor. Being as yet unapprized of the external forms of respect among them, such conduct surprized us a good deal. The chief of the three, a good looking young man, of short stature, I understood to be a person of consideration. He was Governor of the province of Dalla, on the opposite side of the river to Rangoon, which he held on the part of the mother of the Queen, whose jaghire or estate it is. The second, an elderly plain man, said he was Nak-haan-gee; literally, the royal ear. I was afterwards informed he was transmitter of intelligence, or reporter to the imperial court, an office of much confidence. The third, a Seree, an inferior secretary, was a man of little relative importance compared with the other two. We conversed for an hour, through the medium of an interpreter who spoke the language of Hindostan: they were extremely inquisitive, and asked a number of questions concerning the objects of the mission, which were answered in friendly but general terms. Having paid their compliments, they arose to depart, and returned to their boats, making lavish professions of friendship; and whilst the ship sailed before a gentle breeze, they rowed with great velocity round her, performing a variety of evolutions, and exhibiting considerable skill in the management of their vessels, which were of unequal dimensions, from twenty-eight to forty oars: we judged the longest to be between sixty and seventy feet, and from six to eight in breadth: in this manner we proceeded until the town and shipping were in view. The Princess Royal East Indiaman, that had come from Madras for a cargo of timber, fired a salute to the Company's colours; and the Sea-Horse paid a compliment to the battery on shore, of eleven guns, which were returned by an equal number: the pilot came to, below the town, apart from the other ships about half a mile. As soon as the Sea-Horse dropped anchor, all the boats withdrew, without further notice or explanation.

Being desirous of sending some of our attendants on shore to refresh themselves, particularly the Hindoos, whose religion enjoins them not to eat victuals dressed on board, and who were on that account put to great inconvenience, being obliged at sea to subsist on dried fruits, sweetmeats, and parched pulse, I sent one of the attendants to the Governor of Dalla, to acquaint him with my wish. He, in reply, desired that I would defer landing till the following day, when a habitation that was preparing for our reception would be in readiness: with this request I acquiesced, and communicated the same to Captain Thomas, and the gentlemen of the deputation, who forbad their servants to leave the ship without express permission.

About five o'clock in the afternoon the interpreter returned on board, and informed me, that the Raywoon, or Governor of the town, meant to wait on me next day at the dwelling assigned to us; intimating also, that he was ordered to remain on board to receive my commands. This plea of attention was probably only a cloak to cover another motive: his business seemed to be rather to watch our motions, and learn our views, than to obviate inconveniences, or manifest respect. He spoke the Hindoo language fluently; and I desired the Moonshee, a discreet and sensible man, to entertain him. The night passed without any communication with the shore, or with the other ships in the river.

Next morning, the 21st, at ten o'clock, the Seree, or under-secretary, came on board, accompanied by a man of Portugueze extraction, who spoke very imperfect English. The Seree told me he was about to depart for Pegue, charged with dispatches for the Maywoon, or Viceroy, and requested to know whether we had any commands: I replied in the affirmative; adding, that it was my wish to send a confidential person to his Excellency, to deliver to him a letter from the Governor General of India, and another from myself. The Seree, finding I would not intrust my dispatches to him, promised to call at noon, and convey my messenger to Pegue (about ninety miles distant) in his own boat, a promise which he omitted to perform.

At four o'clock in the afternoon, Mr. Wood, Dr. Buchanan, and myself, landed, and were conducted to a spacious temporary building, which had been prepared for our reception; it was situated on the verge of the river, about 500 yards below the town, opposite to where the Sea-Horse was moored; it consisted of only one story, raised three feet from the ground, supported on posts driven into the earth; an elevation very necessary to the comfort of its inhabitants, as the high spring tides washed the foundation pillars, and almost insulated the building, by filling a channel which the rains had excavated. This edifice, about ninety feet in length, was entirely composed of bamboos and strong cane mats, and divided into several compartments; the roof was lofty, and covered with the same materials, which were laid in such a manner as to afford protection from rain, and shade from the sun: the floor, a bamboo grating, was likewise spread with mats; and in one apartment small carpets were laid, doubtless designed as a mark of distinction. On landing, we were received by the Seree, who made a frivolous excuse for not having called according to his promise, saying, that another person had been sent in his stead. On entering the virando or balcony, we were saluted by the sounds of very discordant music, issuing from the instruments of a band of musicians, that had been sent by the Governor to welcome us; to these he had obligingly added a set of dancing girls, and tumbling boys, who exhibited a variety of movements in attitudes, some of which were not ungraceful. Having dismissed this noisy assemblage, and taken a cursory view of our habitation, we were unanimous in opinion, that for the present it would be more advisable, and more commodious, to sleep on board, at least for that night, as we had brought no conveniences on shore with us. Leaving therefore part of the guard, and a few of our attendants to occupy the house, we returned at dusk, and passed the night on board the Sea-Horse, better lodged, and much more comfortably than if we had continued in our new dwelling.

Surprize and disappointment were a good deal excited, to find, that during all this time, not a boat of any description came to our ship, either from the English merchantmen in the river, or from shore; a circumstance that bore the appearance of distrust and prohibition on the part of the government. Captain Thomas therefore ordered his pinnace to be launched, and rowed to the nearest vessel: being informed that the commander was on shore, he directed his boat to the town quay, and, landing without ceremony, proceeded to the residence of a gentleman, with whom he was acquainted, where he met several masters of merchant ships, who informed him that they had received an order from the Rhoom, or public court in which the council of government assembled, enjoining them not to go on board the Sea-Horse themselves, or suffer any intercourse with their ships, as matters of etiquette had not yet been adjusted; but added, sailor like, that they had agreed to ask permission next morning to pay their respects to the representative of their nation, and if refused, to go without permission; a resolution from which Captain Thomas prudently dissuaded them, saying, they could not more oblige the person they meant to honour, than by an implicit compliance with the wishes of the Birman government.

On the following morning, Captain Thomas and the gentlemen of the deputation accompanied me on shore to our habitation. We found no person of distinguished consequence there, but crowds of the lower class, both men and women, were collected from curiosity. In a short time several baskets were brought, with the Raywoon's, or Governor's compliments, containing venison, ducks, chickens, bread, and roots: the same company of musicians that had performed on the preceding day, attended to amuse us. At twelve o'clock the approach of a person of condition was announced, when a tall elderly man, of a graceful appearance, followed by several attendants, was ushered in, under the title of Baba-Sheen, whose manners were easy and respectful. After informing me, through the medium of a Portugueze interpreter, that he was second in authority at Rangoon, and held the office of Ackawoon, he apologized for the absence of the Raywoon, or Governor of the town, who, he said, was prevented from waiting on me by indisposition; and added, that he would be happy to shew me every attention in his power. I expressed my sense of his politeness; remarking, that my wants were confined to permission to purchase a few necessaries, and the means of sending a messenger to the Viceroy of Pegue, with a letter from the Governor General of India, and one from myself, which I was desirous should be delivered as speedily as possible; to this he replied, that he would forward by express any commands I might have; observing, that it was an useless trouble to send a servant of my own. His meaning was obvious; and as this was his first visit, which might be considered rather as ceremonious, than as intended to discuss business, I did not press the matter farther: being, however, determined not to protract the purposes of the mission longer than was necessary, I acquainted him that Mr. Wood would return his visit the same evening, after which, I would converse with him further on the objects of the deputation. He endeavoured to wave the visit, by saying it might put Mr. Wood to an inconvenience; but that it was his duty to wait on me, which he would do at any time, on the shortest notice, either on board the ship, or at our habitation. In the course of conversation he informed me, that though a native of the Birman country, he was of Armenian extraction, and professed belief in our Saviour. We parted about two o'clock; and at his desire, my Moonshee wrote a list of such articles as we stood in need of, and tendered payment beforehand; an offer that was declined. As our baggage and necessaries had not yet been disembarked, we returned to dine on board. Early in the afternoon the Ackawoon's boat was perceived rowing towards the house, with design, as we imagined, to prevent by anticipation the promised visit. Captain Thomas ordered his barge to be manned, and accompanied me on shore. To this interview Baba-Sheen brought with him, as interpreter, a Mussulman merchant, who spoke Persian tolerably well, through whom I was enabled to convey my sentiments with more ease than at our former meeting.

After an interchange of compliments, I told him that the friendly inclinations which had long subsisted between the British government in India and his Birman Majesty, had been a source of so much satisfaction to the Governor General of India, that, with a view to perpetuate an union mutually advantageous to both countries, he had deputed me, in the character of public minister, and a confidential person, to strengthen the bonds of amity, by the delivery of friendly letters; and to offer, in his name, assurances of a perfect regard. In proof of this, I had brought certain products of our country, which, together with the letters, I was charged to present in person to his Majesty at Ava, and to the Viceroy of Pegue; that, coming in such a capacity, I felt much chagrined at finding, on the part of the Rangoon government, an apparent want of confidence, for which I could assign no cause; and experiencing a degree of restraint, imposed on myself and my people, so inconsistent with what I expected: that I could no otherwise account for such conduct, than by attributing it either to their misunderstanding my intentions, or my own want of knowledge of their customs; that I wished exceedingly to ascribe it to the latter, but found it difficult to persuade myself that such obvious marks of distrust could be altogether matter of form, without any other meaning.

To this the interpreter replied on the part of his superior, in a very verbose and affected style, that nothing was farther from the intention of Baba-Sheen and the council of Rangoon than to give umbrage or offer disrespect; that it was the custom of their nation; and that the restraint which was now so irksome to me, would, he had no doubt, speedily be removed. I replied, that it was my earnest desire to manifest my regard for the Birman government, by acquiescing in every ceremonial that their customs prescribed for persons in the capacity I held, provided such ceremonials were not derogatory from the dignity of the state I represented: but there was one point in which the conduct of the council of Rangoon could not be justified, under any plea of form or custom; this was, the interdiction laid on the captains of the English ships in the river, against going on board the Sea-Horse, to pay me that mark of respect to which he well knew I was entitled, as agent from the English government, and which those gentlemen were solicitous to offer me in that character; that this prohibition, contrary to the usage of all civilized states, was too disrespectful to be passed over in silence, and could only arise from unworthy suspicions, or from an intention to give offence: I desired that he would favour me with an explanation of such extraordinary and unexpected treatment.

To this requisition, Baba Sheen replied in vague and unsatisfactory language; assuring me that what had been done was only in conformity to long established usage, which he begged I would not take amiss, or consider in a mistaken point of view; that if I would entrust my letters for the Viceroy to him, he would forward them by a safe messenger, who would return in two or three days, and probably bring with him an invitation from his Excellency to pay him a visit at Pegue, whither he should have the honour to attend me.

Being furnished with duplicates of all my official papers, and apprised that the letter from the Governor General to the Viceroy was merely complimentary, I thought it a fit opportunity to manifest a confidence in him, in the hope that it might produce a liberal return. I therefore told him, that although it was contrary to our practice to entrust official papers to other than a confidential servant, yet, to manifest the reliance I had on his good will, I would take upon me, in the present case, to wave all form, and with pleasure commit to him the delivery of the letter from the Governor General, together with one from myself. During this conference I discovered that Baba-Sheen understood my meaning in Persian, although he could not himself speak it; he, however, spoke the language of Hindostan in an imperfect manner, but sufficient to express intelligibly what he wished to convey, and we soon understood each other so well, as no longer to stand in need of an interpreter. It was now late, and he took his leave, with lavish professions of respect and good inclination.

The delicacy of my present situation caused me to consider seriously on what were the most eligible steps to pursue. The vigilant suspicion with which I was guarded, and the restriction, little short of imprisonment, imposed on myself and my attendants, aggravated by the humiliating prohibition against holding any intercourse with my own countrymen, seemed to augur an unfavourable issue to the mission, and were sufficient to warrant my availing myself of a clause in my instructions, that gave me a discretionary power to return, without further explanation, in case I judged it expedient. Reflecting, however, that to withdraw in disgust, before I had further communication with higher authority, would, in the present stage of the business, only serve to confirm their suspicions, and substantiate that jealousy which it was the primary object of the mission to remove. Adverting also to the probability that the persons who ruled at Rangoon were inimical to the deputation, as inconsistent with their own interests, and perhaps were ignorant and at a loss how to act. Weighing these considerations, together with the ceremonious and respectful manner in which the deputation had been received on its first arrival, I judged it most prudent to submit, for some time longer, to the irksomeness of my situation, rather than take a step so decided as to exclude every avenue of future communication.

This morning I went on shore to our habitation, accompanied by Captain Thomas, and Doctor Buchanan; we remained till noon, and returned to the ship without seeing any person of note: wherever we directed our steps, three or four Birman centinels followed us closely. Whilst we were at the house, a present of milk, venison, fowls, and vegetables, came from the Governor; and eleven baskets of rice, with a large tub of gee,* were sent on board the Sea-Horse for the use of the people. Payment was offered, but positively refused; the messenger saying he was instructed to receive my commands for whatever necessaries we might require. Not any person belonging to the mission was yet allowed to enter the town, or purchase articles at the market, nor could a servant go to a well a few yards from our dwelling to fetch water, without the attendance of a Birman centinel; no country boat was suffered to approach us, nor did any intercourse pass between the Sea-Horse and the vessels in the river.

In this state of unpleasant restraint we passed the 24th and 25th; our excursions from the ship extended no farther than the insulated habitation.

* Clarified butter.

Every morning the usual present for our table was regularly brought, to which was sometimes added fish of a good quality, that which is called in Bengal the sable fish. On the morning of the 26th I went on shore at an early hour, accompanied by Doctor Buchanan; the spring tides, which prevailed since the time of our arrival, had now subsided, and left a dry foot-path in the rear of the house, across the water-course that surrounded it, thereby opening a free communication with the country. Doctor Buchanan and myself took the liberty to pass the boundary for the first time: When the Birman centinels perceived our intention, they consulted together, as we imagined, whether or not they should interpose and prevent us; they however contented themselves with following us, and vigilantly observing all our actions. Passing over some dry rice grounds, we reached the place where the ceremony of burning the dead is usually performed: whilst we were examining the ruins of a decayed temple, a messenger came to inform me that Baba-Sheen had arrived at the house: we immediately went back, and found him waiting for us. After the usual salutation, I asked him if the courier he had dispatched to Pegue, was returned? He answered in the affirmative; and added, that as the letters contained nothing more than a notification of my arrival, and customary compliments, the Viceroy had sent a verbal reply, to signify that he would be glad to see me and the rest of the English gentlemen at Pegue; at the same time commanding him to provide suitable boats, and every requisite for our journey, which Baba-Sheen said would be in readiness in two or three days; and that it was his intention to precede us, in order to make the necessary arrangements for our reception. This intimation was answered on my part with a cool acknowledgment of the Viceroy's civility: after expressing my surprize that he had not written, either to notify having received the Governor General's letter, or desire our company, I added, that my paying a visit to his Excellency was a matter which could not at that time be determined. Baba-Sheen hoped that no impediment might arise to prevent it, and begged to be favoured with a sight of the presents intended for the Viceroy: I promised to gratify his wish, provided he would come on board the Sea-Horse; he appointed the following morning, and took his leave: in this visit he was accompanied by the Nakhaan, or news writer beforementioned.

At nine o'clock in the morning Baba-Sheen came on board; we were likewise honoured by the visit of an unexpected personage. The Raywoon, or governor, who had before excused himself on account of indisposition, found his health sufficiently mended to venture to the ship, and by his looks plainly evinced that he had not been long an invalid: his appearance bespoke him sixty years of age; his dress was military; he carried a sword, and wore a tight coat of European broad cloth, with gold buttons of a conical form, a fillet of muslin surrounded his head, a piece of checquered Pegue silk, wrapped round his waist, and half concealed his thighs; on his feet he wore the sandal of Pegue, which resembles those used by the Sepoys of India: he was attended by seven or eight servants armed with sabres, one of whom carried a painted box containing beetle leaf and areca nut, another his writing materials, and a third a flaggon of water, on the neck of which was suspended a large gold cup, that served as a cover to the flaggon, and a vessel to drink out of: all these, I afterwards understood, were appendages of his dignity, as well as articles of convenience. After a slight obeisance, for the Birmans are not ceremonious in their salutations, he sat down on a chair placed on the quarter-deck, and in his conversation displayed more knowledge than I had as yet discovered in any of his countrymen: he informed me his name was Seree Nunda Kiouza, that he had commanded the troops which first entered the British territories, and met General Erskine on the borders of Chittagong, mentioning circumstances that left no room to doubt his veracity. He seemed exceedingly pleased to hear that the fugitive delinquents had been given up to the justice of their country; and expressed himself in handsome terms of General Erskine, whose moderation and good sense, he observed, prevented the effusion of much blood; intimating also great doubt, as to what might have been the issue of the contest, had matters been pushed to extremity. Of this little ebullition of vanity I took no notice, and, at the request of Baba-Sheen, ordered the presents designed for the Viceroy to be displayed: they consisted of several pieces of gold, silver, and plain muslin, three pieces of broad cloth, a piece of velvet, and one of flowered satin, a high finished fowling-piece, a corabah of Persian rose-water, specimens of cut glass, and some smaller articles. Our visitants examined them with close attention; one of their attendants wrote an inventory on the spot, and, I afterwards understood,* calculated the value of each distinct article. The Raywoon expressing approbation of the cloth, particularly that of a blue colour, I requested permission to send a piece to his house: he returned a civil answer, in general terms, without either declining or accepting my offer. After some unimportant conversation, they withdrew; and at my desire, Captain Thomas saluted the Raywoon with seven guns: shortly afterwards I sent a

* Similar curiosity was expressed by the mandarines at Canton, to learn, from the India Company's Commissioners, the particulars and value of the presents that were brought by Lord Macartney, for the Emperor of China. Sir George Staunton's Embassy, Vol. I. chap. 9th.

servant to him, with compliments, and the piece of cloth I had promised, which, to my no small surprise, he declined, and returned by the same messenger, apologizing for his refusal, by saying, that certain reasons prevented him at that time from receiving my present. For this ambiguous conduct I could no otherwise account, than by ascribing it to that suspicious distrust which was so plainly indicated in all the actions of this singular people.

The circumstances I have related, together with many other petty marks of authorised disrespect from different quarters, determined me to come to a full and satisfactory eclaircissement with the government of Rangoon, before I would consent to visit the Viceroy at Pegue. In pursuance of this resolution, I sent early in the morning to Baba-Sheen, desiring to see him as soon as convenient. He came to the house about ten o'clock. After recapitulating the various causes of umbrage which had been given me, I added, that all these reasons combined, which were still further strengthened by the Viceroy's having returned a vague, and verbal, reply to the Governor General's letter, contrary to their known usage, rendered it impossible for me to proceed to Pegue, until he should explain the motives of such mysterious conduct; and I desired, that if any doubts were entertained respecting the objects of my mission, or the nature of my designs, that he would express himself freely, and give me an opportunity, by removing them, to undeceive their government. He replied, as usual, in equivocal terms, and by an assurance, that it was no more than what was conformable to custom. I said, I was sorry for it, as our customs were so incompatible with theirs: that I could not, consistent with what I owed to the dignity of my own government, longer submit to my present situation: that as their forms and ours differed so widely, and, from what he said, were not likely to correspond; without a derogatory concession on one part or the other, there was no help for it; we could not apply the remedy, and should part as we had met, on terms of mutual good will and friendship. As I had thus far acquiesced, Baba-Sheen did not expect that matters would take such a turn: intelligence of my arrival had been forwarded to the court, and the authors of my departure would be subject to its displeasure: he appeared alarmed, and earnestly asked,—"What is it you desire?" I replied, immediate release from all personal restraint; that the spies which were stationed on board the Sea-Horse, and the centinels that accompanied every boat that left, or came to, the ship, should be removed; that my servants should have the same liberty that the servants of other strangers enjoyed, with leave to purchase what they wanted; that boats from the shipping in the river should have free access, and the commanders permission to visit me; that Mr. Wood should have safe conduct to the Viceroy of Pegue, to receive in person either a verbal acknowledgment of the Governor General's letter, and an invitation to me to visit Pegue, or bring with him a written reply: that unless these reasonable requisitions were acceded to, I must beg leave to depart, which I should do on the most amicable terms; and only regret that the public character I had the honour to fill, did not admit of concessions on my part, which would be considered as humiliating by my countrymen. To this Baba-Sheen answered in his former strain, endeavouring to amuse me by a story quite impertinent to the subject. I told him it was very well; the English and Birman nations, I hoped, would long continue to maintain a friendly intercourse: at the same time begged to be favoured with his commands to Calcutta. He then entreated of me to lay aside my intention, and assigned as a reason for the Viceroy's not writing, that he had no person with him who understood either Persian or English: this was not true, for I knew, that the Mussulman merchant, who interpreted on the 22nd, carried the letters* to him, in order to explain them. Finding that I was determined, he said he would consult the Raywoon, and give me a reply in the afternoon: he then took his leave.

At four o'clock, Mr. Wood and myself met the Raywoon and Baba-Sheen, at our habitation; they came accompanied by a numerous train of followers; among others, the Nak-haan attended to listen to, and note the conversation. At this interview every persuasive art was used to prevail on me to forego my intention of departure, without their assenting to my propositions; they even condescended to ask it as a favour. I, however, continued inflexible; at their desire, I recapitulated the terms on which alone I would consent to remain. After talking for three hours to no purpose, and offering to yield in some things, they at length agreed to give up every point. Mr. Wood was to accompany Baba-Sheen to Pegue; the captains of the English ships were to have free access; our attendants liberty to purchase what they wanted, and to go where they pleased; the spies stationed on board the Sea-Horse were to be removed; and boats suffered to pass from the ship to the shore without a Birman centinel. These matters being stipulated, and a punctual performance solemnly promised, I relinquished my design of going away for the present, and we parted with apparent contentment and good humour on both sides.

The morning of the 29th produced a satisfactory adjustment of every point in contention, by an unqualified acquiescence on the part of the

* The letters of the Governor General to the Emperor and the Viceroy, were written in Birman, Persian, and English. I always wrote in Persian, and in English.

Rangoon government, to my several requisitions. At ten o'clock the captains of the principal English ships in the river visited me at the house, accompanied by Baba-Sheen; the spies were withdrawn from the ship, and our people permitted to go to the Bazar, or market, without molestation.

CHAPTER III.

Consent to go to Pegue before the return of Mr. Wood.—Suspicions of the Birmans awakened by designing Persons.—Hospitable Reception experienced by Foreign Merchants at Rangoon—Characters of Men in Office—Arts used to counteract the English Deputation.—Mr. Wood departs from Rangoon—politeness of the Raywoon.—Embark for Pegue—bring to during the Ebb of Tide—appearance of the Country—find the Remains of two Deer, half devoured by Tigers.—Rich Soil—Country destitute of Population, and infested by wild Beasts.

At the earnest solicitation of Baba-Sheen, I consented to embark for Pegue on the 31st of March, and not wait the return of Mr. Wood, as I had at first intended. The annual festival at the great temple of Pegue was about to be celebrated with sumptuous magnificence; and the Viceroy had expressed a particular desire that the English gentlemen should witness the rejoicings. I told Baba-Sheen that I would relinquish my original determination on this point, as a mark of my confidence in him, and perfect conviction of the friendly inclinations of the Viceroy.

Previous to this amicable termination of a disagreement, which at first bore an inauspicious appearance, I had conjectured what were the real motives of their distrust, and my conclusions afterwards proved to be rightly founded. Pride, the natural characteristic of the Birmans, was inflamed by the arts of designing men, and suspicion was awakened by misrepresentation. The Birmans, sensible of the advantages of commerce, but inexpert in the practice, desirous to improve, but unacquainted with the principles of trade, had of late years given toleration to all sects, and invited strangers of every nation to resort to their ports; and being themselves free from those prejudices of cast, which shackle their Indian neighbours, they permitted foreigners to intermarry, and settle amongst them. But their country had been so much harassed by wars with neighbouring nations, and torn by revolts and domestic dissensions, that trade was frequently interrupted, and sometimes entirely stopped; property rendered insecure, and even the personal safety of settlers endangered. During the short intervals of tranquillity, obscure adventurers, and outcasts from all countries of the east, had flocked to Rangoon, where they were received with hospitality by a liberal nation: among these, the industrious few soon acquired wealth by means of their superior knowledge. The Parsees, the Armenians, and a small proportion of Mussulmen, engrossed the largest share of the trade of Rangoon; and individuals from their number were frequently selected by government to fill employments of trust that related to trade, and transactions with foreigners, the duties of which the Birmans supposed that such persons could perform better than themselves. Baba-Sheen, born in the Birman country, of Armenian parents, had obtained the high office he held by his skill in business, and his general knowledge. The descendant of a Portuguese family, named Jaunsee, whose origin was very low, and who in the early part of his life had been accused as an accessary to a piratical seizure of an English vessel, was invested with the important office of Shawbunder or intendant of the port, and receiver of the port customs. This man appeared to perform the duties of his station with diligence. The town of Rangoon was indebted to his activity for the pavement of its streets, for several well built wooden bridges, and a wharf, which, extending into the river, and raised on posts, enabled the ships to deliver and receive cargoes without the assistance of river craft: under his direction also, a spacious custom house had lately been erected. This is the only lay building in Rangoon that is not constructed of wood; it is composed of brick and mortar, and the roof covered with tiles; within, there are a number of wooden stages for the reception of bale goods. Notwithstanding the respect which the energy of Jaunsee's character had obtained, the Birmans were by no means insensible of the meanness of his extraction: his want of education was a matter of derision among them: although an inhabitant of the Birman country near forty years, and a great part of the time an officer of government, he could neither read nor write, and even spoke their language imperfectly. We were unfortunate in his happening to be at Ava at the time of our arrival, whither he had gone to render up his annual accounts: had he been on the spot, it is probable he would have obviated several of the inconvenient circumstances attending our first introduction.

The character of Baba-Sheen was strikingly contrasted with that of the Shawbunder; he was a man of general knowledge, and deemed by the Birmans an accomplished scholar; he was better acquainted with the history, politics, and geography of Europe, than any Asiatic I ever conversed with: his learning was universal, being slightly versed in almost every science; but his information, extensive as it was, although it gained him employment, could not procure him confidence: he was said to be deficient in other essential requisites.

Several private merchants had also acquired influence in Rangoon. Bawangee, a Parsee of considerable credit, had interest to procure a partial mitigation of duties on his merchandize, in consideration of supplying annually a certain number of firelocks for the royal arsenal. Jacob Aguizar, an Armenian, to whom I had letters of credit, dealt largely in foreign commodities. These people naturally behold with a jealous eye, any advance of a commercial nature, that might tend to diminish their influence, and deprive them of that dictatorial power, which they assume and exercise over all merchants and mariners that resort to Rangoon; but of none are they so apprehensive as of the English; a connection with whom might teach the Birmans to transact foreign business without their assistance, and give them a more adequate sense of their own interests. Under these fears they had long been disseminating the seeds of suspicion, and warning the Birmans to be on their guard against British fraud, as well as British force; but no sooner did they hear of the present deputation, than the alarm bell was sounded from all quarters. They represented (as I was credibly informed) our designs to be of the most mischievous tendency; and even endeavoured to work on the superstition of the people, by the solemn promulgation of a prophecy, that in less than twelve months the English colours would fly on the Rangoon flag-staff. These artifices, however, which were not now practised for the first time, although they could not deceive the Birmans, still it is probable were not altogether void of effect; nor is it to be wondered at, that our reception, though respectful from the deputation that came down to meet us, was not perfectly cordial. There is also reason to conclude, that the provincial officers of Rangoon knew not in what manner they ought to act, not having received precise instructions for the regulation of their conduct towards us, in matters of ceremony.

Conformably to our recent arrangement, Mr. Wood left us on the preceding night, and, accompanied by Baba-Sheen, set out for Pegue in a commodious boat, well protected from the weather. This day the captains of the principal ships in the river dined with me on shore. The Raywoon, knowing that I was to have company, sent a whole antelope, with Indian vegetables in abundance; and acquainted me, that boats would be in readiness for us on the following day at noon, as I had promised to leave Rangoon by the evening's tide.

The morning of the following day was spent in preparation for our journey to Pegue. Having now come to a right understanding with persons in power, I did not scruple to send on shore part of my heavy baggage, which was deposited in the house, under charge of three soldiers, and some servants, whom we were obliged to leave behind on account of indisposition. The presents for his Majesty were not taken out of the ship, as many of the articles were of a brittle nature, and liable to injury from removal. I likewise drew up a short letter of instructions for Captain Thomas, leaving him in most cases a latitude to act from the dictates of his own discretion, on which I knew I might with safety rely; at the same time I pointed out the propriety of using every means to conciliate the inhabitants, and cautioned him to repress, in his European crew, that thoughtless intemperance which is the characteristic of British seamen when they get on shore.

About noon three boats were in readiness at the creek near our dwelling. The one designed for my conveyance was comfortable, according to Birman notions of accommodation. It consisted of three small compartments, partitioned by fine mats, neatly fastened to slips of bamboo cane: the inner room was lined with Indian chintz; the roof, however, was so low as not to admit of a person standing upright; an inconvenience scarcely to be endured by an European, but not at all regarded by Asiatics. It was rowed by twelve Birman watermen, who used short oars, made in the English form, and who seemed to understand their business. A large heavy boat was provided for the soldiers and our domestics, and a small cutter attended as a kitchen: the boat destined for Dr. Buchanan did not arrive until it was dark, and being a very indifferent one, we imagined it was kept out of sight for that reason.

The mouth of the Siriam or Pegue river, where it joins with that of Rangoon, is about three miles below the town; we therefore waited till the ebb tide was nearly spent, in order to drop down, and take the first of the flood to ascend the river of Pegue. At eight o'clock at night we embarked, accompanied by two war-boats, in one of which was the Nakhaan of Rangoon, and in the other an inferior officer; a black Portugueze in the service of the provincial government, who spoke the language of Hindostan, came as official interpreter: we had likewise another Portugueze, named Pauntchoo, who engaged in my service at the Andaman island, whither he had come from Bassien, as a trader in tobacco and small articles, for the supply of the colony. This man was a valuable acquisition to me during the mission; he spoke the Birman language fluently, and that of Hindostan intelligibly: the latter was the medium I commonly used in my conversations with Birmans, and was seldom at a loss to find some person that understood it. On arriving at the mouth of the Pegue river, we brought to, and waited an hour for the turn of tide, which, during the springs, runs with considerable violence. On the first of the flood, we weighed, and used our oars: neap tides prevailing, the boats made but slow progress, about four miles an hour, continuing at that rate for seven hours, when we again stopped, and fastened our boats to the bank.

Early in the morning Dr. Buchanan and myself walked out with our guns, accompanied by half a dozen attendants: the country round, as far as our view could reach, displayed a level plain, with clumps of trees at distant intervals; a thick reedy grass had grown in some places very high; in others, where it had been burnt, there appeared good pasturage for cattle: we saw the embanked divisions of a few rice plantations, and discovered the vestiges of former culture and population; but during a walk of two hours the eye was not gratified with the sight of house or inhabitant: desolated by the contentions of the Birmans and Peguers, the country had not yet recovered from the ravages of war. In our walk we observed many tracks of wild elephants, the spots where hogs had rooted, and deer lain, and found the remains of two antelopes that had recently been killed, and were half devoured by tigers. The Doctor and myself fired at deer without success. The banks on each side the river are low, and the land seems adapted to produce excellent crops; but it is now quite deserted, and become the undisputed domain of the wild beasts of the forest.

CHAPTER IV.

Arrive at Pegue—polite Reception—invited to the Celebration of the Annual Festival—Procession described.—Sports in honour of the Day—Pugilistic Exercises—Birmans expert at Wrestling.—Formal Introduction to the Maywoon, or Viceroy.—Companies from the different Districts of the Province pass in Review.—Grand Display of Fire-works—orderly and sober Demeanour of the Populace.—Curiosity of the Birmans.—Attention of the Viceroy to our Accommodation.—Invited to a Dramatic Representation.—Siamese Actors—an extraordinary Performer—Description of the Play.—Birmans close the Year with a purificatory Ceremonial, in which the English Gentlemen bear a part.

At noon we got under way, and soon passed a village on the right, consisting of about twenty houses; the river gradually diminished in breadth, and at this place was not more than forty yards wide, the banks covered with coppice and long reeds: after passing another and larger village, where there was a chokey or watch-house, we proceeded through a cultivated country, and numerous villages appeared on each side. At seven in the evening we were in sight of Pegue, and judged the distance by water from Rangoon to be about ninety miles, most part of the way in a northward direction; but the windings of the river are so great, that the road in a straight line must be much less. When we approached the landing place, Mr. Wood came down to meet us, and the favourable account he gave of his reception, added not a little to the satisfaction of having finished our journey: we also found Baba-Sheen on the bank waiting our arrival. This personage conducted us with great civility to our habitation, which we were pleased at finding far superior to that we had left. It was situated on a plain, a few hundred yards without the principal gate of the present town, but within the fortified lines of the ancient city. Like Birman houses in general, it was raised between three and four feet from the ground, composed wholly of bamboos and mats, and indifferently thatched: this is a defect that extends universally to their own dwellings, and affords matter of surprise, in a country where the coarse grass used for thatching, is so plentiful. We had each a small apartment, as a bed-chamber, with carpets spread over the mats, and a larger room to dine in, and to receive visitors: huts were also erected for our attendants; and a bamboo palisade, inclosing a court sufficiently spacious, surrounded the whole. We altogether had reason to be satisfied with our dwelling; it was commodious, according to the ideas of the people themselves, and we had no right to complain of that which was well intended. Shortly after our arrival, two officers of government waited on me, with compliments of congratulation from the Maywoon; they stayed but a short time, perceiving that we were busy in arranging conveniences for the night.

Our servants were occupied during the greater part of the next day, in bringing up our baggage from the boats to the house, a distance of nearly half a mile. In the afternoon an officer called Che-Key, second in rank to the Maywoon, and the Sere-dogee, or secretary of the provincial government, accompanied by Baba-Sheen, paid us a visit to tea. They informed me that the Maywoon, or Viceroy, who had been much engaged in directing the preparations for the ensuing festival, hoped that we would wave ceremony, and give him our company on the following morning at the great temple of Shoemadoo, to view the amusements of the first day; an invitation that I gladly accepted from motives of curiosity, as well as of respect.

At eight o'clock in the morning Baba-Sheen arrived, in order to conduct us to the temple; he brought with him three small horses, equipped with saddles and bridles, resembling those used by the higher ranks of the inhabitants of Hindostan. After breakfast, Mr. Wood, Doctor Buchanan, and myself, mounted; and attended by Baba-Sheen, and an Ackedoo, an officer belonging to the Maywoon's household, also on horseback, set out to view the ceremony. We entered the new town by the nearest gate, and proceeded upwards of a quarter of a mile through the principal street till we came to where it was crossed at right angles by another, which led from the Maywoon's residence to the temple: here our progress was stopped by a great concourse of people, and we perceived on each side of the way, troops marching by single files in slow time, towards the temple. By the advice of Baba-Sheen, we occupied a convenient spot to view the procession. The troops that we saw, were the Maywoon's guard; five or six hundred men passed us in this manner, wretchedly armed, and equipped; many had muskets that appeared in a very unserviceable state, with accoutrements not in a more respectable condition; some were provided with spears, others with sabres; whilst their dress was as motley as their weapons. Several were naked to the middle, having only a Kummerband, or waistcloth, rolled round their waist, and passed between their legs; some were dressed in old velvet, or cloth coats, which they put on regardless of size or fashion, although it scarce covered their nakedness.

or trailed on the ground: it was finery, and finery in any shape was welcome. Some wore Dutch broad brimmed hats, bound with gold lace, others the crowns of hats, without any brim at all: the officers of this martial band, who were for the most part Christian descendants of Portugueze ancestors, exhibited a very grotesque appearance. The first personages of rank that passed by were three children of the Maywoon, borne astride upon men's shoulders; the eldest, a boy about eight years of age; the youngest, a girl not more than five; the latter only was legitimate, being the first born of his present wife; the two elder were the offsprings of concubines. The Maywoon followed at a short distance, mounted on the neck of a very fine elephant, which he guided himself. His dress was handsome and becoming, he had on a dark velvet robe with long sleeves, trimmed with broad gold lace, and on his head he wore a conical cap of the same material, richly embroidered: a number of parade elephants in tawdry housings brought up the rear. As we had not been formally introduced, he passed by, without honouring us with any notice. Proceeding to the foot of the steps that lead to the pagoda, his elephant knelt down to suffer him to alight. Whilst he was in the performance of this act, the parade elephants knelt also, and the crowd that followed squatted on their heels. Having ascended the flight of steps, he put off his shoes, and walked once round the temple without his umbrella, which was laid aside out of reverence to the sanctity of the place. When he had finished this ceremony, he proceeded to the scene of amusement, a sort of theatre erected at an angle of the area of the temple. Two saloons, or open halls, separate from the great building, formed two sides of the theatre, which was about fifty feet square, covered by an awning of grass, spread on a flat roof of slender canes, supported by bamboo poles. Beneath the projecting verge of the roof of one of the saloons, there was an elevated seat, with a handsome canopy of cloth, for the accommodation of the Maywoon and his three children; and on a bare bench beneath him sat the principal officers of his court. On the left side of the theatre, a similar canopy and chair were erected for the Maywoon of Martaban, who happened at this time to be passing by to take possession of his government. Opposite to him, under the roof of the other saloon, seats were provided for the English gentlemen, covered with fine carpeting, but without any canopy. The diversions of this day consisted entirely of boxing and wrestling. In order to prevent injury to the champions, the ground had been prepared, and made soft with moistened sand. At the latter exercise they seemed to be very expert: a short, stout man was particularly distinguished for his superior skill and strength; we were told, that in former contests he had killed two of his antagonists. The first that encountered him on the present occasion, though much superior in size, was, after a short struggle, pitched on his head, and, as the bystanders said, severely hurt. Many others displayed great activity and address; but in the art of boxing they seemed very deficient, notwithstanding they used fists, knees, and elbows. The battles were of short duration; blood drawn on either side terminated the contest; and even without it, the Maywoon would not suffer them to contend long. At the end of an engagement both combatants approached the Maywoon's throne, and prostrated themselves before him, with their foreheads to the ground, whilst an attendant spread on the shoulders of each two pieces of cotton cloth, as the reward of their exertions, which they carried away in a crouching position, until they mingled with the crowd. The places of those who retired were immediately filled by fresh pugilists. This amusement lasted for three hours, until we became quite weary of it; tea and sweetmeats in great profusion were afterwards served to us, in the name of the Maywoon. We departed without ceremony, and got home about four o'clock, extremely oppressed by the intense heat of the weather.

In the morning an early message came from the Maywoon, intimating that he hoped to see us that day at the government-house. Baba-Sheen also made a tender of his services to introduce us to the Praw, or lord; who being ready at the hour appointed, we set out on horseback to pay our visit of ceremony, preceded by the soldiers of the guard, and our personal attendants. Six Birmans also walked in front, bearing the articles intended as a present, which consisted of silks, satins, velvets, gold, flowered and plain muslins, some broad cloth, and a handsome silver-mounted fowling piece. In this order we marched through the town, the objects of universal curiosity, till we reached the gate of an inclosure surrounding the Maywoon's dwelling. It was made of boards nailed to posts twelve or thirteen feet high, and comprehended a spacious square, in the centre of which stood the governor's residence. There were likewise some smaller houses irregularly disposed, appropriated, as we understood, to the several members of the Maywoon's family. We pulled off our shoes at the bottom of the stairs, and were ushered into a saloon, from whence, turning to the right, we ascended three steps into a hall, where a number of persons, ranged on each side, were sitting with their legs inverted, waiting the entrance of the Maywoon. Instructed by Baba-Sheen, we took our seats on small carpets spread in the middle of the room, in front of a narrow gallery, elevated about two feet from the floor, and railed in; with the presents placed before us on trays. In a few minutes the Maywoon entered by a door at one end of the gallery; we made no obeisance, as none was desired, but his attendants crouched to the ground. He sat down, and silence was kept for some time, which I first interrupted, by telling him, through Baba-Sheen, that the Governor-General of India, having received his friendly letter, and being well assured of the amicable disposition of the Birman government towards the English nation, had charged me with the delivery of letters and presents to his Majesty at Ava, and had likewise requested his acceptance of a few articles which I had brought with me. I then rose, and presented the Governor-General's letter; he laid it on the tray before him, talked of indifferent matters, and was extremely polite in his expressions and manner, but carefully avoided all discourse that had the least relation to business, or the objects of the embassy. After half an hour's conversation, chiefly on uninteresting topics, he invited us to a grand display of fireworks, which was to take place on the following day, and soon after withdrew unceremoniously: tea and sweetmeats were then served up. Having tasted of what was set before us, we were conducted by Baba-Sheen to the outer balcony, to view the different companies pass by that intended to exhibit fireworks on the following day.

It is the custom, on this occasion, for the several Mious or districts, whose situation is not too remote, to select and send a number of men and women from their community to represent them at the general festival: these companies vie with each other in the magnificence of their fireworks, and on the eve of celebration pass the government house in review before the Maywoon and his family, each company distinct. A small waggon, drawn by four buffaloes, profusely decorated with peacocks' feathers, and the tails of Thibet cows, led the procession, on which were laid the fireworks of that particular company; next advanced the men belonging to it, dancing and shouting; the females, in a separate troop, came last, singing in full chorus, and clapping their hands in accurately measured time. They, for the most part, appeared to be girls from sixteen to twenty years of age, comely, and well made, but their features were without the delicacy of the damsels of Hindostan, or the bloom of the soft Circassian beauties. In every company of young women, there were a few aged matrons, probably as a check on the vivacity of youth; the seniors, however, seemed to join in the festivity with juvenile sprightliness. Refreshments were again served up to us, and we returned home about two o'clock.

At eight in the morning great crowds had assembled on the plain without the stockade of the present town, but within the walls of ancient Pegue; three temporary sheds were erected on the middle of the green, apart from each other, one for the reception of the Maywoon and his family, another for the Martaban governor, and a third for our accommodation. Common spectators, to the number of many thousands, were scattered in groups over the plain; each division or company exhibited in turn its own fireworks: the display of rockets was strikingly grand, but nothing else merited attention. The cylinders of the rockets were trunks of trees hollowed, many of them seven or eight feet long, and from two to three feet in circumference; these were bound by strong ligatures to thick bamboos, eighteen or twenty feet in length; they rose to a great height, and in descending emitted various appearances of fire that were very beautiful. The time appointed for the amusement considerably diminished the effect, but it was chosen from an humane apprehension of injury to the people by the fall of extinguished rockets, which must have rendered the diversion, during the night, extremely dangerous. Notwithstanding this precaution, a man was unfortunate enough to be in the way of one that killed him on the spot. Each company, after contributing its share towards the general entertainment, marched past the Maywoon, to the sound of musical instruments; after which they proceeded to our shed with songs and dances, "the pipe and the tabor," manifesting every lively demonstration of joy.

It was a spectacle not less pleasing than novel to an European, to witness such a concourse of people of all classes, brought together for the purposes of hilarity and sport, without their committing one act of intemperance, or being disgraced by a single instance of intoxication. What scenes of riot and debauchery would not a similar festival in the vicinity of any capital town of Great Britain inevitably produce! The reflection is humiliating to an Englishman, however proud he may feel of the national character.

During the four following days we enjoyed a respite from public shows and ceremonials, and had leisure for observation; notwithstanding our hall, in a morning, was generally crowded, as every person of distinction in Pegue paid me the compliment of a visit, except the Maywoon, who, within the precincts of his own government, where he represents the king, never returns a visit. Numbers, both of men and women, prompted by harmless curiosity, surrounded the paling of the inclosure from morning till night; those of a better class usually came in, some previously asking permission, but many entered without it. Perfectly free from restraint among themselves, the Birmans scruple not to go into your house without ceremony, although you are an utter stranger. To do them justice, however, they are not at all displeased at your taking the same freedom with them. This intrusion is confined wholly to your public room; they do not attempt to open a door, and where a curtain dropped denotes privacy, they never offer to violate the barrier. On entering the room they immediately descend into the posture of respect. Of all our customs none seemed to surprise them more than the preparations for dining: the variety of utensils, and our manner of sitting at a table, excited their wonder: they never took any greater liberty than merely to come into the room, and sit down on the floor; they meddled with nothing, and asked for nothing, and when desired to go away always obeyed with cheerfulness. Had untold gold been placed before them, I am confident not a piece would have been purloined. Among the men of rank that visited us, an officer called Seree Dogee favoured us with his company more frequently than the rest; he held, by commission from the King, the place of chief provincial secretary, and junior judge of the criminal court; this gentleman often partook of our dinner, and seemed to relish our fare, but could not be prevailed on to taste wine or strong liquors; he was much pleased with the English mode of making tea, of which he drank copiously; indeed it is a beverage highly palatable to all ranks of Birmans.

Although, from the established forms of diplomatic etiquette, we had little personal intercourse with the Maywoon, yet he was not deficient in attention; he sent large supplies of rice, oil, gee, preserved tamarinds, and spices, for our Indian attendants; presents also of fruit and flowers were daily brought to me in his name. As their religion forbids the slaughter of any but wild animals for the purposes of food, he did not offer any thing for the use of the table; but our servants had liberty to purchase whatever they wanted. Fowls, kid, and venison constituted our principal dishes; the two first we procured in abundance, and of a good quality; the venison was meager, but well tasted, and made excellent soup; it was chiefly the wild antelope, with which the country abounds. Having among my people two bakers, and a person who understood making butter, we were seldom without these essential articles of a tolerable quality. Whatever we had occasion to kill was slain in the night, to avoid offending the prejudices of the people, who, so far from seeking cause of offence, were inclined to make every liberal allowance for the usage of foreigners. The Maywoon politely ordered a pair of horses of the Pegue breed, small, but handsome and spirited, to be selected, and sent to us, from his own stud, accompanied by two grooms, one to attend on each horse; a temporary stable was erected for them within the paling of our court, where they continued whilst we remained at Pegue, and afforded us the means of exercise and pleasing recreation. Being now commodiously settled, I invited Captain Thomas from Rangoon, to spend a few days with us; he accepted my invitation, and came up in a boat provided by the intendant of the port, having previously arranged the concerns of his ship, and the mode of supplying the crew during his absence.

The solar year of the Birmans was now drawing to a close, and the three last days are usually spent by them in merriment and feasting; we were invited by the Maywoon to be present on the evening of the 10th of April, at the exhibition of a dramatic representation.

At a little before eight o'clock, the hour when the play was to commence, we proceeded to the house of the Maywoon, accompanied by Baba-Sheen, who, on all occasions, acted as master of the ceremonies. The theatre was the open court, splendidly illuminated by lamps and torches; the Maywoon and his lady sat in a projecting balcony of his house; we occupied seats below him, raised about two feet from the ground and covered with carpets; a crowd of spectators were seated in a circle round the stage. The performance began immediately on our arrival, and far excelled any Indian drama I had ever seen. The dialogue was spirited, without rant, and the action animated, without being extravagant: the dresses of the principal performers were showy and becoming. I was told that the best actors were natives of Siam, a nation which, though unable to contend with the Birmans and Peguers in war, have cultivated with more success the refined arts of peace. By way of an interlude between the acts, a clownish buffoon entertained the audience with a recital of different passages, and by grimace, and frequent alterations of tone and countenance, extorted loud peals of laughter from the spectators. The Birmans seem to delight in mimickry, and are very expert in the practice, possessing uncommon versatility of countenance. An eminent practitioner of this art amused us with a specimen of his skill, at our own house, and, to our no small astonishment, exhibited a masterly display of the passions, in pantomimic looks and gestures: the transitions he made from pain to pleasure, from joy to despair, from rage to mildness, from laughter to tears; his expression of terror, and, above all, his look of idiotism, were performances of first rate merit in their line, and we agreed in opinion, that had his fates decreed him to have been a native of Great Britain, his genius would have rivalled that of any modern comedian of the English stage.

The plot of the drama performed this evening, I understood, was taken from the sacred text of the Ramayan of Balmiec*, a work of high authority amongst the Hindoos. It represented the battles of the holy Ram and the impious Rahwaan, chief of the Rakuss, or demons, to revenge the rape of Seeta, the wife of Ram, who was forcibly carried away by Rahwaan, and bound under the spells of enchantment. Vicissitudes of fortune took place

* Called by Sir William Jones, Valmiec.

during the performance, that seemed highly interesting to the audience. Ram was at length wounded by a poisoned arrow; the sages skilled in medicine consulted on his cure; they discovered, that on the mountain Indragurry grew a certain tree that produced a gum, which was a sovereign antidote against the deleterious effects of poison; but the distance was so great that none could be found to undertake the journey: at length Honymaan,* leader of the army of apes, offered to go in quest of it. When he arrived at the place, being uncertain which was the tree, he took up half the mountain, and transported it with ease; thus was the cure of Ram happily effected, the enchantment was broken, and the piece ended with a dance, and songs of triumph.

On the 12th of April, the last day of the Birman year, we were invited by the Maywoon to bear a part ourselves in a sport that is universally practised throughout the Birman dominions on the concluding day of their annual cycle. To wash away the impurities of the past, and commence the new year free from stain, women on this day are accustomed to throw water on every man they meet, which the men have the privilege of retorting; this licence gives rise to a great deal of harmless merriment, particularly amongst the young women, who, armed with large syringes and flaggons, endeavour to wet every man that goes along the street, and, in their turn, receive a wetting with perfect good humour; nor is the smallest indecency ever manifested in this or in any other of their sports. Dirty water is never cast; a man is not allowed to lay hold of a woman, but may fling

* Honymaan is worshipped by the Hindoos under the form of an ape, and is one of the most frequent objects of their adoration: almost every Hindoo pagoda has this figure delineated in some part of it. Honymaan is the term used by the Hindoos to denote a large ape.

as much water over her as he pleases, provided she has been the aggressor; but if a woman warns a man that she does not mean to join in the diversion, it is considered as an avowal of pregnancy, and she passes without molestation.

About an hour before sunset we went to the Maywoon's, and found that his lady had provided plentifully to give us a wet reception. In the hall were placed three large china jars, full of water, with bowls and ladles to fling it. Each of us, on entering, had a bottle of rose-water presented to him, a little of which we in turn poured into the palm of the Maywoon's hand, who sprinkled it over his own vest of fine flowered muslin; the lady then made her appearance at the door, and gave us to understand that she did not mean to join in the sport herself, but made her eldest daughter, a pretty child, in the nurse's arms, pour from a golden cup some rose-water mixed with sandal-wood, first over her father, and then over each of the English gentlemen; this was a signal for the sport to begin. We were prepared, being dressed in linen waistcoats. From ten to twenty women, young and middle aged, rushed into the hall from the inner apartments, who surrounded and deluged without mercy four men ill able to maintain so unequal a contest. The Maywoon was soon driven from the field; but Mr. Wood having got possession of one of the jars, we were enabled to preserve our ground till the water was exhausted; it seemed to afford them great diversion, especially if we appeared at all distressed by the quantity of water flung in our faces. All parties being tired, and completely drenched, we went home to change our clothes, and in the way met many damsels who would willingly have renewed the sport; they, however, were afraid to begin without receiving encouragement from us, not knowing how it might be taken by strangers; but they assailed Baba-Sheen and his Birman attendants with little ceremony. No inconvenient consequences were to be apprehended from the wetting; the weather was favourable, and we ran no risk of taking cold. Having put on dry clothes, we returned to the Maywoon's, and were entertained with a dance and puppet-show that lasted till eleven.

CHAPTER V.

Public Rejoicings cease.—Site of the ancient City of Pegue—Fortifications.—Encouragement given to Settlers.—Description of the new Town—Public Buildings.—Dread of Fire—Precautions used against it.—An Account of the Temple of Shoemadoo.—Visit the Siredaw, the superior Rhahaan, or High Priest of the Country.—Desolated State of the Environs of Pegue—monastic Retreats of the Rhahaans.—Manufactures at Pegue—Officers of the provincial Government—Administration of Justice.—Monsoon threatens.—Prepare to depart—take Leave of the Viceroy.

Sports and festivities ceased with the departed year, a circumstance that gave us great pleasure, as, from attending them, we were frequently exposed to the influence of a burning sun, which at this season is most powerful; but though the heat from noon till five in the evening was intense, yet the nights were cool, and the mornings pleasant and refreshing. I generally took advantage of two temperate hours, from the dawn of day till the sun became inconvenient, to walk or ride through the city and its environs; and in all my excursions I never once experienced insult or molestation; curiosity and astonishment were often expressed, but unaccompanied by personal incivility, or by the slightest indication of contempt.

The fate that befel this once flourishing city has already been recounted in the preceding pages. The extent of ancient Pegue may still be accurately traced by the ruins of the ditch and wall that surrounded it; from these it appears to have been a quadrangle, each side measuring nearly a mile and a half: in several places the ditch is choked up by rubbish that has been cast into it, and the falling of its own banks; sufficient, however, still remains to show that it was once no contemptible defence; the breadth I judged to be about sixty yards, and the depth ten or twelve feet: in some parts of it there is water, but in no considerable quantity. I was informed, that when the ditch was in repair, the water seldom, in the hottest season, sunk below the depth of four feet. An injudicious faussebray, thirty feet wide, did not add to the security of the fortress.

The fragments of the wall likewise evince that this was a work of magnitude and labour; it is not easy to ascertain precisely what was its exact height, but we conjectured it at least thirty feet, and in breadth, at the base, not less that forty. It is composed of brick, badly cemented with clay mortar. Small equidistant bastions, about 300 yards asunder, are still discoverable; there had been a parapet of masonry, but the whole is in a state so ruinous, and so covered with weeds and briars, as to leave very imperfect vestiges of its former strength.

In the centre of each face of the fort there is a gateway about thirty feet wide; these gateways were the principal entrances. The passage across the ditch is over a causeway raised on a mound of earth, that serves as a bridge, and was formerly defended by a retrenchment, of which there are now no traces.

It is impossible to conceive a more striking picture of fallen grandeur, and the desolating hand of war, than the inside of these walls displays.

Alompra, when he got possession of the city in the year 1757, razed every dwelling to the ground, and dispersed or led into captivity all the inhabitants. The temples or praws, which are very numerous, were the only buildings that escaped the fury of the conqueror; and of these the great pyramid of Shoemadoo has alone been reverenced and kept in repair.

The present King of the Birmans, whose government has been less disturbed than that of any of his predecessors, early in his reign turned his thoughts to the population and improvement, as well as the extension, of his dominions, and seemed desirous to conciliate his subjects by mildness, rather than govern them by terror. He has abrogated some severe penal laws imposed by his predecessors upon the Taliens, or native Peguers. Justice is now impartially distributed, and the only distinction at present between a Birman and a Talien, consists in the exclusion of the latter from places of public trust and power.

No act of the Birman government is more likely to reconcile the Peguers to the Birman yoke, than the restoration of their ancient place of abode, and the preservation and embellishment of the temple of Shoemadoo. The King, sensible of this, as well as of the advantages that must arise to the state from an increase of culture and population, five years ago issued orders to rebuild Pegue, encouraged settlers by grants of ground, and invited the scattered families of former inhabitants to return and repeople their deserted city.

His Birman Majesty, more effectually to accomplish this end, on the death of the late Maywoon, which happened about five years ago, directed his successor, the present governor, to quit Rangoon, and make Pegue his future residence, and the seat of provincial government of the thirty-two districts of Henzawuddy.*

These judicious measures have so far succeeded, that a new town has been built within the site of the ancient city; but Rangoon possesses so many advantages over Pegue, in a commercial point of view, that persons of property who are engaged in business will not easily be prevailed upon to leave one of the finest sea-ports in the world, to encounter the difficulties of a new settlement, where commerce, if any can subsist, must be very confined, from the want of a commodious navigation. The present inhabitants, who have been induced to return, consist chiefly of Rhahaans, or priests, followers of the provincial court, and poor Talien families, who were glad to regain a settlement in their once magnificent metropolis. The number altogether perhaps does not exceed six or seven thousand; those who dwelt in Pegue during its former days of splendor are now nearly extinct, and their descendants and relatives scattered over the provinces of Tongho, Martaban, and Talowmeou; many also live under the protection of the Siamese. There is little doubt, however, that the respect paid to their favourite temple of worship, and the security and encouragement held out to those who venture to return, will, in time, accomplish the wise and humane intentions of the Birman monarch.

Pegue, in its renovated and contracted state, seems to be built on the plan of the former city, and occupies about one half of its area. It is fenced round by a stockade from ten to twelve feet high; on the north and east sides it borders on the old wall. The plane of the town is not yet filled with houses, but a number of new ones are building. There is one main

* The Shanscrit name given to the province of Pegue by the Birmans.

street running east and west, crossed at right angles by two smaller streets not yet finished. At each extremity of the principal street, there is a gate in the stockade, which is shut early in the evening, after that hour entrance during the night is confined to a wicket. Each of these gates is defended by a wretched piece of ordnance, and a few musqueteers, who never post centinels, and are usually asleep in an adjoining shed. There are two inferior gates on the north and south side of the stockade.

The streets of Pegue are spacious, as are those of all the Birman towns that I have seen. The new town is well paved with brick, which the ruins of the old plentifully supply; on each side of the way there is a drain to carry off the water. Houses of the meanest peasants of Pegue, and throughout the Birman empire, possess manifest advantage over Indian dwellings, by being raised from the ground either on wooden posts or bamboos, according to the size of the building. The kioums or monasteries of the Rhahaans, and the habitations of the higher ranks, are usually elevated six or eight, those of the lower classes from two to four feet.

There are no brick buildings either in Pegue or Rangoon, except such as belong to the King, or are dedicated to their divinity Gaudma: his Majesty has prohibited the use of brick or stone in private buildings, from the apprehension, I was informed, that if people got leave to build brick houses, they might erect brick fortifications, dangerous to the security of the state. The houses, therefore, are all made of mats, or sheathing boards, supported on bamboos or posts; but from their being composed of such combustible materials, the inhabitants are under continual dread of fire, against which they take every precaution. The roofs are lightly covered, and at each door stands a long bamboo, with an iron hook at the end, to pull down the thatch: there is also another pole, with a grating of iron at the extremity, about three feet square, to suppress flame by pressure. Almost every house has earthen pots, filled with water, on the roof; and a particular class of people,* whose business it is to prevent and extinguish fires, perambulate the streets during the night.

The Maywoon's habitation, though not at all a magnificent mansion for the representative of royalty, is, notwithstanding, a building of much respectability, compared to the other houses of Pegue; from an outside view we judged it to be roomy, and to contain several apartments, exclusive of that in which he gives audience: it possesses, however, but few ornaments. Gilding is forbidden to all subjects of the Birman empire; liberty even to lacker, and paint the pillars of their houses is granted to very few: the naked wood gave an unfinish'd appearance to the dwelling of the Maywoon, which, in other respects, seemed well adapted for the accommodation of a Birman family.

The object in Pegue that most attracts, and most merits notice, is the noble edifice of Shoemadoo,† or the Golden Supreme. This extraordi-

* These people are called Pagwaat; they are slaves of government; men who have been found guilty of theft, and, through mercy, had their lives spared; they are distinguished by a black circle on each cheek, caused by gunpowder and punctuation; as well as by having on their breast, in Birman characters, the word *thief*, and the name of the article stolen, as, on one that I asked to be explained to me, Putchoo Khoo, *cloth thief*. These men patrole the streets at night, to put out all fires and lights, after a certain hour. They act as constables, and are the public executioners.

† Shoe or Shuœ, in the Birman tongue, signifies golden; and there can be no doubt that Madoo is a corruption of Mahadeva, or deo. I could not learn from the Birmans the origin or etymology of the term; it was explained to me as signifying a promontory that overlooked land and water. Praw imports lord, and is always annexed to the name of a sacred building;

Drawn by Singey Bey. *Engraved by T. Maitland*

Shoemadoo, the Great Temple at Pegue.

Ground Plan of Shoemadoo Praw

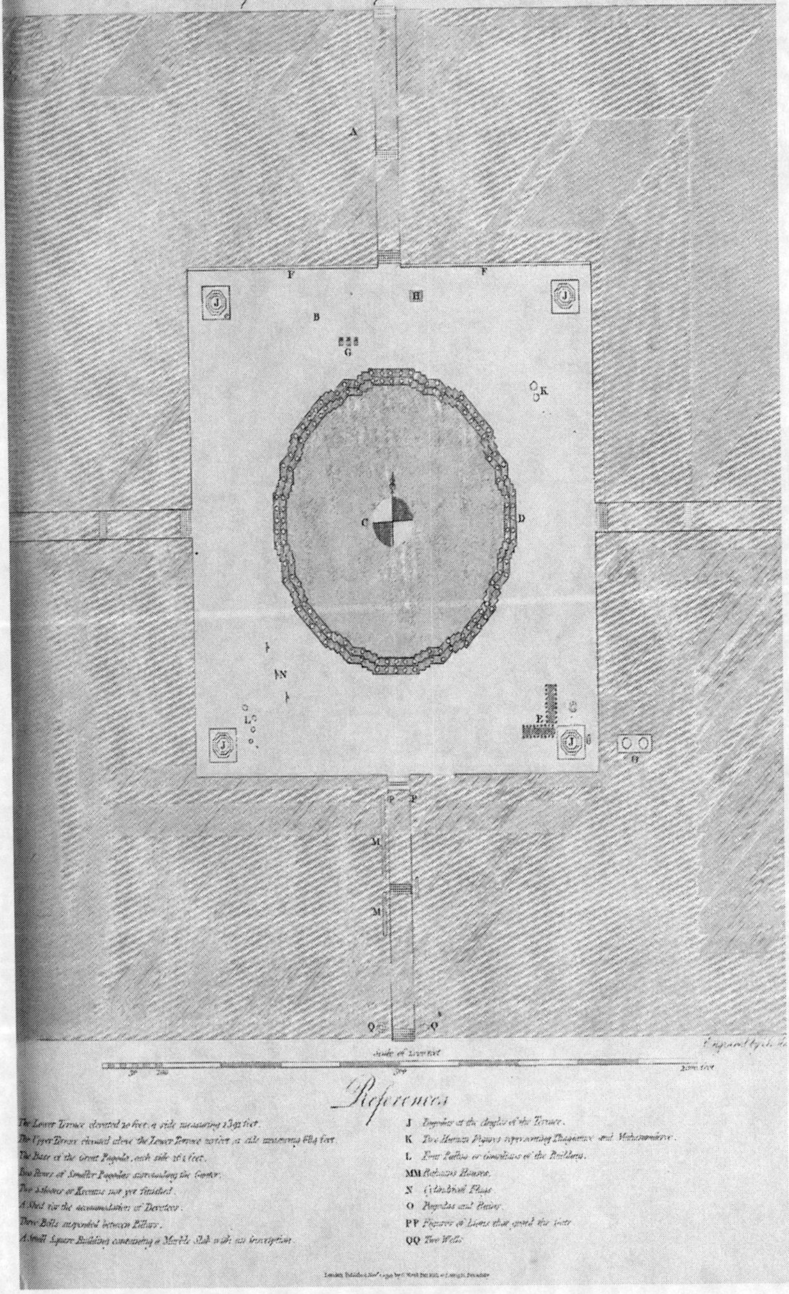

Engraved by J. ...

Scale of 1000 feet

50 100 500 1000 feet

References

The Lower Terrace elevated 20 feet, a side measuring 1391 feet.

The Upper Terrace elevated above the Lower Terrace 10 feet, a side measuring 684 feet.

The Base of the Great Pagoda, each side 162 feet.

Two Rows of Smaller Pagodas surrounding the Center.

Two Houses or Kioums not yet finished.

A Shed for the accommodation of Devotees.

Three Bells suspended between Pillars.

A Small Square Building containing a Marble Slab with an Inscription.

J Pagodas at the Angles of the Terrace.

K Two Human Figures representing Thagiamee and Mahasumdere.

L Four Pillars or Standards of the Buildings.

MM Rahaans Houses.

N Cylindrical Flags.

O Pagodas and Ruins.

PP Figures of Lions that guard the Gate

QQ Two Wells

London, Published Nov. 1799 by G. Nicol Pall Mall & J. Wright Piccadilly

nary pile of building is erected on a double terrace, one raised upon another: the lower and greater terrace is about ten feet above the natural level of the ground, forming an exact parallelogram: the upper and lesser terrace is similar in shape, and rises about twenty feet above the lower terrace, or thirty above the level of the country. I judged a side of the lower terrace to be 1391 feet; of the upper, 684. The walls that sustained the sides of the terrace, both upper and lower, are in a ruinous state; they were formerly covered with plaster, wrought into various figures; the area of the lower is strewed with the fragments of small decayed buildings, but the upper is kept free from filth, and is in tolerably good order. There is reason to conclude that this building and the fortress are coeval; as the earth of which the terraces are composed, appears to have been taken from the ditch; there being no other excavation in the city, or in its neighbourhood, that could have afforded a tenth part of the quantity.

The terraces are ascended by flights of stone steps, which are now broken

it is likewise a sovereign and a sacerdotal title, and is frequently used by an inferior when addressing his superior. The analogy between the Birmans and ancient Egyptians, in the application of this term, as also in many other particulars, is highly deserving of notice.

Phra was the proper name under which the Egyptians first adored the sun, before it received the allegorical appellation of Osiris, or Author of Time; they likewise conferred the same title on their kings and on their priests.

In the first book of Moses, chap. xli. Pharaoh gives " Joseph to wife, the daughter of Potiphera, or the priest of On." In the book of Jeremiah a king of Egypt is styled Pharaoh *Ophra;* and it is not a very improbable conjecture, that the title of Pharaoh, given to successive kings of Egypt, is a corruption of the word Phraw or Praw, in its original sense signifying the sun, and applied to the sovereign and priesthood, as the representatives on earth of that splendid luminary.

and neglected; on each side are dwellings of the Rhahaans, raised on timbers four or five feet from the ground; these houses consist only of a large hall; the wooden pillars that support them are turned with neatness; the roofs are covered with tiles, and the sides are made of boards; there are a number of bare benches in every house, on which the Rhahaans sleep; we saw no other furniture.

Shoemadoo is a pyramidical building, composed of brick and mortar, without excavation or aperture of any sort; octagonal at the base, and spiral at top; each side of the base measures 162 feet; this immense breadth diminishes abruptly, and a similar building has not unaptly been compared in shape to a large speaking-trumpet.*

Six feet from the ground there is a wide projection that surrounds the base, on the plane of which are fifty-seven small spires of equal size, and equidistant; one of them measured twenty-seven feet in height, and forty in circumference, at the bottom. On a higher ledge there is another row, consisting of fifty-three spires of similar shape and measurement.

A great variety of mouldings encircle the building, and ornaments somewhat resembling the fleur-de-lys surround the lower part of the spire: circular mouldings likewise girt it to a considerable height, above which there are ornaments in stucco not unlike the leaves of a Corinthian capital, and the whole is crowned by a *Tee*, or umbrella, of open iron-work, from which rises a rod with a gilded pennant.

The tee or umbrella is to be seen on every sacred building that is of a spiral form: the raising and consecration of this last and indispensable appendage, is an act of high religious solemnity, and a season of festivity and relaxation. The present king bestowed the tee that covers Shoemadoo.

* See Mr. Hunter's Account of Pegue.

It was made at the capital: many of the principal nobility came down from Ummerapoora to be present at the ceremony of its elevation.

The circumference of the tee is fifty-six feet; it rests on an iron axis fixed in the building, and is farther secured by large chains strongly rivetted to the spire. Round the lower rim of the tee are appended a number of bells, which, agitated by the wind, make a continual jingling.

The tee is gilt, and it is said to be the intention of the King to gild the whole of the spire. All the lesser pagodas are ornamented with proportionable umbrellas of similar workmanship, which are likewise encircled by small bells.

The extreme height of the edifice, from the level of the country, is 361 feet, and above the interior terrace, 331 feet.

On the south-east angle of the upper terrace there are two handsome saloons, or kioums, lately erected, the roofs composed of different stages, supported by pillars; we judged the length of each to be about sixty feet, and the breadth thirty: the ceiling of one is already embellished with gold leaf, and the pillars are lackered; the decoration of the other is not yet completed. They are made entirely of wood; the carving on the outside is laborious and minute: we saw several unfinished figures of animals and men in grotesque attitudes, which were designed as ornaments for different parts of the building. Some images of Gaudma, the supreme object of Birman adoration, lay scattered around.

At each angle of the interior and higher terrace there is a temple sixty-seven feet high, resembling, in miniature, the great temple; in front of that, in the south-west corner, are four gigantic representations, in masonry, of Palloo, or the evil genius, half beast, half human, seated on their hams, each with a large club on the right shoulder. The Pundit, who accompanied me, said that they resembled the Rakuss of the Hindoos. These are guardians of the temple.

Nearly in the centre of the east face of the area are two human figures in stucco, beneath a gilded umbrella; one, standing, represents a man with a book before him, and a pen in his hand; he is called Thasiamee, the recorder of mortal merits and mortal misdeeds; the other, a female figure kneeling, is Mahasumdera, the protectress of the universe, so long as the universe is doomed to last; but when the time of general dissolution arrives, by her hand the world is to be overwhelmed and everlastingly destroyed.

A small brick building near the north-east angle contains an upright marble slab, four feet high, and three feet wide: there is a long legible inscription on it. I was told it was an account of the donations of pilgrims of only a recent date.

Along the whole extent of the north face of the upper terrace there is a wooden shed for the convenience of devotees who come from a distant part of the country. On the north side of the temple are three large bells of good workmanship, suspended nigh the ground, between pillars; several deers horns lie strewed around; those who come to pay their devotions first take up one of the horns, and strike the bell three times, giving an alternate stroke to the ground: this act, I was told, is to announce to the spirit of Gaudma the approach of a suppliant. There are several low benches near the foot of the temple, on which the person who comes to pray, places his offering, commonly consisting of boiled rice, a plate of sweetmeats, or cocoa nut fried in oil; when it is given, the devotee cares not what becomes of it; the crows and wild dogs often devour it in presence of the donor, who never attempts to disturb the animals. I saw several plates of victuals disposed of in this manner, and understood it was the case with all that was brought.

There are many small temples on the areas of both terraces, which are neglected, and suffered to fall into decay. Numberless images of Gaudma lie indiscriminately scattered. A pious Birman, who purchases an idol, first procures the ceremony of consecration to be performed by the Rhahaans; he then takes his purchase to whatever sacred building is most convenient, and there places it within the shelter of a kioum, or on the open ground before the temple; nor does he ever again seem to have any anxiety about its preservation, but leaves the divinity to shift for itself. Some of those idols are made of marble that is found in the neighbourhood of the capital of the Birman dominions, and admits of a very fine polish; many are formed of wood, and gilded, and a few are of silver; the latter, however, are not usually exposed and neglected like the others. Silver and gold is rarely used, except in the composition of household gods.

On both the terraces are a number of white cylindrical flags, raised on bamboo poles; these flags are peculiar to the Rhahaans, and are considered as emblematic of purity, and of their sacred function. On the top of the staff there is a henza, or goose, the symbol both of the Birman and Pegue nations.

From the upper projection that surrounds the base of Shoemadoo, the prospect of the circumjacent country is extensive and picturesque; but it is a prospect of nature in her rudest state; there are few inhabitants, and scarcely any cultivation. The hills of Martaban rise to the eastward, and the Sitang river, winding along the plains, gives an interrupted view of its waters. To the north-west, about forty miles, are the Galladzet hills, whence the Pegue river takes its rise; hills remarkable only for the noisome effects of their atmosphere. In every other direction the eye looks over a boundless plain, checquered by a wild intermixture of wood and water.

Not being able to procure any satisfactory information respecting the antiquity of Shoemadoo, I paid a visit to the Siredaw, or superior Rhahaan of the country; his abode was situated in a shady grove of tamarind trees, about five miles south-east of the city; every object seemed to correspond with the years and dignity of the possessor. The trees were lofty, a bamboo railing protected his dwelling from the attack of wild beasts; a neat reservoir contained clear water, a little garden supplied roots, and his retreat was well stocked with fruit trees: some young Rhahaans lived with him, and administered to his wants with pious respect. Though much emaciated, he seemed lively, and in full possession of his mental faculties; he said his age was eighty-seven. The Rhahaans, although subsisting on charity, never solicit alms, or accept of money; I therefore presented this venerable prelate of the order with a piece of cloth, which was repaid by a grateful benediction. He told me, that in the convulsions of the Pegue empire, most of their valuable records had been destroyed, but it was traditionally believed that the temple of Shoemadoo was founded 2300 years ago, by two merchants, brothers, who came to Pegue from Tallowmeou, a district one day's journey east of Martaban. These pious traders at first raised a temple one Birman cubit* in height; Sigeamee, or the spirit that presides over the elements, and directs the thunder and lightning, in the space of one night increased the size of the temple to two cubits; the merchants then added another cubit, which Sigeamee doubled in the same short time; the building thus attained the magnitude

* Twenty-two inches.

of twelve cubits, when the merchants desisted; that the temple was afterwards gradually increased by successive monarchs of Pegue, the registers of whose names, with the amount of their contributions, had been lost in the general ruin; nor could he inform me of any authentic archives that escaped the wreck.

In the afternoon Dr. Buchanan accompanied me in a ride about a mile and a half to the eastward of the fort; thorns and wild bamboos grew in this direction close to the ditch, and the road lay through woods, intersected by frequent pathways. We saw no other habitation, than here and there a poor Peguer's hut, beneath the shelter of a clump of bamboos; but the memorials of former populousness were thickly strewed: hillocks of decayed masonry, covered with the light mould which time generates upon a heap of rubbish, and the ruins of numerous temples, met the eye in every quarter. From these melancholy monuments we could trace the extent of the suburbs, which retained scarce any vestiges of former grandeur; they merely served to point out "campos ubi Troja fuit." We saw no gardens or inclosures, nor any cultivation on that side of the fort, but the pathways being trod by cattle indicated that the country farther on was better inhabited, and probably in a state of higher improvement.

Returning from our excursion, we met Mr. Wood, who, early in the morning, attended by his own servants, and some Birman guides, had crossed to the west side of the river, to amuse himself with a day's shooting; he found an inconsiderable village on the opposite bank, in the neighbourhood of which there were rice plantations that extended a mile westward; beyond these he entered a thick wood, consisting chiefly of the bamboo and pipal trees. Through this wilderness he penetrated nine or ten miles, without meeting an inhabitant, or seeing a single dwelling. Some water-fowls and wood-pigeons were the reward of his toil.

South of Pegue, about a mile beyond the city walls, there is a plain of great extent, for the most part overgrown with wild grass and low brushwood, and bare of timber trees, except where a sacred grove maintains its venerable shade. A few wretched villages are to be seen, containing not more than twenty or thirty poor habitations. Small spots of land have been prepared by the peasants for tillage, who seem to live in extreme poverty, notwithstanding they possess in their cattle the means of comfortable subsistence; but they do not eat the flesh, and I was told what is remarkable enough, that they seldom drink the milk. Rice, gnapee, a species of sprat which, when half putrified, is made into a pickle, and used as a seasoning for their rice, oil expressed from a small grain, with salt, are almost their only articles of food. Their cows are diminutive, resembling the breed on the coast of Coromandel; but the buffaloes are noble animals, much superior to those of India. I saw here, for the first time, some of a light-cream colour; they are used for draft and agriculture, and draw heavy loads on carts or small waggons, constructed with considerable neatness and ingenuity.

The groves beforementioned are objects of no unpleasing contemplation; they are the retreats of such Rhahaans or priests as devote themselves to religious seclusion, and prefer the tranquillity of rural retirement to the noise and tumults of a town. In their choice of a residence they commonly select the most retired spots they can find, where shady trees, particularly the tamarind and banyan, protect them from the noon-day sun. In these groves they build their kioums, and here they pass their solitary lives. All kioums or monasteries, whether in town or country, are seminaries for the education of youth, in which boys of a certain age, are taught their letters, and instructed in moral and religious duties. To these schools the neighbouring villagers send their children, where they are educated gratis, no distinction being made between the son of the peasant and him who wears the tsaloe, or string of nobility. A piece of ground contiguous to the grove is inclosed for a garden, where they sow vegetables and plant fruit trees; the Indian sweet potatoe, and the plantain, being the most nutritious, are principally cultivated; the charity of the country people supply them abundantly with rice, and the few necessaries which their narrow wants require. Abstracted from all worldly considerations, they do not occupy themselves in the common concerns of life. They never buy, sell, or accept of money.

The only article of consequence manufactured at Pegue, is silk and cotton cloth, which the women weave for their own and their husbands' use. It is wrought with considerable dexterity; the thread is well spun, and the texture of the web is close and strong; it is mostly checquered like the Scotch tartan. They make no more than what suffices for their own consumption.

In the town of Pegue there are only three persons, besides the Maywoon or viceroy, whose rank entitles them to distinction: these are, the Raywoon, Chekey, and the Sere-dogee. The first is an old man turned of seventy, still vigorous and active, who, it seems, had distinguished himself by his prowess in former wars, and obtained his present post as the reward of valour: he is also invested with high military insignia, and has the privilege of wearing on his head a gilded helmet, or bason, which is never used except on state occasions, when he exhibits a formidable representation of the meager knight adorned with Mambrino's helmet. The Chekey is a middle aged man, dull and plethoric; and, last in office, our acquaintance, the Sere-dogee, about forty, sadly afflicted with the rheumatism. The assiduous attentions of this good natured man, though perhaps dictated by policy, were both pleasing and useful, and, to appearance at least, perfectly disinterested. I had presented him with some trifles, a piece of muslin, one of silk, and a few yards of broad cloth, which he accepted, he said, not for their value, but as a token of my good opinion. He one day brought his daughter, a child of six years old, with him, to pay me a visit; after taking notice of her I spread a piece of Bengal silk over her shoulders, as is the custom when one makes a present to an inferior. The father thanked me with great cordiality, but returned the piece, saying, he feared I might think he brought the child with a view to extract a present; and that I should have occasion for all the articles I had got to give away, if I expected to satisfy every body who would look for a gratification; I disclaimed the first supposition, but could not overcome the delicacy of his scruples.

These officers exercise the function of magistrates, and hold separate courts at their own houses, for the determination of petty suits; each has his distinct department; but this private jurisdiction is very limited; all causes of importance relating to property, and matters of an high criminal nature, are solemnly tried in open court. The three before mentioned officers unite, and form a tribunal, which sits at the Rhoom,* or public hall of justice, where they hear the parties, examine witnesses, and take depositions in writing: these depositions are sent to the Maywoon, who represents the king, and the judges transmit their opinions along with the evidence, which the Maywoon either confirms or rejects, as he thinks

* Called Roundaye by Europeans.

proper; and in cases of capital conviction, orders execution, or pardons the culprit. From his judgment there lies no appeal, except when it happens that an offender, who holds an office under a royal commission, is brought to trial; in that case the minutes of the evidence taken in court, must be forwarded to the council of state, to be by them submitted to the king, who himself applies the law, and awards the sentence.

We had now spent nearly three weeks at Pegue, and seen every thing worthy of notice, which, in a place so lately rescued from a desert, could not be very interesting or various. Gathering clouds, and a gloomy horizon foretold the approach of the south-west monsoon; and we had reason shortly to expect the arrival of a royal messenger, to notify his Majesty's pleasure in regard to our further progress. Having also several arrangements to make at Rangoon, preparatory to our departure, it became expedient to appoint a day for quitting Pegue; I therefore intimated to the Maywoon my intention, and fixed on the 25th to take my leave, on which day I visited him in form. After half an hour's cheerful conversation, he asked me with much earnestness, whether we were pleased with the reception and treatment we had received; in return, I gave him the most ample assurances of our entire satisfaction, expressed my sense of his past kindness, and my reliance on his future friendship; he seemed happy to find that we were contented, and handsomely apologized for the restraint and apparent rudeness we had sustained on our first coming to Rangoon, which, he said, originated in misconception. Thus we parted with perfect complacency on both sides.

Nor was this acknowledgment, on my part, mere matter of empty compliment; although I thought, that on certain occasions, he might have relaxed from the ostentatious dignity which he cautiously preserved; yet he never was deficient in politeness. His attentions to our accommodation and convenience were unremitting; and we experienced during the term of our residence, uniform civility from all his dependents, which, in fact comprise the whole of the inhabitants of Pegue.

CHAPTER VI.

Leave Pegue.—Reach the Village of Deesa.—Abundance of Game.—Buffaloes—their Antipathy to the Colour of red, or scarlet.—Deesa infested by Tigers, and wild Elephants.—Reach Rangoon.—Geographical Position of Pegue erroneously laid down in modern Maps.—Members of the English Deputation reside within the Fortifications of Rangoon.—Mistrust evinced by the principal Inhabitants.—Description of the Town of Rangoon—Swine and Dogs numerous.—Receive much useful Information from an Italian Missionary.—Account of the People called Careaners—of the Temple of Shoedagong.—Birmans fond of religious Processions.—Account of the Rhahaans, or Ecclesiastics.—Meet the Seredaw, or High Priest of Rangoon—his Character.—Virgin Priestesses.—Reason of the Abolition of their Order.

CAPTAIN Thomas and Dr. Buchanan, with a proportion of the baggage and servants, left Pegue on the 21st, to return to Rangoon; Mr. Wood and myself were ready to embark on the 26th. We went on board in the afternoon, attended by the Nakhaan, two inferior officers of government, and the public interpreter; the remainder of our domestics followed in a separate boat. The heavy rains that fell during the night incommoded the rowers, and retarded our progress; next morning the weather cleared up, but towards noon the sky again became overcast, and seemed to promise a stormy night. About two o'clock we reached a village on the east bank, called Deesa; at this place we found two commodious houses unoccupied, close to the river. Our boatmen being fatigued, and there appearing no probability of being able to reach Rangoon by the night's tide, I judged it most advisable to take up our quarters here until the morning.

Shortly after our arrival had been announced, the Miou-gee, or chief person of the village, came to pay his respects; he informed me, that at this season of the year his village, and those adjacent, were nearly deserted by men, who were all sent on the service of government, to make salt by the sea side, leaving their wives, children, and aged parents at home. The article of salt produces a considerable revenue to the state: the peasantry are employed in preparing it during the hot season: as soon as the monsoon sets in, they return to their habitations, and till their lands until the time comes round for a renewal of their annual labour on the coast, which does not occupy more than four months in the year.

Making enquiries respecting what game the country produced, the Miou-gee told me that it abounded in various kinds, particularly deer; and that if I chose to walk out with my gun, he would be my guide, and undertake to shew me a herd of antelopes at no great distance. I accepted the offer with pleasure: we went through the village, which did not contain more than fifty houses, comfortable in appearance, and well raised from the ground: the women and children flocked to their doors, and screamed with astonishment at seeing such a phænomenon as an English officer dressed in his uniform. Proceeding to the eastward, about a mile from the town, we came on an extensive plain, where the tall rank grass had been consumed by fire, to allow the growth of the more delicate shoots, as pasturage for the cattle. Here we soon discovered a herd of deer, but so watchful and wild, that I could only get near enough to fire a random shot from a rifle, which did not take effect. In endeavouring to approach them unperceived, I left my servants and guide at a considerable distance, and took a circuit by myself, out of sight of my companions. A drove of buffaloes belonging to the villagers happened to be nigh at the time that I discharged my gun; alarmed at the noise, the whole troop raised their heads, and, instead of running away, seemed to stand on the defensive. I walked leisurely from them, when two came out of the herd, and, with their tails and heads erect, trotted towards me, not in a strait line, but making a half circle, as if afraid to advance; they were too nigh for me to think of escaping by flight, I therefore kept on at a moderate pace, in an oblique direction, stopping at times, with my face towards them, on which they also stood still, and looked at me; but when I resumed my way, they immediately advanced; in this circuitous manner one of them came so close that I felt my situation extremely awkward. I had reloaded my rifle whilst I walked, but reserved it for an extremity. As the beast approached, I stopped more frequently, which always checked his progress for a time; but he had now drawn so nigh, that I expected every instant to have a direct charge made at me: fortunately the Miou-gee from a distance discovered my situation; he hallooed out, and made signs by taking off his blue cotton jacket, holding it up in the air, and then throwing it down. I immediately comprehended his meaning, and, whilst I edged away, slipped off my scarlet coat, which I flung, together with my hat, into some long grass, where they lay concealed; the buffalo instantly desisted from the pursuit, and returned towards the herd, quietly grazing as he retired. This circumstance proves that the buffalo entertains the same antipathy to the colour of red or scarlet that some other animals are known to do. The Miou-gee, when I joined him, seemed quite as much alarmed as I was; he said, that if I had sustained any injury, his head would have paid the forfeit of the accident.

The country inland appeared to be cleared of trees and brushwood, to a considerable distance; but on the banks of the river to the north and south, the thickets bordered on the village, and, I was told, abounded in jungle* fowl, and peacocks; but my guide requested I would not venture in, for fear of tigers, which, he said, frequently came prowling round the village at night, and sometimes carried away their dogs, but durst not attack their buffaloes, who, to all appearance, were a match for any tiger, and almost as fierce. The inhabitants also complained of being much molested in the wet season by wild elephants, that occupy, in great numbers, a forest twelve miles to the north-east. These powerful animals, allured by the early crops of rice and sugar cane, make predatory excursions in large troops, and do a great deal of mischief, devastating more than they devour. The poor peasantry have often to lament the destruction of their most exposed plantations.

Next morning before daylight we left Deesa with the first of the ebb; at ten o'clock we reached Rangoon, and landed at our former dwelling below the town. Baba-Sheen, who had travelled all night, arrived about the same hour from Pegue.

How much it is to be lamented, that the country we had just left, one of the fairest and most healthful on the globe, should remain, for the greater part, a solitary desert, whilst so many of the human race are condemned to languish away life in noxious regions, or extract, by incessant labour, a

* This is a bird well known to sportsmen in India; it differs little from the common barn-door fowl, except that the wild sort are all of one colour—a dark red, with black breast and legs. The flesh is very delicate.

scanty subsistence from a barren soil. The natives of the adjacent islands of Nicobar, whose swollen limbs and diseased bodies evince the pestilential atmosphere they breathe, might here prove useful members of general society, live in the enjoyment of a salubrious climate, supply their own, and contribute to relieve the wants of others. But it must require a long and uninterrupted term of peace to renew the population of Pegue. Should it ever be so fortunate, there can be little doubt that Peguc will be numbered amongst the most flourishing and delightful countries of the East.

The authorities on which the geography of the city and river of Pegue has been laid down, though doubtless the best that could be procured, are nevertheless far from being accurate. The Pegue river is called by the natives, Bagoo Kioup, or Pegue rivulet, to distinguish it from Mioup, or river. It is navigable but a very few miles to the northward of the city of Pegue, and for this it is indebted wholly to the action of the tide. It has no communication with the sea, except by the Rangoon river, and in the fair season, at low water, is almost dry. There seems to have been a mistake of this stream for the Sitang river, about fifteen miles east of Pegue, which is a great and independent body of water, that partly describes the course that is given in the map, to what is called the Pegue river.

Nor does the meridian measurement of the city of Pegue, as reported by former travellers, at all correspond with later observations. Mr. Wood, an accurate astronomer, and furnished with excellent instruments, places Pegue in 17° 40′ north latitude, above forty geographical miles south of the position assigned to it in the map. The difference in longitude is less than that of latitude. Mr. Wood, from a mean of observations of the immersion and emersion of Jupiter's satellites, determines Pegue to be in 96° 11′ 15″, about thirty-two miles west of its supposed situation. This eastward error may have given occasion to the mistake of the Sitang river for that of Pegue. Indeed the authorities for the geography of this country are, in most places imperfect, and in some altogether erroneous.

The ruinous state, and the uncomfortable situation of the dwelling assigned to us on our first arrival, rendered it desirable to remove into the town; and, as a proper understanding was now established with the Rangoon government, no objection whatever was made to taking up our abode wherever we thought proper. I accordingly hired two large houses, one for the gentlemen of the deputation, the other for our attendants; these were made of timber, sufficiently spacious, but ill adapted to the climate, being close, and covered with tiles, which retained and transmitted the heat long after the sun had set: they were, however, the best that could be procured, and we felt ourselves more at ease from residing within the inclosure of what is called the Fort of Rangoon.

Being freed from the restraint imposed on us before we went to Pegue, we now enjoyed the full liberty of collecting information, and seeing whatever was worth notice. Although a liberal licence was thus granted to us, I still found, on the part of those persons who were best capable of communicating knowledge, a mistrustful unwillingness to reply to my questions, which they evaded, rather than declined answering; a conduct that created in me more regret than surprise; it was a natural jealousy, which at this time I did not think it prudent to increase by minute enquiries into the internal state of the country, and the political œconomy of their government.

Increasing trade, and consequent population, have extended the present town far beyond the limits that formerly comprehended Rangoon, as it was originally founded by Alompra. It stretches along the bank of the river about a mile, and is not more than a third of a mile in breadth. The city or miou* is a square, surrounded by a high stockade, and on the north side it is further strengthened by an indifferent fosse, across which a wooden bridge is thrown; in this face there are two gates, in each of the others only one. Wooden stages are erected in several places within the stockade, for musqueteers to stand on in case of an attack. On the south side, towards the river, which is about twenty or thirty yards from the palisade, there are a number of huts, and three wharfs, with cranes for landing goods. A battery of twelve cannon, six and nine-pounders, raised on the bank, commands the river, but the guns and carriages are in such a wretched condition, that they could do little execution. Close to the principal wharf are two commodious wooden houses, used by the merchants as an exchange, where they usually meet in the cool of the morning and evening to converse, and transact business. The streets of the town are narrow, and much inferior to those of Pegue, but clean, and well paved: there are numerous channels to carry off the rain, over which strong planks are laid, to prevent an interruption of intercourse. The houses are raised on posts from the ground; the smaller supported by bamboos, the larger by strong timbers. All the officers of government, the most opulent merchants, and persons of consideration, live within the fort; shipwrights, and people of inferior rank, inhabit the suburbs; and one entire street, called Tackally, is exclusively assigned to common prostitutes, who are not permitted to dwell within the precincts of the fortification.

Swine are suffered to roam about the town at large: these animals, which are with reason held unclean, do not belong to any particular

* Miou is a term applied either to a city or a district.

owners; they are servants of the public, common scavengers; they go under the houses, and devour the filth. The Birmans are also fond of dogs, numbers of which infest the streets; the breed is small, and extremely noisy; whenever we walked out, the inhabitants were apprized of our approach by the loud barking of these troublesome curs.

I was now honoured occasionally with visits from all the men of official consequence in Rangoon; but although they paid me this compliment, the greatest formality and caution were still preserved in their deportment and language. Baba-Sheen was the only person with whom we held familiar intercourse, and through him every attention was paid to our wants. From this conduct, however, I judged it prudent to suspend the astronomical observations which Mr. Wood was desirous to make, and not to employ my draftsman until a longer acquaintance had removed their suspicions.

Amongst the foreigners who came to pay their respects to the English gentlemen, was an Italian missionary, named Vincentius Sangermano, who had been deputed to this country about twenty years before, by the Society de propaganda: he seemed a very respectable and intelligent man, spoke and wrote the Birman language fluently, and was held in high estimation by the natives for his exemplary life and inoffensive manners. His congregation consisted of the descendants of former Portugueze colonists, who, though numerous, are in general very poor; they, however, had erected a neat chapel, and purchased for their pastor a piece of ground a mile from the town, on which a neat comfortable dwelling was built, and a garden inclosed. He is indebted for his subsistence to voluntary contributions of his flock; in return for their charity he educates their children, instructs them in the tenets of the Romish faith, and performs mass twice a day at the chapel.

From this reverend father I received much useful information; he told me of a singular description of people called Carayners, or Carianers, that inhabit different parts of the country, particularly the western provinces of Dalla and Bassien, several societies of whom also dwell in the districts adjacent to Rangoon. He represented them as a simple, innocent race, speaking a language distinct from that of the Birmans, and entertaining rude notions of religion. They lead quite a pastoral life, and are the most industrious subjects of the state: their villages form a select community, from which they exclude all other sects, and never reside in a city, intermingle, or marry with strangers. They profess, and strictly observe, universal peace, not engaging in war, or taking part in contests for dominion, a system that necessarily places them in a state of subjection to the ruling power of the day. Agriculture, the care of cattle, and rearing poultry, is almost their only occupation. A great part of the provisions used in the country is raised by the Carianers, and they particularly excel in gardening. They have of late years been heavily taxed and oppressed by the great Birman landholders, in consequence of which numbers have withdrawn into the mountains of Arracan. They have traditional maxims of jurisprudence for their internal government, but are without any written laws: custom, with them, constitutes the law. Some learn to speak the Birman tongue, and a few can read and write it imperfectly. They are timorous, honest, mild in their manners, and exceedingly hospitable to strangers.

The temple of Shoedagon,* or Dagoung, about two miles and a half north of Rangoon, is a very grand building, although not so high, by twenty-

* The name of this temple, which signifies Golden Dagon, naturally recalls to mind the

five or thirty feet, as that of Shoemadoo at Pegue. It is much more ornamented; the terrace on which it stands is raised on a rocky eminence, considerably higher than the circumjacent country. It is ascended by above an hundred stone steps, that have been suffered to fall into decay. The situation renders Shoedagon a conspicuous object at the distance of many miles. The tee and the whole of the spire are richly gilded, which, when the sun shines, exhibit a singularly splendid appearance.

The small auxiliary buildings are yet more numerous than those that surround the base of the Pegue temple. Perceiving that several of these were in a ruinous state, whilst the foundations of others were just laid, and some half finished, I asked, why they did not repair the damages of the old before they erected new ones, and was told, that to mend a decayed praw or temple, though an act of piety, was not so meritorious as to erect a new one; that sometimes the old ones were repaired by those

passage in the Scriptures where the "house of Dagon" is mentioned, and the image of idolatry bows down before the holy ark.

" Next came one
" Who mourn'd in earnest, when the captive ark
" Maim'd his brute image, head and hands lopt off
" In his own temple, on the grunsel edge,
" Where he fell flat, and sham'd his worshippers:
" Dagon his name, sea monster, upward man
" And downward fish: yet had his temple high
" Rear'd in Azotus, dreaded through the coast
" Of Palestine, in Gath and Ascalon,
" And Accaron and Gaza's frontier bounds. MILTON, B. I.

The resemblance is too striking to pass unnoticed; at the same time it should be observed, that analogies of this kind, though always pleasing, are often deceptive.

who were unwilling or unable to be at the expence of a complete building; but this entirely depended on the means and inclination of the donor.

The borders of the terrace on which the temple is raised, are planted with shady trees in regular rows; from this eminence there is a beautiful and extensive prospect; the Pegue and Rangoon rivers are seen winding through a level woody country, and the temple of Syriam, little inferior to those that have been described, stands near the junction of the streams. The rainy monsoon had now set in, and inundations were formed in several places. It would have been a more pleasing, though perhaps less picturesque scene, had the plains been cleared, and the fields laid out for cultivation: we could observe few marks of improvement: woods, lakes, and rivers, presented themselves on every side.

The road leading from the city to the temple is formed with care; a wide causeway in the centre prevents the rain from lodging, and throws it off to the sides: numberless little spires are ranged along the edge of the road, in which are niches to receive small images of their divinity Gaudma. Several kioums or monasteries lay in this direction, generally removed a short distance from the public way, under the shade of pipal or tamarind trees.

The Birmans, like all the natives of the East, are fond of processions; scarce a week passes that there is not a religious display in Rangoon; either a funeral of some person who leaves sufficient to defray the expence of a pompous public burning, or the ceremony of admitting youths into the convents of the Rhahaans; on the latter occasion parents vie with each other, and spare no cost: the principal charge consists in entertainments, and the customary presents to the Rhahaans. The age of induction is generally from eight to twelve years. When a boy is to be introduced into a convent, either as a temporary resident, or with a view to future consecration, his friends prepare their offerings of cloth, rice, preserves, fruit, fans, cushions, mats, and household utensils. On an appointed day he parades the streets, dressed in yellow, and mounted on a horse richly caparisoned, led by two servants: a band of music goes before, and a party of Rhahaans encircle him: his male friends follow in a troop, and the females of their families bring up the rear, the latter carrying on their heads the offerings meant for the Rhahaans. Thus they proceed to the convent of which the novice is to become a member, where he is presented in form to the senior of the brotherhood. This ceremony is repeated three times, and at each perambulation fresh presents are to be provided.

The kioums or convents of the Rhahaans are different in their structure from common houses, and much resemble the architecture of the Chinese; they are made entirely of wood; the roof is composed of different stages, supported by strong pillars; the inside comprehends one large hall; the whole house is open at the sides: some are curiously carved with various symbolic representations of the divinity. There are no apartments for the private recreation of the Rhahaans; publicity is the prevailing system of Birman conduct; they admit of no secrets either in church or state.

From the many convents in the neighbourhood of Rangoon, the number of Rhahaans and Phonghis* must be very considerable; I was told it exceeded 1500. This estimate must include those in their novitiate. Like the Carmelites, they go barefooted, and have their heads close shaven, on which they never wear any covering.

Yellow is the only colour worn by the priesthood; they have a long loose cloke, which they wrap round them so as to cover most part of the

* The inferior order of priests, vulgarly called Tallapoins.

Drawn by Singey Bey. Engraved by T. Medland.

(A Rhahan or Priest.)

London, Published Nov.r 1799 by G. Nicol Pall Mall, & J. Wright Piccadilly

body: they profess celibacy, and abstain from every sensual indulgence. The prescribed punishment for a Rhahaan detected in an act of incontinence, is expulsion, and public disgrace; the delinquent is seated on an ass, and his face daubed with black paint, interspersed with spots of white; he is thus led through the streets, with a drum beating before him, and afterwards turned out of the city: but such instances of degradation are very rare. The juniors are restricted from wandering about licentiously, either by day or night. There is a prior in every convent, who has a discretionary power to grant permission to go abroad.

The Rhahaans never dress their own victuals, holding it an abuse of time to perform any of the common functions of life, which, so long as they occupy, must divert them from the abstract contemplation of the divine essence. They receive the contributions of the laity, ready cooked, and prefer cold food to hot. At the dawn of the morning they begin to perambulate the town, to collect supplies for the day: each convent sends forth a certain number of its members, who walk at a quick pace through the streets, supporting with the right arm a blue lackered box, in which the donations are deposited; these usually consist of boiled rice mixed with oil, dried and pickled fish, sweetmeats, fruit, &c. During their walk they never cast their eyes to the right or to the left, but keep them fixed on the ground; they do not stop to solicit, and seldom even look at the donors, who appear more desirous to bestow, than the others to receive. The Rhahaans eat but once a day, at the hour of noon. A much larger quantity of provision being commonly procured than suffices for the members of the convent, the surplus is disposed of as charitably as it was given, to the needy stranger, or the poor scholars who daily attend them, to be instructed in letters, and taught their moral and religious duties.

In the various commotions of the empire, I never heard that the Rhahaans had taken any active share, or publicly interfered in politics, or engaged in war: by this prudent conduct they excited no resentment: the Birmans and Peguers professing the same religion, who ever were conquerors, equally respected the ministers of their faith.

I had heard much of the veneration paid to the Seredaw, or head of the Rhahaans at Rangoon, and by chance had an opportunity of seeing him; he lived in a very handsome monastery, half a mile from town, on the road leading to Shoedagon. One evening, taking my customary walk, I met him returning from the pagoda; there was nothing to distinguish him from the common Rhahaans; he wore the same yellow dress, and his head and feet were bare; his years and abstracted appearance induced me to ask who he was; on being told, I turned and joined company with him, for he would not have stopped or gone out of his way had a monarch accosted him. He entered freely into conversation, but kept his eyes fixed invariably on the ground before him; he was a little old man, of seventy-five, and still walked with firm step on even ground, but when he ascended the stairs of his dwelling, he required support. He goes every day, at the same hour, to the temple, to offer his devotions, and performs the journey, which, going and returning, cannot be less than four miles, on foot. Approaching his grove, he civilly asked me to come in and rest myself; I followed him, and we took our seats on mats spread on the floor, in the centre of a large and lofty hall. Several younger Rhahaans who had attended him in his walk, ranged themselves at a small distance. I was, however, disappointed in the expectations I had formed; he betrayed a worldly pride inconsistent with his years and sacred function; he announced, with much pomp, that he was the head of the church at Rangoon, and ostentatiously displayed his sacerdotal titles, engraven on iron plates, that had been conferred on him by the present and the late king. He seemed to possess little of the humility which distinguished the aged prelate of Pegue, and I left him impressed with much less reverence than I had entertained for his character before our interview.

I was told, that formerly there were nunneries of virgin priestesses, who, like the Rhahaans, wore yellow garments, cut off their hair, and devoted themselves to chastity and religion; but these societies were long ago abolished, as being injurious to the population of the state. At present there are a few old women who shave their heads, wear a white dress, follow funerals, and carry water to the convents. These venerable dames have some portion of respect paid to them.

CHAPTER VII.

Population of Rangoon—an Asylum for insolvent Debtors.—Religious Toleration granted to Foreigners.—Province of Dalla, and Town of Maindu.—Mima-Shun-Rua, or the Village of Prostitutes.—Barbarous Law respecting the female Relations of insolvent Debtors.—Treatment of the Women.—River of Rangoon commodious for Ship-building—several Ships of burthen on the Stocks.—Birman Shipwrights—Imperial Mandate arrives for the English Deputation to proceed to the Capital—the Maywoon of Pegue ordered to accompany it.—Huntsmen employed to catch Alligators and Rhinoceroses.—Reverence of the Birmans for their braminical Astrologers—they declare a propitious Day for the Maywoon to depart—he leaves Rangoon—English Deputation prepares to follow.—Description of the Boats, &c.

THE population of Rangoon is considerable; there are 5000 registered taxable houses in the city and the suburbs; if each house be supposed to contain six people, the estimate will amount to 30,000. Rangoon, having long been the asylum of insolvent debtors from the different settlements of India, is crowded with foreigners of desperate fortunes, who find from the Birmans a friendly reception, and, for the most part, support themselves by carrying on a petty trade, which affords a decent subsistence to those who act prudently. Here are to be met fugitives from all countries of the East, and of all complexions: the exchange, if I may so call the common place of their meeting, exhibits a motley assemblage of merchants, such as few towns of much greater magnitude can produce; Malabars, Moguls, Persians, Parsees, Armenians, Portugueze, French, and English, all mingle here, and are engaged in various branches of commerce. The members of this discordant multitude are not only permitted to reside under the protection of government, but likewise enjoy the most liberal toleration in matters of religion; they celebrate their several rites and festivals, totally disregarded by the Birmans; who have no inclination to make proselytes. In the same street may be heard the solemn voice of the Muezzin, calling pious Islamites to early prayers, and the bell of the Portugueze chapel tinkling a summons to Romish Christians. Processions meet and pass each other without giving or receiving cause of offence. The Birmans never trouble themselves about the religious opinions of any sect, or disturb their ritual ceremonies, provided they do not break the peace, or meddle with their own divinity Gaudma; but if any person commit an outrage, which the Mussulmen, in their zeal for the true faith, will sometimes do, the offender is sure to be put into the stocks, and if that does not calm his turbulent enthusiasm, they bastinado him into tranquillity.

The violence of the rainy monsoon prevented our making distant excursions, which, in the present stage of the mission, I should perhaps have avoided, had the weather been favourable. Our morning rides and evening walks seldom extended beyond the great temple, that being the best road. Dr. Buchanan one morning went across to the west side of the river, on the bank of which, opposite to Rangoon, is a considerable town, called Maindu, the residence of the governor of the province of Dalla, who has already been mentioned as having come down to meet the deputation on its first arrival. This government is entirely distinct from Rangoon, on the east side: the rank of the governor is much inferior to that of the Maywoon of Pegue, notwithstanding which, the latter cannot apprehend a criminal within the jurisdiction of Dalla, by his own authority. The city of Dalla, from whence the province takes its name, is said to be on the west side of the China Buckier river, and was formerly a place of considerable importance. The town of Maindu is composed of one long street, at the east end is a creek, which goes all the way to Bassien, and has twelve feet depth of water, at high tide; on the west side is a smaller creek, on the bank of which stands a village called Mima-Shun-Rua, or the village of prostitutes, being inhabited wholly by women of that description.

Prostitution in this, as in all other countries, is the ultimate resort of female wretchedness, but here it is often attended with circumstances of peculiar and unmerited misery. Many who follow this course of life are not at their own disposal, or receive the earnings of their unhappy profession; they are slaves sold by creditors to a licensed pander, for debts more frequently contracted by others, than by themselves. According to the laws of Pegue, he who incurs a debt which he cannot pay, becomes, the property of his creditor, who may claim the insolvent debtor as his slave, and oblige him to perform menial service until he liquidates the debt; nor does the unhappy man always suffer in his own person alone, his immediate relatives are often included in the bond, and when that is the case, are liable to be attached and sold, to discharge the obligation. The wretchedness into which this inhuman law plunges whole families is not to be described. Innocent women are often dragged from domestic comfort and happiness, and from the folly or misfortune of the master of the house, in which they perhaps have no blame, are sold to the licensed superintendant of the Tackally, who, if they possess attractions, pays a high price for them, and reimburses himself by the wages of their prostitution.

In their treatment of the softer sex the Birmans are destitute both of delicacy and humanity, they consider women as little superior to the brute stock of their farms. The lower class of Birmans make no scruple of selling their daughters, and even their wives, to foreigners who come to pass a temporary residence amongst them. It reflects no disgrace on any of the parties, and the woman is not dishonoured by the connection.

Respecting the trade of Rangoon, the commodities which the country is capable of producing, the present state of its commerce, and the obstacles that check its growth, I shall have occasion to speak more at length in another part of this work: it is sufficient here to observe; that teak, the most durable wood that is known, and best adapted for the construction of ships, is produced in the forests of the Birman and Pegue empires in inexhaustible abundance. The river of Rangoon is equally commodious for the construction of ships; the spring tides rise twenty feet in perpendicular height; the banks are soft, and so flat that there is little need of labour for the formation of docks: vessels of any burden may be built. Nature has liberally done her part to render Rangoon the most flourishing seaport of the eastern world.

There were at this time several ships from 600 to 1000 tons burden on the stocks; one belonging to the Maywoon of Pegue, about 900 tons, was considered by professional men as a specimen of excellent workmanship; it was entirely wrought by Birman carpenters, and formed on a French model, as are most of the ships built in this river, the Birmans having received their first rudiments of the art from that nation. Three or four vessels of burden were likewise in a state of forwardness, belonging to English adventurers, and one still larger than the rest, almost ready to be launched, the property of the Governor of Maindu, the town on the opposite side. If this ship was not composed of prime materials, the building at least was well attended to; every morning the governor's wife crossed the river in her husband's barge, attended by two or three female servants; after landing she commonly took her seat on one of the timbers in the yard, and overlooked the workmen for some hours, after which she returned home, and seldom missed coming back in the evening, to see that the day's task had been completed. The slip on which the ship was built happened to be contiguous to our first habitation, a circumstance that caused us to remark her constant visits: curiosity, however, did not prompt her, or any of her attendants, to come within our precincts, whilst decorum deterred us from making advances towards an acquaintance. Her husband never accompanied her, and she did not seem to require his aid. Women in the Birman country are not only good housewives, but likewise manage the more important mercantile concerns of their husbands, and attend to their interests in all outdoor transactions: they are industrious to the greatest degree, and are said to be good mothers, and seldom, from inclination, unfaithful wives. If this be a true character, they meet with a most ungenerous return, for the men treat them as beings of a very subordinate order.

Whilst we admired the structure and materials of these ships, we could not overlook the mode in which the work was executed, and the obvious merit of the artificers. In Bengal a native carpenter, though his business is commonly well done, yet in his manner of performing it, he excites the surprise and ridicule of Europeans; he cuts his wood with a diminutive adze, in a feeble and slow manner, and when he wants to turn a piece of timber, has recourse to a coolee, or labourer, that attends him; numbers there compensate for the want of individual energy; notwithstanding this, they finish what they undertake in a masterly manner. The Birman shipwrights are athletic men, and possess, in an eminent degree; that vigour which distinguishes Europeans, and gives them pre-eminence over the enervated natives of the East; nor do I imagine that the inhabitants of any country are capable of greater bodily exertion than the Birmans.

The month of May was now far advanced, and we became a little impatient at remaining so long in a state of uncertainty, especially as the officers of government did not at all relax in the formality and coldness of their deportment, nor were we yet assured what might be the nature of our reception at court. From this unpleasant state of suspense we were agreeably relieved by the arrival of a letter from the Maywoon of Pegue, to the council of Rangoon, acquainting them that he had received the imperial mandate to make preparations for our conveyance by water to the capital; and that it was his Majesty's farther pleasure that he should accompany the deputation in person. Baba-Sheen lost no time in imparting to me the intelligence, which was soon after communicated by an official message from the Raywoon, inviting me to the Rhoom, or public hall, to hear the order formally announced in council. This was a ceremony which I begged leave to decline, but I sent my Moonshee, or Persian secretary, to attend the meeting.

Our visit to Ummerapoora being now a measure decided on by the highest authority, it became requisite to make some enquiries respecting our accommodations for the voyage. Being well aware that no steps could be taken except through the regular channels of authority, I applied to the Raywòon to obtain permission to purchase suitable boats for the use of the deputation: an inferior officer waited on me, to represent on the part of the Raywoon, that it was inconsistent with the usage of their government to admit of a public minister being at any expence for his conveyance; and that the superintendant of the port had received instructions to prepare as many boats as I thought necessary. This, I understood, was an established point of etiquette from which they could not possibly recede. I expressed regret at putting the government to so great an expence, but requested, as the season was boisterous, and the voyage not a short one, that the vessels might be examined by an English shipwright, and such alterations made as would render them commodious to Europeans, which the boats of the natives, both from their structure and insufficient covering, are far from being. My desire met a cheerful compliance.

Conformably to the imperial mandate, the Maywoon left Pegue, and arrived at Rangoon on the 25th of May; his retinue was numerous, and as no person of high official consequence, when summoned to attend the Golden Feet, can assure himself of returning to his government, or office, in order to be prepared for whatever might occur, he brought with him his wife and family, as the companions of his voyage. On the day after his arrival I paid him a visit, he was extremely civil, and assured me of his ready services on every occasion.

About this time an order came from court to the provincial government of Pegue, which furnished a subject of much conversation. I was told that the Emperor of China, having never seen a rhinoceros or an alligator, entertained an ardent desire to view those formidable animals before his death, and had intimated his wish, through a provincial legate from Yunan, who had lately arrived at Ummerapoora for the purpose of settling some mercantile arrangements. The King of Ava, solicitous to gratify his august brother of China, had signified his pleasure to his chief minister, who sent the order beforementioned, the purport of which, I understood, was to catch twenty alligators, and as many of the rhinoceros tribe, and convey them to the metropolis, whence they were to be transported to the imperial city of Pee-Kien. Those who made elephant hunting their profession, were dispatched to the forests, and strong nets were thrown across the Pegue river, on the sands of which, when the tide ebbed, I had seen, in the course of my journey to Pegue, a much greater number than his majesty required. The fishermen began successfully; several alligators were taken in two or three days, and put into boats, in the bottom of which wells were constructed. The crocodile and alligator, although they are accounted amphibious animals, cannot long support life out of the water. The rhinoceros hunters, I afterwards learned, were not equally fortunate.

In a former part of this work it has been mentioned, that the Birmans, notwithstanding they are Hindoos of the sect of Boodh, and not disciples of Brahma, nevertheless reverence the Brahmins, and acknowledge their superiority in science over their own priests or Rhahaans. The partiality which the King, who is guided in every movement by astrological advice, manifests in their favour, has given celebrity to their predictions, and brought them so much into fashion, that there is not a viceroy or Maywoon who has not in his household some of these domestic sages, whom he consults on all important occasions, and sometimes on occasions of no importance whatever. The Maywoon of Pegue, whose viceroyalty, though not the most extensive, is the most lucrative in the empire, maintains a number of Brahmins, whose counsel he desired on the most fortunate day and hour to commence the journey. After due deliberation, the 28th of May, at eight o'clock in the morning, was pronounced the most propitious for departure, and that time was accordingly appointed. Unluckily our boats could not be got in readiness quite so soon, but as there was no resisting the stars, the Maywoon declared his regret at the supernatural necessity that compelled him to precede us, promising, however, to wait at the head of the Rangoon river, where it branched from the great stream of the Irrawaddy, until we should join him, the distance being not more than a two day's journey. I acquiesced in the propriety of submitting every temporal concern to the disposal of fate, and hoped that he would not suffer any consideration for us, to interfere with his own arrangements. On the day fixed, at seven in the morning, he passed our habitation, and proceeded with much pomp to the water-side, himself on horseback, his lady in a palanquin, and his children carried astride on men's shoulders. His own barge was very handsome, and of the structure appertaining to nobility; it was attended by several war boats ready manned, with a number of common vessels; some belonging to his retinue, others to merchants, who took the opportunity of his protection to transport their merchandize duty free. The Maywoon reposed for a short time in the house that is used as an exchange, and when the great drum that proclaimed the hour struck the first stroke, he stepped on board, and was followed by his family; in an instant every boat pushed from the shore with a loud shout; the oars were vigorously plied, and the flood tide setting strong, the fleet was soon carried to the northward of the city.

The boats, six in number, that had been provided for our accommodation, were now ready to receive us; Dr. Buchanan, Mr. Wood, and myself, had each a separate vessel; the Hindoo Pundit, whose religious prejudices rendered it irksome to him to mingle with Mussulmen, had likewise a small boat to himself. The guard, and such attendants as we did not immediately require, occupied another of a larger size, in which our heavy baggage, field equipage, &c. were stowed: a kind of cutter was equipped as a kitchen, which was seldom wanted, as our own barges were sufficiently spacious to admit of all culinary purposes, without inconvenience to the inhabitants. Those barges were of a very different construction from the flat-bottomed vessels called budgerows, that are used on the Ganges; ours were long and narrow, and required a good deal of ballast to keep them steady; even with ballast they would have been in constant danger of oversetting, had they not been provided with outriggers, which, composed of thin boards, or oftener of buoyant bamboos, make a platform that extends horizontally six or seven feet on the outside of the boat, from stem to stern. Thus secured, the vessel can incline no farther than until the platform touches the surface of the water, when she immediately rights; on this stage the boatmen ply their oars, or impel the boat forward by poles; such an addition affords a convenience unknown to the navigation of the Ganges; it is the place exclusively appropriated to the crew, who sleep on it at night, and, by putting up mats, or spreading a sail from the roof of the boat to the outside edge, shelter themselves from the weather. My barge was sixty feet in length, and not more than twelve in the widest part; by taking away one thwart beam near the stern, laying a floor two feet below the gunwale, and raising an arched roof about seven feet above the floor, a commodious room was formed, fourteen feet long, and ten wide, with a closet behind it; at the stern there was a stage, on which the Leedegee, or steersman, stood, and a vacant space of seven or eight feet, where a kettle might be boiled, or dinner provided. On each side of the cabin a small door opened on the platform, and there were three windows which, when raised, admitted a free circulation of air. The roof was made of bamboos, covered with mats, and over all was extended a painted canvass that effectually secured us from the heaviest rain. The inside was neatly lined with matting. The conveyances of the other gentlemen were nearly of the same size and construction. Twenty-six boatmen composed the crew of my vessel, exclusive of the Leedegee, who is the chief or captain.

CHAPTER VIII.

Depart from Rangoon.—Alteration in the Temperature of the Air.—Reach Panlang.—Mosquitoes unusually numerous and troublesome.—Pass Kettoree-Rua, or Parroquet Village.—Towns of Yangain-Chain-Yah, and Denoobew.—A handsome Temple.—Segahghee—Summeingtoh—Yeoungbenzah.—Singular Appearance of a Tree.—Taykyatt—Terriato, or Mango Village—Taambooterra—Kioumzeik, or Convent Stairs.—Indigo Plant—Birman Method of preparing it for Use.—Manufactory of Cotton Cloth.—Shwaye-Gaim—Sabbaymeoun—Gnapeezeik.—Violent Current.—Yeagaim—Kanounglay, or Little Kanoung.—Rich Plantations.—Kanoungghe, or Great Kanoung.—Slow Progress.—Meyahoun—gilded Temples, and spacious Convents—numerous trading Boats—Country fruitful.—Pasheem—Kianggain.—Violent Gust of Wind.—Tirroup-miou, or Chinese Town.—Mountains.—Tzeezau.—Peeing-ghee.—A Ship on the Stocks.—Beautiful Appearance of the Banks.—Great Difficulty in surmounting the Stream—extraordinary Exertions of the Boatmen—Fleet dispersed—Baggage-boat lost.—The Fleet reassembles.—Reach the City of Peeaye-mew, or Prome.

On the 29th of May we were ready to depart: our baggage and attendants had been previously sent on board, and the boats containing the royal presents had received their lading from the Sea-Horse. We embarked in the evening, slept on board, and at 10 o'clock next morning, when the tide served, pushed off, accompanied by our civil acquaintance, the Sere-dogee of Pegue, Baba-Sheen, Jacob Aguizar, the Armenian merchant, and the chief interpreter of Rangoon; these personages had boats of their own. Pauntchoo, my Portugueze servant, being with me, and three or four of the boatmen speaking a little of the Hindostan language, I was at no loss to make myself understood. An under Seree, or inferior clerk, was stationed in my boat, professedly to attend to my wants, and receive my orders, and probably with a view to observe and report my actions. It was, however, an ostensible compliment, and accepted by me in that light.

We rowed without intermission until three in the afternoon. A short way from Rangoon the river becomes narrower, with a winding course, owing to which we did not advance more than three leagues in a direct line. We passed a small village on the left: the banks on each side were shaded with trees. The fleet brought to on the north side of the river, when Doctor Buchanan went on shore, and found an extensive plain covered with short grass, beyond which there was a large village. We experienced a pleasing alteration in the temperature of the air on the water, from what we had felt on shore. The day before our departure, at two o'clock in the afternoon, the thermometer in the house stood at 98°; next day, at the same hour, the quicksilver only reached 90° on the river. When the flood made, we got under way, rowed hard all night, and anchored in the morning near a town called Panlang, which, the Seree informed me, had once been a city of considerable magnitude, and from which the Rangoon river is frequently called the Panlang-mioup. The number of boats that were moored near it, indicated that it was still a place of some importance. The soil is rich, but there appeared to be little cultivation in its neighbourhood: here a branch of the river shapes its course to the south. At two in the afternoon we pursued our voyage, and continued rowing till seven in the evening, when we brought to, having passed three small villages in the way, one of which was surrounded by thick groves of plantain trees. At this place we spent a very comfortless night; it is a part of the river remarkable for being infested by mosquitoes of an unusual size, and venomous beyond what I ever felt in any other country: two pair of thick stockings were insufficient to defend my legs from their attacks; when in bed the curtains afforded some protection, but the servants, and even the boatmen, got no rest all night. A kind of reed that grows on the bank, breeds and harbours these insects in the utmost abundance; fortunately the colony does not extend many miles; a war boat that rows quick can escape them, but a heavy vessel must lie for one tide within their action.

On the first of June, at daybreak, we left Panlang, and stopped about nine o'clock at a hamlet on the right, where we saw a few gardens, and several travellers passing along a road at some distance on the plain. The river here contracts greatly, and does not appear to be more than two hundred yards across. Our people having taken refreshment, we continued our voyage. After leaving Panlang the influence of the tide becomes much weaker, and the water, during the ebb, is fresh. Our progress was but slow, having neither wind nor stream to befriend us. In three hours we reached Kettoree-Rua, or Parroquet village; and in two hours more came to Yangain-Chain-Yah. Here we entered the great river, and stopped for the night, our boats being fastened with hawsers to the bank. The course of the stream was nearly north and south, and about a mile wide.

Next morning, at the dawn of day, we pushed off, and at one o'clock, joined the Maywoon, who with his suite, and a vast concourse of boats, was waiting our arrival; he sent a polite message, with a present of some milk, fine rice, and fruit. Heavy rains falling, we remained here all day: the banks were steep, and there was nothing to attract notice. At a distance on the opposite shore we could perceive the temple of Denoobew.

At eight o'clock in the morning of the 3d of June the whole fleet got under way. Being now in the great river, and no longer sheltered by high and close banks, we spread our canvass, and favoured by a strong southerly wind, sailed against the stream. At nine we passed Denoobew, an extensive town, ornamented with a lofty temple, resembling Shoedagon in form, but of a less size. The adjacent fields appeared cultivated; several large mercantile boats were lying here, and more at a small village on the opposite side; the river was still low; the rains, although set in, had not yet materially affected it. We passed, in the course of our day's journey, many islands of sand formed by different streams of the river, in the dry season, but which are entirely covered when the waters swell; on some of these islands there are trees and verdure. We left the towns of Segahghee on the east, and Summeingtoh on the west. Our journey this day was very delightful; the weather turned out fine, and the wind was so favourable, that though the stream was strong, we passed the banks at the rate of three miles an hour: there were not less than an hundred sail of boats of different sorts in company; the whole was a cheerful and pleasing sight. The Maywoon being considered as commodore of the fleet, his movements regulated the rest. We stopped at sunset near the town of Yeoungbenzah, where I missed the Sere-dogee of Pegue, who seldom failed making an evening visit to drink tea, and ask questions about England. Baba-Sheen told me that he was left behind at the head of the Rangoon river, where he was bargaining for another boat, his own being rather crazy, and so deeply laden with merchandize, that he durst not venture it on the great river.

We left Yeoungbenzah at daybreak, and passed in our course several islands of sand. In one place we perceived the roots and stump of a tree growing close to the water's edge, under a high bank, about fourteen feet beneath the surface of the soil: this singular appearance is to be accounted for by supposing, that where the bank was now raised, there had formerly been a sand level with the water, on which a tree took root, and had been covered by annual accumulations from the river during the season of inundation. It is probable that the tall reeds and coarse grass, which every year rot and incorporate with the sand of the river, form the fine soil of the plains; thus aquatic exuviæ are to be discovered every where deep in the earth: the stream, however, washes away on one side as much as it deposits on the other, and as is the case with all rivers flowing through champaign countries, is continually changing its channel. In the morning we passed Taykyatt, a long and straggling town on the west side; also Terriato, or Mango village, small, but beautifully situated on a high commanding bank that overlooks the country on the opposite side to a great distance; it is surrounded by groves of mango trees, from which it takes the name. Taambooterra, on the same side, is a long town. The country, in this journey, did not appear so well inhabited as that we passed through the day before. At half past four we came to for the night at Kioumzeik, or Convent Stairs; a long sand intervened between us and the town; at this season the convex side of the windings of the river always terminates in a level sand. Two temples, not large, but gilded on the outside from top to bottom, made a very brilliant appearance. There were here many monasteries, the Rhahaans belonging to them were strolling up and down the banks, as curiosity led them. Near the river side were some fields planted with indigo, which throve in full luxuriance, and was nearly ripe; the natives prepare it without any skill: a large quantity of the weed was steeping in an old boat sunk in the river, which was substituted in the room of a vat. They do not take the trouble, or perhaps do not know how, to purify and reduce it to a hard refined consistence, but are satisfied with it in a liquid state; they use it to colour a coarse kind of cotton cloth, which is manufactured here in great quantities. The indigo is very cheap, and doubtless might, by proper management, be cultivated in this country to the highest advantage.

The town of Kioumzeik is well built, and seems to be in a state of improvement: there are several interruptions in it, caused by water-courses, over which good wooden bridges are built. The manufacture of cotton cloth is the source of its prosperity. A town called Henzadah, near to Kioumzeik, is of much greater antiquity. Numerous cart-roads and pathways evince that there is an extensive communication maintained with the interior country, but we saw little cultivation of grain, and only a few gardens. Buffaloes and other cattle were grazing in large herds on the neighbouring plain.

On the next day, June 5th, we put off at the first dawn, and passed in the course of our journey several small villages, none of which presented any thing worth notice; Sekayebeeim, on the east, was the most considerable. The bank on one side was high, and the sands extensive on the other. The course of the river runs deep beneath an overhanging bank, at a sluggish rate, not exceeding a mile in the hour. The southerly wind was not so strong as usual, and the temperature of the air had become much hotter; the thermometer, which on the preceding day stood at 78°, on this rose to 86°; still the heat was not oppressive. We brought to in the afternoon, south of a town called Ackeo; the evening was cloudy and threatened a thunder storm; a long and low strand lay between the boats and the town; I did not go on shore: Dr. Buchanan, however, ventured, and met with nothing to repay the trouble he took in traversing a plain of heavy sand.

We set off the following morning at the usual hour, and saw a few villages, but none remarkable; one on the east bank was situated in a large garden of plantain trees. At noon our boatmen tracked the boats along the sands, and made greater progress thus than they could either by rowing or setting with poles. Notwithstanding the general name of the river is Irrawaddy, I learned that different parts of it are distinguished by different appellations, taken from places of note on its banks, as though we should call the Thames, at appropriate places, the Gravesend river, the London river, &c. At two o'clock the sky lowered, and black clouds in the north-west quarter threatened one of those violent gusts which are frequent at this season; the Ledeegee, of his own accord, brought to on the west side, under the shelter of an high bank. As soon as the boat was made fast, the Doctor and I clambered up the steep; the country round was covered with reeds as tall as a man's head; there were many pathways leading through them, but we were dissuaded by the Birmans from entering, for fear of tigers, which are numerous here, and particularly frequent that kind of cover. The storm broke before it reached us, and, after a delay of two hours, we set sail with a southerly wind: passing a large village on the west, the Seree told me it was named Shwaye-Gaim, and that the inhabitants sometimes, during the rainy season, found gold dust in the sand of the river, which is washed down by the periodical rains.

A town nearly opposite, on the east side, is called Sabbaymeoun. It was eight o'clock in the evening when we stopped close to the town of Gnapeezeik. Gnapee, or Napee, a sort of sprat half pickled and half putrid, has already been described as a favourite and universal sauce used by the Birmans, to give a relish to their rice; Zeik signifies a landing place, whence we concluded that this town is an emporium for that commodity, which, in itself, forms an extensive branch of traffic.

Early in the morning we left Gnapee, and had to contend against a strong current, with very little assistance from the wind; the western bank was planted with pipal and mango trees. Yeagaim, on the right, and Kanounglay, or Little Kanoung, on the left, were the most remarkable places; near the latter we saw several plantations of fruit trees, the mango, plantain, jack-fruit, and custard apple. The fields near it were regularly laid down, and well fenced; many boats, some of them of a large size, were building on the banks, and the general aspect of things denoted peace and plenty. A little time brought us to Kanoungghe, or Great Kanoung, a long town, with a good quay, and well constructed wooden stairs, consisting of one hundred steps, descending to the water's edge. The population of this part of the country must be considerable. In getting round a bluff point we found much difficulty, owing to the rapidity of the current; the fleet was, in consequence, widely scattered, some surmounting the stream with more ease than others; the wind was but faint, and the weather exceedingly sultry. At two o'clock the thermometer rose to 94°. Our boatmen being harassed, I brought to early in the evening, under a pleasant bank; the Maywoon had got far a-head. Before tea I walked out with my gun, but had no success, seeing only a few quails and some wild pigeons. The country was tolerably well cleared, and though there was not much cultivation, it seemed in a state of preparation for the husbandman.

Our progress on the following day was more expeditious; we soon reached the neighbourhood of Meyahoun, formerly Loonzay, rendered memorable in the wars between the Birmans and Peguers. It is a very ancient city, stretching two miles along the margin of the river. Houses in cities or in villages differ very little; but this town was distinguished by numerous gilded temples, and spacious convents: a great variety of tall wide-spreading trees gave the place an air of venerable grandeur; under the shade of these several Rhahaans were luxuriously reposing. We saw not less than two hundred large boats at the different quays, which, on an average might be reckoned each at sixty tons burthen, all provided with good roofs, and masted after the country manner. They seemed much better constructed than the unwieldy wullocks* of Bengal. I was informed that the neighbourhood of Mayahoun is uncommonly fruitful in rice, and that a large quantity is exported annually to the capital. Here also were capacious granaries belonging to the King, built of wood, and covered with thatch; these are always kept filled with grain ready to be transported to any part of the empire in which there happens to be a scarcity, a misfortune that sometimes occurs to the higher provinces, where the annual rains are neither so certain nor so copious as in the southern districts: this wise and humane institution strongly evinces the solicitude of the monarch for the welfare of his people. Leaving Mayahoun, we passed Pasheem, whence a nullah, or water-course, leads to the south-west, also Kianggain; at both these places there were a number of trading boats. At half past two o'clock we were assailed by a violent

* A heavy boat used on the river Ganges.

north-west gust of wind, that, acting with the current, drove us back nearly two miles before we could reach the shore. The river here was more than a mile wide, although it had not yet attained its full monsoon height. At four we again got under way, and saw, on the east side, Tirroup-miou, or Chinese Town. During our journey this day we plainly discerned the Anoupectoumiou, or great western hills that divide this country from Arracan; the particular mountains in sight, the boatmen said, were named Taungzo. The districts we passed through this day were exceedingly populous, and in most parts cultivated. We brought to late in the evening, under a steep bank, near the inconsiderable village of Tzeezau.

We left, before daylight, a very uncomfortable situation: the night was sultry, and the high bank that hung over us prevented a free circulation of air; added to this, we were annoyed with myriads of stinking insects that issued from the reeds and coarse grass. The pleasantness of the day compensated for the inconveniences of the night. As we advanced, the western range of hills closed upon the river, and in some places displayed very beautiful scenery. Approaching the town of Peeing-ghee, on the west side, the rocky banks rose abruptly to the height of two or three hundred feet, the sides of which were richly clothed with hanging trees of variegated foliage. The confinement of the water in this place increased its rapidity, and I could not but admire the exertions made by the boatmen in stemming so violent a stream: oars were useless, and the perpendicular banks afforded no footpath to track; it therefore became necessary to impel the boat forward by bamboo poles, a labour at which the Birmans are uncommonly expert. When the pole is firm in the ground, they place the top of it against the muscles of the shoulder, just above the collar bone, then raising that shoulder, and bending forward, they bring the whole weight of the body to bear upon the end of the pole; in this manner they traverse the platform from stem to stern, following each other in quick succession on both sides of the boat, having small thwart bamboos fastened on the platform, a yard asunder, to prevent their feet from slipping. Owing to this mode of fixing the end of the pole against the muscles that reach from the back of the neck to the shoulder, a callosity is formed, and a Birman boatman always appears to be high shouldered. I could not discover why they preferred that method to the more obvious and easy one of pushing with the flat of the shoulder; they, however, performed what I am persuaded none but Birmans could effect. We were an hour in passing the extreme force of the current, which did not exceed four hundred yards.

The town of Peing-ghee, and that of Sahlahdan, a little above it, export a great part of the teak timber that is carried to Rangoon. The forests extend along on the western mountains, and were in sight from the boats. The trees are felled in the dry season, and when the monsoon sets in, are borne by the torrents to these towns. There was a ship on the stocks close to Peeing-ghee, of 400 tons burthen; a Mussulman merchant from Surat, out of economy, chose this place for building at, in preference to Rangoon; he meant, as soon as the hull should be finished, to float it down the stream. I was told that there was a good deal of hazard in the navigation, the distance of which, including the windings of the river, probably exceeds 150 miles; but he calculated the difference of expence to be adequate to the risk. This adventurer furnished a proof of the confidence that might be placed in the Birman government, and the security that a stranger has for his property. The teak tree, although it will grow on the plains, is a native of the mountains. The forests, like most of the woody and uncultivated parts of India, are extremely pestiferous; an inhabitant of the champaign country considers a journey thither as going to inevitable destruction. The wood-cutters are a particular class of men, born and bred in the hills; even they are said to be unhealthy, and seldom attain longevity.

The difficulty of this day's journey had dispersed the fleet; the lightest and best manned boats of course got a-head of the rest, and several were obliged to join their crews, and carry up each vessel singly by their united strength. Half a mile above Sahlahdan I overtook the Maywoon, who had arrived some time before me, and was waiting for us. The boatmen being greatly harassed, he recommended us to pass the night here. In the evening we took a walk together: the Maywoon was attended by eight or ten servants armed with spears and musquets: we both fired at game without success. The Birmans, even the common boatmen, are fond of fowling to a degree of childish delight; sooner than not shoot they will fire at sparrows. I never was more importuned than by them for shot, which they do not know how to fabricate. No schoolboy could be more pleased than the Leedegee of my boat, when I one evening lent him a gun to shoot wild pigeons. In this, as well as many other particulars, their disposition is strikingly contrasted with the habits of apathy and indolence that characterize the natives of Asia in general. My companions, Dr. Buchanan and Mr. Wood, not joining the party before dark, I expressed my apprehensions about them to the Maywoon, who was so good as to dispatch a war-boat to their assistance; the Doctor came about ten o'clock, but Mr. Wood's people being quite exhausted, he was obliged to stop three miles short of us, and the baggage-boat did not arrive at all. A little after midnight I was awakened to receive the unpleasant intelligence that she was wrecked: the boatmen, it seems, had nearly surmounted the difficult passage below Peeing-ghee, when, either from a remission of their efforts, or a more impetuous gush of water than usual, the boat suddenly got stern-way, and when once she lost ground there was no recovering it; the boatmen resigned her to the current, which swept her back with irresistible violence; fortunately she set towards the side, where a landing was practicable, and taking the ground on a rocky bottom, she bulged, and filled with water. The people got on shore safe, and it was expected that most of the articles on board would be recovered, but such as were liable to injury from the water were irretrievably spoiled.

Early the next morning, June 10th, Mr. Wood joined company, and the Maywoon sent an officer to Peeing-ghee with directions to procure a proper conveyance for my people, and render them every possible assistance; he likewise intimated to me his desire to remain three or four days at Meeayday, a town and district two days journey north of Prome, which he holds in jaghire by a grant from the king. This intention was far from being disagreeable to me or to any of the party, as our boatmen were fatigued, and the servants and the guard required a short time to adjust their conveniences for the remainder of the voyage.

The country contiguous to the river in this day's journey, was pleasingly diversified with hill and valley, and with spots of cleared ground and hanging woods: the range of mountains retired in a westerly direction as we advanced to the north, but smaller hills still skirted the river. We sailed before a fine southerly breeze, and enjoyed a climate far more temperate than I ever experienced in Hindostan at the same season of the year.

We left, a-stern on the west, Podangmew, a large and populous city, and on the right Shwaye-do-mew was the most important town. About noon we stopped to avoid a squall from the north-west: in the evening, my boat being a-head, I reached the city of Peeaye-mew, or Prome, on the east side; the other gentlemen did not cross the river till next morning.

CHAPTER IX.

Description of Prome.—Surprise excited by an European.—Prome sometimes called Terre-kelteree—Origin of the Name—singular Analogy.—Village of Pouoodang—Temple—Zee-ain—Kamma—Neoungbenzeik.—Gale of Wind.—Yeoungbenzeik—Serraipmew—Trees—Soil.—Meeaday—House erected for the English Agent—Mode of Structure—Birmans punctilious in whatever relates to Rank.—Town of Meeaday—Indulgence to Strangers—Cultivation—invited by the Maywoon to visit his Gardens—Remarks—meet a Caravan—curious Stone—numerous Visitants—leave Meeaday.—Pass Meealsah-gaim.—Reach Loonghee.—Visit a Kioum.—Tradition respecting Loonghee.—Romantic Scenery.—Tigers numerous.—Cattle—Soil—Produce.—Excursion of the Portugueze Pantchoo.—Tangho—a Fort and City of importance.—Beetle Nut.—Kayns, or Mountaineers.—Shawbunder arrives—His whimsical Appearance.

Prompted by curiosity to view a place so renowned as Prome is in Birman history, for having been the scene of many long sieges and bloody conflicts, as soon as my boat was made fast I hastened on shore, and a short way from the bank entered a long strait street, in which I walked for near a mile. The buildings were not remarkable; but though I saw little to notice, I found that I was myself an object of universal wonder: the singular appearance of an English officer dressed in uniform was a phænomenon perhaps never before seen in this part of the world. My attendants also created no little surprise; the dogs, numbers of which infested the streets, set up a horrid barking; the men gaped, the children followed me, and the women, as usual, expressed their astonishment by loud laughter, and clapping their hands; yet not the least indication of contempt was manifested, nor any thing done that could be construed into an intention to offend. Whichever way I turned, the crowd respectfully opened, and the most forward were restrained by others. The notice I took of a little girl, who was alarmed at our appearance, seemed to be very gratifying to the parents, and the mother encouraging her child, brought her close to me. Had I entered a house, I have no doubt but the owners would have offered me the best of what it contained. Kindness to strangers is equally the precept and the practice of Birmans.

At the upper end of the present city are to be seen the ruins of the ancient fort of Prome; it had been a small pentagon, built of brick, and from its situation must have been very strong. The modern fort is nothing more than a palisaded inclosure, with earth thrown up behind it. Low hills, on the eastern side approach the town, in which the rains have formed channels down to the river, that are crossed by wooden bridges. I passed some stone-cutters' yards, where artificers were manufacturing flags for pavements, and slabs and vases for the use of temples, out of a fine freestone which is found in that neighbourhood. Adjacent to the town there is a royal menagery of elephants, consisting of two rows of lofty well built stables, in which these animals are lodged during the rains. I saw some that had been lately caught, under the discipline necessary to render them docile.

The city of Prome, and the province in which it stands, are the jaghire, or estate, of the second son of the king; they likewise give him his title. Prome is sometimes called Terreketteree, or single skin; the Birmans have an old legendary tale respecting the origin of this name: it is related that a favourite female slave of Tutebong-mangee, or the mighty sovereign with three eyes, importuned her lord for a gift of some ground, and being asked of what extent, replied in similar terms with the crafty and amorous Eliza, when she projected the site of ancient Carthage. Her request was granted, and she used the same artifice. The resemblance of the stories is curious.

I had not leisure to go through the whole of the town, but was informed that it contained more inhabitants than Rangoon, and had a better supplied market. The Seree told me that the ruins of a large fort and city, much surpassing the present, stood about a league eastward of the town: the lateness of the hour prevented me from continuing my researches.

We departed from Prome at an early hour on the 11th of June, and sailed before a strong southerly gale till we came to Pouoodang, a small village built on the western bank of the river. A high hill of a conical form rises abruptly behind it, on the top of which there is a temple of peculiar sanctity, having once been the abode of Gaudma; the impression made by the foot of the divinity is shewn indented on a slab of marble. The Maywoon had gone before us to perform his devotions at this place of worship. The hill seemed difficult of ascent; several of our people went up, but the day being wet and stormy I declined the undertaking. We afterwards made head against a violent current by the aid of a tempestuous wind: there was, for a long way, little improvement close to the river; obscure hamlets at distant intervals just served to shew that the country was not without inhabitants. Zeeain, on the west, appeared a pretty village. Towards evening we reached Kammah, on the east side: it is the chief town of a district that bears the same name, and makes large exports of teak timber for the Rangoon market. We did not stop here, but continued our course as far as Neoungbenzeik, where we arrived too late to make many observations: this also is a town of some respectability. We were here on a lee shore, under a high and rocky bank. The Maywoon not liking the appearance of the weather, and thinking it unsafe to remain in such a situation all night, ordered the boatmen to row across to a long sand, where we might be secure from danger in the event of a storm; nor was this precaution ill timed; about midnight it blew a hurricane: we, however, ran no risk; our boats touched the soft sand, and were moored by strong hawsers reaching from the stem and stern to the shore. Mr. Wood and Dr. Buchanan, who had not come up, found shelter in a creek, where they passed the night. As soon as the storm commenced, the Maywoon detached a war-boat to their assistance.

Our associates joined the fleet betimes in the morning, and we sailed immediately. Our journey this day was disagreeable, from the violence of the southerly wind, which, meeting the stream, caused a heavy swell: the boats pitched deep, and were very uneasy. We passed a small village on the left bank, whence, I was told, a road leads through the mountains to Arracan. Yeoungbenzeik, or Indian fig-tree stairs, on the east side, is a fine village, situated in a romantic country; so also is Pelon, a place remarkable for boat building; and Samban, famed for its iron manufactory. At a particular part the river was divided into two distinct branches, separated by a sand; each branch we judged to be a mile wide; and when the water rises so as to overflow the sands, the breadth cannot be less than four miles from bank to bank. Every village we saw was ornamented with one or more small temples. In the evening we brought to, at a town called Sirraipmew. The country around was pleasingly diversified with swelling grounds covered with stately trees, particularly with the tamarind and mango; Dr. Buchanan measured one of the latter, and found it, at the height of his shoulder from the ground, twelve feet in circumference: some of the tamarind and pipal trees seemed still larger. Many of the rising grounds were planted with indigo, but the natives suffer the hills, for the most part, to remain uncultivated, and only plough the rich levels: they everywhere burn the rank grass once a year to improve the pasture. We saw many people at labour. The soil is a fine mould, and would produce abundant crops in proper hands; but the Birmans will not take much pains; they leave half the work to nature, which has been very bountiful to them. Their thirst for conquest does not seem to have enriched their country.

In the morning, when we left Sirraipmew, the wind blew as usual from the southward with great violence. At noon we reached Meeaday, the personal estate of the Maywoon of Pegue, who is oftener called, from this place, Meeaday Praw, or Lord of Meeaday, than by his viceroyal titles. Here, in compliance with the wishes of the Maywoon, we proposed staying a few days.

It is a mark of respect, and a distinction of rank, for a person journeying on the water to have houses built for his accommodation on the banks, at the places where he means to stop. When the king goes on the river, or travels by land, buildings of the royal order of architecture are erected wherever he is to halt. In the manner of constructing houses, whether temporary or lasting, strict observance is paid to the form, which is indicative of the rank of the occupant; nor dare any subject assume a mode of structure to which he is not legally entitled: the distinction consists chiefly in the number of stages of which the roof is composed. The subordination of rank is maintained and marked by the Birmans with the most tenacious strictness, and not only houses, but even domestic implements, such as the beetle box, water flaggon, drinking cup, and horse furniture, all express and manifest, by shape and quality, the precise station of the owner; nor can one person intrude upon the rights of another, under penalty of incurring a most severe punishment, which is never remitted. The Maywoon had obligingly given directions to have a house constructed on the bank for us, of the order appertaining to nobility, but of what particular class I could not easily ascertain, and refrained from minute inquiries, as it might appear fastidious, and give an unfavourable impression to those whom it was my inclination to conciliate.

The materials of which these houses are made, are always easy to be procured; and the structure is so simple, that a spacious, and by no means uncomfortable dwelling, suited to the climate, may be erected in one day. Our habitation, consisting of three small rooms, and a hall open to the north, in little more than four hours was in readiness for our reception: fifty or sixty labourers completed it in that time, and, on emergency, could perform the work in much less. Bamboos, grass for thatching, and the ground rattan, are all the materials requisite; not a nail is used in the whole edifice: a row of strong bamboos, from eight to ten feet high, are fixed firm in the ground, which describe the outline, and are the supporters of the building; smaller bamboos are then tied horizontally by strips of the ground rattan, to these upright posts; the walls, composed of bamboo mats, are fastened to the sides, with similar ligatures; bamboo rafters are quickly raised, and a roof formed, over which thatch is spread in regular layers, and bound to the roof by filaments of rattan; a floor of bamboo grating is next laid in the inside, elevated two or three feet above the ground; this grating is supported on bamboos, and covered with mats and carpets: thus ends the process, which is not more simple than effectual. When the workmen take pains, a house of this sort is proof against very inclement weather. We experienced, during our stay at Meeaday, a severe storm of wind and rain, but no water penetrated, or thatch escaped, and if the tempest should blow down the house, the inhabitants would run no risk of having their brains knocked out, or their bones broken: the fall of the whole fabric would not crush a lady's lap-dog.

Having got possession of our dwelling, Mr. Wood, Dr. Buchanan, and myself, took a walk to view the town and adjacent country: our boats had brought to at the southern extremity of Meeaday. It is a place of no great magnitude, but extremely neat: there are two principal streets, and at the north end of the present town are to be seen the ruins of a brick fort, which, like all other forts of masonry in the Birman empire, is in a state of dilapidation. At a short distance there is a pleasant river which flows through a fertile plain affording some rich pasture-ground; and interspersed with plantations of tobacco. On the south and south-east sides, the town is inclosed by a deep ravine, the banks of which are cut perpendicular, and the remains of an old brick wall were discoverable, which was probably a defence to the former suburb. We observed many small temples and convents apart from the town, situated in groves of mango, tamarind, and pipal trees of uncommon stateliness and beauty. The Maywoon had a residence here, also a pleasure house and beetle garden at some distance. Notwithstanding his manners were still very formal, and evidently desirous of little personal intercourse, he continued invariably attentive, and daily sent me such presents as he thought would be acceptable, such as fruit, fish, and milk. Although it is sinful, according to the Birman tenets, to deprive any being of life to satisfy a carnivorous appetite, yet the inhabitants do not scruple to kill game of all kinds, and abstain only from domestic animals; even in this they often relax, and always grant a most liberal indulgence to strangers. I was allowed to send my Portugueze servant to the neighbouring villages to purchase fowls, which we got very good, and sometimes were able to procure kids. The Birman farmers do not breed sheep, goats giving so much more milk. It was privately intimated to me, that there would be no crime if a servant of mine should shoot a fat bullock when he met one; that it would be ascribed to accident, and I might make reparation to the owner, who would think himself amply recompensed for his loss by two tackals, about six shillings; and the beast being dead, there could be no sin in eating it; but that a public sanction could not previously be given to slaughter one. I declined supplying our table by this evasive logic, and preferred the want of beef to the risk of giving offence, and wounding the feelings of people who omitted no opportunity to manifest towards us hospitality and kindness.

North of the town about a mile, there is a good deal of cultivation, chiefly of rice; the fields were well laid down, and fenced. This quarter is beautifully wooded, and diversified with rising grounds. We observed many cart-roads and pathways leading into the country in various directions. The soil is composed of clay and sand, and in some places is very stony, particularly near the river. Early on the 14th the Maywoon politely sent us an invitation to accompany him on the same evening to his garden-house; I was not well, and excused myself; Mr. Wood was otherwise engaged, but the Doctor undertook to represent us. The Maywoon supplied him with a horse for his conveyance, and rode himself; they crossed the small river beforementioned, and traversed a country partly cultivated, and partly wooded: the road was indifferent, and led through two very neat villages. They also passed several straggling houses, which, considered as country cottages, were extremely comfortable. In their way they saw a caravan of waggons, which had come from a great distance, loaded with goods of different sorts for traffic. The inhabitants in many places were employed in clearing the ground, and burning the long grass and brushwood. On arriving at the garden, about five miles distant, the Maywoon and his company, among whom the Doctor was the most distinguished, were regaled with tea and sweetmeats, and returned late in the evening nearly by the same road.

In the course of our walks, not the least curious object that presented itself was a flat stone, of a coarse gray granite, laid horizontally on a pedestal of masonry, six feet in length, and three wide, protected from the weather by a wooden shed. This stone, like that at Pouoodang, was said to bear the genuine print of the foot of Gaudma; and we were informed that a similar impression is to be seen on a large rock situated between two hills, one day's journey west of Memboo. On the plane of the foot upwards of one hundred emblematical figures are engraven in separate compartments: two convoluted serpents are pressed beneath the heel, and five conch shells, with the involutions to the right, form the toes: it was explained to me as a type of the creation, and was held in profound reverence. There is said to be a similar impression on a rock* on Adam's Peak, in the island of Ceylon; and it is traditionally believed, both by the Birmans, the Siamese, and the Cin-

* See Baldæus; also Knox's Historical Relation of Ceylon.

galeze, that Gaudma or Boodh, placed one foot on the continent, and the other on the island of Ceylon. The neighbouring Rhahaans had no objection to my painter's taking a copy of it, a task that he performed with great exactness.*

On our return, we met a caravan of waggons travelling from the southern country towards the capital, eighteen in number: these vehicles were well constructed, and more commodious and neat than the clumsy gawries or carts of India. Each waggon was drawn by six bullocks, and several spare ones followed, to supply the place of any that might fall sick or lame. A good tilted roof of bamboo, covered with painted cloth, threw off the rain. They contained not only merchandize, but also entire families, the wives, children, monkies, cats, parroquets, and all the worldly substance of the waggoner. Each bullock had a bell under his throat. The wheels not being greased, a horrid noise announced the approach of the caravan long before it could be seen. They travel slowly, from ten to fifteen miles a day. At night the waggons are disposed in a circle, and form a barrier, within which, the carriers feed their cattle, light fires, and dress their victuals, secure from the attacks of tigers, which much infest the less populous parts of the empire.

We remained at Meeaday until the 22d of June. During our stay I made short excursions to different parts of the country, and found little variation in its appearance; it was very beautiful, though but half cultivated, and I was everywhere treated with respect. The news of the mission had reached the place before we arrived, and excited a general curiosity to see the Boomien of the Colars, or the general of the strangers, as

* Annexed is a plate of the impression, to enable the learned antiquary to compare this curious symbolic representation with the sacred hieroglyphics of the ancient Egyptians.

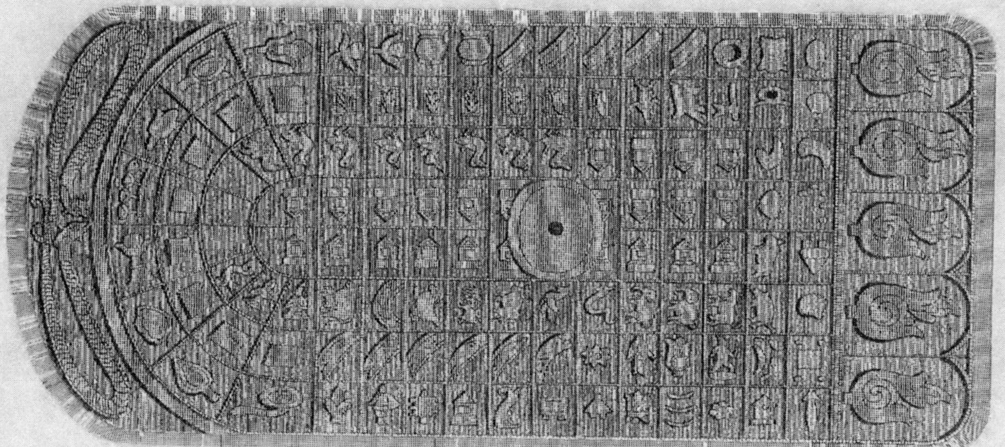

Drawn by Singey Bey. Engraved by J. Medland

Impression of the Foot of Gaudma

London Published Nov.r 1. 1799 by G. Nicol Pall Mall & J. Wright, Piccadilly.

they were pleased to denominate me. Not only the better class of the inhabitants of Meeaday came to visit us, but likewise people of condition from all the towns and villages twenty miles round: I have sometimes received eight or ten different companies in a morning. When a party wished to be introduced, a message was sent to ask permission, which being obtained, they entered the room in a crouching position, and sat down on their heels, men and women alike; they always brought a gift of something, whatever they supposed might be acceptable; tobacco, onions, fine rice, &c.: no company presented themselves empty handed; it would not have been respectful; of course their offerings drew from me a suitable return, such as fillets of Indian muslin to the women, and a Cossembuzar silk handkerchief to the men. Several parties of women came unaccompanied by their husbands, or any of their male friends; and according to the notions entertained by them, there was nothing indecorous in it; they were unconscious of any thing but an innocent desire to gratify curiosity, and manifest respect; women of a better class were always accompanied by a train of female attendants, and, like the sex every where, were more lively, good humoured, and inquisitive than the men.

Early on the 22d of June matters were arranged for the prosecution of our journey, and the fleet was in readiness to depart. The articles saved from the boat that had been wrecked below Peeing-ghee, were dried, our attendants, however, had suffered a material loss: but a serviceable boat had been provided for them in lieu of the one that was lost. At eleven o'clock we pushed off, the Maywoon leading the van: the day turned out tempestuous and gloomy, and the wind blew hard from the south. In a short time we passed Meealsah-gain, on the west, a large village at the foot of a fine swelling wooded lawn, ornamented with some neat temples. Our way through the water was very rapid, not less than five miles an hour, and at one time it blew so violently that we were obliged to make for the shore. The range of hills, which in our course this day approached nearest to the river, were covered with a blue mist. We passed some villages of no note: the country seemed populous, and herds of cattle were grazing on the banks. About seven o'clock we brought to for the night on the west side.

At seven in the morning, after a night of unremitting rain, we left an uncomfortable situation, and sailed till we came to an extensive island, which divided the river into two branches; we took the eastern side, and on account of the inclemency of the weather, brought to at the lower town of Loonghee, opposite the south extremity of the island. The width of the stream between the main land and the island is about 500 yards. In the afternoon the rain ceased, but the wind continued. Dr. Buchanan and I walked to a convent of Rhahaans, that seemed to be of more than ordinary note: we found it a good building, and ascending a flight of steps took the liberty of entering without ceremony. The neatness of the inside corresponded with the external appearance: a number of Gaudmas, richly gilt, and of various sizes, were ranged on a bench to receive the adorations of the pious. It was the eighth day of the moon, which is the Birman sabbath, and several persons were sauntering up and down, waiting for the hour of prayer. The superior, a man advanced in years, was sitting on his elevated seat when we went in: he expressed much surprise at our appearance and dress, but was extremely civil: he presented me with a scroll, written with a stylus on a papyrus leaf, which, he said, contained a sacred exhortation, and requested I would preserve it in remembrance of Shoedagonga Sere-daw, which, it seems, was his title. He asked why the Doctor did not wear a scarlet dress like mine, and being informed of his profession, begged a prescription for a sore throat, which almost hindered him from articulating. The Doctor promised to send him a gargle, and we took our leave.

The infant son of the Maywoon had been unwell for some time, and his illness had now increased to a dangerous height: the anxious parent sent Baba-Sheen to me to intimate his desire of remaining where we were until his child grew better, the tempestuousness of the weather agitating the boat so much, that he was afraid it might increase the fever. I had no scruple in indulging so natural a wish, and as the spot we were in was much exposed, and had many disadvantages, we moved to a more commodious situation, two miles higher up, opposite the north end of the island. A war-boat was dispatched express to the capital to bring down medicine, and a celebrated professor of physic; in the mean time all the physicians of the country, to the number of twenty, were assembled, to consult and prescribe for the sick infant.

Loonghee, or Great Cable, takes its name from the following circumstance: a curious ligament of stone unites a pointed rock, which rises in the middle of the stream, with the opposite bank; it has the appearance of a petrified cable, and the natives relate, that one hundred years ago a large rope, floating down the river, ceased its course at this place, and that one end adhering to the rock, and the other to the bank, the rope was changed into stone. They also say that the opposite island formerly constituted a part of one, situated fifteen miles higher up, but was severed from it by an earthquake, and carried down to the place where it now rests. The quality which the waters of the Irrawaddy possess of changing wood into stone, of which we afterwards saw innumerable instances, renders the transmutation of the cable by no means an impossible circumstance. The

Birmans, however, are deeply tainted with that credulity which ignorance is ever disposed to pay, to tales of fiction and to miraculous events.

Whether removed by an extraordinary convulsion of nature, and by a still more extraordinary transportation, or whether encircled by the river from the disposition that all large streams flowing through a level country have to change their channel; whatever may have been the cause, the island now constitutes a principal object in one of the finest sylvan scenes I ever beheld. From a temple above Loonghee, that stands by the river side, on a commanding cliff whose summit overhangs its base, the eye is gratified by a most delightful combination of natural beauties: a fine sheet of water three miles in breadth, broken by an island about a mile long, and half a mile wide, covered with trees of luxuriant foliage; eminences on the opposite shore, that rise from gently swelling grounds clothed in wood, to brown and rugged mountains, which, receding in an oblique direction, leave to the view a long and level plain: these altogether form a landscape which I never saw equalled, and, perhaps, is not to be excelled. How much I regretted that my draftsman, though skilful in copying figures and making botanical drawings, was unacquainted with landscape painting and perspective, and that not one of ourselves possessed any knowledge of that delightful art. Had Mr. Daniel, in his Oriental Travels, visited this part of the world, the view from Loonghee would have stood conspicuous among those faithful and excellent representations by which he has locally introduced India into England, and familiarized the European eye to the rich scenery of the East.

We continued at this charming place until the 2d of July, when the child of the Maywoon, notwithstanding the prescriptions of twenty doctors, was declared out of danger. So long as recovery continued doubtful,

I sent the Hindoo Pundit every morning to enquire after his health: this attention was taken in good part, and the Pundit obtained the honour of being introduced into the sick chamber, where he witnessed the most amiable demonstrations of parental tenderness: both the father and mother were kneeling by the side of the infant's bed, and attended on him themselves day and night. The disorder proved to be an inflammatory fever, and their treatment of it was perfectly simple: tea made of wild thyme, and decoctions of several vegetable productions, were the only medicines administered; the rest was left to nature, who accomplished her part. They did not, however, neglect to call in the aid of supernatural remedies; incantations were used, and amulets applied, to the efficacy of which much was attributed. Whatever might have been the cause, the recovery of the child afforded very general satisfaction; every body seemed to feel an interest in his fate.

We made several short excursions during our continuance at Loong-hee; the country to the southward was well cultivated, and the fields inclosed by strong hedges of thorn: the soil is light and sandy, with many loose stones; the ground, for the most part, uneven, and rising into gentle acclivities. There were several neat villages, within the distance of two or three miles; a deep ravine, formed by the monsoon rains, extended inland from the river, the banks of which were covered with stunted trees. Dr. Buchanan, in following its course, perceived in the sand the fresh tracks of a tiger, and prudently returned. On enquiring I understood that the adjacent woods contained many of these destructive beasts, who frequently at night come down the bed of the water-course to quench their thirst at the river. I went the next day with the Doctor and an armed party to the place, and plainly traced in the sand the footsteps of two tigers, a large and a small one; this discovery rendered us cautious of pursuing game into the forests. We found partridges, hares, quails, and wood pigeons, in the open fields, but the jungle-fowl, or wild poultry, kept close in the thick coverts, where we heard the cocks crow, but did not dare to venture after them. We saw on the island, which is a very romantic spot, a few deer, and three buffaloes; the former were extremely wild; we fired at them without success, but were more fortunate in killing a number of pigeons of a beautiful plumage, and excellent to eat.

The cattle used for tillage and draft in this part of the country are remarkably good; they put only a pair in the plough, which differs little from the plough of India, and turns up the soil very superficially. In their large carts they yoke four, and often six: walking out one day I met a waggon drawn by four stout oxen, going at a hand gallop, and driven by a country girl standing up in her vehicle, who seemed to manage the reins and a long whip with equal ease and dexterity: this was a novel sight to a person accustomed to the slow moving machines of India, in which the women are almost too timorous to ride, much less to attempt to guide.

The soil in the neighbourhood of Loonghee is very favourable for the cultivation of cotton; we saw many fields planted with it, in which the shrub was growing strong and healthy. In one field a man was sowing sesamum: the light dry grains answer here better than rice, which thrives only in low and moist grounds.

My Portugueze servant Pauntchoo, whom I had dispatched along with a Birman, in quest of fowls and kids, was absent for three days, a circumstance that gave rise to some uneasiness on his account, from the fear of his having been devoured by tigers: he, however, returned safe, and informed me that he had been to a town nine leagues distant, and in his way passed through several villages, and a country thickly inhabited. When he had concluded his bargain, he procured a small cart to carry his purchase to Loonghee, and could not prevail on the owner to accept of any thing more than a Cossembuzar silk handkerchief. All the manufactures of India are highly prized by the Birmans, although many articles are not at all superior to what they make themselves. Pauntchoo also reported, that there was a well frequented road leading to the city of Tongho, which was distant fifteen days journey, the capital of a rich and populous province that bears the same name, and is governed by one of the King's sons, who takes his title from it, being called Tongho Teekien, or Prince of Tongho; he added that its inhabitants excelled in the manufacture of cotton cloth, and their country produced the best beetle nut in the empire, a luxury in which Birmans of all ranks indulge so freely, that it is become with them almost a necessary of life. In one of Pauntchoo's expeditions across the river he met with a village inhabited by Kayns, a race of mountaineers perfectly distinct from the Carianers, and speaking a language differing radically both from theirs and that of the Birmans. They were originally inhabitants of the Arracan mountains, whom the Birmans, since their conquest of that kingdom, have prevailed on, partly by force, and partly by mild treatment, to abandon their native hills, and settle on the plain. There are several small societies of these people established near the foot of the mountains farther north. The Carianers are not to be found higher up than the city of Prome.

Every thing was now in readiness for us to take our next departure, and the first of July was fixed upon to leave Loonghee. On the morning of the 29th of June we were surprised by an unexpected visit from the Portugueze Shawbunder of Rangoon, who has already been mentioned as having been at Ummerapoora, the capital, at the time of our first arrival. He had been ordered down from court to meet the deputation, and came with all the pomp that his station would allow him to display; his barge was profusely decorated with colours, and his boatmen were dressed in uniform. On landing, he first paid his compliments to the Maywoon, and afterwards waited on me at my boat.

The appearance of this naturalized Portugueze was calculated rather to excite laughter than respect: he wore a long tunic of old velvet, decorated with tarnished gold lace, and on his head a broad brimmed hat flapped, bound also with gold. He spoke the language of Hindostan imperfectly, but well enough to make himself understood. After an awkward salutation, half in the Birman, half in the European manner, he informed me that he had been sent by an order from the Lotoo, or Grand Council, to meet the English deputation, and to acquaint me that his Majesty had been pleased to direct that three officers of distinguished rank should proceed to Pagahm-mew, a city seven days journey below Ummerapoora, to wait our arrival, and escort us to the capital. The King, he observed, had done me the extraordinary honour to send a royal barge for my personal accommodation, with two war-boats to tow it: this was considered as a flattering mark of his Majesty's good inclination, and we drew from it a favourable omen. To have our barge drawn by war-boats was an honorary privilege granted only to persons of the first consequence; it is grounded on the idea, that it is inconsistent with the dignity of a man of high rank to be in the same boat with people of such mean condition as common watermen; it is a singular refinement, and furnishes an additional instance of the characteristic pride of the nation. The Shawbunder displayed great shrewdness in his conversation. He asked me several questions respecting the powers with which I was invested; and as the visit might in some degree be considered as official, I in part gratified his curiosity, by explaining in general terms the nature of the mission, and the capacity in which I expected to be received, without at all disclosing the specific objects I had in view.

CHAPTER X.

Leave Loonghee.—Extensive Island—Keendoo Praw—Meegheoung-yay, or Crocodile Town—Meein-yah—Patanagoh—Magway—Spanziek—strong Current—Hills clothed with Wood—Maynbu—Shoe-Lee-Rua, or Golden Boat Village—Gold the Type of Excellence—Yaynangheoum, or Petroleum Creek—petrified Wood—barren Country—Pengkioum—Sembewghewm—Sillahmew—Manufactory of Silk—Crotolaria Juncea—Mountain of Poupa—Seenghoo—Bullock slain by a Tiger.—Yoos, an ugly Race.—Temple of Logah-nundah.—City of Pagahm—Neoundah—Birman Deputies—Music—Dancing—beautiful Manufactory of lackered Ware.—Temple of Shoezeegoon—destructive Conflagration—numerous religious Buildings—gigantic Figure of the Divinity in a recumbent Posture—another Image erect—Oil Mills.

The Shawbunder left Loonghee on the first of July, to announce our approach to the Birman officers, who were already arrived at Pagahm: we postponed our departure until the following day, and at seven in the morning quitted this pleasing and rural place. In our journey we passed many towns and villages; sometimes we went swiftly through the water, at others we were stationary, and even lost ground, as the wind frequently subsided, and the stream was very rapid. The range of Arracan mountains appeared to recede westward, and about three o'clock we came to a large island formed by separate arms of the river; there was a pyramidical temple on it, called Keendoo Praw, and several smaller ones raised on a high terrace. I estimated the extent of the island to be two miles: at the upper end we crossed the river, and stopped a mile above Meegheoung-yay, at past seven in the evening.

Meegheoung-yay, or Crocodile Town, is a place of much trade and importance; there were not less than 100 large boats, and several smaller ones, lying at different stairs, which, my people said, were taking on board rice, onions, garlic, and oil, for the consumption of the capital. It stands on a very high bank, and has fewer religious buildings than any town we had seen of equal magnitude. Dr. Buchanan went on shore at daybreak, and observed in his walk some neat farms, each of them containing four or five cottages, better built than houses in towns usually are: they were fenced round with wide inclosures to receive the cattle, of which there was great abundance. The fields were divided by thorn hedges; the low grounds prepared for rice, and the higher planted with leguminous shrubs, or left for pasture.

Early on the 3d we passed Meeinyah: between that and Patanagoh, on the eastern shore, there was a sloping bank planted with indigo, which was then ripe, and the villagers were cutting it. Melloon, on the west side, seemed rich in temples, but the town was no way distinguished. Patanagoh had only one temple, which was splendidly gilded; it is a long straggling village, and every house had a comfortable garden, enclosed by a bamboo railing, with orchards of palmyra, plantain, and mango trees: here, likewise, were many boats of burthen waiting to receive a cargo. Numerous villages were scattered along the banks, which, as the wind blew strong, and we were obliged to keep in the middle of the river, there was no opportunity of examining. This day we passed some sandy islands, and brought to early in the evening, on the eastern side, between the towns of Magway and Spanzeik. I took a walk before tea, and could discover little cultivation in the vicinity of the river: the land was stony, and covered with low thorn trees, in which we saw jungle-fowl, and other game. Herds of young cattle were grazing among the thickets: we crossed some cart roads, and met several peasants.

At daybreak next morning, we set sail with a fair and steady wind, by the force of which the fleet stemmed a strong current. Low woody hills skirted the river, particularly on the eastern side; on the summits of some of these hills temples were raised, and one on the western bank, called Maynbu, appeared to be considerable. The river, except where it was interrupted by islands, could not be less than two miles across. We passed a village named Shoe-Lee-Rua, or Golden-boat Village, from its being inhabited by watermen in the service of the King, whose boats, as well as every thing else belonging to the Sovereign, have always the addition of shoe, or golden, annexed to them; even his Majesty's person is never mentioned but in conjunction with this precious metal. When a subject means to affirm that the King has heard any thing, he says, "It has reached the golden ears;" he who has obtained admission to the royal presence, has been at the golden feet; the perfume of otta of roses, a nobleman observed one day, "was an odour grateful to the golden nose." Gold, among the Birmans, is the type of excellence: although highly valued, it is not used for coin in the country; it is employed sometimes in ornaments for the women, and in utensils and ear-rings for the men; but the greatest quantity is expended in gilding their temples, in which vast sums are continually lavished.

The Birmans present the substance to their gods, and ascribe its qualities to their king.

After passing various sands and villages, we got to Yaynangheoum, or Earth-oil (petroleum) Creek, about two hours past noon. The country now displayed an aspect differing from any we had yet seen; the surface was broken into small separate hills, entirely barren, and destitute of vegetation, except some stunted bushes that grew on the declivities, and in the dells, and a few unhealthy trees immediately in the neighbourhood of the villages: the clay was discoloured, and had the appearance of red ochre. We were informed that the celebrated wells of petroleum, which supply the whole empire, and many parts of India, with that useful product, were five miles to the east of this place. The Seree brought me a piece of stone, which he assured me was petrified wood, and which certainly had much the appearance of it. In walking about, I picked up several lumps of the same, in which the grain of the wood was plainly discernible; it was hard, silicious, and seemed composed of different lamina. The Birmans said it was the nature of the soil that caused this transmutation, and added that the petrifying quality of the earth at this place was such, that leaves of trees shaken off by the wind, were not unfrequently changed into stone before they could be decayed by time. The face of the country was altered, and the banks of the river were totally barren; the ground was superficially covered with quartz gravel, and concreted masses of the same material were thickly scattered. The mouth of the creek was crowded with large boats, waiting to receive a lading of oil, and immense pyramids of earthen jars were raised within and round the village, disposed in the same manner as shot and shells are piled in an arsenal. This place is inhabited only by potters, who carry on an extensive manufactory, and find full employment. The smell of the oil was extremely offensive; we saw several thousand jars filled with it ranged along the bank; some of these were continually breaking, and the contents, mingling with the sand, formed a very filthy consistence. Mr. Wood had the curiosity to walk to the wells, but though I felt the same desire, I thought it prudent to postpone visiting them until my return, when I was likely to have more leisure, and to be less the object of observation.

At seven in the morning, on the 5th of July, we left the neighbourhood of Earth-oil Wells. After passing Pengkioum, where a small river unites with the Irrawaddy, the face of the country resumed its verdant appearance, and the trees shot up with their usual vigour. The bed of the river, from bank to bank, was very wide; we judged it to be four miles, but the stream being divided into different channels, formed low intermediate islands of sand, which are covered when the waters attain their utmost height. On the left we saw the town of Sembewghewn, from whence there is a road that leads through the western hills into Arracan, which is accounted much the least difficult passage: this is the place to which all Bengal articles of merchandize imported by way of Arracan are brought, and are here embarked on the Irrawaddy. Shortly after, we saw a large town on the eastern side, with several neat temples; it was called Pakang-yay: lofty palmyra, the tamarind, and banyan trees, spread a pleasant shade around it; here also were some heavy trading boats. The western shore seemed rich and level; we brought to about six in the afternoon, a little below Sillah-mew, a large town remarkable for its manufactories of silk. The fleet had not long been moored when the retail merchants flocked down to the water side to dispose of their wares: they carried in lackered boxes pieces of silken cloth, and of silk and cotton mixed, which they offered for sale at what I considered a very high price. I was asked fifteen tackal, about £2. sterling, for a piece, of moderate fineness, five yards long, and barely one yard wide: they were mostly woven in patterns adapted to the Birman dress. The silk, of which these goods are made, comes from Yunan, the south-west province of China: it is brought from Ummerapoora to this place in a raw state, and is returned in the web. The colours are bright and beautiful, but do not appear to be durable; the texture is close and strong; it wears, I was informed, much longer than any China or Indian manufacture.

Sillah-mew is a handsome town, shaded by wide spreading trees, and embellished with several temples. A smooth bank sloping to the river, and clothed with the finest verdure, adds much to its beauty. The soil in general is but poor; some fields were regularly fenced, and cattle in large herds were grazing in the neighbourhood. Dr. Buchanan informed me that he saw the crotalaria juncea growing spontaneously, which would yield good hemp or flax.

On the sixth of July we made but little way, the current was violent, and the wind not strong enough to enable us to stem it; we were obliged to have recourse to poles, and were pushed forward with excessive labour by the boatmen; in one place where an island contracted the stream, we sent out an anchor a-head in a small cutter, and hauled on it by a hawser. The Arracan mountains appeared to the west, and a conspicuous hill, lofty, and of a conical form, called Poupa, was in sight to the eastward: a few villages, and many temples, skirted the banks. In the afternoon the fleet made fast to the eastern shore; there was neither town nor village nigh; it was about four miles below Seenghoo, and though we saw little cultivation there were several herds of cattle. Dr. Buchanan, whose ardour for botanical researches often made me apprehensive for his safety, in wandering through the thickets in quest of plants, heard the report of a musket at a distance; on his approach to the spot, he found some peasants about to skin a bullock that had just been killed by a tiger: the shot had caused the animal to abandon his prey, and in its retreat it most fortunately took another way from that which the Doctor came. This was not the only time that his thirst after knowledge, and reliance upon his gun, led him into danger. A musket is a very precarious defence against the sudden assault of the most ferocious and terrible of all animals.

Whilst we were at tea, the Seree informed us, that further on there is a small river which enters the Irrawaddy at a place called Yoo-wa, and that two days journey up this river is a large town called Yoo-miou; he observed also, that an extensive tract of country is inhabited by a people called Yoo, whom he represented as exceedingly ugly, having protuberant bellies, and white teeth. The Birmans, both men and women, colour their teeth, their eyelashes, and the edges of their eyelids, with black.* The Yoos are subjects of the Birman state, and observe the same religious worship; they speak the language of Tavay, which is nothing more than a provincial dialect of the Birman tongue.

We left our nightly station at the customary hour, and favoured by a fair breeze, sailed through a country diversified by small barren hills, on which there was little vegetation, and by green fertile valleys, cultivated, and laid out in farms. The petrifactions, like those we found at Yaynangheoum,

* This custom is not confined to the Birmans, particularly the operation of colouring the eyelashes; the women of Hindostan and Persia commonly practice it; they deem it beneficial, as well as becoming. The collyrium they use is called Surma, the Persian name of antimony.

were frequent here: indigo was growing in one of the valleys. About twelve o'clock we came to a rocky point that projected far into the river, round which the current set with such excessive rapidity, that our boats were a long time in getting past, and did not at length effect it without difficulty and some danger. The Maywoon obligingly sent his war-boats to our assistance. After we had surmounted this impediment, we came to a green level bank, where there was a wide range of pasturage, and many cattle feeding. Seenghoo is a large town; in its neighbourhood, and for a great distance along the eastern bank, small temples were built close to the river. We did not make much way in this day's journey, although our labour was great. In the evening we brought to near Keahoh, a poor village, where the inhabitants get their livelihood by extracting molasses from the palmyra tree, of which they make tolerably good sugar.

Although the soil near the river is in most places unproductive and barren, yet, as we advanced northwards on the following day, population increased. Every little hill and rising ground was crowned with a temple; that of Logah-nunda is distinguished for its superior size; it is a clumsy inelegant mass of building, elevated on a semicircular terrace; the base is painted with different colours, and the cupola is richly gilded.

Leaving the temple of Logah-nundah, we approached the once magnificent city of Pagahm. We could see little more from the river than a few straggling houses, which bore the appearance of having once been a connected street: in fact, scarcely any thing remains of ancient Pagahm, except its numerous mouldering temples, and the vestiges of an old brick fort, the ramparts of which are still to be traced. The town of Neoundah, about four miles to the north, which may be called a continuation of Pagahm, has flourished in proportion as the latter has decayed. We passed a small river named, in the days of splendour, Shoe-kiaung, or the Golden Stream: here we spent a night, rendered unpleasant by the stormy weather.

We reached Neoundah early on the 9th of July. At this place the deputation from the capital, which I had been apprized of by the Shawbunder, was waiting my arrival. The Seree informed me that a temporary house, which I saw on a clear piece of ground about 100 yards from the brink, had been erected as a compliment to me; it was much larger than that which the Maywoon had prepared at Meeaday. Early in the afternoon I left my boat, and was received at the house by the Birman officers with every formal testimony of respect; on a part of the floor, elevated a few inches, a carpet was spread, on which I took my seat. The principal person of the deputation was a Woondock, or junior counsellor of state; the others were, the governor of a district called Miengdong, north of Ava, the governor of Pein-keing, bordering on China, and the commandant of the Siamese guards. The Woondock was a lively man, about forty-five years old; the rest appeared of more advanced age, not less than sixty-five or seventy: they all wore the tsaloe, or chain of nobility. The Woondock, though from his station he had precedence of the rest, yet was not of such high rank as the two governors. The utmost decorum was preserved at this meeting; the Woondock spoke in the name of the others, and Baba-Sheen interpreted in the language of Hindostan. After pompously expatiating upon the honour which his Birman Majesty had been pleased to confer on me, by sending a deputation to welcome me, and a barge with war-boats to tow it, he asked some trivial questions, and offered his services to procure whatever we stood in need of. Having discoursed for a short time, a band of music and a company of dancing girls were introduced; drums, gongs, the Indian syrinda, or guitar, the Birman harp, and fiddle, with loud and harsh clarionets, almost deafened us with their noise. Among the dancers, one girl much excelled her companions in symmetry of form and elegance of movement; she was richly dressed, and in shewing the modes of dancing practised in different countries, displayed a fine person to great advantage. The manner of Cassay is most consonant to the English taste, in which the time varies suddenly from quick to slow. The entertainment, however, seemed entirely lost upon the elders, who sat in solemn insensibility, chewing their beetle nut, and regarding with profound gravity the voluptuous attitudes of a very beautiful woman. The amusement did not end till past nine o'clock. I directed a few pieces of silver to be distributed among the musicians and dancers. The Birman officers retired without ceremony, and we passed the night on board our respective boats.

The next morning I was again visited in form, with the additional honour of the company of the Maywoon of Pegue, a compliment which, either from pride or policy, he had never before condescended to pay; the Woondock, however, was here his superior. We conversed for an hour on indifferent subjects, and the Maywoon informed his friends that Dr. Buchanan was a botanist, and had made several drawings of plants. On a wish being expressed to see them, the Doctor obligingly gratified their curiosity with a sight of some that had been executed by the Bengal painter, under his own inspection; these were instantly recognized by the Birmans, who mentioned the names of the originals: they are themselves fond of vegetable productions, which they use very generally in medicine. About eleven o'clock the assembly broke up, and it was settled that we should pursue our journey on the following day.

The remaining time was spent in viewing as much of this once flourishing city, as the shortness of our stay would admit. On entering the town, we came into a long, narrow, winding street, about thirty feet wide; the houses were built of bamboo, and raised from the ground: this street was full of shops, containing no other articles than lackered ware: boxes, trays, cups, &c. varnished in a very neat manner, were displayed in the front of the shops; they were of various colours, some had figures painted on them, others wreaths of flowers. Leaving this street we crossed a water-course on a good wooden bridge, and came to the bazar, or provision market: the green-stalls seemed to be well provided with rice, pulse, greens, garlic, onions, and fruit; there were also fresh-fish, Gnapee, and dead lizards, which latter the Birmans account a delicacy; but there was not any meat. In our progress, we passed over another bridge, and saw several streets running in parallel lines; some of these were inhabited by carriers, whose cattle were feeding on rice straw, round their houses. Having reached the extremity of the town in this direction, we came upon a well paved road, that led to the great temple named Shoezeegoon, to which we proceeded. On each side of the road there was a range of small temples, neglected and in ruins: the kioums, or monasteries, were in good repair, and we saw some handsome houses for the accommodation of strangers. Shoezeegoon is neither so large nor so well built as the temples at Rangoon or Pegue; the height does not exceed 150 feet: it is surrounded by a spacious area paved with broad flags, on which there are a number of lesser buildings, profusely gilded, and laboriously carved. A staircase on the outside leads up to a gallery, about a third of the height of the principal temple, from whence we had an extensive prospect of the country, which appeared to be exceedingly unproductive and barren: the ruins of innumerable religious buildings were to be seen in every direction, which cover a space of ground not less than six or seven miles along the river, and three miles inland. Pagahm is said to have been the residence of forty-five successive monarchs, and was abandoned 500 years ago in consequence of a divine admonition: whatever may be its true history, it certainly was once a place of no ordinary splendour. Returning by a different way, we walked through an alley occupied by blacksmiths' shops, furnished with bill-hooks, spike-nails, adzes, &c. A little farther on we saw the ruins of a street that had been consumed by fire only two days before; from seventy to eighty houses were destroyed by the conflagration. It was the Tackally, and the sufferers were the already wretched, the miserable public prostitutes.

In the afternoon I directed my walk southward, and was much surprised at the number of religious edifices I beheld. They differ in structure from those we had seen in the lower provinces; instead of a slender spire rising to a great height from an expanded base, the temples of Pagahm, in general, carry up a heavy breadth to very near the top, and then come abruptly to a point, which gives a clumsy appearance to the buildings. Many of the most ancient temples at this place are not solid at the bottom; a well arched dome supports a ponderous superstructure; within, an image of Gaudma sits enshrined; four gothic doorways open into the dome; in one of these I saw a human figure standing erect, which the Seree* told me, was Gaudma; and another of the same personage, lying on his right side asleep, both of gigantic stature. The divinity, however, is rarely to be found in these attitudes; the posture in which he is

* I suspect the authenticity of my information on this point, which, I imagine, proceeded from ignorance in the Seree. Of these figures, which he called Gaudma, I conceive the one erect to be the Hindoo Ananda, the other, Nà-rà-yàn, sleeping on the waters.

generally depictured, is sitting cross-legged on a pedestal, adorned with representations of the leaf of the sacred lotus carved upon the base; the left hand of the image rests upon his lap, and the right is pendent. Passing through the suburbs, we came to a part where the inhabitants were employed in expressing oil from the sesamum seed: the grain is put into a deep wooden trough, in which it is pressed by an upright timber fixed in a frame; the force is increased by a long lever, on the extremity of which a man sits and guides a bullock that moves in a circle, thus turning and pressing the seed at the same time: the machine was simple, and answered the end effectually. There were not less than 200 of those mills within a narrow compass. From the circumstance of the cattle being in good order, we concluded that they are fed on the seed after the oil is extracted. The land about Pagahm scarcely yields sufficient vegetation to nourish goats.

CHAPTER XI.

Embark on board the royal Barge—leave Pagahm—singular Caves—Birman Hermits.—Pass Sirraykioum—Gnerroutoh—Country populous.—Shwayedong—Keonzeec—Toucheec—Læpac, or pickled Tea——Kiouptaun, or Line of Rocks—Tanoundain—Tirroup-mew, or Chinese Town.—The Keenduem a large River—Cassay Boatmen—Yandaboo—Manufactory of earthen Ware—Summeikioum—Manufactory of Salt-petre, and Gunpowder.—Gnameaghee—Tobacco Plantations.—Sandaht, or Elephant Village—Meahmoo—Yapadain—the Shawbunder returns.—Kiouptaloun—periodical Risings of the River—ancient Ava—Description of it—Temple of Shoegunga Praw.—Beautiful Situation of Chagain.—Appearance of Ummerapoora, the Capital—Tounzemahn—spacious Lake—Residence of the British Deputation, and Reception on our landing.

AT nine o'clock in the morning of the 11th of July I took possession of the royal barge with ceremonious formality, accompanied by the Woondock and Baba-Sheen. The platform on the outside contained space for thirty two rowers, sixteen on each side; but on this occasion the oars were not fastened, as it was meant to be drawn by war-boats: the inside was divided into three small apartments, handsomely fitted up; the roof and sides were lined with white cotton, and the floor covered with carpets and fine mats. I proceeded in this barge till one o'clock, and then returned to my own boat, which was a much more convenient, though less dignified conveyance.

After leaving Neoundah, the eastern bank of the river rises to a perpendicular height, eighty or one hundred feet above the river. In the side of the cliff, rather more than half way up, we saw some apertures resembling doorways, and were told that they were entrances into caves which had formerly been inhabited by hermits, who, desirous of withdrawing from the world, had excavated these abodes with their own hands, and dwelt in them for the remainder of their lives, preserving no farther intercourse with their fellow creatures, than what was necessary to receive their food, which was lowered down to them by a rope. The Birmans do not inflict on themselves disgustful tortures, after the manner of the Hindoos, but they deem it meritorious to mortify the flesh by the voluntary penance of abstemiousness and self-denial. Solitary seclusion has, at some period or other, been accounted praiseworthy in most countries: during the reign of monkish superstition, it prevailed very commonly throughout Europe: our legendary tales are not wholly unfounded: the Hermit of Warkworth is said to have had its origin from a fact. Birmans, however, though bigotted, are not gloomy, and are in general blessed with a disposition too cheerful to retire from the world in hopeless despondency, or sullen discontent.

Our journey this day was slow, and we perceived little that differed from what has already been described: the islands formed by the river were long, and succeeded each other with such small intervals, that the full breadth of the river, from bank to bank, seldom could be seen; we judged it to be in most places three miles wide: our boats kept near the eastern shore, and passed, on that side, the towns of Sirraykioum and Gnerroutoh. During the latter part of the day, the country seemed fertile, and the soil richer than in the neighbourhood of Pagahm: the number of inhabitants and cattle denoted a considerable population. In the evening we brought to near Shwayedong, a small but neat town, containing about 300 houses, ranged in a regular street; each dwelling had a small garden, fenced with a bamboo railing. Two monasteries and a few small temples, did not claim particular notice, but the tall and wide-spreading trees that overshadowed them, were objects of pleasing contemplation.

On the next day, July 12th, we continued our journey, sometimes going fast, at others slow, and with difficulty, as the wind favoured us, the reaches of the river winding so much, that we had it on all quarters. Keozee, on the eastern side, was the place of most consequence, and was ornamented with several neat temples. At half past five in the evening I went on shore, and found the adjacent country divided into fields, which, at a proper season, are cultivated; the remains of a tobacco plantation that had produced a crop in the former year, were yet lying on the ground: detached hills appeared to the eastward. We brought to, and spent the night near a small village called Toucheec, to the north of Yebbay. Here the inhabitants get their livelihood by selling Læpac, or pickled tea-leaf, of which the Birmans are extremely fond. The plant, I was informed, grows at a place called Palong-miou, a district to the north-east of Ummerapoora; it is very inferior to the tea produced in China, and is seldom used but as a pickle.

On the following day we kept close to the eastern shore, and the breadth of the river being in most places from three to five miles, it was not easy minutely to distinguish objects on the western bank. The country, as we advanced north, increased in population and improved in agriculture; the land everywhere indicated a deficiency of rain, being parched, and broken into deep fissures, owing to the want of moisture. We understood the season had been remarkably dry; rain, however, was shortly expected. The river, notwithstanding the failure of the monsoon, continued to rise. We passed, on the eastern side, Kiouptaan, or the Line of Rocks, Tanoumdain, a respectable town, with several other towns and villages. In the evening we brought to at an island opposite Tirroup-mew, or Chinese City; there is a small district that bears the same name, called so in commemoration of a victory gained here over an army of Chinese that invaded the Birman empire some centuries ago, at the period when Pagahm was the seat of government, whence it appears that the Chinese have long considered this kingdom as a desirable conquest, and have made more than one fruitless attempt to accomplish its subjection.

The next day we stopped five miles above Tirroup-mew, where the Keenduem mingles its waters with those of the Irrawaddy; this great river comes from the north-west, and divides the country of Cassay from that of Ava. The Birmans say that it has its source in a lake three months journey to the northward: it is navigable, as far as the Birman territories extend, for vessels of burthen. An intelligent man belonging to Dr. Buchanan's boat, informed him, that the most distant town, in the possession of the Birmans, on the Keenduem, was named Nakioung, and the first Shaan town* was called Thangdat. The entrance of the Keenduem, seemed somewhat less than a mile wide: the Irrawaddy, immediately above the junction, became much narrower; but I imagine a stream was concealed,

* Shaan, or Shan, is a very comprehensive term given to different nations, some independent, others the subjects of the greater states: thus the Birmans frequently mention the Melap-Shaan, or Shaan subject to the Birmans; the Yoodra-Shaan, subject to the Siamese; the Cassay-Shaan, to the Cassayers.

and that what appeared to be the limits of the river was the bank of an island formed by another branch.

In the men who rowed the war-boats that accompanied the barge from Ummerapoora, I had remarked features differing much from the other boatmen, and a softness of countenance that resembled more the Bengal than the Birman character of face; on enquiry I learned that they were Cassayers, or the sons of Cassayers, who had been brought away from their native country, at times when the Birmans carried their predatory incursions across the Keenduem. Eastern invaders, who do not intend to occupy the territories they over-run, usually adopt the policy of conveying away the inhabitants, particularly children, whom they establish within their own dominions, and thus acquire additional strength by augmenting the number of their subjects. This has been a practice of Asiatic warfare from time immemorial: the last contest of the English with Hyder Ally depopulated the Carnatic. Children, until they attain a certain age, may be transplanted with safety, and will assimilate to any soil, but after arriving at the years of maturity, the most lenient treatment will hardly reconcile the human mind to coercive detention in a foreign country. The spot where a person has passed the tender years of life, the long remembered and impressive interval between infancy and manhood, be it where it may, is ever dear to him. I should willingly have conversed with the Cassay boat people respecting their nation, but my situation forbad me, either to gratify my own curiosity, or sanction the enquiries of others.

At ten o'clock we reached the town of Yandaboo, remarkable for its manufactories of earthen ware; and in the course of the day we passed many towns and villages, on each side, agreeably shaded by trees, particularly by the palmyra and the tamarind. Early in the evening we brought to in a creek which leads up to a large town named Summei-kioum: after dinner Dr. Buchanan and myself took a walk along the margin of the creek, which carried us to the town by a wide circuit: we found the houses, though numerous, mean, and very irregularly built; the grounds in the neighbourhood were embanked for the cultivation of rice. The soil appeared to be good, but the inhabitants expressed the utmost anxiety on the subject of rain; not a drop had yet fallen here, although, in the common course of seasons, the monsoon should have commenced three weeks earlier. The poor people were carefully husbanding their rice straw, for the support of their cattle, large herds of which were endeavouring to pick up a subsistence from the parched blades of grass, in fields that were covered with dust instead of verdure. The appearance of these animals bespoke excessive poverty if not actual famine.

At Summei-kioum there is the greatest manufactory of saltpetre and gunpowder in the kingdom: here also is prepared the gunpowder that is required for the royal magazines; it is the sole occupation of the inhabitants. Neither saltpetre nor gunpowder are suffered to be exported under any plea, nor can the smallest quantity be sold without a special license from some man in power.

Early in the morning we left the neighbourhood of gunpowder and saltpetre: temples and villages lined the banks so thickly that it would be tedious to enumerate them. At nine o'clock we stopped at Gnameaghee, celebrated for producing the best tobacco in the Birman empire; many brick kilns were on fire, preparing materials for building temples, of which there appeared to be already a sufficient number. Pursuing our journey, we passed numerous islands; some of them were cultivated, and had houses, inhabitants, and trees. Towards evening the wind suddenly rose to a storm; Mr. Wood and myself reached Sandaht, or Elephant Village; Dr. Buchanan's boat could not make head against wind and stream, and dropped an anchor; perceiving his situation, I dispatched one of the war-boats to his aid, when the united efforts of both crews soon brought him in safety to the fleet. Sandaht is a small town which, together with the lands adjacent, is occupied entirely by the elephant-keepers belonging to the royal stables. The King is the sole proprietor of all the elephants in his dominions, and the privilege to ride on, or keep one of these animals, is an honour granted only to men of the very first rank and consequence: his Birman Majesty is said to possess 6000. In India, female elephants are prized beyond males, on account of their being more tractable; but in Ava it is the reverse; females are never used on state occasions, and seldom for ordinary riding, which causes the other sex to be of much higher value; it however rarely happens that either one or the other is to be purchased, the King's exclusive right, and the limited use that is made of them, prevent their becoming an article of common sale.

We set out at an early hour next morning; Meahmoo, on the western side, appeared from the water to be a large town, shaded by groves of palmyra trees; it is remarkable for a manufactory of coarse checkered cotton cloth, such as is worn by the lower class of people. Yapadain, a town on the eastern side, was distinguished by several temples, and a handsome monastery. About twelve o'clock the Shawbunder, who, after the interview at Loonghee, had returned to Ava, again met us; he had travelled with great expedition, having been at court, and made his report: the present visit was a spontaneous act of civility: he possessed a small jaghire, or personal estate, in the neighbourhood, where he had prepared some refreshments, of which he requested I would stop to partake. I complied with his desire, and accompanied him to a bower formed in a clump of bamboos, on the bank of the river, and shaded from the sun by an artificial awning of grass: here we found a profusion of fruits, milk, butter, and preserves, in dishes laid out on carpets; a company of dancing girls and musicians from a neighbouring village entertained us with their music and graces. I remained as short a time as was consistent with civility, and then pursued my voyage. We passed in our progress several populous villages pleasantly situated, and adorned with well enclosed gardens and orchards of plantain, guava, and other fruit trees. At night we brought to at Kiouptaloum, where a large temple, surrounded by several small buildings, was the only object that merited particular attention.

Next day we got under way at the customary hour, and made but slow progress, the wind heading us so far, that the square sails of the Birman boats could not keep full; oars and poles were plyed with vigour. The river, which, though it had not yet risen to its utmost periodical height, had overflowed its banks, filled all the water-courses, and inundated the low grounds adjacent to its bed. As the force of the current lay in the middle of the stream, in order to avoid its influence we frequently navigated through fields, in which the tall grass and reeds appeared above the surface of the water, and the trees had their stems immersed beneath the flood. The swelling of the Irrawaddy is not influenced by the quantity of rain which falls in the vallies, but by the torrents that rush down from the mountains. Notwithstanding the drought in the champaign country had been greater this year than usual, the river was swollen to its regular height, which, I was informed, it rarely fell short of, or exceeded: indeed this part of the country is seldom refreshed by copious rains, but, like Egypt, depends on the overflowing of its river to fertilize the soil. The Irrawaddy, during the monsoon months, rises and subsides three or four times. As our distance from Ummerapoora diminished, towns and villages on each side recurred at such short intervals, that it was in vain to enquire the name of each distinct assemblage of houses; each, however had its name, and was for the most part inhabited by one particular class of people, professing some separate trade, or following some peculiar occupation. We were shewn a tomb erected to the memory of a person of high distinction, who had been accidentally drowned near that place fifteen years before; it was an oblong brick building, one story high, with eight or nine doors opening towards the river. Many beautiful temples and kioums would have engaged our attention, had we not already seen such numbers, and been assured that all we had viewed fell far short of those, which we should have an opportunity of beholding at the capital. We brought to late in the evening, at the lower landing place of what was once the city of Ava, and the metropolis of all the Birman empire.

In the morning I took a hasty view of Aungwa, or Ava; it is divided into an upper and lower city, both of which are fortified; the lower, which is the most extensive, I judged to be about four miles in circumference; it is protected by a wall thirty feet high, at the foot of which there is a deep and broad fosse. The communication between the fort and the country is over a mound of earth crossing the ditch, that supports a causeway; an embankment of earth in the inside sustains the wall; the upper or smaller fort, which may be called the citadel, and does not exceed a mile in circuit, was much stronger, and more compact than the lower, but neither the upper nor the lower had a ditch on the side of the river. The walls are now mouldering into decay; ivy clings to the sides, and bushes, suffered to grow at the bottom, undermine the foundation, and have already caused large chasms in the different faces of the fort. The materials of the houses, consisting chiefly of wood, had, on the first order for removing, been transported to the new city of Ummerapoora: but the ground, unless where it is covered with bushes, or rank grass, still retains traces of former buildings and streets. The lines of the royal palace, of the Lotoo, or grand council hall, the apartments of the women, and the spot on which the Piasath, or imperial spire, had stood, were pointed out to us by our guide. Clumps of bamboos, a few plantain trees, and tall thorns, occupy the greater part of the area of this lately flourishing capital. We observed two dwelling houses of brick and mortar, the roofs of which had fallen in; these, our guide said, had belonged to Colars, or foreigners: on entering one, we found it inhabited only by bats, which flew in our faces, whilst our sense of smelling was offended by their filth, and by the noisome mildew that hung upon the walls. Numerous temples, on which the Birmans never lay sacrilegious hands, were dilapidating by time. It is impossible to draw a more striking picture of desolation and ruin.

Among the religious buildings within the fort, one named Shoegunga Praw, no ways distinguished for size or splendour, was in former times held peculiarly sacred, and is still reverenced above the rest. At the present day, when an officer of rank is about to enter on a great public trust, or a new commander is appointed to the army, the oath of allegiance is administered in this temple with great solemnity, a breach of which is considered the most heinous crime a Birman can be guilty of, and is invariably punished by the severest tortures. How Shoegunga obtained this distinction I was not able to learn. We were informed that a temple of much greater magnitude, named Logatherpoo Praw, stood a short distance to the westward of the fort, in which was a colossal figure of Gaudma, formed out of a solid block of marble. This temple and image we had a better opportunity of viewing on our return.

Leaving Ava in our rear, the river bends again to the northward, when the opposite city of Chagain, and the spires, the turrets, and the lofty Piasath of Ummerapoora, create an unexpected pleasure, and exhibit a fine contrast to the gloomy and deserted walls of Ava. Chagain, on the north side, once, too, the seat of imperial residence, is situated partly at the foot, and partly on the side, of a rugged hill that is broken into separate eminences, and on the summit of each stands a spiral temple; these temples, rising irregularly one above another to the top of the mountain, form a beautiful assemblage of objects, the effect of which is increased by their being carefully whitewashed, and kept in repair. As we sailed near the opposite shore, the sun shone full upon the hill, and its reflected rays displayed the scenery to the highest advantage; in addition to this, the swollen state of the river gave to the waters, the semblance of a vast lake, interspersed with islands, in which the foundations of Ummerapoora seemed to be immersed. Numberless boats were passing up and down, and the houses on the western, or rather southern shore, appeared, from their uninterrupted succession, to be a continued town, or suburbs of a city.

At twelve o'clock we came to the mouth of the channel that communicates with the lake of Tounzemahn, through which it receives its waters from the river. The situation of Ummerapoora has already been described; the southern face of the fort is washed, during the rainy season, by the waves of the lake, and the houses of the city and suburbs extend along the bank as far as the extreme point of land. Across the lake, and opposite to the fort, stands the small village of Tounzemahn, near which, in a tall grove of mango, palmyra, and cocoa nut trees, a dwelling was prepared for the British deputation. On entering the lake, the number of boats that were moored, as in a harbour, to avoid the influence of the sweeping flood, the singularity of their construction, the height of the waters, which threaten inundation to the whole city, and the amphitheatre of lofty hills that nearly surrounded us, altogether presented a novel scene, exceedingly interesting to a stranger. We rowed towards the grove, whilst the greater part of the fleet went to the opposite side: on reaching the bank, I perceived a war-boat belonging to the Maywoon of Pegue, who, I understood, was at the grove waiting our arrival. I was received on landing by Baba-Sheen, and some inferior officers; they accompanied me to the house, which was situated about 300 yards from the brink of the lake, overshadowed by lofty trees, that completely defended it from the meridian sun. When we came to the entrance of the virando, or balcony, the Maywoon of Pegue, the Governor of Bamoo, a province bordering on China, and the Woondock beforementioned, welcomed me to the capital. Being seated on carpets spread along the floor, the conversation turned on general topics, and particularly on European geography, a subject on which the Governor of Bamoo appeared very desirous of information. After some time, the Woondock addressing himself to me, said, that his Birman Majesty had been absent a few months, at a country residence named Meengoung, where he was erecting a magnificent temple to their divinity Gaudma, but was expected to return soon to Ummerapoora; that, in the mean time, instructions had been given to his ministers to provide every thing requisite for the accommodation of the English gentlemen, and that Baba-Sheen was commanded to reside near us, in order to supply our wants, and to communicate our wishes: to this the Maywoon of Pegue added, that the two inferior Serees, or provincial under secretaries, who had accompanied us from Rangoon, were likewise directed to attend to our orders, and being persons to whom we were accustomed, would probably be more agreeable to us than entire strangers.

These polite and hospitable attentions were received and acknowledged by me with real satisfaction; nor was it at all diminished by the freedom with which the Woondock informed me, that it was contrary to the etiquette of the Birman court, for a public minister from a foreign nation, to go abroad before his first audience. He therefore hoped I would not cross the lake in person, or suffer any of my people to do so, until the ceremonials were past; but as our customs differed from theirs, and the Europeans habituated themselves to take exercise, I was at full liberty to walk or ride into the country, or over the plains that lay between our dwelling and the hills, as far as I thought proper; recommending to me at the same time, not to go to any great distance, as it would be considered by the common people in the light of a derogation from my own consequence. I thanked him for his counsel, which was delivered with many expressions of civility, and readily acquiesced in what he assured me was an established custom.

This usage of debarring a public minister from entering the capital previous to his first formal presentation, I understood was neither recent nor uncommon; it has long been the known practice of the Birman and Siamese governments; Monsieur Loubere makes mention of it in his Account of an Embassy to Siam, sent from the court of Louis the Fourteenth. It is founded on that cautious policy which governs all nations eastward of India in their intercourse with foreign states.

CHAPTER XII.

Place of Residence described.—Deputation from China provincial—not Imperial.—Rhoom, a Building sometimes attached to private Houses—Reason of it.—Munificence of the Birman Government.—Letter from General Erskine—opened by the Birman Minister—Apology.—Appearance of the adjacent Country—parched for Want of Rain.—Cassay Farmers—Women industrious—row the Boats—fond of singing.—Chinese Music discordant and troublesome—Indolence of the Chinese.—King returns to the Capital.—Eclipse of the Moon.—Reason of Delay—Pride of the Court—its Punctiliousness—Letter from the Governor-General translated—present a Memorial—Embassies usually consist of three Members.—Visit from the junior Deputies from China—whimsical Ceremony.—Return the Visit—Subject of Conversation.

As soon as my visitors took their leave, I made a survey of our new habitation; it was a spacious house of one story, raised from the ground somewhat more than two feet, and better covered than Birman houses usually are; it consisted of two good sized rooms, and a large virando, or balcony; the partitions and walls were made of cane mats, with latticed windows in the sides: the shape of the roof was such as distinguishes the houses of nobles: it was altogether a comfortable habitation, and well adapted to the climate. Mr. Wood had a smaller house erected behind mine, and parallel to it, and Dr. Buchanan another at right angles. Small separate huts were constructed for the guard, and for our attendants; the whole was surrounded by a strong bamboo paling, which inclosed a court yard. There were two entrances by gates, one in front of my house, the other backwards; at each of these, on the outside of the paling, was a shed, in which a Birman guard was posted to protect us from thieves, keep off the populace, and probably to watch and report our movements.

On the skirts of the same grove, in a line with our dwelling, similar houses were erected for three Chinese deputies, who had arrived at Ummerapoora about two months before us: these personages were represented as composing a royal mission from the imperial city of Pekin, but circumstances early led me to suspect that their real character did not rise higher than that of a provincial deputation from Manchegee, or Yunan, the south-west province of China, which borders on the kingdom of Ava, a conjecture that was afterwards confirmed. They had accompanied the Governor of Bamoo, which is the frontier province, to the capital; and I understood that their business was to adjust some mercantile concerns relating to the jee, or mart, where the commodities of the two empires are brought and bartered. It was not at all improbable that the mission had been sanctioned by the authority of the Emperor of China, especially as the principal member of it was a native of Pekin, and had lately come from thence: but the false pride of the Birman court suggested the puerile* expedient of representing it to us as an imperial embassy, a distinction to which, I was privately informed from an authentic source, it possessed no

* The Chinese seem to have been actuated by a policy equally absurd, when they informed Sir George Staunton, at the time of the formal introduction of Lord Macartney, that "Embassadors from Pegue" were present; and that "Siam, Ava, and Pegue were tributary to China:" such unworthy deceptions not being expected, could hardly be guarded

pretensions whatever. The members, however, were treated apparently with much personal respect and attention.

The building denominated Rhoom, has already been described as the official hall of justice, where the members of provincial governments, and all municipal officers, are accustomed to assemble for the transaction of public business. Every man of high rank in the Birman empire is a magistrate, and has a place of this description and name contiguous to his dwelling, but always on the outside of the enclosure of his court yard, and not surrounded by any fence or railing, in order to manifest publicity, and shew that it is the seat of majesty and justice, to which all mankind may have free access. An imperial mandate to a governor, or an order from a governor to a petty miougee, or chief of a small town or district, is invariably opened and read aloud in this sanctified hall. The Birman government, in the administration of public affairs, suffers no such thing as privacy or concealment. The rhoom is likewise an appendage of dignity, as it denotes him to whose habitation it is annexed, to be a person of rank and consequence; a building of this sort was erected within a few yards of the front gate of our inclosure.

For two days after our landing, the boatmen and servants were employed in transporting our baggage from the boats to the house, and our time was chiefly taken up in arranging the domestic economy of our new residence, in which we found a liberal provision of all such necessaries as the natives themselves require; my rooms were carpeted, but the chairs, tables, &c. were my own. Rice, gee (clarified butter), firewood,

against. The courts of Ava and Pekin appear to resemble each other in many points, but in none more than in their vanity, which often manifests itself in a manner not less ridiculous than contemptible.

and pots for dressing victuals, were supplied to our people in abundance. A few stalls, or petty shops, were established in the grove, to afford the smaller ingredients of cookery, such as greens, spices, salt, tamarinds, &c. Here also tobacco and beetle leaf were sold; and to enable our attendants to purchase such articles, one hundred tackal, about £12. sterling, were distributed amongst them: this was an act of munificence which I with great difficulty avoided the obligation of, in my own person, but no remonstrance could prevail on the Birman officer to dispense with it in the instance of our domestics.

The delinquent refugees, of whom mention has been made in a former part of this work, as having been surrendered by order of the Governor-General, to the justice of their country, had reached Ummerapoora some weeks previous to our arrival. The Birman guard that escorted them had brought a letter directed to me from General Erskine, the English commander at Chittigong; this letter the Birman minister, as it was alleged, through mistake, but more probably by design, caused to be opened, and procured a translation from an Armenian interpreter. The circumstance was reported to the King, who ordered that the letter should be safely deposited in the Lotoo, and given to me on my arrival: the royal injunctions were punctually obeyed; an officer, in his dress of ceremony, brought it over. A proposal was first made, that I should go myself to the rhoom, solicit its restoration, receive it as an act of grace, and do homage to the King, by bowing with my face towards the palace. From this I entirely dissented, as the cause of complaint was with me, and confidence had in some measure been violated by their breaking the seal. I do not imagine that the proposition originated from any authority, as it was immediately given up, and the letter, in a silk wrapper, was formally presented to me on a tray, by the officer who conveyed it across the lake.

Being now comfortably lodged, we had leisure to take a view of the circumjacent country, and observe the objects that immediately surrounded us. Behind the grove in which we lived was a smooth extensive plain, intersected by the embankments of what, in the past year, had been fields of rice, but which promised, this season, to be an unproductive waste, owing to the uncommon drought: notwithstanding the spot we were on was elevated very little above the present level of the lake, which had now nearly reached its utmost height, yet the ground was parched up, and divided into chasms from want of moisture. Dark and rugged mountains, about eight miles distant, bounded the prospect to the southwest: several small villages were scattered over the plain, and on the skirts of the grove, inhabited, as we were informed, by native Cassayers, or the descendants of Cassayers, who had been carried into captivity by the Birman invaders during their predatory expeditions across the Keenduem.

The Seree who accompanied me said, that these people, whom he called Munniporeans, from Munnipore, the capital of Cassay, were in general become reconciled to their state of servitude, owing to their having been brought away very young from their own country: the superior industry and skill which they possess over the Birmans in different branches of handicraft, supplied them with a comfortable subsistence. Those in our neighbourhood were farmers and gardeners, who cultivated pulse, greens, onions, and such vegetables as Birmans use; these articles they transport at an early hour across the lake to the city, where they retail them in the market, and bring home the produce at night; this business is mostly performed by females; one man, commonly a person in years, accompanies each boat, in which, standing erect, he acts as steersman, whilst the women, usually from ten to fourteen in number, sitting with their legs across, row short oars, or use paddles, according to the size of the vessel: when they set out in a morning, they proceed in silence, but returning at night, they join in jocund chorus, and time the stroke of their oars to the bars of their song. We were serenaded every evening from dusk till ten o'clock by successive parties of these joyous females, whose strains, though unpolished, were always melodious and pleasing. The Birmans, both men and women, are fond of singing whilst at work; it lightens their labour: "song sweetens toil, how rude soe'er the sound." Unfortunately our music was not confined to these passing chantresses; there were other performers, less agreeable, nearer to us. Our neighbours, the deputies from China, unluckily for the repose of those from Britain, happened to be amateurs in their way, and had amongst their dependants a select band of musicians, such as I certainly had never heard equalled; it is impossible to describe the horrible noises that issued from gongs, drums, cymbals, an instrument with two strings, which may be called a fiddle, and something like a clarionet, that sent forth a sound more grating to the ear than all the rest. This was their constant nocturnal amusement, which never ended before midnight, and was not once remitted, till the principal personage of the embassy became so indisposed that he could endure it no longer. Whilst he lingered we enjoyed tranquillity, but after his decease the concert recommenced, and continued, to our great annoyance, till they quitted the grove to return to their native country.

The opposite habits of different nations were here strikingly evinced in the dissimilarity between the manners of the English, and those of the

Chinese; the latter never left the precincts of their habitation, or manifested a desire to leave it, except to loll in easy chairs, and smoke their long pipes in the cool of the evening on the margin of the lake, about two or three hundred yards in front of their house. The English gentlemen accustomed themselves either to walk or ride three or four miles in the morning before breakfast, and the same distance in the afternoon, a circumstance that did not escape the notice of the Birmans. My customary route was in a southern direction, over pathways that led through rice fields, in my return making a circuit along the green border of the lake. Although there was not the least cause to apprehend either injury or insolence, I was always attended in my excursions by six or eight soldiers, and by as many of my private servants, armed with sabres, who seemed to attract no less notice than myself. When I met any of the natives, particularly women, they squatted down into the posture of respect. As soon as the novelty of my appearance had a little worn off, I was told that they were still anxious to know why a person consulting his own amusement, and master of his own time, should walk so fast; but on being informed that I was " a Colar," or stranger, and that it was the custom of my country, they were reconciled to this as well as to every other act that did not coincide with their own prejudices and usage.

In a few days the return of the King was announced by the discharge of rockets, and by the general bustle that so important an event caused among all classes of people: we saw nothing of the display, which we understood, on this occasion, was not at all pompous.

The period of our arrival occurred at a juncture that supplied the Birman court with a plausible excuse for postponing the consideration of public business, and delaying my formal reception, as well as the delivery of the letter from the Governor-General to the King. It so happened that in the ensuing month there was to be an eclipse of the moon, an operation of nature, which they ascribe to the interference of a malignant demon. On such an occasion affairs of state, and all important matters of business, that will admit of procrastination, are put off to the following month. The astrologers were assembled to consult on the first fortunate day after the lapse of that inauspicious moon, when they discovered that the seventeenth of the month Touzelien, corresponding with the 30th of August, was the earliest that would occur, and that day was accordingly appointed for the public reception of the English embassy.

Caution and policy had, perhaps, as great a share with the Birmans as superstition, in thus retarding the ceremony of our introduction: it was to them a novel incident; they were desirous to penetrate thoroughly into the objects we had in view, before any part of the subject came into formal discussion. They might probably also wish to have an opportunity to judge of our national character, and to determine, from our conduct, in what manner to regulate their own; if such were their motives, they were consistent with that sagacity, which I found invariably displayed by the Birman government in all its resolutions and acts of a public nature

But the prevailing characteristic of the Birman court is pride; like the sovereign of China, his Majesty of Ava acknowledges no equal; indeed it is the fixed principle of all nations eastward of Bengal, to consider foreign ministers as suppliants come to solicit protection, not as representatives who may demand redress; rather as vassals to render homage, than as persons vested with authority to treat on equal terms. Of this system I was early apprized, and felt no disappointment at hearing of a general rumour current among the higher ranks of Birmans, that a deputy had arrived from the English government, bearing tribute for their King. Reports of this nature were no otherwise regarded than as an admonition to regulate my actions with scrupulous circumspection.

Amongst other regulations of this punctilious court, I was given to understand, that it was not customary for the King to receive any letter in a formal manner without being previously apprized of its contents. This created some difficulty in respect to the letter from the Governor-General, which was at length surmounted by an agreement on my part to admit of a copy being made in my presence, but it was stipulated by them that it should be transcribed in the rhoom adjacent to my house, and not in my private residence. In this proposal I acquiesced, and accordingly a formal deputation, consisting of seven or eight officers of state, was directed to proceed to the rhoom, where they were to open the letter, and see it properly transcribed: these personages came with much parade, apparelled in their robes of ceremony; on landing they walked directly to the rhoom, and having taken their seats, sent a Terrezogee, or inferior officer, along with Baba-Sheen, to request I would come, and bring with me the Governor-General's letter; I obeyed this summons, accompanied by the other gentlemen and our usual attendants. On entering the rhoom I was civilly desired, as the occasion was a solemn one, to make obeisance towards the piasath, or spire of the royal palace, which was more than two miles distant, a ceremony I complied with by raising my right hand to my head, and making a slight inclination of my body, after the manner of the Mahomedan Salaam. Being seated, I delivered the letter, which was written in English and in Persian, to the Woondock, or superior officer; it was immediately opened by a secretary: and an Armenian interpreter, named Muckatees, who spoke and wrote English fluently, was ordered to make a copy in English, whilst a Mussulman moonshee made another in Persian. When the writing was finished, I delivered a paper, which I desired might be laid before his Majesty's council, declaratory, in general terms, of the friendly wishes and views of the Governor-General in deputing me to the Birman court, and expressing my desire to maintain a confidential intercourse with such persons as his Majesty, or his council, should think proper to authorize.

The business being concluded I returned to my house, and received a ceremonious visit from the Birman officers, among whom there were some personages of high distinction; a Woondock, but not the one that met me at Pagahm, presided; the master of the elephants, the old governor of Peenkeing, two Sere-dogees, or secretaries of state, and some other officers, whose names and stations I did not learn, were present; their robes, which were very graceful, were made either of velvet or flowered satin, with wide bodies, and loose sleeves: they all were invested with the chain of nobility, and wore caps covered with light-green taffety. Three of higher rank than the rest, had a wreath of gold leaves encircling the bottom of their caps, not unlike the strawberry leaves in a ducal coronet; their attendants, who were numerous, carried a variety of utensils, such as their beetle box, water flaggon, drinking cup, and spitting pot, of which latter, from their filthy practice of chewing beetle, they stood in constant need. I regaled them with tea, and English raspberry jam spread on biscuits: although they praised, I do not think they much relished our preserve; they ate sparingly, and refreshed themselves with copious bowls of tea, unadulterated either by cream or sugar.

About this time the Chinese minister, who has already been mentioned as labouring under severe indisposition, sent me a polite message, expressing his regret that he had it not in his power to visit me in person, but that his two colleagues would wait on me whenever I should be at leisure to receive them; I returned my acknowledgments, and appointed the following day.

It is customary among nations eastward of Bengal, when a public deputation is sent to a foreign court, to nominate three members, who constitute a council; although the president or chief of these is invested with all the power, and controls the proceedings of the rest, yet the distinction between them is not so wide as to preclude the juniors from a high degree of consequence being attached to their stations; and in case of the demise of the principal, the senior survivor executes all diplomatic functions, thus wisely guarding against any impediment which a casualty might throw in the way of negotiation.

The two junior members of the Chinese deputation came at the appointed hour, accompanied by seven or eight attendants. There is no personage on earth so solemn and ceremonious as a Chinese officer of state; his dignity is preserved by profound silence, unless when occasion renders it necessary to exercise the faculty of speech, which is always slow, monotonous, and dull; even gentlemen in the familiarity of private life, seldom depart from their gravity, or relax into a smile. On entering a room where there is company, good breeding is evinced by a modest but pertinacious refusal to sit down till the master of the house is first seated, which would be an equal violation of decorum on his part. This custom, I was told, sometimes produces a very ludicrous scene, and the guests are not unfrequently obliged to be dragged to their chairs, and placed in them almost by compulsion. My house being about to undergo some alteration, I had caused a suite of tents, which I had brought with me, to be pitched for our temporary accommodation; in these I made arrangements to receive my visitors, who were exact to their time. On entering the door of the marquee they both made an abrupt stop, and resisted all solicitation to advance to chairs that had been prepared for them, until I should first be seated; in this dilemma Dr. Buchanan, who had visited China, advised me what was to be done; I immediately seized on the foremost, whilst the Doctor himself grappled with the second; thus we soon fixed them in their seats, both parties, during the struggle, repeating Chin Chin, Chin Chin, the Chinese term of salutation. The conversation was not at all lively or interesting, for though I sat between them, our words had to make a wide circuit before they reached each other's comprehension. I spoke in the language of Hindostan to a Mussulman who understood Birman, he delivered it to a Birman who spoke Chinese, this Birman gave it to the first official domestic, who repeated it to his master in the Chinese tongue. Our wines, port, claret, and Madeira, all excellent of their kind, were served up; these, however, were too cold for Chinese palates; my visitants did not seem to relish them; but when cherry-brandy was introduced, their approbation was manifested by the satisfaction with which each of them swallowed a large glass full of the liquor: they tasted our tea, and, before they departed, politely presented me with some fans, two or three pieces of silk, two small boxes of tea, and three bottles of shouchou, a very fiery spirit distilled from rice, of which the Chinese are extremely fond. I returned the visit on the following day, and was received with as much pomp and ostentation as circumstances would admit: in front of the house a silk ensign waved, on which was embroidered the imperial dragon of China, and at their gate were suspended whips and chains, importing the power which the owner possessed to inflict corporal punishment. The two junior members met me at the threshold of their habitation, apologized for the unavoidable absence of the chief personage, and introduced me into a hall, the walls of which were concealed by screens of silk, and the chairs covered with loose pieces of satin; this interview was rendered more interesting than the former, by a spontaneous question on the part of the senior Chinese, to know whether I had heard of the safe arrival of Lord Macartney in England. His lordship having left China only the preceding year, it was not possible to have had accounts of his reaching England, and the issue of his lordship's negotiations was at that time wholly unknown; consequently, being unacquainted both with the objects and event of that splendid mission, I felt myself rather on delicate ground in regard to the enquiries which I, on my part, wished to make. In order to draw some conclusion from their discourse, I encouraged them to pursue the topic, by asking how his lordship's health had borne the vicissitudes of climate; they replied that they only knew of the embassy from report, and seemed reluctant to enter into particulars, with which, it is probable, they were entirely unacquainted; I did not, therefore, press the subject farther; but I was not suffered to remain long in doubt what their sentiments were. Chinese vanity scarcely yields to that of the Birmans; here was an opportunity, by exaggeration and misrepresentation, of indulging their own pride at the expence of the English nation, which, in the accounts circulated by them at Ummerapoora respecting the embassy to China, they did not neglect. They treated us with tea and sweetmeats, and smoked their long pipes with unrelaxed solemnity. I repaid their civilities by giving them some broad-cloth and brandy, and took my leave.

The alterations in my own dwelling, which I had suggested, were quickly carried into effect, and by an order from the Lotoo or grand council, a small additional building, of a square form, and raised from the ground, was erected within the enclosure of our court, for the reception of the presents intended for his Majesty. I was given to understand that this building was meant as a compliment to what they thought proper to term, among themselves, "tribute from the King of England;" but as no such arrogant assumption was ever publicly professed, I could not take notice of mere rumour: it was, however, privately intimated to me, that keeping our tents pitched, would be considered by the court in the light of a reflection upon its hospitality, and an inference would be drawn from it, that we were discontented with our habitation. I immediately ordered the marquees to be struck, nothing being farther from my intention than to give umbrage, or express dissatisfaction, for which indeed, in the present instance, there was certainly no ground.

The interval that elapsed between the time of our arrival at Ummerapoora, and of our formal introduction at court, afforded us leisure to acquire some insight into the customs, religious tenets, and moral economy of the Birman nation. Instead, therefore, of filling up the chasm by an unimportant journal, in which the acts of one day differed but little from those of the preceding, I shall dedicate a few pages to a more general account of the country, and endeavour, as far as our own circumscribed observation, and the information of others enabled us, to illustrate the character of this people from their manners, and their state of society from the progress which the arts had made, and from the usages of the inhabitants in common life.

CHAPTER XIII.

Religion of the Birmans—their Laws—Jurisdiction of the Metropolis —Lawyers—the Royal Establishment—Council of State—Officers—Honours not hereditary—Insignia of Rank—Dress—Resemblance to the Chinese.—Marriages—Funerals—Population—Revenue.

AFTER what has been written, there can be little necessity to inform my readers that the Birmans are Hindoos: not votaries of Brahma, but sectaries of Boodh, which latter is admitted by Hindoos of all descriptions to be the ninth Avatar,* or descent of the deity in his capacity of preserver. He reformed the doctrines contained in the Vedas, and severely censured the sacrifice of cattle, or depriving any being of life: he is called the author of happiness: his place of residence was discovered at Gaya in Bengal, by the illustrious Amara,† renowned amongst men, "who caused an image "of the supreme Boodh to be made, and he worshipped it: reverence be "unto thee in the form of Boodh; reverence be unto thee, Lord of the "Earth; reverence be unto thee, an incarnation of the deity; and, eternal "one, reverence be unto thee, O God in the form of Mercy."

* Sir William Jones, on the Gods of Greece, Italy, and India.

† See the translation of a Shanscrit inscription on a stone found in the temple of Boodh, at Gaya, by Mr. Wilkins. Asiat. Research. Vol. I. I am indebted for the annexed representation of the image of Boodh, at Gaya, to the kindness of Lord Teignmouth. The reader will observe the close resemblance it bears to that of the Birman Gaudma.

Drawn by Captn. Crooke.

Image of Boodh at Gaya in Bengal.

Gotma, or Goutum, according to the Hindoos of India, or Gaudma, among the inhabitants of the more eastern parts, is said* to have been a philosopher, and is by the Birmans believed to have flourished above 2300† years ago: he taught, in the Indian schools, the heterodox religion and philosophy of Boodh. The image that represents Boodh is called Gaudma, or Goutum, which is now a commonly received appellation of Boodh himself: this image is the primary object of worship in all countries situated between Bengal and China. The sectaries of Boodh contend with those of Brahma for the honour of antiquity, and are certainly far more numerous. The Cingaleze in Ceylon are Bhoodhists of the purest source, and the Birmans acknowledge to have originally received their religion from that island.‡ It was brought, say the Rhahaans, first from Zehoo (Ceylon) to Arracan, and thence was introduced into Ava, and probably into China; for the Birmans assert with confidence that the Chinese are Boodhists.

This is a curious subject of investigation, and the concurrent testimony of circumstances, added to the opinions of the most intelligent writers, seem to leave little doubt of the fact. It cannot, however, be demonstrated beyond the possibility of dispute, till we shall have acquired a more perfect knowledge of Chinese letters, and a readier access to their repositories of learning. Little can at present be added to the lights cast on the subject by the late Sir William Jones, in his Discourse delivered to the Asiatic Society on the Chinese: that great man has expressed his conviction in positive terms, that "Boodh was unquestionably the Foe of

* Sir William Jones on the Gods of Greece, Italy, and India.

† This agrees with the account of the Siamese computation given by Kæmpfer.

‡ The Birmans call Ceylon, Zehoo.

China," and that he was also the god of Japan, and the Woden of the Goths, an opinion which corresponds with, and is perhaps grafted on, the information of the learned and laborious Kæmpfer,* corroborated afterwards by his own researches. On whatever grounds the latter inference rests, it will not tend to weaken the belief of his first position, when I observe that the Chinese deputies, on the occasion of our introduction to the Seredaw or high priest of the Birman empire, prostrated themselves before him, and afterwards adored an image of Gaudma with more religious fervour than mere politeness, or acquiescence in the customs of another nation, would have excited: the Bonzes also of China, like the Rhahaans of Ava, wear yellow as the sacerdotal colour, and in many of their customs and ceremonies there may be traced a striking similitude.

Whatever may be the antiquity of the worship of Boodh, the wide extent of its reception cannot be doubted. The most authentic writer † on the eastern peninsula calls the image of Gaudma, as worshipped by the Siamese, Somona-codom: being unacquainted with the language of Siam, which from so short a residence as four months, it was impossible he could

* Speaking of the Budz, or Seaka, of the Japanese, Kæmpfer says, "I have strong reasons "to believe, both from the affinity of the name, and the very nature of this religion, that its "author and founder is the very same person whom the Bramins call Budha, and believe to "be the essential spirit of Wishna, or their deity, who made his ninth appearance in the world "under this name: the Peguers call him Samana Khutama." Hist. Japan, Book IV. ch. 6.

Treating on the introduction of Boodh into China, the same author says, "About the "year of Christ 518, one Darma, a great saint, and twenty-third successor on the holy see "of Seaka (Budha), came over into China from Seitenseku, as the Japanese writers explain "it, that is, from that part of the world which lies westward with regard to Japan, and laid, "properly speaking, the first firm foundation of the Budsdoism in that mighty empire." Book. IV. ch. 6.

† Loubere.

have acquired, he confounds two distinct words, Somona, and Codom, signifying Codom, or Gaudma, in his incarnate state; the difference between the letters C and G may easily have arisen from the mode of pronunciation in different countries; even in the Birman manner of uttering the word, the distinction between these letters is not very clear. The Boodh of the Indians and the Birmans, is pronounced by the Siamese Pooth, or Pood, by the vulgar, Poo; which, without any violence to probability, might be converted by the Chinese into Foe;* the Tamulic termination *en*, as Mr. Chambers remarks, creates a striking resemblance between Pooden and the Woden of the Goths; every person who has conversed with the natives of India knows that Boodh is the Dies Mercurii, the Wednesday, or Woden's day, of all Hindoos. Chronology, however, which must always be accepted as a surer guide to truth, than inferences drawn from the resemblance of words, and etymological reasoning, does not, to my mind, sufficiently establish that Boodh and Woden were the same. The period of the ninth incarnation of Vishnu was long antecedent to the existence of the deified hero of Scandinavia. Sir William Jones determines the period when Boodh appeared on the earth to be 1014 years before the birth of Christ. Odin, or Woden, flourished at a period not very distant from our Saviour, and was, according to some, a cotemporary of Pompey and of Julius Cæsar. The author of the Northern Antiquities places him 70 years after the Christian era. Even the Birman Gaudma, conformably to their account, must have lived above 500 years before Woden. So immense a space can hardly be supposed to have been overlooked: but if the supposition refers, not to the war-

* M. Gentil asserts that the Chinese admit, by their own accounts, that Foe, their object of worship, was originally brought from India.

rior of the north, but to the original deity Odin, the attributes of the latter are as widely opposed to those of Boodh, who was himself only an incarnation of Vishnu, as the dates are incongruous. The deity, whose doctrines were introduced into Scandinavia, was a god of terror, and his votaries carried desolation and the sword throughout whole regions; but the Ninth Avatar* brought the peaceful olive, and came into the world for the sole purpose of preventing sanguinary acts. These apparent inconsistencies will naturally lead us to hesitate in acknowledging Boodh and Woden to be the same person: their doctrines are opposite, and their eras are widely remote.

Had that distinguished genius,† whose learning so lately illumined the East, been longer spared for the instruction and delight of mankind, he would probably have elucidated this obscurity, and have removed the dusky veil that still hangs over the religious legends of antiquity. The subject,‡ as it now stands, affords an ample field for indulging in pleasing theories, and fanciful speculations; and as the probability increases of being able to trace all forms of divine worship to one sacred and primeval source, the inquiry in proportion becomes more interesting, and awakens a train of serious ideas in a reflecting mind.

It would be as unsatisfactory as tedious, to attempt leading my reader through the mazes of mythological fable, and extravagant allegory, in which the Hindoo religion, both Braminical and Boodhic, is enveloped

* See the account of the Ninth Avatar, by the Rev. Mr. Maurice, in his History of Hindostan, Vol. II. Part 3.

† I need hardly observe that I mean Sir William Jones.

‡ General Vallancey, so justly celebrated for his knowledge of the antiquities of his country, has expressed his perfect conviction that the Hindoos have been in Britain and in Ireland. See Major Ouzeley's Oriental Collection, Vol. II. Much attention is certainly due to such respectable authority.

and obscured; it may be sufficient to observe, that the Birmans believe in the Metempsychosis, and that, after having undergone a certain number of transmigrations, their souls will at last either be received into their Olympus on the mountain Meru,* or be sent to suffer torments in a place of divine punishments. Mercy they hold to be the first attribute of the divinity: "Reverence be to thee, O God, in the form of Mercy;" and they worship God by extending mercy unto all his creatures.

The laws of the Birmans, like their religion, are Hindoo; in fact there is no separating their laws from their religion: divine authority revealed to Menu the sacred principles in a hundred thousand slocas, or verses; Menu promulgated the code; numerous commentaries† on Menu were composed by the Munis, or old philosophers, whose treatises constitute the Dherma Sastra, or body of law.

The Birmans generally call their code Derma Sath, or Sastra; it is one among the many commentaries on Menu: I was so fortunate as to procure a translation of the most remarkable passages, which were rendered into Latin by Padre Vincentius Sangermano, and, to my great surprise, I found it to correspond closely with a Persian version of the Arracan code, which is now in my possession. From the inquiries, to which this circumstance gave rise, I learned that the laws, as well as the religion of the

* Meru properly denotes the pole, and, according to the learned Captain Wilford, it is the celestial north pole of the Hindoos, round which they place the garden of Indra, and describe it as the seat of delights.

† The code of Gentoo laws, translated by Mr. Halhed, I am informed, is a compilation from the different commentaries on Menu, who was "the grandson of Bramah, the first of created beings," and whose work, as translated by Sir William Jones, is the ground of all Hindoo jurisprudence.

Birmans, had found their way into the Ava country from Arracan, and came originally from Ceylon.* The Birman system of jurisprudence is replete with sound morality, and, in my opinion, is distinguished above any other Hindoo commentary for perspicuity and good sense; it provides specifically for almost every species of crime that can be committed, and adds a copious chapter of precedents, and decisions to guide the inexperienced, in cases where there is doubt and difficulty. Trial by ordeal and imprecation are the only absurd passages in the book; but on the subject of women it is, to an European, offensively indecent; like the immortal Menu, it tells the prince and the magistrate their duty, in language austere, manly, and energetic; and the exhortation at the close is at once noble and pious; the following extracts will serve as a specimen;

" A country may be said to resemble milk, in which oppression is like " to water; when water is mingled with milk, its sweetness immediately " vanishes; in the same manner oppression destroys a fair and flourishing " country. The royal Surkaab† will only inhabit the clearest stream; so " a prince can never prosper in a distracted empire. By drinking pure " milk the body is strengthened and the palate is gratified, but when " mingled with water, pleasure no longer is found, and the springs of " health gradually decline.

* As an incontestible proof that the Birmans acknowledge the superior antiquity of the Cingaleze, and the reception of their religion and laws from that quarter, the King of Ava has sent, within these few years, at separate times, two messengers, persons of learning and respectability, to Ceylon, to procure the original books on which their tenets are founded; and, in one instance, the Birman minister made an official application to the Governor-General of India, to protect and assist the person charged with the commission.

† Bittern. This is a Persian term, used by the Mahomedan translator.

"A wise prince resembles a sharp sword, which at a single stroke cuts "through a pillar with such keenness that the fabric still remains un-"shaken; with equal keenness his discernment will penetrate advice.

"A wise prince is dear to his people, as the physician is to the sick "man, as light to those that are in darkness, as unexpected sight to the "eyes of the blind; as is the full moon on a wintery night, and milk to "the infant from the breast of his mother."

The commentator then proceeds to denounce tremendous judgments against an oppressive prince and a corrupt judge; the latter is thus curiously menaced:

"The punishment of his crimes, who judges iniquitously, and decides "falsely, shall be greater than though he had slain one thousand women, "one hundred priests, or one thousand horses."

The book concludes as follows:

"Thus have the learned spoken, and thus have the wise decreed, that "litigation may cease among men, and contention be banished the land; "and let all magistrates and judges expound the laws, as they are herein "written; and to the extent of their understanding, and according to the "dictates of their conscience, pronounce judgment agreeably to the tenor "of this book: let the welfare of their country, and the benefit of their "fellow-creatures, be their continual study, and the sole object of their "attention: let them ever be mindful of the supreme dignity of the Rou-"lah* and the Bramins, and pay them that reverence which is due to "their sacred characters: let them observe becoming respect towards all "men, and they shall shield the weak from oppression, support the help-"less, and, in particular cases, mitigate the severity of avenging justice.

* The Arracan name for Rhahaan.

" It shall be the duty of a prince, and the magistrates of a prince, wisely " to regulate the internal police of the empire, to assist and befriend the " peasants, merchants, farmers, and those who follow trades, that they " may daily increase in worldly wealth and happiness; they shall promote " all works of charity, encourage the opulent to relieve the poor, and " liberally contribute to pious and laudable purposes; and whatsoever " good works shall be promoted by their influence and example, whatsoever " shall be given in charity, and whatsoever benefit shall accrue to mankind " from their endeavours, it shall all be preserved in the records of heaven, " one-sixth part of which, though the deeds be the deeds of others, yet shall " it be ascribed unto them; and at the last day, at the solemn and awful " hour of judgment, the recording spirit shall produce them, inscribed on " the adamantine tablet of human actions. But, on the other hand, if the " prosperity of the nation be neglected, if justice be suffered to lie dor-" mant, if tumults arise, and robberies are committed, if rapine and foul " assassination stalk along the plains, all crimes that shall be thus perpe-" trated through their remissness, one-sixth part shall be brought to their " account, and fall with weighty vengeance on their heads; the dreadful " consequences of which surpass the power of tongue to utter, or of pen " to express."

Laws, thus dictated by religion, are, I believe, in general, conscientiously administered. The criminal jurisprudence of the Birmans is lenient in particular cases, but rigorous in others; whoever is found guilty of an undue assumption of power, or of any crime that indicates a treasonable intent, is punished by the severest tortures. The first commission of theft does not incur the penalty of death, unless the amount stolen be above 800 kiat, or tackal, about £100. or attended with circumstances of atrocity, such as murder, or mutilation. In the former case the culprit has a round mark imprinted on each cheek by gunpowder and punctuation, and on his breast the word thief, with the article stolen; for the second offence he is deprived of an arm, but the third inevitably produces capital punishment: decapitation is the mode by which criminals suffer, in the performance of which the Birman executioners are exceedingly skilful.

The city of Ummerapoora is divided into four distinct subordinate jurisdictions, in each of which a Maywoon presides. This officer, who, in the provinces, is a viceroy, in the metropolis resembles a mayor, and holds a civil and criminal court of justice; in capital cases he transmits the evidence in writing, with his opinion, to the Lotoo, or grand chamber of consultation, where the council of state assembles; the council, after close examination into the documents, reports upon them to the King, who either pardons the offender, or orders execution of the sentence: the Maywoon is obliged to attend in person, and see the punishment carried into effect.

Civil suits may be transferred from the courts of the Maywoons to the Lotoo; this removal, however, is attended with a heavy expence. There are regular established lawyers, who conduct causes, and plead; eight only are licensed to plead in the Lotoo; they are called Ameendozaan: the usual fee is five tackal, equal to sixteen shillings, but the government has large profits on all suits that are brought into court.

There is no country of the East in which the royal establishment is arranged with more minute attention than in the Birman court; it is splendid without being wasteful, and numerous without confusion; the most distinguished members, when I was at the capital, were: the Sovereign, his principal queen, entitled Nandoh Praw, by whom he has no sons; his second wife, Myack Nandoh, by whom he has two sons; the Engy Teekein,* or Prince Royal, and Pêe Teekien, or Prince of Prome. The princes of Tongho, Bassien, and Pagahm, are by favourite concubines. Meedah Praw is a princess of high dignity, and mother of the chief queen. The prince royal is married, and has a son and two daughters, all young; the son takes precedence of his uncles, the crown descending to the male heirs in a direct line. These were the principal personages of the Birman royal family.

Next in rank to the princes of the blood royal are the Woongees,† or chief ministers of state. The established number is four, but the place of one has long been vacant: these form the great ruling council of the nation; they sit in the Lotoo, or imperial hall of consultation, every day, except on the Birman sabbath, from twelve till three or four o'clock, or later, as there happens to be business; they issue mandates to the Maywoons, or viceroys of the different provinces; they control every department of the state, and, in fact, govern the empire, subject always to the pleasure of the King, whose will is absolute, and power undefined.

To assist in the administration of affairs, four officers, called Woondocks, are associated with the Woongees, but of far inferior authority; they sit in the Lotoo, in a deliberative capacity, having no vote; they give their opinions, and may record their dissent from any measure that is proposed, but the Woongees decide: the Woondocks, however, are frequently employed to carry into execution business of great public importance.

Four Attawoons, or ministers of the interior, possess a degree of in-

* Often called Engy Praw.

† Woon signifies burthen; the compound word implies, Bearer of the Great Burthen.

Drawn by Singey Bey. Engraved by T. Medland.

A Woongee or Member of the Chief Council & his Wife in their dress of ceremony.

London. Published Nov.r 1, 1799, by G. Nicol Pall Mall & J. Wright Piccadilly

fluence that sometimes counteracts with success the views and wishes of the Woongees; these the King selects to be his privy counsellors, from their talents, and the opinion he entertains of their integrity: they have access to him at all times; a privilege which the principal Woongee does not enjoy.

There are four chief secretaries, called Sere-dogees, who have numerous writers, or inferior Serees, under them.

Four Nachaangee sit in the Lotoo, take notes, and report whatever is transacted.

Four Sandohgaan regulate all ceremonials, introduce strangers of rank into the royal presence, and are the bearers of messages from the council of state to the King.

There are nine Sandozains, or readers, whose business it is to read all official writings, petitions, &c. Every document, in which the public is concerned, or that is brought before the council in the Lotoo, is read aloud.

The four Maywoons, already mentioned, are restricted to the magisterial superintendance of their respective quarters of the city; they have nothing farther to do with the Lotoo, than to obey the commands they receive from thence.

The Assaywoon, or paymaster-general, is also an officer of high importance; the place is at present held by one of the Woongees, who is called Assay Woongee.

There are several other officers of distinction, who bear no ostensible share in the administration of public affairs, such as the Daywoon, or King's armour-bearer; the Chaingeewoon, or master of the elephants; also the Woons of the Queen's household, and that of the prince royal. Each of the junior princes has a distinct establishment.

In the Birman government there are no hereditary dignities or employments; all honours and offices, on the demise of the possessor, revert to the crown.

The tsaloe, or chain, is the badge of the order of nobility, of which there are different degrees, distinguished by the number of strings, or small chains, that compose the ornament; these strings are fastened by bosses where they unite: three of open chain work is the lowest rank; three of neatly twisted wire is the next; then of six, of nine, and of twelve; no subject is ever honoured with a higher degree than twelve; the King alone wears twenty-four.

It has already been noticed, that almost every article of use, as well as ornament, particularly in their dress, indicates the rank of the owner; the shape of the beetle-box, which is carried by an attendant after a Birman of distinction wherever he goes, his ear-rings, cap of ceremony, horse furniture, even the metal of which his spitting-pot and drinking-cup are made (which, if of gold, denote him to be a man of high consideration), all are indicative of the gradations of society; and woe be unto him that assumes the insignia of a degree which is not his legitimate right.

The court dress of the Birman nobility is very becoming; it consists of a long robe either of flowered satin or velvet, reaching to the ankles, with an open collar and loose sleeves; over this there is a scarf, or flowing mantle, that hangs from the shoulders, and on their heads they wear high caps made of velvet, either plain, or of silk embroidered with flowers of gold, according to the rank of the wearer. Ear-rings are a part of male dress; persons of condition use tubes of gold about three inches long, and as thick as a large quill, which expands at one end like the mouth of a speaking-trumpet; others wear a heavy mass of gold beaten into a plate,

Drawn by Singey Bey. Engraved by I. Medland

An Attawoon, or Minister of the Interior, and his Wife. A Soredogee, or Secretary of State: In their dress of ceremony.

London. Publish'd [illegible] by G Nicol Pall Mall & J Wright Piccadilly

and rolled up; this lump of metal forms a large orifice in the lobe of the ear, and drags it down by the weight to the extent sometimes of two inches. The women likewise have their distinguishing paraphernalia; their hair is tied in a bunch on the top of the head, and bound round with a fillet, the embroidery and ornaments of which express their respective ranks; a short shift reaches to the pit of the stomach, is drawn tight by strings, and supports the breasts; over that is a loose jacket with close sleeves; round their waist they roll a long piece of silk, or cloth, which, reaching to their feet, and sometimes trailing on the ground, encircles them twice, and is then tucked in. When women of condition go abroad, they put on a silk sash, resembling a long shawl, which crosses their bosom, and is thrown over the shoulders, gracefully flowing on each side. The lowest class of females often wear only a single garment, in the form of a sheet, which, wrapped round the body, and tucked in under the arm, crosses their breasts, which it scarcely conceals, and descends to their ankles; thus, when they walk, the bottom of the cloth, where it overlaps, is necessarily opened by the protrusion of the leg, and displays to a side view as high as the middle of the thigh; such an exposure, in the opinion of an European, bears an indecent appearance, although it excites no such idea in themselves. There is an idle and disgusting story related by some writers, respecting the origin of this fashion, which, being wholly unfounded, does not deserve repetition: it has been the established national mode of dress from time immemorial, and every woman, when walking, must shew great part of her leg, as what may be called their petticoat is always open in front, instead of being closed by a seam.

Women, in full dress, stain the palms of their hands, and their nails, of a red colour, for which they use a vegetable juice, and strew on their bosoms powder of sandal wood, or of a bark called Sunneka, with which some rub their faces. Both men and women tinge the edges of their eyelids, and their teeth with black; this latter operation gives to their mouths a very unseemly appearance in the eyes of an European, which is not diminished by their being constantly filled with beetle leaf. Men of rank wear, in common dress, a tight coat, with long sleeves made of muslin, or of extremely fine nankin, which is manufactured in the country, also a silk wrapper that encircles the waist: the working class are usually naked to the middle, but in the cold season a mantle or vest of European broad cloth is highly prized.

The Birmans in their features bear a nearer resemblance to the Chinese than to the natives of Hindostan. The women, especially in the northern part of the empire, are fairer than Hindoo females, but not so delicately formed; they are, however, well made, and in general inclined to corpulence: their hair is black, coarse, and long. The men are not tall in stature, but active and athletic; they have a very youthful appearance, from the custom of plucking their beards instead of using the razor: they tattoo their thighs and arms into various fantastic shapes and figures, which they believe operate as a charm against the weapons of their enemies. Neither the men nor women are so cleanly in their persons as the Hindoos of India, among whom diurnal ablution is a religious as well as a moral duty. Girls are taught at an early age to turn their arms in such a manner as to make them appear distorted: when the arm is extended the elbow is inverted, the inside of the joint being protruded, and the external part bending inwards; from this cause the pendent arm in the plates seems as though it were broken; the representation is nevertheless perfectly faithful.

Drawn by Singey Bey — Engraved by T. Medland

A Woondock and his Wife in their dress of ceremony.

London Published Novr 1. 1799, by G. Nicol Pall Mall, & J. Wright Piccadilly.

Marriages among the Birmans are not contracted until the parties attain the age of puberty: the contract is purely civil; the ecclesiastical jurisdiction having nothing to do with it. The law prohibits polygamy, and recognizes but one wife, who is denominated Mica; concubinage, however, is admitted to an unlimited extent. A man may repudiate his wife under particular circumstances, but the process is attended with a heavy expence. Concubines, living in the same house with the legitimate wife, are, by law, obliged to perform menial services for her, and when she goes abroad they attend her, bearing her water-flaggon, beetle-box, fan, &c. When a husband dies, his concubines, if bound in servitude to him, become the property of the surviving widow, unless he shall have emancipated them by a specific act, previous to his decease. When a young man is desirous to espouse a girl, his mother, or nearest female relation, first makes the proposal in private; if the suit be well received, a party of his friends proceed to the house of the parents of the maiden, with whom they adjust the dotal portion. On the morning of the bridal day the bridegroom sends to the lady three loongees, or lower garments, three tubbecks, or sashes, and three pieces of white muslin; such jewels also, ear-rings, and bracelets, as his circumstances will admit: a feast is prepared by the parents of the bride, and formal writings are executed: the new-married couple eat out of the same dish, the bridegroom presents the bride with some læpack, or pickled tea, which she accepts, and returns the compliment; thus ends the ceremony, without any of that subsequent riot* and resistance on the part of the young lady and her female friends, with which the Sumatrian damsels oppose the privileges of an ardent bridegroom.

When a man dies intestate, three-fourths of his property go to his

* See Marsden's Account of Sumatra, page 230.

children born in wedlock, but not in equal proportions, and one-fourth to the widow, who is the guardian both of the property and the children, until the latter attain the age of maturity. A Birman funeral is solemnized with much religious parade, and external demonstration of grief; the corpse is carried on a bier, on men's shoulders; the procession moves slowly; the relations attend in mourning, and women, hired for the occasion, precede the body, and chant a dirge-like air. The Birmans burn their dead, unless the deceased is a pauper, in which case he is either buried or cast into the river, as the ceremony of burning is very expensive. The bier is placed on a funeral pile six or eight feet high, made of billets of dried wood, laid across, with intervals to admit a circulation of air, and increase the flame. The Rhahaans walk round the pile, reciting prayers to Gaudma, until the fire reaches the body, when the whole is quickly reduced to ashes: the bones are afterwards gathered and deposited in a grave. Persons of high distinction, such as the Seredaw, or chief ecclesiastic of a province, a Maywoon, a Woongee, or a member of the royal family, are embalmed, and their remains preserved six weeks or two months after decease, before they are committed to the funeral pile: during this period the body is laid in state in some kioum or religious building, but at the capital it is placed in a sacred saloon, beautifully ornamented with gilding, and exclusively appropriated to that pious purpose. I was told that honey is the principal ingredient made use of to preserve the body from putrefaction.

Of the population of the Birman dominions I could only form a conclusion, from the information I received of the number of cities, towns, and villages, in the empire; these, I was assured by a person who might be supposed to know, and had no motive to deceive me, amount to eight thousand, not including the recent addition of Arracan. If this be true, which I have no reason to doubt, and we suppose each town, on an average, to contain three hundred houses, and each house six persons, the result will determine the population at fourteen millions four hundred thousand. Few of the inhabitants live in solitary habitations; they mostly form themselves into small societies, and their dwellings thus collected compose their Ruas, or villages; if, therefore, we reckon their numbers, including Arracan, at seventeen millions, the calculation may not be widely erroneous; I believe it rather falls short of than exceeds the truth. After all, however, it is mere conjecture, as I have no better data for my guidance than what has been related.

With regard to the revenue of the Birman state, I confess myself to be without the means of forming even a rude estimate of the amount. According to the sacred law in the chapter which treats of the duties of a monarch, Dhasameda,* or a tenth of all produce, is the proportion which is to be exacted as the authorized due of the government; and one-tenth is the amount of the King's duty on all foreign goods imported into his dominions. The revenue arising from the customs on imports, and from internal produce, is mostly taken in kind, a small part of which is converted into cash, the rest is distributed, as received, in lieu of salaries, to the various dependants of the court. Princes of the blood, high officers of state, and provincial governors, receive grants of provinces, cities, villages, and farms, to support their dignity, and as a remuneration of their services: the rents of these assignments they collect for their own benefit. Money, except on pressing emergency, is never disbursed from the royal coffers; to one man the fees of an office are allotted; to another a station

* See Appendix.

where certain imposts are collected; a third has land; each in proportion to the importance of his respective employment; by these donations, they are not only bound in their own personal servitude, but likewise in that of all their dependants; they are called slaves of the King, and in turn their vassals are denominated slaves to them; the condition of these grants include also services of war, as well as the duties of office. Thus the Birman government exhibits almost a faithful picture of Europe in the darker ages, when, on the decline of the Roman empire, the principles of feodal dependance were established by barbarians from the north.

Although it seems difficult, and perhaps impossible, under such a system, to ascertain, in any standard currency, the amount of the royal revenue, yet the riches which the Birman monarch is said to possess are immense, a supposition that may readily be admitted, when it is considered that a very small share of what enters his exchequer, returns into circulation. The hoarding of money is a favourite maxim of oriental state policy; an eastern potentate cannot be brought to comprehend that the diffusion of property among his subjects is a surer source of wealth to himself, and of security to his throne, than the possession of Lydian treasures, locked up in vaults, and concealed in secret recesses, contrived by sordid avarice and foolish cunning.

Drawn by Singey Boy — Engraved by T. Holland

(A _ Berman _ Peasant and his Wife.)

London, Published Nov.r 1 1799 by G. Nicol, Pall Mall & J. Wright, Piccadilly

CHAPTER XIV.

Military Establishment—Infantry—Cassay Cavalry—Artificers—War-boats—Gunpowder long known—Weapons—Food—Climate—Soil—Produce — Minerals — precious Stones — Commerce — Currency—Weights—Measures—Character of the Natives—not jealous of their Women—ferocious in War—Beggars unknown.—Animals—Division of Time— Music—Language—Extent of the Empire—Rivers.

THE Birmans may be denominated a nation of soldiers, every man in the kingdom being liable to be called upon for his military services; and war is deemed the most honourable occupation; the regular military establishment of the Birmans is nevertheless very inconsiderable, not exceeding the numbers of which the royal guard is composed, and such as are necessary to preserve the police of the capital. When an army is to be raised, a mandate issues from the golden palace, to all viceroys of provinces, and Miougees of districts, requiring a certain number of men to be at a general rendezvous, on an appointed day, under command, sometimes of the viceroy himself, but oftener that of an inferior officer: the levy is proportioned to the population of the province, or district, estimated from the number of registered houses it contains. The provincial court determines the burthen which each house is to bear; commonly every two, three, or four houses are to furnish among them one recruit, or to pay 300 tackal in money, about £40. or £45.; this recruit is supplied with arms, ammunition, and, I believe, with a certain daily allowance of grain from government, but is not entitled to pay. The families of these conscripts are carefully retained in the district which they inhabit, as hostages for the good conduct of their relation. In case of desertion or treachery, the innocent wife, children, and parents of the guilty person, are dragged to execution without the least remorse or pity; even cowardice subjects the family of the delinquent to capital punishment. This barbarous law, which is rigorously enforced, must have a powerful effect in securing the allegiance of the troops, and of impelling them to vigorous exertion, and it is, perhaps, the only sure mode of inciting to enterprises of danger, men who are not actuated by any innate sense of honour, and who do not feel any national pride.

Infantry and cavalry compose the regular guards of the king; the former are armed with muskets and sabres, the latter are provided with a spear about seven or eight feet long, which they manage on horseback with great dexterity, seldom requiring or making use of any other weapon. The infantry are not uniformly clothed; I heard various accounts of their numbers: 700 do constant duty within the precincts, and at the several gates of the palace: I think that on the day of my public reception, I saw about 2000, and have no doubt but all the troops in the city were paraded on that occasion. I was told that there were only 300 cavalry in Ummerapoora, but that 2000 were scattered, in small detachments, throughout the neighbouring districts. All the troopers in the king's service are natives of Cassay, who are much better horsemen than the Birmans. Mr. Wood, who saw some of them at exercise, informed me that they nearly resembled those he had met with in Assam; they ride, like all orientals, with short stirrups and a loose rein; their saddle is hard and high, and two large circular flaps of strong leather hang down on each side, painted or gilded, according to the quality of the rider. Their dress is not unbecoming; they wear a tight coat, with skirts reaching down to the middle of the thigh, and on

Drawn by Singey Bey. Engraved by T. Medland

A Cassay Horseman.

London. Published Nov.r 1, 1799, by G. Nicol, Pall Mall & J. Wright, Piccadilly

their head a turban of cloth, hard rolled and plaited, that ſorms a high cone, which bends backward in a graceful manner. The breed of horses in Ava are small, but very hardy and active; contrary to the practice of other eastern countries, they castrate their horses, and are thus enabled to maintain them with little trouble and expence, and can also turn a number loose in a field together, without any risk of their injuring one another. Horses are frequently exported in timber ships bound for Madras, and other parts of the coast, where they are disposed of to considerable advantage.

The government of Ava is extremely attentive to provide, in times of peace, for the contingencies of war; the royal magazines, I was told, could furnish 20,000 firelocks, which, if they resembled the specimens I saw, cannot be very formidable; these have been imported, at different periods, into the country, by ships trading to Rangoon and other parts of the empire, and are either of French manufacture, or condemned muskets from the English arsenals in India. The Birmans are very fond of their arms, of which they take great care; their gunsmiths, who are all natives of Cassay, keep them in repair, but they are in general so bad as to be out of the power of art, to render them serviceable. I saw a tolerably good fowling piece, which they said was entirely the work of a Cassay artificer; this, however, was allowed to be an extraordinary effort of genius; the person who shewed it to me, presented me, at the same time, with a bamboo, which threw out a short spear of iron by means of a spring; it was executed by the maker of the gun, and seemed to be formed after a model of an English walking stick, that contained a concealed spike; the imitation evinced much ingenuity, although the workmanship was coarse, and the iron badly polished.

By far the most respectable part of the Birman military force is their establishment of war-boats. Every town of note, in the vicinity of the river, is obliged to furnish a certain number of men, and one or more boats, in proportion to the magnitude of the place. I was informed that the king can command, at a very short notice, 500 of these vessels: they are constructed out of the solid trunk of the teak tree, which is excavated partly by fire, and partly by cutting; the largest are from eighty to one hundred feet long, but the breadth seldom exceeds eight feet, and even this space is produced by artificially extending the sides after the trunk has been hollowed. They carry from fifty to sixty rowers, who use short oars that work on a spindle; the prow is solid, and has a flat surface, on which, when they go to war, a piece of ordnance is mounted, a six, a nine, or even a twelve pounder; the gun carriage is secured by lashings to strong bolts on each side, and swivels are frequently fixed on the curvature of the stern.

The rowers are severally provided with a sword and a lance, which are placed by his side whilst he plies the oars. Besides the boatmen, there are usually thirty soldiers on board, who are armed with muskets: thus prepared, they go in fleets to meet the foe, and, when in sight, draw up in a line, presenting their prows to the enemy. Their attack is extremely impetuous; they advance with great rapidity, and sing a war-song, at once to encourage their people, daunt their adversaries, and regulate the strokes of their oars; they generally endeavour to grapple, and when that is effected, the action becomes very severe, as these people are endued with great courage, strength, and activity. In times of peace they are fond of exercising in their boats, and I have often been entertained with the dexterity they display in the management of them. The vessels being low in the water, their greatest danger is that of being run down by a larger boat striking on their broadside, a misfortune which the steersman is taught to dread, and to avoid, above all others. It is surprising to see the facility with which they steer, and elude each other in their mock combats. The rowers are also practised to row backwards, and impel the vessel with the stern foremost; this is the mode of retreat, by means of which the artillery still bears upon their opponent. The largest of the war-boats do not draw more than three feet water. When a person of rank is on board, there is a sort of moving tilt or canopy, for his particular accommodation, placed sometimes in the centre, and sometimes on the prow. The sides of the boat are either gilt as far as the water's edge, or plain, according to the rank of the person it carries. Gilded boats are only permitted to princes of the blood, or to persons holding the highest stations, such as a Maywoon of a province, and a minister of state.

It is by no means improbable that the use of gunpowder was well known in India before its effects were discovered in the west; yet there is not any reason to believe that the natives of Ava applied it to the purpose of musquetry, till Europeans instructed them in the art. According to Indian accounts, cannon were fabricated in the east long before the era of European conquest; their artillery, however, was not capable of being transported with facility, or at all used in the field: they were made of iron bars beaten into a cylindrical form, rudely put together, but of great strength, and enormous weight, from which, when raised on a rampart or tower, they threw huge stones to annoy the enemy. The musquet was first introduced into the Pegue and Ava countries by the Portugueze, and is an implement of war which the inhabitants unwisely prefer to their own native weapons, the spear and sabre, a partiality that is highly prejudicial to themselves, for nothing can be less formidable than such fire arms as they possess, or have the means of procuring. The proper indigenous weapons of the country are the spear, the javelin, which is thrown from the hand, the cross-bow, and the sabre; the latter is used by the Birmans not only as an implement of war, but is likewise applied to various purposes as an instrument of manual labour; with this the peasant fells trees, shapes timbers, cuts bamboos, or defends himself against an enemy, and wild beasts; he never travels without it, and generally, when on a journey, carries a shield on his left arm: they encumber themselves with less baggage than perhaps any other people; and are satisfied with a scanty portion of the hardest fare.

In their food the Birmans, compared with the Indians, are gross and uncleanly. Although their religion forbids the slaughter of animals in general, yet they apply the interdiction only to those that are domesticated; all game is eagerly sought after, and in many places it is publicly sold; reptiles also, such as lizards, guanas, and snakes, constitute a part of the subsistence of the lower classes. During our voyage up the river, the boatmen, after we had brought to, used frequently to hunt for camelions and lizards among the thickets. They are extremely fond of vegetables; at those places where garden greens were not to be procured, they gathered wild sorrel, and sometimes substituted the tender leaves of trees; these, boiled with rice, and moistened with a little oil, or seasoned with gnapee, or pickled sprat, compose a meal with which a Birman peasant or boatman is satisfied; the higher ranks, however, live with more delicacy, although their fare is never very sumptuous.

The climate of every part of the Birman empire, which I have visited, bore testimony to its salubrity, by the best possible criterion, the appearance and vigour of the natives. The seasons are regular, and the extremes of heat and cold are seldom experienced; at least the duration of that intense heat, which immediately precedes the commencement of the rainy season, is so short, that it incommodes but for a very little time. During our residence in the country we lost only one man by disease; another met an accidental death; in wandering through the woods he became the prey of a tiger.*

The soil of the southern provinces of the Birman empire is remarkably fertile, and produces as luxuriant crops of rice as are to be found in the finest parts of Bengal. Farther northward the country becomes irregular and mountainous; but the plains and vallies, particularly near the river, are exceedingly fruitful; they yield good wheat, and the various kinds of small grain which grow in Hindostan; as likewise legumes, and most of the esculent vegetables of India. Sugar canes, tobacco of a superior quality, indigo, cotton, and the different tropical fruits, in perfection, are all indigenous products of this favoured land.

Besides the teak tree, which grows in many parts of the Birman empire, as well to the north of Ummerapoora, as in the southern country, there is almost every description of timber that is known in India. Dr. Buchanan, in one of his afternoon excursions, perceived a large log of fir, which, his attendant informed him, had been washed down by the torrents from a mountainous part of the country, four days journey northward of the capital, where it grows in abundance, and of considerable magnitude: the natives call it Tænyo; they extract the turpentine, which they turn to use, but consider the wood of little value, on account of its softness. If they could be prevailed upon to transport it to Rangoon, it might prove a beneficial

* This unfortunate man belonged to the Sea-Horse.

material to the navigation of India. Top-gallant masts and yards made of teak are thought to be too heavy. European and American spars are often bought for these purposes at a very exorbitant price, an inconvenience which the fir of Ava, if conveyed to the market, would probably obviate.

The kingdom of Ava abounds in minerals; six days journey from Bamoo, near the frontiers of China, there are mines of gold and silver, called Badouem: there are also mines of gold, silver, rubies, and sapphires at present open on a mountain near the Keenduem, called Wooboloo-taun; but the most valuable, and those which produce the finest jewels, are in the vicinity of the capital, nearly opposite to Keoum-meoum. Precious stones are found in several other parts of the empire. The inferior minerals, such as contain iron, tin, lead, antimony, arsenic, sulphur, &c. are met with in great abundance; amber, of a consistence unusually pure and pellucid, is dug up in large quantities near the river; gold, likewise, is discovered in the sandy beds of streams which descend from the mountains. Between the Keenduem and the Irrawaddy, to the northward, there is a small river called Shoe Lien Kioup, or the Stream of Golden Sand.

Diamonds and emeralds are not produced in any part of the Ava empire, but it affords amethysts, garnets, very beautiful chrysolites, jasper, loadstone, and marble; the quarries of the latter are only a few miles from Ummerapoora; it is equal in quality to the finest marble of Italy, and admits of a polish that renders it almost transparent. Blocks of any size that it is possible to transport might be procured, but the sale is prohibited; nor is it allowed to be carried away without a special license. Images of Gaudma being chiefly composed of this material, it is on that account held sacred. Birmans may not purchase the marble in mass, but are suffered and indeed encouraged to buy figures of the deity ready made. Exportation of their gods out of the kingdom is strictly forbidden. The city of Chagain is the principal manufactory of these marble divinities.

An extensive trade is carried on between the capital of the Birman dominions and Yunan in China. The principal article of export from Ava is cotton, of which I was informed there are two kinds, one of a brown colour, of which nankeens are made, the other white, like the cotton of India; I did not see any of the former. This commodity is transported up the Irrawaddy in large boats, as far as Bamoo, where it is bartered at the common jee, or mart, with Chinese merchants, and conveyed by the latter, partly by land, and partly by water, into the Chinese dominions. Amber, ivory, precious stones, beetle nut, and the edible nests brought from the eastern Archipelago, are also articles of commerce: in return, the Birmans procure raw and wrought silks, velvets, gold leaf, preserves, paper, and some utensils of hardware.

The commerce between the capital and the southern parts of the empire is facilitated by the noble river that waters the country; its principal objects are the necessaries of life: several thousand boats are annually employed in transporting rice from the lower provinces to supply Ummerapoora, and the northern districts; salt and gnapee may likewise be reckoned under the same head. Articles of foreign importation are mostly conveyed up the Irrawaddy; a few are introduced by way of Arracan, and carried over the mountains on the heads of coolies, or labourers; European broadcloth, a small quantity of hardware, coarse Bengal muslins, Cossembuzar silk handkerchiefs, China ware, which will not admit of land carriage, and glass, are the principal commodities. Cocoa nuts also, brought from the Nicobar Islands, where they are of uncommon excellence, are looked upon as a delicacy, and bear a high price: merchants carry down silver, lac, precious stones, and some other articles, to no great amount. A considerable sum of money is annually laid out at the capital in the purchase of marble statues of Gaudma, which are all fabricated at Chagain, opposite Awa-haung, or ancient Ava: they are not permitted to be made at any other place.

The Birmans, like the Chinese, have no coin; silver in bullion, and lead, are the current monies of the country; weight and purity are, of course, the standard of value, and in the ascertainment of both, the natives are exceedingly scrupulous and expert. What foreigners call a tackal, properly kiat, is the most general piece of silver in circulation; it weighs ten penny-weights ten grains and three-fourths; its subdivisions are, the tubbee, two of which make one moo; two moo one math; four math one tackal, and one hundred tackal compose one viss. Money scales and weights are all fabricated at the capital, where they are stamped, and afterwards circulated throughout the empire; the use of any others is prohibited.

Rice is sold by a measure called Tayndaung, or basket; the weight is sixteen viss, about fifty-six pounds. There are many subdivisions of measurement. The average price of rice at the capital is one tackal, rather more than half-a-crown, for a basket and a half. At Rangoon and Martaban one tackal will purchase four or five baskets.

The bankers, called by foreigners Pymon, are likewise workers in silver, and assayers of metal: this is a class of people very numerous, and indispensably necessary, as no stranger can undertake either to pay or receive money without having it first examined. Every merchant has a banker of this description, with whom he lodges all his cash, and who, for receiving and paying, gets an established commission of one per cent.; in consideration of which he is responsible for the quality of what goes through his hands; and in no instance did I ever hear of a breach of trust committed by one of these bankers. The quantity of alloy varies in the silver current in different parts of the empire: at Rangoon it is adulterated twenty-five per cent.; at Ummerapoora, pure, or what is called flowered silver, is most common; in this latter all royal dues are paid. The several modifications are as follows:

Rouni, or pure silver.	
Rounika,	5 per cent. of alloy.
Rounizee,	10 per cent.
Rouassee,	20 per cent.
Moowadzoo,	25 per cent.
Woombo,	30 per cent.

Any person may have his silver either purified or depreciated to whatever standard he chuses; the nearest silversmith will be glad to perform the work, free from charge for his labour, as the bringer by the operation must lose a trifle, which the artist gains: the small quantity of metal that adheres to the crucible is his profit. I was informed that the silversmith can sell these crucibles afterwards to refiners for forty tackals a thousand, and that an adequate gain accrues to the purchaser from the metal extracted from the pot after it is broken.

The Birman measures of length are, a Paul-gaut, or inch, eighteen of which compose the Taim, or cubit.

The Saundaung, or royal cubit,* equal to twenty-two inches.

The Dha, or Bamboo, which consists of seven royal cubits; 1000 dha make one Birman league, or Dain, nearly equal to two British miles and

* This cubit varies according to the will of the monarch.

two furlongs; the league is also subdivided into tenths. The Birmans keep their accounts in decimals, after the manner of the Chinese.

It has already been noticed, that the general disposition of the Birmans is strikingly contrasted with that of the natives of India, from whom they are separated only by a narrow range of mountains, in many places admitting of an easy intercourse. Notwithstanding the small extent of this barrier, the physical difference between the nations could scarcely be greater, had they been situated at the opposite extremities of the globe. The Birmans are a lively, inquisitive race, active, irascible, and impatient; the character of their Bengal neighbours is too well known, as the reverse, to need any delineation; the unworthy passion of jealousy, which prompts most nations of the east to immure their women within the walls of an haram, and surround them with guards, seems to have scarcely any influence over the minds of this extraordinary and more liberal people. Birman wives and daughters are not concealed from the sight of men, and are suffered to have as free intercourse with each other as the rules of European society admit; but in other respects women have just reason to complain of their treatment; they are considered as not belonging to the same scale of the creation as men, and even the law stamps a degrading distinction between the sexes; the evidence of a woman is not received as of equal weight with that of a man, and a woman is not suffered to ascend the steps of a court of justice, but is obliged to deliver her testimony on the outside of the roof. The custom of selling their women to strangers, which has before been adverted to, is confined to the lowest classes of society, and is perhaps oftener the consequence of heavy pecuniary embarrassment, than an act of inclination; it is not, however, considered as shameful, nor is the female dishonoured; partly perhaps from this cause, and partly from their habits of education, women surrender themselves the victims of this barbarous custom with apparent resignation. It is also said that they are very seldom unfaithful to their foreign masters, indeed they are often essentially useful, particularly to those who trade, by keeping their accounts and transacting their business: but when a man departs from the country, he is not suffered to carry his temporary wife along with him; on that point the law is exceedingly rigorous: every ship, before she receives her clearance, is diligently searched by the officers of the custom-house: even if their vigilance were to be eluded, the woman would be quickly missed; and it would be soon discovered in what vessel she had gone, nor could that ship ever return to a Birman port but under penalty of confiscation of the property, and the infliction of a heavy fine and imprisonment on the master: female children also, born of a Birman mother, are not suffered to be taken away. Men are permitted to emigrate; but they think that the expatriation of women would impoverish the state, by diminishing the sources of its population.

One vice is usually the parent of another: the Birmans, being exempt from that of jealousy, do not resort to the diabolical practice of emasculating male children, to educate them as spies over their women. Chastity, they know, is more safely guarded by principles of honour and attachment than by moats or castles. When Arracan was conquered by the Birmans, several eunuchs were made prisoners, belonging to the prince of the country, who had adopted that degenerate custom of Mahomedan growth. These people are maintained by the Birman monarch rather as memorials of his conquest, than for any services they are required to perform. Infidelity is not a characteristic of Birman wives; in general they have too much employment to leave leisure for the corruption of their minds. A woman of the highest rank seldom sits in idleness at home; her female servants, like those of Grecian dames of antiquity, ply " the various labours of the loom:" whilst the mistress superintends and directs their industry. On the occasion of a formal visit to the mother of the present Queen, we observed in one of the galleries of her palace, three or four looms at work, wrought by the damsels of her household. Weaving is chiefly a female occupation. Most Birman families make all the cotton and silk cloth that is required for their domestic consumption.

The Birmans, in some points of their disposition, display the ferocity of barbarians, and in others, all the humanity and tenderness of polished life: they inflict the most savage vengeance on their enemies; as invaders, desolation marks their track, for they spare neither sex nor age; but at home they assume a different character; there they manifest benevolence, by extending aid to the infirm, the aged, and the sick: filial piety is inculcated as a sacred precept, and its duties are religiously observed. A common beggar is no where to be seen: every individual is certain of receiving sustinence, which, if he cannot procure by his own labour, is provided for him by others.

During the several excursions which we made into the country, we did not perceive any of the feathered tribe that were peculiar to this part of the world, or that were not to be met with in India, the ornithology of which is already well known. The Henza, the symbol of the Birman nation, as the eagle was of the Roman empire, is a species of wild fowl, called in India the Braminy goose; but the natives of Ava do not deify the bird. Of the beasts of Ava, the only one I saw, with which I was unacquainted, was the ichneumon, or the rat of Pharaoh, called by the natives Ounbaii. It is a singular circumstance that there should not be such an animal as the jackal in the Ava dominions, considering that they are so numerous in the adjoining country. Pegue abounds in elephants; for though they are to be met with in other parts of the empire, that seems to be their favourite abode. One of his Birman Majesty's titles is, Lord of the White Elephant, and of all the Elephants in the World.

The Birmans divide their time as follows:

The space in which the finger can be raised and depressed is called charazi; ten charazi make one piaan; six piaan one bizana, (about a minute). The day, of twenty-four hours, commencing at noon, is divided into eight portions, or yettee, of three hours each, thus denominated:

Moon Yettee, or noon.
Loung Yettee, 3 P. M.
Lay Yettee, 6 P. M.
Gneah Yettee, 9 P. M.
Gneah Gnek Yettee, midnight.
Gneah Laghee Loung Yettee, 3 in the morning.
Mioh Ling Yettee, 6 A. M.
Gneah Tek Yettee, 9 A. M.

These divisions of time are ascertained by a machine, resembling the hour-glass, and sometimes by a perforated pan placed in a tub of water: they are announced by a stroke on an oblong drum, which is always kept near the dwelling of the chief magistrate of the city, town, or village; it is commonly raised on a high bamboo stage, with a roof of mats to protect it from the weather.

The edifice at the royal palace for the reception of this instrument is of masonry, and very lofty, whence the sound is said to be distinctly conveyed to the remotest extremes of the city.

The Birman year is divided into twelve months, which, strictly speaking, cannot be called synodical, although they comprehend the same number of days. A revolution of the moon, in passing from one conjunction with the sun to another, is performed in 29 days 12 hours and 44 minutes; but the Birman lunations consist of 29 and 30 days, alternate, which causes a difference between the Newtonian and Birman lunar account of 8 hours and 48 minutes. The Birman months are as follow:

	Days.
Tagoo contains - - - -	29
Kayoung - - - - -	30
Nay Young - - - -	29
Wazoo - - - - -	30
Wagoung - - - - -	29
Toozelien - - - - -	30
Sandaing Guite - - - -	29
Tazoung Moang - - - -	30
Gnadoh - - - - -	29
Peeazoo - - - - -	30
Taboodway - - - - -	29
Taboung - - - -	30
	354

In order to complete a solar revolution, they intercalate in every third year a month of 30 days, which is called Toodea Wazoo; in this third year the months of Tagoo and Nay Young have each 30 days instead of 29; they likewise suppress or pass over a day, which, if reckoned, would either be the 31st Taboung or the 1st of Tagoo: by these means the number of days in three solar years is thus computed:

	Days.
Three lunar years, of 354 days each - -	1062
Intercalary month in the third year - - -	30
Two intercalary days in Tagoo and Nay Young -	2
Suppressed or passed over at the end of the year -	1
	1095

This computation corresponds, in the number of days, with three years; every fourth year however will occasion the difference of a day on account of our bissextile or leap year; of this the Birmans are fully sensible, as well as of many other defects in their manner of reckoning: to remedy the confusion likely to ensue from such erroneous calculations, their style or mode has frequently been altered by arbitrary authority. His present Birman Majesty, however, is so desirous to ascertain and establish, by accurate tables, a permanent and unvarying measurement of time, that he made an application to the late Governor General of India to send to his capital a Bramin well versed in astronomy, to assist the deliberations of his council of professors, among whom his Majesty always presides in person, and he is said to be no inconsiderable proficient in the science of astronomy.

The manner in which the Birman month is subdivided, I imagine, is peculiar to their nation; instead of reckoning the days progressively from the commencement to the close of the month, they advance no farther than the full moon, from which they recede by retrogressive enumeration until the month is finished.

Thus the new moon is called,

Lahzan terrait gnay, or first day of the increasing moon.

Lahzan gnerait gnay, second day, &c.

Lahzan loungrait gnay, third day, &c.

Lahzan layrait gnay, fourth day, &c.

Lahzan narait gnay, fifth day, &c.

Lahzan kioukrait gnay, sixth day, &c.

Lahzan koonrait gnay, seventh day, &c.

Lahzan sheaseddainrait gnay, eighth day, &c.

Lahzan karait gnay, ninth day, &c.

Lahzan sayrait gnay, tenth day, &c.

Lahzan say terrait gnay, eleventh day, &c.

Lahzan say-gnerrait gnay, twelfth day, &c.

Lahzan say soungrait gnay, thirteenth day, &c.

Lahzan tassay sayrait gnay, fourteenth day, &c.

Lah bee, fifteenth day, &c.

Lah bee-goo terrait gnay, or the first day of the decreasing moon.

The seventeenth, eighteenth, &c. correspond with the second and third of the increasing moon, substituting Lah Bee-goo for Lahzan. The last day of the month, whether of twenty-nine or thirty days, is called Lah gnay.

The Birman month is divided into four weeks of seven days each; the days are distinguished by the following names:

Tamaing nuaye, Sunday, the first day of the Birman week.

Talain lah, - Monday.

Aing gah, - Tuesday.

Boodt-hoo, - Wednesday.

Keah-subbeday, Thursday.

Zoup keah, - Friday.

Sunnay, - Saturday.

The eighth day of the increasing moon, the fifteenth or full moon, the eighth of the decreasing moon, and the last day of the moon, are religiously observed by Birmans as sacred festivals. On these hebdomadal holidays no public business is transacted in the Rhoom; mercantile dealings are suspended; handicraft is forbidden; and the strictly pious take no sustenance between the rising and the setting of the sun; but this latter instance of self-denial is not very common, and, as I understood, is rarely practised, except in the metropolis, where the appearance of sanctity is sometimes assumed, as a ladder by which the crafty attempt to climb to promotion. The Sovereign himself is a great favourer of the austerities of the Birman religion; and his chief minister, or Woongee, has for many years on a Birman sabbath abstained from food so long as the sun continues above the horizon.

The Birmans are extremely fond both of poetry and music; they call the former Yeddoo: when repeated by a scholar it flows soft and measured, to the ear; it is sometimes in successive, and often in alternate rhimes. A line is called Tageoung; a stanza, Tubbouk. They have epic as well as religious poems of high celebrity, and they are fond of reciting in heroic numbers the exploits of their kings and generals. I was informed that the prowess of Alompra is recorded in verses not unworthy of a monarch.

Music is a science which is held in considerable estimation throughout the Birman empire, and is cultivated at the present day more generally than in India, notwithstanding it is there termed, as by the ancient Greeks, the language of the gods. The royal library of Ummerapoora is said to contain many valuable treatises on the art. Some of the professional musicians display considerable skill and execution, and the softer airs are pleasing even to an ear unaccustomed to such melody. The principal instruments are a Soum, or harp, made of light wood, hollowed and varnished, in shape somewhat like a canoe with a deck; at the extremity a piece of hard wood is neatly fastened, which tapers to the end, and rising curves over the body of the harp; from this curvature, the strings, usually made of wire, are extended to a bridge on the belly of the instrument: there are two sounding holes, one on each side of the bridge. The size of the Soum varies from two to five feet in length.

The Turr resembles our violin; it has only three strings, and is played on with a bow. I at first imagined it had been of European introduction, and brought to Pegue by the Portugueze, but I was assured it was an original instrument of the country.

The Pullaway, is a common flagelet.

The Kyezoup, is a collection of cymbals, which are suspended in a bamboo frame; these cymbals, varying in size, produce modulated gradations of sounds; there were eighteen in the Kyezoup that I saw.

The Patola, or guitar, is a curious instrument; it is the exact form of a crocodile in miniature; the body of which is hollow, with sounding holes on the back; three strings of wire extend from the shoulder to the tail, and are supported on bridges at each extremity; the strings are tuned by means of pegs in the tail, to which they are fastened; it is played on by the finger, and is generally used to accompany the voice.

The Boundaw is a collection of drums, oblong in form, and varying in size, which are suspended perpendicularly in a wooden frame by leather thongs. The whole machine is about five feet in diameter and four feet high. The performer stands in the centre, and beats on the drums with a small stick. This instrument is always introduced when there is a full band, and is much used in processions, being carried by two men, whilst the performer shuffles along in the inside, playing as he goes.

The Heem is the pipe of Pan, formed of several reeds neatly joined together, and sounded by a common mouth-piece; when played with skill, it produces a very plaintive melody.

These are the principal instruments of music in use among the Birmans. Dr. Buchanan purchased a complete concert set, for fifty-four tackal, which is about five or six guineas. Melody has charms for all mankind: among the boatmen that rowed my barge, I doubt whether there was one who did not possess an instrument of some sort; he who could procure no better, had what we call a Jew's harp, with which he delighted to beguile half an hour of a cool evening, after a day of hard labour under a burning sun.

Of the ancient Pallis,* whose language constitutes at the present day the sacred text of Ava, Pegue, and Siam, as well as of several other countries eastward of the Ganges; and of their migration from India to the banks of the Cali, the Nile of Ethiopia, we have but very imperfect information. As a nation they have long ago ceased to exist: they are said to have possessed, in former times, a dominion stretching from the Indus as far as Siam, and to have been conquered by the Rajaputras, who changed the

* In Captain Wilford's elaborate and learned Dissertation on Egypt and the Nile, from the ancient books of the Hindoos, there is the following passage:

" The history of the Pallis cannot fail to be interesting, especially as it will be found " much connected with that of Europe; and I hope soon to be supplied with materials for a " full account of them. Even their miserable remains in India must excite compassion, " when we consider how great they once were, and from what height they fell, through the " intolerant zeal and superstition of their neighbours. Their features are peculiar, and their " language different, but perhaps not radically, from that of the other Hindoos. Their vil- " lages are still called Palli." Asiat. Research. Vol. III.

name of their country from Palisthan to Rajaputra. In the old books of the Hindoos they are called Paliputras, and it may I think be concluded that they were the Palibothri of the ancients.

It has been the opinion of some of the most enlightened writers* on the languages of the East, that the Pali, the sacred language of the priests of Boodh, is nearly allied to the Shanscrit of the Bramins; and there certainly is much of that holy idiom engrafted on the vulgar language of Ava, by the introduction of the Hindoo religion. The character in common use throughout Ava and Pegue is a round Nagari, derived from the square Pali, or religious text; it is formed of circles and segments of circles, variously disposed and combined, whilst the Pali, which is solely applied to the purposes of religion, is a square letter, chiefly consisting of right angles.

The Birman language contains thirty-three simple sounds, to represent which, their alphabet, commonly called Kagye Kague, consists of an equal number of distinct characters, exclusive of various marks and contractions, that supply the place of long and short vowels, diphthongs, &c. These are explained and enumerated in separate series, in the Birman Spelling-book, entitled, Kaynboungie, in which every possible combination is given and exemplified.

It should be observed here, that there is no representation of the vowel corresponding with our short ă, as from the frequent occurrence of that sound in the middle and at the end of words, it was found convenient to omit it in writing; it is nevertheless to be pronounced after every simple sound or consonant not supplied with another vowel, unless it be forbidden

* Captain Wilford on Egypt and the Nile. Loubere's Account of Siam. Chambers on the Ruins of Mavalipuram. Asiat. Research. Vol. I.

by a mark of elision placed over the letter, or excluded by the junction of two or more consonants, in the form of a compound character. These singularities, I am informed by Mr. Wilkins, are common to all the alphabets of the Hindoo class.

The Birmans write from left to right, and though they leave no distinguishing space between their words, they mark the pauses of a sentence and the full stops. Their letters are distinct, and their manuscripts are in general very beautiful.

The common books of the Birmans, like those of the Hindoos, particularly of such as inhabit the southern parts of India, are composed of the palmyra leaf, on which the letters are engraved with a stylus; but the Birmans far excel the Braminical Hindoos in the neatness of the execution, and in the ornamental part of their volumes. In every Kioum, or monastery, there is a library or repository of books, usually kept in lacquered chests. Books in the Pali text, are sometimes composed of thin stripes of bamboo, delicately plaited, and varnished over in such a manner, as to form a smooth and hard surface upon a leaf of any dimensions; this surface is afterwards gilded, and the sacred letters are traced upon it in black and shining japan. The margin is illumined by wreaths and figures of gold, on a red, green, or black ground.

In the recitation of poetry, the language is exceedingly melodious; even the prose of common conversation appears to be measured, and the concluding word of each sentence is lengthened by a musical cadence, that marks the period, to the ear of a person wholly unacquainted with the meaning.

The annexed Plate exhibits the simple elementary characters, with the sound that each expresses, and the name in the Birman tongue: this name has an appropriate meaning, such as "great ka," "spiral ka," "circular za," &c. but some of these characters are very rarely used, such as No. 4, 9, 11, 12, 13, 14, 15, 19, 23, and 32.

To this alphabet is added the Shanscrit elementary character, analogous to each of the Birman characters; also the Birman cyphers, and a specimen of the ancient Pali, taken from a very beautiful manuscript in my possession, which contains an account of the ceremony used in the consecration of Rhahaans.*

It is difficult to ascertain with precision the exact limits of the Birman empire. Dr. Buchanan, who accompanied me, sought for geographical information with the most diligent inquiry; he procured, but not without considerable trouble and expence, sketches of every part of the Birman territories; and he has transmitted the materials which he thus collected to the East-India Company. Those sketches, however, being contained in various and detached pieces, not forming any connected body, nor yet reduced to a graduated scale, can hardly be brought into the shape of a regular map without the aid of some further communications; they are nevertheless documents of much intrinsic value and importance; it is therefore to be hoped that, with the aid of some additional lights, a vacuum on the terrestrial globe will, ere long, be filled up, and a portion of the earth delineated, which heretofore has been very imperfectly known. On a probable calculation from Dr. Buchanan's papers of the extent of the present Birman empire, it appears to include the space between the 9th and 26th degrees of north latitude, and between the 92d and 107th degrees of longitude east of Greenwich, about 1050 geographical miles in length, and 600 in breadth: these are the ascertainable limits, taken from the

* I am indebted for the Shanscrit character, to the kindness of my friend Mr. Wilkins.

The BIRMAN ALPHABET called ကကြီးခခွေး KAGYE-KAGUE.

BIRMAN	SANSCRIT	SOUND	NAME	IN ENGLISH
က	क	Kă	ကကြီး	Kă-gyĕ
ခ	ख	'Kă	ခခွေး	'Kă-guè
ဂ	ग	Gă	ဂငယ်	Gă-ngay
ဃ	घ	'Gă	ဃကြီး	'Gă-gyĕ
င	ङ	Ngă	င	Ngă
စ	च	Ză	စလုံး	Ză-loun
ဆ	छ	'Ză	ဆလိမ်	'Ză-lein
ဇ	ज	Să	ဇကွဲ	Să-guè
ဈ	झ	Să	ဈမျဉ်းဆွဲ	Să-miayn-sua
ည ဉ	ञ	Gnă	ည	Gnă
ဋ	ट	Tă	ဋသန်လျင်းချိတ်	Tă-thă-gnayn-gieit
ဌ	ठ	'Tă	ဌဝမ်းဘဲ	'Tă-wum-bă
ဍ	ड	Dă	ဍရင်ကောက်	Dă-yayn-gauk
ဎ	ढ	'Dă	ဎရေမှုတ်	'Dă-rè-moup
ဏ	ण	Nă	ဏကြီး	Nă-gyĕ
တ	त	Tă	တဝမ်းပူ	Tă-wum-bu
ထ	थ	'Tă	ထဆင်ထူ	'Tă-zayn-thu
ဒ	द	Dă	ဒထွေး	Dă-dué
ဓ	ध	Dhă	ဓအောက်ချိုက်	Dhă-auk-kiaik
န	न	Nă	နငယ်	Nă-ngay
ပ	प	Pă	ပစောက်	Pă-zauk
ဖ	फ	'Pă	ဖဦးထုပ်	'Pă-out-toup
ဗ	ब	Bă	ဗထက်ချိုက်	Bă-tek-kiaik
ဘ	भ	'Bă	ဘကုန်း	'Bă-goum
မ	म	Mă	မ	Mă
ယ	य	Yă	ယပက်လက်	Yă-pet-lek
ရ	र	Ră	ရကောက်	Ră-gauk
လ	ल	Lă	လ	Lă
သ	व	Thă Să	သ	Thă Să
ဝ	श	Wă	ဝ	Wă
ဟ	ष	Hă	ဟ	Hă
ဠ	स	Lă	ဠကြီး	Lă-gye
အ	ह	ă	အ	ă

BIRMAN NUMERALS.

1 ၁	2 ၂	3 ၃	4 ၄	5 ၅	6 ၆	7 ၇	8 ၈	9 ၉	10 ၁၀	11 ၁၁	20 ၂၀	100 ၁၀၀
တစ်	နှစ်	သုံး	လေး	ငါး	ခြောက်	ခုနစ်	ရှစ်	ကိုး	တဆယ်	ဆယ့်တစ်	နှစ်ဆယ်	တရာ

The PALI, or RELIGIOUS TEXT of the BIRMANS.

[illegible]

A line of Connected Writing in the Birman Character.

[illegible]

Birman accounts; but it is probable that their dominions stretch still farther to the north. It should, however, be remarked, that the breadth often varies, and is in many places very inconsiderable, on what is called the Eastern Peninsula.

Dr. Buchanan, in the summary* or general outline of the geographical materials which he collected, thus expresses himself on the subject of rivers:—It appears " that the Arracan river is not so considerable as " what has been supposed, but takes its rise in hills at no great distance " to the north.

" That the river coming from Thibet, which is supposed to be that of " Arracan, is in fact the Keenduem, or the great western branch of the " Ava river.

" That what is supposed to be the western branch of the Irrawaddy, is " in fact the eastern one; which passes by Ava, and runs to the north, " keeping west from the province of Yunan, and leaving between it and " that part of China a country subject to the Birmans.

" That the Loukiang, which is supposed to be the great branch of the " Irrawaddy, has no communication with that river; but on entering the " Birman dominions assumes the name of Thaluayn, or Thanluayn, and " falls into the sea at Martaban.

" That the river of Pegue, which is supposed to come from China, rises " among hills about 100 miles from the sea, and which form the boundary " between the Birman and Pegue kingdoms.

" That between the Pegue and Martaban rivers there is a lake, from " which two rivers proceed; the one runs north to Old Ava, where it " joins the Myoungnya, or Little River of Ava, which comes from

* Extract from the Bengal Political Letter, 11th of September, 1797.

"mountains on the frontiers of China; the other river runs south from "the lake to the sea, and is the Sitang river in the map.

"That the rivers of China, which are supposed to be the heads of the "Pegue river, are those of the river of Siam.

"That the rivers of Siam and Cambodia communicate by a very con- "siderable branch, called the Annan."

This disposition of the rivers gives an entire new face to the geography of India extra Gangem; and from the diligence and ability with which Dr. Buchanan collated the several accounts that he received, I am inclined to believe that his statement is nearly correct.

CHAPTER XV.

Permission granted to make Astronomical Observations—Message from the King.—River rises.—Present of Wheat.—Bees—Honey.—Bengal Painter employed at Court.—Mode of catching wild Elephants.—King solicitous to introduce the Art of Glass-making.—Attentions from Viceroys to Foreign Ministers.—Letters arrive from Bengal.—Our People healthy—Chinese the reverse—the Cause.—Ceremony arranged—Procession—Manner of Entrance—Introduction into the Lotoo, or Grand Council Hall.—Description of the Court—its Magnificence—King not present.—Questions proposed.—Banquet.—Formalities observed in returning.

THE occurrences that took place in the interval between our arrival and the 30th of August, the day appointed for our formal introduction, were not of sufficient importance to require a minute relation. We enjoyed whatever personal convenience the country could supply; and I gladly embraced every opportunity to evince the most implicit confidence; which I am induced to think was productive of beneficial consequences. To my public character, as will appear in the sequel, the conduct of the Birman court was punctilious and haughty, even to insufferable arrogance; but my accommodation and security as an individual were attended to with all the urbanity that could be expected from the most polished state of Europe.

Geography is the foundation of all historical knowledge, without which history becomes little better than romance. Having hitherto found the most authentic geographical information I could obtain respecting countries eastward of the Ganges to be extremely erroneous, I was on that account more particularly desirous to determine the true situation of the capital of Ava; especially as I had now a favourable opportunity of profiting by the assistance of a gentleman of high professional talents. It however seemed expedient to obtain the sanction of the Birman government, before I authorized Mr. Wood to commence astronomical observations; and, in reply to an application I made through the Maywoon of Pegue, I received the most liberal acquiescence; a compliment that was afterwards enhanced by a gracious message from his Birman Majesty, desiring to know, according to our calculation, the exact time when the expected eclipse of the moon was to take place, and, as it was partial, what portion of the lunar body would be in shade? Mr. Wood satisfied him in both particulars, and we were informed that the King, on comparing Mr. Wood's account with his own predictions, (for he is said to be himself an adept in the science), discovered only a slight difference in the segment of the moon which was to be obscured. Mr. Wood's knowledge procured him considerable respect among the better informed natives, but it excited the terror of the vulgar. Being obliged at night to leave the grove and go out on the plain, in order to have a distinct view of the heavenly bodies, the peasants that inhabited the neighbouring villages believed him to be a necromancer, and his telescope and time-keeper instruments of magic: in their wonder they sometimes crowded about him so as to disturb his operations; but it was nothing more than harmless curiosity; they wanted to discover by what means he held communication with the Natts, the supernatural and invisible agents of the air.

The river, which had now risen to its utmost height, had encroached so much on the grove, as to threaten a general inundation, and we began to think it not improbable that we should be obliged some night hastily to change our residence from the house to the boats. The cause of the swelling of the waters was not apparent, as there had not fallen with us a sufficient quantity of rain to produce the smallest alteration in the body of the river: the Birmans, however, who knew the exact limit to which it would rise, laughed at our proposing to make arrangements for a sudden embarkation, and assured us that, within the memory of man, the floods had never surpassed a certain boundary.

Although, from the nature of the grounds in the neighbourhood of our dwelling, rice was the only grain that could be cultivated, we understood that on the other side of the lake, near the city, there were extensive fields of wheat, which, from the samples brought to us, seemed to be equal in quality to the finest growth of England. The market price at Ummerapoora was one tackal, nearly half a crown, for a taindaung, or basket weighing about fifty-six pounds; but we had no occasion to purchase any, as the provision made by the commissary of government, and the presents from those who visited us, kept our store-room full. Every person who came, brought something, either fruit, flowers, a plate of fine rice, of wheat, or some similar mark of respect. In return, I treated those of the higher order with tea and sweetmeats; of the former they were extremely fond; and I can truly say, that from ten in the morning until evening, the tea equipage was never unemployed. An old man who acted as commissary, and lived in the rhoom adjacent to our dwelling, whose title was Kyewoon, brought all the females of his family to see us; they produced as their offering, fresh honeycombs hanging from branches of the bamboo tree; the honey was dropping from the boughs into pans. I was told that the bees were wild in the woods, and in such plenty that wax formed a staple article of commerce. The natives have a mode of gathering the honey without destroying the insect. The soldiers of the guard and our domestics continued to receive two tackal, at stated periods, in addition to their allowance of rice; and beetle-leaf was to be had fresh from gardens belonging to the adjacent villages. In one of these plantations, which very much resembled an English hop-garden, I saw a man watering his plants by means of a wheel, which raised water out of a well from a considerable depth. The machine was constructed with much ingenuity.

The reputation that my Bengal draughtsman had acquired by his botanical drawings, performed under the inspection of Dr. Buchanan, having come to the knowledge of his Birman Majesty, or, in the Birman phrase, having reached the Golden Ears, the King was pleased to desire a specimen of his skill, and sent over a painting on glass, executed by a Siamese artist in his own service, signifying his royal will that it should be copied upon paper. This picture, which was a tolerable performance, represented the mode of catching wild elephants in the forests. It was thus described to me: the hunters, mounted on tame elephants that are trained to the business, by lying flat on their backs, introduce themselves unnoticed into a wild herd, and take an opportunity to cast a running noose in the track of the one that is meant to be secured. The other end of the rope is fastened to the body of the tame elephant, who immediately throws the wild one down; a battle then ensues, in which the trained elephant, being assisted by its associates, soon overpowers the inhabitant of the woods, who is deserted by all the others; it is afterwards borne away a prisoner, fast bound to two of its captors, whilst another moves on at its head, and a fourth

Drawn by Singey Bey. Engraved by T. Medland.

Method of Catching Wild Elephants in Ava.

London, Published Nov.r 1 1799, by G. Nicol, Pall Mall & J. Wright Piccadilly.

urges it behind. In a few weeks, by proper discipline, the animal becomes docile, and submits to its fate. Those that are taken in the manner delineated in the Plate, I was told, are for the most part females. Male elephants are usually enticed by the blandishments of females,* trained for the purpose, into an inclosure or Keddah, from whence they cannot extricate themselves, and are easily secured. My painter performed the task so much to his Majesty's satisfaction, that a request was made for his further services, in executing a drawing of a celebrated image of Gaudma, in which I willingly acquiesced. He was employed on it a week, and when it was finished, his Majesty condescended to express his approbation of the performance, which was certainly much superior to any thing that his own painter could produce.

Among the articles of foreign trade, which had found their way into the Birman country, nothing was held in higher estimation than the European glass ware, imported into Rangoon from the British settlements in India. The art of vitrification has long been known and practised in most countries of the East; but no where can they make a pure transparent substance, like that which is brought from Europe. The Birman monarch, who is a great admirer of the manufacture, was particularly desirous to introduce it into his dominions; and supposing that every Englishman must be versed in the knowledge of making whatever comes from his own country, he sent a message to request I would furnish his artificers with such instructions, as might enable them to fabricate glass of a quality equal to

* For a more ample description of the manner of catching wild elephants in Tipura, near the mountains that divide Bengal from the Birman dominions, see a Paper by John Corse, Esq. in the third Volume of the Asiat. Researches. The practice of Pegue differs somewhat from that of the Bengal hunters.

what was made in England. Unluckily, none of us happened to be skilled in the mystery of a glass-house; all, therefore, that we could do, was to explain the principles of the art, which Dr. Buchanan obligingly undertook; and in order to facilitate the acquirement, and guide them in the practice, I lent them the Encyclopædia Britannica, and pointed out the article where the process is fully explained. Baba Sheen and the Armenian interpreter translated it into the Birman tongue; but I much fear that the theory alone, conveyed in terms of science, will not, without practical experience, advance them very far in an art which his Birman Majesty is so laudably solicitous to bring to perfection among his subjects.

It was a matter too remarkable to pass unnoticed, that of the numbers who did me the honour of a visit, there was not one that had any share in the administration of public affairs, the Woondock that met me at Pegahm excepted, who, though of distinguished rank, is but an inferior minister: none of the Woongees or Attawoons condescended to pay me the compliment. The Maywoon of Pegue sometimes honoured me with his company: his official consequence, however, was here diminished into insignificance, notwithstanding he was of the highest order, except one, of nobility, wearing a tzaloe of nine strings.

When a public minister is delegated from a foreign power to the Birman court, it is the established custom for the Maywoon, or governor of the frontier province which the minister first enters, to provide for his safe conveyance to the capital, and to attend to his convenience so long as he continues to reside in the country; a service which he is frequently obliged to perform in person, as in the present case of the English deputation. The governor of Bamoo, the province bordering on Yunan, performed the office to our Chinese neighbours with the utmost kindness and

Drawn by Singey Bey. Engraved by T. Holland.

Image of the Birman Gaudma in a Temple at Ummerapoora.

London, Published Nov'r 1 1799 by G. Nicol, Pall Mall & J. Wright, Piccadilly.

urbanity, and in his frequent visits to them took the opportunity of calling upon me. He was a sensible man, exceedingly courteous in his manners and address; he said he had been twice to Pekin in the capacity of legate before he obtained his present station: he described the journey as very fatiguing, but, at the proper season, not at all perilous; he was upwards of three months in performing it. The road from the frontiers of the province of Bamoo, until he penetrated far into Manchegee, or Yunan, lay through mountains: during the last thirty days he travelled in a boat on canals and rivers. He informed me that there were two languages spoken in China, one the Tirroup, or native Chinese; the other the Tarrait, or Tartar tongue: the latter is the language of the conquerors. The Birmans have not liberty to pass at will into the Chinese territory, or the Chinese into that of the Birmans; but the Governor has power to grant passports. He gave me an impression of the Chop, or seal, which he was accustomed to affix to such papers, and likewise promised me a chart of his route to Pekin, which he afterwards presented to me. I had various occasions to acknowledge the attentions and kindness of this truly well bred and intelligent man, who seemed to have profited from his travels, and to have overcome that affected reserve which is the national characteristic of a Birman courtier.

On the 15th of August, the arrival of a messenger from Rangoon, sent by Captain Thomas, as the bearer of letters and newspapers that had been brought from Calcutta, diffused among us that satisfaction which they only, who have been in remote countries, and long absent from their friends, can truly estimate; it was the first communication we had received since our departure from Bengal, and the situation of affairs in Europe was at that time extremely interesting.

In addition to the comfort we experienced from living at ease, and having every want liberally supplied, our gratitude was due to providence for the inestimable blessing of health, which we enjoyed to a degree that fully evinced the salubrity of the climate; not a symptom of sickness, in a single instance excepted, had manifested itself among our people; but this was not the case with our Chinese neighbours; they were less fortunate, a dysentery, which had early attacked the senior member of the embassy, began to spread among his domestics; and although they were not numerous, we heard of frequent deaths, and of general illness among them. As no doubt could be entertained of the healthiness of the situation we were in, their malady was to be ascribed to some other cause than the atmosphere. The Governor of Bamoo, however, explained the matter very sensibly, by observing, that the sickness under which they alone laboured, entirely originated in their own indolence, and in the pernicious diet that they used. The Chinese are said to be nationally great lovers of swine's flesh, and these personages possessed all the partiality of their country for that unclean animal; they had erected a pigstye within the inclosure of their dwelling, where they fed pork for their own table, and, as a matter of compliment, sometimes sent a joint of the meat to me; but though it seemed to be good, we could not bring ourselves to use it. In addition to the ill effects of such gross food, they took no exercise, and drank immoderately of shouchow, a fiery and deleterious spirit. The Governor of Bamoo, who accounted for the cause of their ailment, condemned their sensuality, which, he said, he had in vain endeavoured to correct by advice and persuasion. At length the principal legate became so seriously ill that his life was judged to be in danger: the governor, anxious for the preservation of a person whose safety was in some degree entrusted to his care, with a humanity that did him honour, applied to me for medical assistance. Dr. Buchanan willingly accompanied him to the sick man's chamber, and on examining his patient, immediately perceived that the case was desperate. He was an emaciated old man, reduced by a disease of such long continuance, as to leave no prospect of recovery: medicines, however, were administered, which, though they afforded but a temporary relief, raised a fallacious hope in the breast of the sufferer, who expressed the utmost anxiety to be able to attend on the day appointed for our public reception, at which time the Chinese deputies were likewise to be introduced: they had before been admitted to an informal audience of the King, when the court was at Meengoung, soon after their first arrival, where his Majesty met them as though by chance. It is not usual for the King to receive public ministers ceremoniously except in the metropolis.

As the time approached that was appointed for our public entry into Ummerapoora, which as yet we had only viewed from our residence on the opposite bank of the lake, I judged it proper to make some enquiry respecting the ceremonials usually observed on such occasions, and the exterior forms of homage that would be required. I wished also to ascertain the relative degree of rank that would be granted to the agent of the Governor-General of India; and as I was officially given to understand that the Chinese deputies were to be introduced on the same day, I urged my right to precedence, on the thorough persuasion that they did not constitute an imperial embassy, but were merely a provincial legation, although probably sanctioned by the monarch of China.

The necessity of ascertaining these points became evident, from the scrupulous regard to external forms, which the Birmans manifested upon every occasion. The Maywoon of Pegue being the channel of my official communication, I received through him, in reply to my first application, a general assurance of due attention, but an equivocal answer with respect to the Chinese. Repeating the requisition for satisfactory particulars, I was informed that I should be allowed parity of rank with the nobility of the court, and that precedence over the Chinese deputies would be granted to me. With those assurances I remained satisfied.

On the 29th of August, the day preceding that of our formal introduction, I received a message, desiring to know what number of attendants I meant to take with me, and to specify the rank they bore, particularly that of the Pundit, the Moonshee, and painter. I was at the same time acquainted, that it was not customary to admit armed men into the palace, a form to which I readily assented. Late in the evening another message was brought to inform me, that the profession of Dr. Buchanan was held by the Birmans in a less dignified estimation than it bore among us; and that it was unusual, on such solemn occasions, to receive a person of his station into the Lotoo, or great council hall. I took some pains to vindicate the dignity of the liberal and enlightened profession of medicine, and explained to them, that there was no monarch of Europe who did not consider a physician as worthy to hold a place in the most distinguished ranks of society. This difficulty was at length conquered; they agreed to receive the Doctor, but stipulated that he should ride on horseback in the procession, and not be indulged with an elephant, a privilege which, they said, was granted only to persons of the highest consequence.

Preparatory to our visit, the presents intended for his Majesty were carefully assorted, and put into separate boxes: they were both handsome and costly, consisting of various kinds of European and Indian articles, such as mirrors, cut-glass, fire-arms, broad cloths, embroidered muslins, and

Indian silks, all of the finest quality that could be procured; among other things there was a Shanscrit manuscript, superbly illumined, and written with beautiful minuteness; it was a copy of the Bagwaat Geeta, inclosed in a case of gold, and designed as a personal compliment from Sir John Shore, the Governor-General, to his Birman Majesty: there was also an electrical machine, of the effects of which some of the Birmans were not ignorant.* The boxes were covered with red satin, and fastened to poles, for the convenience of being carried on men's shoulders. Every matter was arranged on the day before the ceremony was to take place.

On the 30th of August we took an early breakfast, and about eight o'clock a Sere-dogee, or secretary of the Lotoo, came to acquaint us that boats were prepared to convey us across the lake. Our domestics had received orders to hold themselves in readiness, dressed in the livery of the embassy, and the guard was paraded without arms. The presents having been sent before, we walked to the water side, attended by Baba-Sheen, the Sere-dogee, and several inferior officers; at the same time the two junior members of the Chinese mission, the senior being now at the point of death, came forth from the gate of their enclosure, attended by a retinue comparatively very small. We found three war-boats at the bank ready to receive us; these boats were sufficiently capacious for the number they were destined to contain: the largest was of fifty oars, but they were not above one-third manned, probably with a view to our accommodation, as the vessels are so narrow, that persons unaccustomed to them cannot sit between the rowers without inconvenience: it did not, however, escape our notice, that they were quite plain, without either gilding or paint. We were about twenty minutes in rowing to the opposite side of the lake, and found a crowd of people collected

* An electrifying machine had been introduced several years ago by a Frenchman.

near the water's edge to see us land. The place where we landed appeared to be nearly a mile, in a direct line, below the fort, the southern walls of which are washed by the lake when the waters are swollen. Three elephants and several horses were waiting to convey us, and some Birman officers of inferior consequence attended at the bank, dressed in their robes and caps of ceremony. The furniture of the animals we were to ride was far from being superb. Men of rank in the Birman empire always guide their own elephants, and sit on the neck, in the same manner that the drivers, or mohaats, do in India: owing to this custom they are unprovided with those commodious seats in which an Indian gentleman reposes at ease on the back of this noble beast, whilst the government of it is entrusted to another person. A large wicker basket, somewhat resembling the body of an open carriage, but smaller, without any elevated seat, and covered with carpets at the bottom, was fastened on the back of the elephant by means of iron chains that passed under his belly, and were prevented from chafing him by tanned ox-hides. This equipage was neither comfortable nor elegant; but as I had not learned how to manage an elephant, and ride between his ears, there was no alternative; I was obliged either to take what was provided, or submit to a less dignified conveyance. The drivers, instead of making the beast kneel down to receive his rider, as is the custom in other countries, drove him up to a temporary stage that had been erected for the purpose of mounting. Each of the Chinese deputies was also honoured with an elephant. Mr. Wood and Dr. Buchanan rode on handsome spirited horses, of the small Pegue breed, which had been prepared for them, and were equipped with much better furniture than was assigned to the elephants. The Birman saddles, however, not being well calculated for the ease of an European rider, two of English manufacture, which we had brought with us, were substituted in their stead. The moonshee, the pundit, and the painter were likewise permitted to ride on horseback. After we had adjusted the ceremonial of mounting, the procession was marshalled in the following order:

A Sandohgaan, or master of the ceremonies, on horseback;

An Oniroupseree, or register of strangers, on horseback;

A Letzounseree, or register of presents, on horseback;

dressed in their official robes and caps.

Soldiers that composed the escort.

The elephant of the representative of the Governor-General.

Mr. Wood and Dr. Buchanan, on horseback.

Baba-Sheen, as chief interpreter.

The Chinese deputies, on elephants, preceded by their servants, bearing flags.

A Woondock, or second counsellor of state.

Two Terrezogees, or officers who hold judiciary stations.

The servants of the embassy walked on each side, two by two; and a number of constables attended, with long white rods, to keep off the populace.

The procession being thus arranged, we commenced our march, keeping a moderate pace, so as not to distress the bearers of the presents. After proceeding a short way, we entered a wide and handsome street, that was paved with brick: the houses on each side were low, built of wood, and covered with tiles; they had been evidently prepared for the occasion, being fresh whitewashed, and decorated with boughs and flowers; the shops, which are usually open towards the street, displayed their best goods. In front of each house was a slight latticed railing of bamboo, advanced into the street, to the distance of three or four feet; over this space was spread a shade of bamboo mats, that reached from the eaves of the houses to the railing, forming a sort of covered balcony, every one of which was crowded with spectators, men and women indiscriminately. Boys sat on the tops of the houses, and the streets were so thronged as to leave only a sufficient space for the procession to move without interruption; but what rendered the scene most remarkable was, the posture which the multitude preserved; every person, as soon as we came in sight, squatted on his hams, and continued in that attitude until we had passed by: this was an indication of high respect. Throughout the crowd there was no disturbance or any extraordinary noise; the populace looked up and gazed in silence, nor did they attempt to follow us, but were satisfied with a transient view. The Pagwaats, or constables, armed with long rods, sometimes affected to strike those who were most forward, in order to make them recede; but in this act they humanely avoided hurting any one, generally directing the blow to the ground close to those whom they intended to remove. Thus we passed through several wide streets, running in a strait direction, and often crossed by others at right angles. We perceived only two brick houses, and these we were informed belonged to foreigners. Contiguous to the fort was a small street, entirely occupied by the shops of silversmiths, who exhibited their wares in the open balcony, and displayed a great variety of Birman utensils in plate. The distance from the landing-place to this street we computed to be two miles. Immediately after we crossed the ditch of the fort, which was wide, deep, and faced with brick, but had little water in it: the passage was over a causeway formed on a mound of earth, in which there was a chasm of about ten feet to carry off the rain, and across this a strong bridge of planks was laid. Between the bridge and the foot of the wall, there was a space, eighty or a hundred feet wide, on which two redoubts were raised to defend the passage of the ditch; the rampart, faced by a wall of brick, was about twenty feet high, exclusive of the parapet, which had embrasures for cannon, and apertures for musquetry. Small demi-bastions projected at regular distances beyond the wall, but they did not appear to contain sufficient space to admit of heavy ordnance. The body of the rampart was composed of earth, sustained externally and within by strong walls: the gate was massive, with a wicket in it, and the fort altogether, considered as an eastern fortification, was respectable, but insufficient to resist the approaches of an enemy skilled in the science of war. The Birmans, however, believe it to be impregnable; they put their trust in the height and solidity of their wall, which they conceive to be strong enough to resist all assaults, independent of the cover of a glacis, or any other advanced work than the ditch. I did not attempt to mortify their pride by telling them a disagreeable truth, that a battery of half a dozen cannon would, in a few hours, reduce their walls to a heap of ruins; and, indeed, if I had told them so, it is probable they might not have credited the information.

We entered by the western gate: there was little distinction between the houses in the fort and those of the city, except that the dwellings of persons of official consequence, and the members of the royal family, who resided within the walls, were surrounded by a wooden partition, that inclosed a court. We passed, making several angles in our way, through a market supplied with rice, pulse, and other vegetables, but saw neither meat nor fish. At the distance of two short streets from the palace, we came to a spot where bamboo stages were erected for us to alight, similar to those at the landing-place; here we dismounted, and walked in the same order as we had rode. Coming to the top of a short street leading down to the palace, we were desired by the Sandohgaan, or master of the ceremonies, through Baba-Sheen, to stop and make obeisance to the residence of majesty, by a gentle inclination of the body, and raising the hand to the head, as they did; a desire with which I complied, although I conceived the distance so great as hardly to require that mark of respect. When we had proceeded two or three hundred yards farther, the Sandohgaan repeated the ceremony of bowing, to which I offered no objection, nor should I have felt the smallest reluctance in complying, had not the manner of the Sandohgaan been what I considered extremely disrespectful. Thus we proceeded, until we came to the rhoom, which was a lofty hall, raised four or five feet from the ground, and open on all sides; it was situated about a hundred yards from the gate of the palace court, on the left hand, and in the centre of a spacious area. Putting off our shoes we entered the saloon, and sat down on carpets that were spread for us, with our faces towards the palace gate: here the presents were deposited, whilst the Chinese deputies took their places on the other side.

It was now about ten o'clock, and the Woondock intimated that we must wait until all the princes of the royal family arrived, before it would be proper for us to enter: we had sat but a short time, when the Prince of Pegahm, the junior of the King's sons, in point of rank though not in years, being born of a different mother, made his appearance. He was mounted on the neck of a very fine elephant, which he guided himself, sitting on a scarlet cloth embroidered with gold, whilst a servant behind, on the back of the animal, screened him from the sun with a gilded parasol. About fifty musqueteers led the way; these were followed by a number of halberdiers, carrying spears with gilded shafts, and decorated with gold tassels. Six or eight officers of his household (each of the King's sons have a separate establishment) came next, dressed in velvet robes with embroidered caps, and chains of gold depending from the left shoulder to the right side; these immediately preceded the prince's elephant: another body of spearmen, with his palanquin of state, closed the procession. On entering the gate, he gave to one of his attendants a polished iron hook, with which he governed his elephant; as not any thing that can be used as a weapon is suffered to be brought within the precincts of the palace, not even by his Majesty's sons. The prince's escort halted without the gate, and the greater number of his attendants were stopped, those only being admitted who were of higher rank, together with the men who carried his large beetle-box of gold, and his flaggon of water, which are brought rather for state than for refreshment. When the prince had alighted, his elephant returned, and all the attendants ranged themselves in the area between the rhoom and the palace gate. Soon after the Prince of Pegahm had entered, the Prince of Tongho, the next in precedence, appeared; he was attended by a suite nearly similar to that of his brother; and in succession came the Princes of Bassein and of Prome: the Engy Teekien, or heir apparent, came last; when he arrived it was twelve o'clock, which, the great drum, that proclaims the hours, sounded from a lofty tower near the palace. The state in which the latter personage made his public entrance was highly superb, and becoming his elevated station. He was preceded by a numerous body guard of infantry, consisting of four or five hundred men, armed with musquets, who marched in regular files, and were uniformly clothed and accoutred; next came a party of Cassay troopers, habited in their fanciful dress, with high conical caps bending backwards. We were told that through respect they had alighted from their horses nearly at the same place where we had dismounted. Twenty or thirty men followed these, holding long gilded wands; then came eighteen or twenty military officers of rank, with gilded helmets; next the civil officers of his household and his council, wearing the tzaloe, or chain of nobility, and arrayed in their robes and caps of state, varied according to their respective ranks. The Prince, borne on men's shoulders, in a very rich palanquin, but without any canopy, followed; he was screened from the sun by a large gilded fan, supported by a nobleman, and on each side of his palanquin walked six Cassay astrologers, of the Braminical sect, dressed in white gowns and white caps, studded with stars of gold; close behind, his servants carried his water-flaggon, and a gold beetle-box, of a size which appeared to be no inconsiderable load for a man. Several elephants and led horses with rich housings came after; some inferior officers, and a body of spearmen, with three companies of musqueteers, one clothed in blue, another in green, and a third in red, concluded the procession.

In every part of this ostentatious parade perfect regularity was maintained, which considerably increased the effect. All things seemed to have been carefully predisposed and properly arranged. If it was less splendid than imperial Delhi, in the days of Mogul magnificence, it was far more decorous than any court of Hindostan at the present day. The rabble was not tumultuous, the attendants and soldiery were silent, and every man seemed to know his own place. No noisy heralds, as is the custom in India, ran before, vociferating titles, and overturning people in their way. The display of this day was solemn and dignified, and I doubt much whether, in any other capital, such multitudes could be brought together with so little confusion; as, besides the attendants and the military there were many thousands of spectators.

Our delay in the rhoom had now been protracted to two hours, a circumstance which, though it gratified our curiosity with a novel and most interesting spectacle, yet could not be considered as a mark of respect, especially as we had not the company of any person of distinguished rank, the junior Woondock excepted, who staid with us but a very short time. The attendance of the Maywoon of Pegue, was, according to the usage of the country, on this occasion our undoubted right; and the example of the Viceroy of Bamoo, who paid that compliment to the Chinese deputies, placed the omission in a more striking point of view, whilst the singular character of the people put it out of my power, to attribute the neglect to chance, or to casual inadvertency.

A few minutes after the Engy Teekien, or Prince Royal, had entered, we received a summons, in compliance with which we proceeded from the rhoom, observing the same order as before; the presents carried in front, and the members of the Chinese embassy following the English deputation. As we proceeded, the Sandohgaan was exceedingly troublesome, by calling on us to make frequent superfluous obeisances, whilst his manner of requiring them was conspicuously uncivil. I checked his insolence by observing, through Baba Sheen, that if he wished me to proceed, he must alter his tone and demeanour. This reproof, however, had only a momentary effect; he soon resumed his arrogant behaviour, which he repeated throughout the day, whenever opportunity offered.

On approaching the gate, the greater part of our attendants were stopped, and not permitted to follow us; and we were desired to put off our shoes, with which we immediately complied.

The area we now entered was spacious, and contained the Lotoo, or grand hall of consultation and of audience, where the Woongees meet in council, and where affairs of state are discussed and determined. Within this inclosure there is an inner court, separated by a brick wall, which comprehends the palace, and all the buildings annexed to the royal residence. Within the gate a troop of tumblers were performing their feats, while dancing girls were exhibiting their graces in the open air, and on the bare ground, to the sound of no very harmonious music. We were next ushered up a flight of stairs into a very noble saloon, or open hall, called the Lotoo, where the court was assembled in all the pomp that Birman grandeur could display. On entering this hall, a stranger cannot fail to be surprised at the magnificence of its appearance; it is supported by seventy-seven pillars, disposed in eleven rows, each consisting of seven. The space between the pillars I judged to be about twelve feet, except the central row, which was probably two feet wider. The roof of the building is composed of distinct stages, the highest in the centre. The row of pillars that supported the middle, or most lofty roof, we judged to be thirty-five or forty feet in height; the others gradually diminish as they approach the extremities of the building, and those which sustain the balcony are not more than twelve or fourteen feet. At the farther part of the hall there is a high gilded lattice, extending quite across the building, and in the centre of the lattice is a gilded door, which, when opened, displays the throne; this door is elevated five or six feet from the floor, so that the throne must be ascended by means of steps at the back, which are not visible, nor is the seat of the throne to be seen, except when the King comes in person to the Lotoo. At the bottom of the lattice there is a gilt balustrade, three or four feet high, in which the umbrellas and several other insignia of state were deposited. The royal colour is white, and the umbrellas were made of silk of that colour, richly bespangled with gold. Within this magnificent saloon were seated, on their inverted legs, all the princes and the principal nobility of the Birman empire, each person in the place appropriated to his particular rank and station: proximity to the throne is, of course, the most honourable situation; and this station was occupied by the princes of the blood, the Woongees, the Attawoons, and other great officers of state. The Engy Teekien (or heir apparent) sat on a small stool, about six inches high; the other princes on fine mats. The space between the central pillars that front the throne, is always left vacant, for this curious reason, that his Majesty's eyes may not be obliged to behold those, whom he does not mean to honour with a look. The place allotted for us was next to this unoccupied part, but we afterwards discovered that the Chinese deputies had taken possession of those seats which, according to the etiquette that had been agreed upon, the English gentlemen were to have occupied. So trivial a circumstance would not have merited attention, had it not been followed by circumstances which left no room to suppose, that any act relating to external forms was either accidental or unpremeditated, on the part of those who regulated the ceremonials.

After we had taken possession of mats that had been spread for us, it was civilly intimated that we ought not to protrude the soles of our feet towards the seat of majesty, but should endeavour to sit in the posture that was observed by those around us. With this desire we would readily have complied, if it had been in our power, but we had not yet learned to sit upon our own legs: the flexibility of muscles which the Birmans, and indeed all the natives of India, possess, is such, as cannot be acquired by Europeans. A Birman, when he sits, seldom touches the seat with his posteriors, but is supported by his heels. It is scarcely practicable for an European, dressed in close garments, to place himself in such an attitude; and if he were able, it would be out of his power to continue long in it. We inverted our legs as much as possible, and the awkwardness with which we did this excited a smile from some; not a word, however, was uttered, and our endeavours, I thought, seemed to give satisfaction. In a few minutes eight Bramins, dressed in white sacerdotal gowns, and silk caps of the same colour, studded with gold, assembled round the foot of the throne, within the balustrade, and recited a long prayer in not unpleasing recitative; this ceremony lasted a quarter of an hour. When they had withdrawn, the letter from the Governor-General, which I delivered to a Woondock, was placed on a silver tray in front of the railing, and a Sandohgaan, or reader, advanced into the vacant space, and made three prostrations, touching the ground each time with his forehead; he then read, or rather chanted, in a loud voice, what I understood was a Birman translation of the letter. When this was done, the reader repeated his prostrations, and next proclaimed a list of the presents for the King. These several readings being finished, he repeated his obeisances and retired: after an interval of a few minutes, an officer, entitled Nakhaangee, advanced, and proposed a question to me, as if from his Majesty; on receiving my answer he withdrew, as it might be supposed, to communicate the reply; and returned in an adequate time to ask another: thus he put three separate questions to me, which were as follows: "You come from a distant country; how long is it since you arrived? How were the King, Queen, and royal family of England, when the last accounts came from thence? Was England at peace or war with other nations? and was your country in a state of disturbance?"

The latter question alone contained more than words of compliment and ceremony, and coming in such a solemn manner, required a clear and determinate answer on my part. I replied in the Persian language—"that Great Britain was at enmity with France; that the continent of Europe was the seat of war; but that the kingdom of England enjoyed perfect tranquillity, which it was not probable would be disturbed." This interrogation seemed to indicate that the Birmans had received impressions of our situation in Europe from no very favourable quarter; and I had afterwards occasion to know, that the unremitting and restless industry of French propagators had pervaded even this remote region, and though, in such a country, they dare not avow their equalizing principles, they left no art unpractised, through the means of their emissaries, to insinuate doubts, excite fears, and create distrust of the English.

These were all the questions that were proposed; neither the Chinese nor any other person being interrogated. In a few minutes after my last reply had been conveyed, a very handsome desert was brought in, and set before us; it consisted of a variety of sweetmeats, as well China as Birman; læpack, or pickled tea-leaf, and beetle, formed part of the entertainment, which was served up in silver, china, and glass-ware: there appeared to be not less than an hundred different small dishes: we tasted of a few, and found some of them very palatable; but none of the courtiers partook, or moved from their places. About half an hour had elapsed, when we were informed by the Sandohgaan that there was no occasion for us to remain any longer. The non-appearance of his Majesty was a considerable disappointment, as I had been taught to expect that he would have received the Governor-General's letter in person: it was not, however, until some time afterwards, that I was made acquainted with the true reason of his absence.

When we rose to leave the Lotoo, the Sandohgaan desired us to make three obeisances to the throne, by a slight inclination of the body and raising the right hand to the head; we were then reconducted to the saloon, where we were informed it was necessary we should remain until the princes came forth from the palace, and had got upon their elephants, as their etiquette did not allow any person, on such occasions, to mount before the members of the royal family; we accordingly took our places in this hall as before: shortly afterwards the court broke up with as much form and parade as it had assembled.

The ceremony of departure differed from that of entrance: the Engy Teekien came out first, who went in last; next followed the other members of the royal family in rotation, and after them came the Chobwaas, or petty tributary princes: these are personages who, before the Birmans had extended their conquests over the vast territory they now possess, had held small independent sovereignties, which they were able to maintain so long as the balance of power continued doubtful between the Birmans, Peguers, and Siamese; but the decided success that has attended the Birman arms since the accession of the present family, having deprived them of their independence, their countries are now reduced to subordinate provinces of the Birman empire. As many of their governors as confidence could be placed in, and who were willing to take the oath of allegiance to their conquerors, were continued in the management of their former possessions, and are obliged to make an annual visit to the capital, to pay homage in person at the golden feet. The moderation, as well as the policy of this measure, is said to have fully answered the ends that were proposed.

As soon as the royal family had departed, we returned to the place where we had left our elephants, and proceeded home, with this difference, that the Chinese deputies, who had followed us to the palace, preceded us in our return; a circumstance which, in addition to several others, gave me cause to attribute want of ingenuousness to those, who had the management of the ceremonials. My claim of precedence had been unconditionally stipulated and admitted; a precedence, which the certainty that the Chinese deputies constituted only a provincial mission of very inferior consideration, gave me an undoubted title to demand.

With a people less attentive to punctilio, or less regardful of the privileges and external indications of rank, I should certainly not have considered it necessary to controvert matters of no intrinsic moment in themselves, but which, when intended to produce an effect on the minds of those who can only judge from appearances, become to a person in a public capacity, of real importance. Every occurrence of this day, and every object that presented itself, evinced the previous care that had been bestowed on the minutest points of etiquette: the utmost splendour of the court had been displayed on the occasion; and I was credibly informed, that the non-appearance of his Majesty was neither customary when a foreign minister from a sovereign state was to be introduced, nor owing to any accidental prevention; but that it was a matter predetermined, in order to afford a pretext for spreading abroad that the representative of the English nation had delivered his dispatches, and tendered tribute (for so they denominated the presents), without being honoured by an interview of their King. These apparent indications of arrogance, which were not diminished by the unworthy artifice of making me believe, that his Majesty was to have received in person the letter from the Governor-General, as coming from a sovereign and an equal power, gave me reasonable grounds to be dissatisfied with the manner in which the ceremonials had been conducted, and made me suspect the real light in which it was the wish of the court that I should be considered. As nothing, however, degrading to my public character had yet been avowed, I refrained from any formal declaration of my sentiments till subsequent circumstances confirmed my conjectures, and rendered an explanation unavoidable.

We did not arrive at our dwelling in the grove, till past three o'clock. In our way home the spectators were few, in comparison with the numbers collected to gaze at us when we went. The day had been oppressively hot, we were nevertheless highly gratified by the scene we had beheld, which was uncommonly splendid, and in every respect suited to the dignity of an imperial court. The evening, however, proved cool, and refreshing breezes recompensed us for the sultriness of the day, the transactions of which supplied an interesting topic of conversation until the hour of repose.

CHAPTER XVI.

Presents expected by the principal Officers—of trivial Value—Matter of Form.—Visit the Engy Teekien—Conduct of the public Officers more respectful.—Splendour of the Court.—Engy Teekien—Ceremony at departing.—Chobwas, or tributary Princes.—Meedaw Praw—a Princess of high Dignity—her Court—venerable Person—Curiosity—Politeness.—Visit to the Princes of Prome—of Bassien—of Tongho—and of Pegahm—Reception at their respective Courts.—View the Piedigaut Tiek, or Royal Library.—Noises renewed by the Chinese.—Effects of Despotism.—Pride of the Ministers.—Insurmountable Difficulty in a Point of Etiquette.—Politeness of the Governor of Bamoo.—Visit to the Seredaw Poundagee Praw, or Arch Priest.—Magnificent Kioum.—Numerous religious Buildings.—Knebang Kioum—a beautiful Building—to what Purpose applied.—A Kioum of extraordinary Splendour.—Visit the Arracan Gaudma—enthusiastic Adoration of the Multitude.—Chounda, or Place of Accommodation for Strangers.—Partake of Refreshment.—Return.—Description of the Fort of Ummerapoora.

THE next morning, August 31st, the Shawbunder of Rangoon, and Baba-Sheen, waited on us with information, that as our formal introduction was now past, I might command elephants and horses to go wheresoever I pleased; and that they had received an order to attend, and to shew me whatever was most worthy the notice of a stranger. They intimated also that the Engy Teekien, or heir apparent, was to hold a court on the following day for the purpose of our introduction, and that our attendance would be expected about the hour of noon. These instructions they had received from the Maywoon of Pegue, to whom I wrote in reply, that as the stipulated formalities, which had been agreed to by all parties, had been infringed on the preceding day, it became necessary, before I could accept of the prince's invitation, to receive a positive assurance, that they would be better observed on this occasion. I likewise represented the conduct of the Sandohgaan as obviously disrespectful, and hoped that he would not be allowed to officiate again on our introduction; but, above all, I desired to be explicitly informed, whether or not, the Engy Teekien purposed to appear in person, without which I could not possibly think of attending his court.

To this letter I received a civil reply, in the Persian language, assuring me that some part of what to me seemed objectionable, originated in mistake; that the Sandohgaan should be confined for his improper conduct; and that the prince intended to receive me in person: these assurances, coming from such a quarter, were perfectly satisfactory.

Since my arrival I had been apprized of a circumstance, of which I was before unaware, that it was customary for a person in a public capacity, to present something of the manufacture of his country, or some rarity, to each member of the royal family to whom he is introduced; it was likewise usual, though not indispensably necessary, to pay the same compliment to the chief ministers and the principal officers of the court. This present being no more than a piece or two of muslin, or silk, was too trifling to be regarded by the individuals, for its value; it was, nevertheless, expected, and the omission would be considered as unhandsome: in addition, therefore, to the things that I had brought with me, I gave directions to purchase such articles of European and Indian manufacture, as were most esteemed, and could be procured; these I allotted agreeably to the instructions of Baba-Sheen and the Shawbunder, who were so good as to acquaint me with the established forms, and the proportion to be presented to each person.

At nine o'clock on the first of September we crossed the river, nearly with the same attendance as on the former day. In consequence of an application I had made to the Maywoon of Pegue, elephants were now provided for Mr. Wood and Dr. Buchanan. This was a circumstance which neither the gentlemen themselves, nor I should have deemed of sufficient importance to deserve any attention, had not the junior members of the Chinese embassy been supplied with them; but as these people paid such strict attention to the minutest article, expressive of relative rank, I did not think it right, that the gentlemen with me, should be considered in a degree inferior to the subordinate members of a provincial delegation, of which, an acquiescence in a less dignified mode of conveyance than the Chinese were allowed, would, on my part, have been a tacit admission.

We proceeded through the city by the route we pursued before, with the presents carried in front, and observing the same order of procession. Many of the houses were decorated with flower-pots and garlands, but the spectators were by no means so numerous as when we made our first entrance. We dismounted at the top of a street within a few hundred yards of the surrounding wall of the prince's palace, where stages had been erected for our convenience; from thence we were conducted to the Rhoom, which was situated a little to the right hand of the principal gate; there was another building of a similar kind opposite to us, which we were informed was used only for trials, and the transaction of public business; but the one that we occupied, was appropriated to ceremony and state. In the formalities of this day, a much more respectful demeanour was preserved towards us, than on the former occasion, and we sat in the Rhoom with better company. Two Woondocks, the master of the elephants, and some other officers, bearing emblems of rank, attended us; another Sandohgaan also officiated in the ceremonials, and behaved very differently from the person, whose manners had been so offensive, and whom I did not observe at court on this day. This conduct fully compensated for the former incivility, though perhaps the Sandohgaan did not receive any severe reprehension for what he had done.

The King of the Birmans, who seems to have a parental fondness for all his children, is said to be particularly attached to the Engy Teekien, or eldest prince; and with a liberal policy has granted him a share in the government, almost equal to what he himself exercises. The establishment of the heir apparent is becoming his high station and future expectations; and his Woon or chief minister stands among the foremost of the Birman nobles, in reputation for wisdom and integrity.

There was little in the etiquette of this day, different from that of the visit to his Majesty: we waited in the Rhoom until all the younger princes had arrived, which they did as before, in rotation, beginning with the junior. The members of the royal family went within the gate, before they alighted from their elephants and palanquins, but the ministers and the nobility dismounted on the outside, and proceeded on foot. After each person had entered, the gate was immediately closed, and opened as soon as another visitant presented himself. When we advanced to the gate we expected it would have been instantly thrown open to admit us; a delay, however, occurred, which at first I was inclined to attribute to some accidental circumstance; but after I had waited some minutes under a burning sun, finding that there was an unnecessary and apparently a studied protraction, I turned round and walked towards the Rhoom; on this, the door was immediately opened, and the interior court, on the right hand of the gate, as we entered, displayed several men dancing in masquerade, and on the left was a band of musicians, and a set of dancing girls without masks. A little farther on, there were two handsome houses; one of masonry, with doors and windows closely resembling Gothic structure, flat roofed, and of a peculiar, but far from inelegant, construction; the other was of wood. We were conducted to the latter, and ascended into a capacious saloon, open on three sides. Here we found the court assembled, nearly in the same manner as at the Lotoo. The hall consisted of six rows of pillars, seven in each row: there was neither gilding nor paint bestowed on them, such ornaments being strictly confined to the sovereign and the priesthood. The naked pillars gave a very rude appearance to the apartment, which was disadvantageously contrasted, with the brilliant dresses of the courtiers. We occupied the same relative position to the rest of the assembly, as at the Lotoo, with this difference, that the gentlemen of the English mission had the place assigned to them, which the Chinese deputies, either through mistake, or design, possessed on the former day. At one end of the saloon, against a wainscot, stood the prince's sofa of state, covered with embroidered cloth, and on each side were ranged several utensils of gold of a very large size; such as his beetle-box, cup, spitting-pot, and water-flaggon: above the sofa there was a window in the wainscot, six or eight feet from the ground, with folding shutters, that were closed when we entered the hall. Soon after we had taken our seats, four Bramins dressed in white sacerdotal garments, chanted a prayer that lasted a quarter of an hour; their devotions being finished, the window beforementioned suddenly opened, and discovered the Engy Teekien seated behind it. The courtiers immediately bent their bodies, and sat in a crouching attitude, with their hands joined: the English gentlemen joined their hands like the rest of the company. The prince seemed to be about twenty-eight or thirty years of age, of an open countenance, and rather inclined to corpulency; but of his person we could not judge, as his head and shoulders only were visible. His habit, as much as could be seen of it, shone with gold, and he wore on his head, a pyramidical cap that glistened exceedingly, but of its real richness we could not form any estimate, being at too great a distance. A list of the presents was then recited in a loud voice by a reader, kneeling in front of the sofa; after which total silence prevailed throughout the assembly; not a word was spoken by the prince; he noticed no one, but sat erect and motionless, without appearing to look either to the right or the left. About a quarter of an hour elapsed in this dumb interview, when on a sudden, by some agency invisible to us, the window-shutters were closed, and we saw him no more.

A very handsome desert was then served up, on dishes spread on gilded trays. We tasted of several things, and, when the repast was ended, returned to the Rhoom, in which we remained until the royal family passed by. As much form was observed this day, as when the court assembled at the Lotoo; and the demonstrations of respect manifested towards the Engy Teekien, as well by his brothers, as by inferior subjects, fell little short of what is offered to the sovereign himself, a circumstance that strikingly evinces, the wisdom and policy of the government. The Chobwas, or petty princes, who followed the royal family, were on this day very numerous: we were told that there were all together fifty-six

Chobwas dependent on the Birman state; if it be true, their territories must be very inconsiderable. On the present occasion the Governor of Bamoo walked amongst them in procession, from which we concluded that he is a temporary regent; a station to which the King occasionally appoints Birman officers, when the hereditary prince of the country happens to be a minor, or incapable of the administration of public affairs.

The mother of the principal Queen, named Meedaw Praw, has already been mentioned, as a princess of high dignity, venerable from her years, and illustrious from the affinity that she bears to the royal family; her sister had been the wife of the famous Alompra, the deliverer of his country, and her daughter being espoused to the reigning monarch, she stands in the double relation of aunt and mother-in-law to the king. I had been apprized that a visit to this lady would be an acceptable mark of respect to his majesty, and as the rank she bore, gave her precedence over all the sons of the king, except the heir apparent, it was proper that I should wait upon her before I paid my respects to the junior princes. I gladly embraced the opportunity, which this offer gave me, to attend the drawing-room of an Asiatic princess, and promised myself much gratification from a sight so uncommon, among the jealous nations of the East. When the ceremony at the palace of the Engy Teekien had ended, it was not more than two o'clock, and there was yet sufficient time to wait upon the Meedaw Praw, who, we were informed, had made preparations to receive us. Mounting our elephants, we went in form to attend her, and found her possessed of a very handsome mansion in the neighbourhood of the imperial palace; it was situated in the centre of a court, surrounded by a palisade, at the gate of which there was a stage erected for our convenience in alighting. We entered the inclosure without any of the parade observed in our former visits: at the bottom of the stairs we put off our shoes, and ascended into a handsome hall, supported by several lofty pillars; at the farther end a portion of the floor was elevated six or eight inches, and separated by a neat balustrade from the rest of the room; within this space, under a white canopy, was placed a large cushion of blue velvet fringed with gold, on a carpet covered with muslin. There was a numerous assemblage of both sexes, but particularly women, sitting round the balustrade. As soon as we entered, a space was immediately vacated for us to occupy, in front of the door and opposite to the cushion. After we had been seated a few minutes, the old lady came forth from an inner apartment, and walked slowly towards the elevated seat, supported by two female servants, whilst another held up her train; her long white hair hung loose upon her shoulders, but she wore neither covering nor ornament upon her head; her dress, which was extremely fine, without being gaudy, became her advanced years and high dignity; it consisted of a long robe of white muslin, and over her shoulders was thrown a sash of gauze, embroidered with sprigs of gold. She advanced to where the cushion was placed, and took her seat on the carpet, supporting her head on her arm that rested on the pillow, whilst the two female attendants, neatly dressed, kneeling, one on each side, fanned her with long gilded fans. Every person seemed to pay her profound respect, and when she entered, both men and women bent their bodies in the attitude of submission. I had brought, as a token of my veneration, a string of pearl and some fine muslin. The Sandohgaan announced the offering, and enumerated the articles with a loud voice, entreating, in my name, her gracious acceptance of them. She looked at the English gentlemen with earnestness, but seemed entirely to disregard the Chinese, although their dress was much more showy than ours: her manner was on this occasion extremely complaisant, and she asked several questions, such as, what were our names? how we were in health? what were our ages? on being informed, she obligingly said she would pray that we might attain as great longevity as herself; adding, that she had reached her seventy-second year. I did not perceive, amongst the numerous company that attended, any of the junior princes, or of the principal ministers, although there were several personages of distinction. After she had retired, a very handsome desert was served up: the fruits and preserves were delicious: whatever China could yield, was united with the produce of their own country. Having tasted of various dishes, we withdrew without any ceremony; and as none of the royal family were present, there was no necessity to delay our departure: we accordingly returned home, a good deal oppressed by the heat of the weather, and wearied by the repetition of tedious formalities.

On the two following days we visited the princes of Prome, of Bassien, of Tongho, and of Pegahm, titles taken from the provinces over which they respectively preside. These brothers are not all by the same mother; the prince of Prome alone, being full brother to the Engy Teckien, or heir apparent. In the course of our visits we had a better opportunity than before, of viewing the streets and buildings; the former were invariably laid out in strait lines, crossing each other at right angles. The houses in general differed little from those of Rangoon; they were all covered with tiles, and on the ridge of the roofs was a long range of earthen pots, filled with water, in readiness to be broken in case of fire. The few houses of brick and mortar which we saw, were said to belong to the members of the royal family. Rows of trees were planted in several streets, five or six feet in front of the houses, forming a shady walk for foot passengers. As the younger princes do not assume the state of royalty, our reception was much more gay and less ceremonious at their palaces, than at that of the Engy Teekien. At the palace of the prince of Prome, or, as he is termed, the Pee Teekien, the preparations made for our entertainment were extremely splendid. When the gate of the inclosure was thrown open to admit us, we were surprised with a view of a lane of elephants on one side, and of horses on the other; there were fifteen of the former, some of which surpassed in size and beauty any I had ever seen: the horses were more numerous, and several of them were richly caparisoned. Passing through these, we came to an open space, where rope-dancers and tumblers were performing in the open air. We stopped to look at them, but observed nothing remarkable in their feats; they were much inferior in agility to the tumblers of Southern India. One man, however, surprised us a good deal, by applying the point of a spear to his shoulder and resting the other end against a pillar, thus pushing on it, apparently with great force, until he bent and broke a thick shaft; this he effected without piercing his own skin, which, though the spear was not very sharp, must have been wonderfully firm to have resisted such evident violence.

While we were viewing the sports, a message was brought from the prince to acquaint us that these people had been procured for our amusement; and after we had satisfied our curiosity, he would be glad to see us. We immediately proceeded to the hall of reception, which was a handsome wooden building, but not so large as that of the elder brother. At the upper end there was a sofa, curiously gilded, and decorated with pieces of mirror, disposed in such a manner as to produce a pleasing effect. None of the royal family were present, and we did not observe any of the Woongees or Attawoons. A few minutes after we had taken our seats, the prince entered, splendidly dressed; he proceeded to his sofa with much solemnity, and spoke only a few words. We were, as usual, entertained with a handsome desert, of which the prince himself solicited us to eat. As soon as he withdrew, our attention was called to a select company of figure-dancers, who had commenced their performance in the virando, or balcony of the hall. This band of females did not at all discredit the festival of a prince; three of the number were beautiful, and moved with graceful ease, in perfect harmony to the music: their outer dress was a flowing robe, made of transparent gauze delicately embroidered with flowers of gold and silver, and a profusion of gold chains encircled their necks and arms. We remained a quarter of an hour beholding this elegant spectacle, and then returned to the place where our elephants were waiting. The prince of Prome is in person rather above the middle size; his age does not exceed twenty-seven or twenty-eight years; and, like his elder brother, his appearance promises future corpulency: his countenance is naturally cheerful and pleasing, which we were told was the true index of his mind: he bears an excellent character, and is said to be much esteemed in the province, over which he immediately presides.

Our next visit was to the prince of Tongho, by whom we were received with every mark of attention. His dwelling was much inferior to those of his elder brothers, and the attendance was comparatively small; there were, however, a number of state elephants paraded in the court-yard, and we passed through a line of musqueteers, drawn up in single files on each side. This military array had a very singular appearance; hardly any two were dressed alike, and some of them were without any other clothing, than a fillet that encircled their head, and a cloth rolled round their waist: through respect, they were all seated on their heels, some with their firelocks shouldered, and others with the butts resting on the ground.

Here also we found tumblers, musicians, and dancers; and there were two carriages in waiting, handsomely gilded, with a pair of horses harnessed to each: these vehicles were of a light construction, on four wheels. open at the sides, and covered with a convex canopy. The prince sat on a gilded chair; he was a slender man, and appeared to be older than the prince of Prome, whom he is said not to resemble in any particular. The power which this prince possesses must be considerable, as his government, formerly the independent kingdom of Tongho, is rich, extensive, and populous; and the fort of Tongho is, at the present day, deemed the strongest in the empire. Persons of rank, we observed, were here permitted to introduce their beetle-boxes and spitting-pots, which was not the case at any of the other courts. Our visit being concluded, we returned home. The heat during the early part of this day had been very intense, but a refreshing shower towards evening cooled the air, and rendered the night pleasant. We were not surprised when we came back, to learn that the senior of the Chinese embassy had died during our absence, as he had been so ill in the morning, that his colleagues declined taking a share in the ceremonials of the day.

On the following day, at the customary hour, we crossed the lake, and proceeded with the same attendants as before, to the house of the prince of Bassien. His dwelling was very handsome, and the pillars of his hall, which the law prohibits him either to gild or paint, were covered with flowered satin. Many men of rank graced the assembly, and some who wore high military insignia; but none of the royal family or the principal ministers were present. The prince seemed a very awkward, bashful youth, about seventeen years of age. The situation of his government, which extends along the sea coast, as far south as Cape Negrais, gives him the power either to obstruct or assist, in a material degree, the merchants who trade to Bassien; and ships being sometimes obliged to take shelter in the Negrais river, during the adverse monsoon, his people have frequent opportunities of affording aid to the distressed. After sitting some minutes, and finding he was not inclined to begin a discourse, I broke through the general silence, by addressing him in a complimentary manner, expressing acknowledgment of the kindness, which had been extended by the officers of his government, to British merchants and mariners, as well as my reliance on his future influence in their favour. I spoke in the language of Hindostan; and each sentence was translated by Baba-Sheen. The prince was embarrassed; he twice attempted to reply, but had not the power; two of his courtiers crept towards him, and, in a prostrate attitude near the foot of his seat, suggested what they conceived he ought to say: their aid, however, was ineffectual; his Highness could not utter a connected sentence. At length his Woon, or chief minister, relieved him, by making an apposite reply in his name. Our entertainment was nearly the same as at the other princes. From hence we went to the palace of the junior prince, entitled Pegahm Teekien; a title derived from the ancient city of that name, which is the seat of his government. He seemed livelier than his brother, whom we had just left; and his Woon was a very venerable personage. On this occasion the repast differed in one particular from any we had yet received; a roast fowl was introduced, no doubt in compliment to us; and as their religion does not forbid them to eat meat, but only prohibits the slaughter of animals for the purposes of food, there was no crime in the act of serving it up to us, or partaking of it themselves: the only question was, how the bird came to be deprived of life? to which, no doubt, an exculpatory answer could have been given. This, however, was a matter which it did not become us to discuss;

it was certainly a handsome and liberal testimony of their desire to provide what they thought would be agreeable to their guests.

In addition to the band of dancing girls that performed here for our amusement, there were two comedians, who recited passages, and exhibited various distortions of countenance; but they were far inferior to the inimitable performer we had seen at Pegue.

Having finished our introductory visits to the different members of the royal family, we had now leisure to gratify curiosity, by viewing whatever the capital contained, that was most deserving the notice of strangers. The day not being far advanced, we walked from the palace of the prince of Pegahm, to see the Piedigaut Tiek, or royal library: it is situated at the north-west angle of the fort, in the centre of a court, paved with broad flags, and close to a very handsome Kioum, or monastery. Before we entered the library we ascended the Kioum, and found the inside correspond with the external appearance; the building was spacious and richly gilded; the pillars, the ceiling, and the pannels were entirely covered with gold leaf; and the image of Gaudma shone with brilliant lustre. A balustrade of wood, minutely and beautifully carved, protected the image from intruders. On the pannels of the walls, were represented figures of inferior agents of the divinity, and of prostrate Rhahaans in the act of devotion: these were all shaped in fret-work in the wood, and were of no contemptible workmanship; a well wrought foliage of the same, bordered the pannels. The image of Gaudma, in this Kioum, was large, and made of marble; it was seated on a broad pedestal, entirely gilded; in front of which, within the balustrade, stood a handsome girandole of cut glass, of European manufacture: near the image, was a gilded couch, which, we were informed, was the customary bed of the principal Rhahaan, or head of all the Birman priesthood, when he chose to pass the night in the fort, which rarely happened. It was splendidly gilt; the bottom, however, was only a bare board; pillows were not wanting; there were two, but they were made of wood. A mat spread on the floor, is the highest luxury of repose, in which the Rhahaans indulge.

From the kioum we proceeded to visit the adjacent library; it is a large brick building, raised on a terrace, and covered by a roof of very compound structure. It consists of one square room, with an enclosed virando, or gallery, surrounding it: this room was locked, and as we had not brought a special order for seeing it, the person who had the care of the library said that he was not at liberty to open the doors, but assured us that there was nothing in the inside different from what we might see in the virando, where a number of large chests, curiously ornamented with gilding and japan, were ranged in regular order, against the wall. I counted fifty, but there were many more, probably not less than a hundred. The books were regularly classed, and the contents of each chest, were written in gold letters on the lid. The librarian opened two, and shewed me some very beautiful writing on thin leaves of ivory, the margins of which were ornamented with flowers of gold, neatly executed. I saw also some books written in the ancient Palli, the religious text. Every thing seemed to be arranged with perfect regularity, and I was informed that there were books upon divers subjects; more on divinity than on any other; but history, music, medicine, painting, and romance, had their separate treatises. The volumes were disposed under distinct heads, regularly numbered; and if all the other chests were as well filled, as those that were submitted to our inspection, it is not improbable, that his Birman Majesty may possess a more numerous library, than any potentate from the banks of the Danube, to the borders of China.

It was late when we returned home, and our repose was disturbed by a renewal of the noises which the Chinese were accustomed to make; they sounded all night on loud gongs, the funeral knell of the departed embassador, uttering at intervals horrible cries and lamentations. One of the mourners imitated with his voice, the howling of a dog so naturally, that all the curs belonging to the boat people, and the Cassay huts in our neighbourhood, joined in the chorus. Our proximity to these personages proved to us a source of great molestation.

About this time a ludicrous circumstance happened, which only deserves notice, as it tends to illustrate the character of the people, and shew to what an abject state, despotic tyranny can debase the human mind. The Engy Teekien, or prince royal, took a pleasure in collecting foreign beasts; among others, he had procured male goats from almost every country of the east. A flock of these, consisting of more than thirty, were sent to feed on the borders of the lake, near our dwelling: we happened to have three or four she-goats, that had been brought from Bengal, for the sake of their milk. Allured by the bleat of the females, the whole flock of males one night broke through the paling, and made a forcible irruption into our court; the suddenness of the attack, at such an hour, surprised us not a little; I got up, and ordered the Birman guards that were posted at the gates, to drive them away, which they attempted to do by shouting at them, but without any effect, as the animals, some of which were very large, had now become furious, and after fighting with each other, began to rush through our houses. I then desired the Birmans to make use of sticks, but this they positively refused, saying that the goats were "praws," or lords, meaning that they were ennobled by belonging to the Prince, and that no person dared, on any account, offer injury to to them; having no other alternative, we armed our servants and the soldiers with large bamboos, who subdued these troublesome invaders, though not without much difficulty, and some risk, whilst the Birmans lifted up their hands and eyes in astonishment at our temerity: the Praws, however, were severely beaten. Having at length got rid of them, I returned to rest, and heard no more of the matter.

The intense heat of the three days, spent in the formalities of visiting the princes, made me postpone any further ceremonials until the 6th of the month (September), which day was appointed to pay our respects to the Seredaw Poundagee Praw, or the arch priest of the Birman empire: in the intermediate time a difference of opinion arose, in regard to the etiquette of compliments, in which I did not think myself at liberty to depart from what I considered an attention due to my public character.

The grand ruling council of the Birman nation has already been described as consisting of four chief members, entitled Woongees, and four junior members, called Woondocks, between whom there is a wide disparity of rank. The place of third Woongee was vacant, and the junior bears very small comparative importance with the two seniors, who, in fact, govern the empire. These personages, whose power is so great, possess a corresponding degree of pride; the governors of provinces are in their esteem men of little consequence, and are often treated by these ministers with excessive arrogance, which is not solely confined to those, whose situation and expectations place them in a state of dependence, but is indiscriminately extended to all; nor could I hope to be exempted from receiving a share in common with others. I was informed, that after paying my respects to the royal family and the Seredaw, it was expected that I should wait on the two senior Woongees, and offer them in person the customary presents. I observed in answer, that I had no objection to paying these ministers a mark of attention by the trifling present which usage had established; but to wait on them at their houses, unless I received an assurance that my visit would be returned, was a ceremony I begged leave to decline. This intimation I imagine was rather a disappointment to them, as much pains were taken to induce me to alter my resolution. I however refused to concede, but I offered to meet them at the house of the Maywoon of Pegue, a proposal from which they dissented, remarking, that to visit me, would be more eligible than to go to the Maywoon's house. I replied that our formalities were not less strict than theirs, and that I could no more relinquish my claim to the respect due to my public station, than they could descend from their elevation, and saw no remedy unless they themselves chose to apply that, which was in their own power, and which they must be sensible I had a right to require. Finding that I was not inclined to yield, they requested, if I could not visit them in person, that I would allow the other gentlemen to pay them the compliment; a desire to which I readily acceded, as well from a wish to open a channel of communication, as to manifest on my part a conciliatory disposition. Mr. Wood and Doctor Buchanan obligingly made no objection; I therefore answered that the gentlemen would wait on them, and expressed my regret that I was deprived of the same pleasure.

During this interval of rest the Governor of Bamoo frequently favoured me with a visit, his business bringing him almost daily to the residence of the Chinese. By his desire, I sent them compliments of condolence, with a piece of coarse white muslin, which, it seems, is the etiquette on such occasions. On one of these days the Bamoo Governor brought with him the chart of his journey to Pekin, as he had formerly promised; it was delineated in a curious manner on a sort of black paper commonly used by the Birmans, on which they write with a pencil, made of steatite, or soap-stone. The places were distinctly marked, but not having any scale, the measurement was extremely confused, and so disproportionate, that it was impossible to judge of distances with any degree of precision. We could however trace his progress through the Chinese dominions in the Jesuits map that is prefixed to du Halde's account of China.

On the day appointed for our visit to the Seredaw, we took boat at seven in the morning, and, attended by our usual retinue, crossed the lake; one of the surviving Chinese also accompanied us. Baba-Sheen, the Shaw-bunder of Rangoon, and some Birman officers, met us on the opposite bank, where our elephants were waiting. When we approached the causeway or bridge, instead of crossing it, we turned to the left, and proceeded close to the ditch, parallel with the west face of the fort, till we came to the north-west angle. At this place the river approaches so near to the walls as to render a continuation of the ditch impracticable; we then went along the north side, passing on our left a handsome kioum, crowned with a gilded piasath or spire, which we were told had been erected by Meedaw Praw, the venerable lady whom we had visited. On arriving at the north-east corner, we observed at some distance on the plain, another religious edifice of distinguished splendor, it was dignified by the title of Kioumdogee, or royal convent, where we were informed that the Seredaw or chief priest intended to receive us, and not at his usual residence, which was at a Kioum about two miles farther. The articles I designed to present to him, having been sent forward to his customary abode, we were obliged to wait in an adjoining house until they could be brought back. Being prepared, we were conducted into a spacious court, surrounded by a high brick wall, in the centre of which stood the kioum, an edifice not less extraordinary from the stile of its architecture, than magnificent from its ornaments, and from the gold that was profusely bestowed on every part. It was composed entirely of wood, and the roofs, rising one above another in five distinct stories, diminished in size as they advanced in height, each roof being surrounded by a cornice, curiously carved and richly gilded. The body of the building, elevated twelve feet from the ground, was supported on large timbers driven into the earth after the manner of piles, of which there were probably 150 to sustain the immense weight of the superstructure. On ascending the stairs, we were not less pleased than surprised, at the splendid appearance which the inside displayed; a gilded balustrade, fantastically carved into various shapes and figures, encompassed the outside of the platform. Within this, there was a wide gallery that comprehended the entire circuit of the building, in which many devotees were stretched prostrate on the floor. An inner railing opened into a noble hall, supported by colonnades of lofty pillars; the centre row was at least fifty feet high, and gilded from the summit to within four feet of the base, which was lackered red. In the middle of the hall there was a gilded partition of open latticed work, fifteen or twenty feet high, which divided it into two parts, from north to south. The space between the pillars varied from twelve to sixteen feet, and the number, including those that supported the galleries, appeared to be not fewer than one hundred, which, as they approached the extremities, diminished in height; the outermost row not exceeding fifteen feet. The bottom of these was cased with sheet lead as a defence against the weather. A marble image of Gaudma, gilded, and sitting on a golden throne, was placed in the centre of the partition; and in front of the idol, leaning against one of the pillars, we beheld the Seredaw sitting on a satin carpet. He was

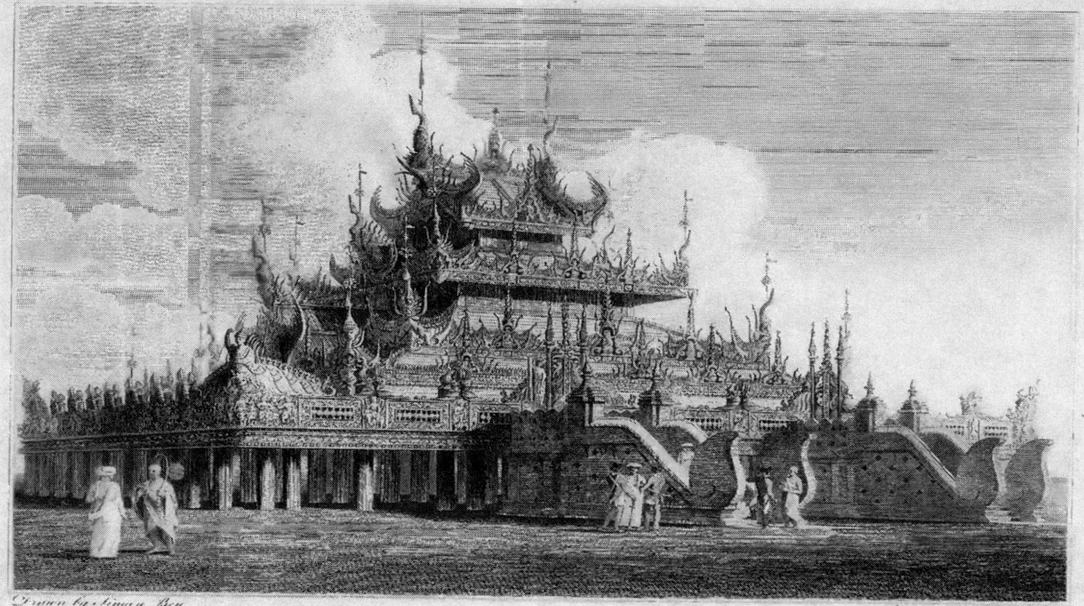

Drawn by Singey Bey — Engraved by T. Medland

A Kioum or Monastery

London, Published Nov.r 1 1799 by G. Nicol, Pall Mall & J. Wright Piccadilly

encompassed by a circle of Rhahaans, from whom he could be no otherways distinguished, than by his preserving an erect position; whilst the others bent their bodies in an attitude of respect, with their hands joined in a supplicating manner. On entering the hall, the Birmans and the Chinese, who accompanied us, prostrated themselves before the figure of Gaudma, after which they kneeled down and made their reverence to the Seredaw, touching the ground with their foreheads, whilst we took our seats on fine mats, that were spread at a little distance from him. He received us with much politeness, and in his looks and demeanour affected more liveliness and complaisance, than any of the fraternity I had hitherto seen. His appearance denoted him to be about forty years of age; not meagre and austere as they generally are, but fat and jocular. I presented to him my offering, which consisted of a piece of yellow cloth, the sacerdotal colour; some sandal wood, and a few wax candles covered with gold leaf. He asked several questions respecting England, such as how long the voyage usually was from thence to India: being told this, he observed that we were an extraordinary people to wander so far from home. I noticed the magnificence of the kioum: he replied, that such sublunary matters did not attract his attention; he was on earth but as a hermit. I desired his prayers; he said they were daily offered up for the happiness of all mankind, but that he would recommend us, to the particular protection of Gaudma. He made some observations on our appearance, which I did not understand, and he even smiled; a relaxation very unusual in a Rhahaan. We retired without ceremony, and mounting our elephants, proceeded along a wide road leading to the northward, which soon brought us to an extensive plain, that seemed to stretch in an uninterrupted level, to the foot of a range of mountains, ten or twelve miles distant. The soil was a poor clay, and the pasturage indifferent. We saw at a distance some fields of grain, and understood that capacious reservoirs had been constructed with great labour and expence, by order of the king, in the vicinity of the mountains, which enabled the inhabitants of the low countries to water their grounds, and render the earth productive in a season of drought. Several kioums and villages were scattered over the plain; but when we had advanced about two miles, religious edifices increased, beyond our power to calculate the number. The first that we entered was called Knebang Kioum, or the Kioum of Immortality, from the centre of which rose a royal Piasath, to the height of a hundred and fifty feet: the roofs were of the customary complicated structure, one above another. This was the place where the embalmed bodies of deceased Seredaws are laid in state: the building rested on a terrace of brick, and was not elevated on pillars, as Kioums and dwelling-houses usually are. The hall was very handsome, about seventy feet square, surrounded by a wide gallery: the roof was sustained by thirty-six gilded pillars, the central forty feet in height. Mats were spread in different parts for the repose of the Rhahaans, and on each was placed a hard pillow; there was also a tray containing books on the duties of Rhahaans, on religion, and the forms of religious worship.

Having rested here for a short time, we next visited the Kioum, which was the ordinary residence of the Seredaw. This building far exceeded, in size and splendour, any we had before seen, and is perhaps the most magnificent of its kind in the universe; it is constructed entirely of wood, and resembled in the style of its structure and ornaments, that in which we had an interview with the Seredaw, but was much more spacious and lofty. The numerous rows of pillars, some of them sixty feet high, all of which were covered with burnished gilding, had a wonderfully splendid effect: it would be difficult to convey, either in language or by pencil, an adequate description of this extraordinary edifice. The boundless expenditure of gilding on parts exposed to the weather, as well as in the inside, cannot fail to impress a stranger with astonishment, at the richness of the decoration, although he may not approve of the taste with which it is disposed: I could not have formed in my imagination a display more strikingly magnificent. This Kioum was also divided by a partition, which separated it in the middle from north to south. There was a small room on one side, made of gilded boards, which we were told was the bedchamber of the Seredaw. Mats were spread on the outside for the attendant Rhahaans. The figure of Gaudma was made of copper, and an European girandole of cut-glass stood before his throne.

Leaving this building, we passed through many courts crowded with smaller temples and Kioums. Several gigantic images of Rakuss, the Hindoo demon, half beast, half human, made of brass, were shewed to us, as composing a part of the spoils of Arracan. From these we were conducted to a magnificent temple which is erecting for the image of Gaudma, that was brought from the same country. The idol is made of polished brass, about ten feet high, and sitting in the usual posture, on a pedestal within an arched recess: the walls are gilded, and adorned with bits of different coloured mirrors, disposed with much taste. Peculiar sanctity is ascribed to this image, and devotees resort from every part of the empire, to adore the Arracan Gaudma, which is not exposed at all hours, to the view of the vulgar. The doors of the recess are only opened when persons of particular consequence come to visit it, or at stated times, to indulge the populace. As we approached, a crowd of people thronged after us with tumultuous enthusiasm, striving for admittance to offer up a prayer to this brazen representative of the divinity. We soon turned from these wretched fanatics, and the object of their stupid adoration, to view the noble Piasath, or royal spire, that crowned the building, and attracted much more of our attention and respect, than an image, from which even the statuary could claim no praise. The spire rose in seven separate stages, above the roof of the Kioum, and the gold leaf, which had recently been applied, glistening in the sun-beams, reflected a brilliant lustre. This temple, with its auxiliary buildings, which are yet in an unfinished state, will, when completed, be the most elegant in the empire, though perhaps not so spacious as that which is the present residence of the Seredaw. From hence we were conducted to what is called the Chounda, or place for the reception and repose of strangers, who come from a distance to offer up their devotions. It communicates on the north side with the great temple, and is also a very beautiful specimen of Birman architecture; it comprehends five long galleries separated by colonnades, each consisting of thirty-four pillars, or two hundred and four all together; the two central rows were about twenty-five feet high, but the external ones did not exceed fourteen; they were painted of a deep crimson ground, enlivened by festoons of gold leaf, encircling them in a very fanciful and pleasing manner, and in a style much more conformable to European taste, than an unvaried surface of gold. The ceiling likewise was embellished with a profusion of carved work, executed with great labour and minuteness. Measuring by our steps, we judged the length to be five hundred and seventy-six feet, and the breadth of each distinct gallery about twelve; the central rather wider than those on either side. A low railing extended along the outer pillars, to prevent improper persons and dogs, from defiling the place. It is built upon a terrace of brick, elevated three feet from the ground;

the floor is made of Chunam, or fine stucco, composed of lime, pounded steatites, and oil, the cohesion of which forms a hard and smooth surface, that shines like marble. Our conductor informed us that this edifice had been lately erected at the sole expence of the senior Woongee. It certainly reflects credit on the projector, and is an ornament to the country.

The heat of the day, which had now attained its greatest force, and our having been in constant exercise from seven in the morning till two o'clock in the afternoon, rendered a place of repose extremely acceptable; and here we not only rested ourselves, but likewise found a plentiful collation prepared for us. Our conductors, aware that the attention of strangers could not fail to be engaged for some hours, by such a multitude of new and striking objects, thought it would be more prudent for us to wait under the shade of this hospitable roof till the afternoon, than expose ourselves unnecessarily, to a burning sun. We had brought with us, at the instance of our friends, wine, bread and butter, and cold fowl, to which the Shawbunder had added a turene of excellent vermicelli soup, and a tolerable good pillaw. We sat down to our repast about two o'clock, and after it was finished, continued to recline upon our mats until evening, fanned by a cool and refreshing breeze from the west, whilst we conversed, and contemplated the scene around. The crowd of people, whom the novelty of our appearance had collected, were neither intrusive nor troublesome. On such an occasion, in most other countries of the East, it is probable that, from the prejudices of bigotry, we should not have been suffered to depart without receiving some insult, or remarking some indication of contempt; but here, notwithstanding we entered their most sanctified recesses, we were every where treated with uniform civility. The presence of those who accompanied us had doubtless some influence in commanding the awe of the multitude; and if their respect was owing to this motive, it speaks highly for the state of their police; but I am inclined also to give them credit for a disposition naturally kind and benevolent.

In the afternoon we returned home by the same road that we came, and our attention being less engaged than in the morning, we had a better opportunity to judge of the form and extent of the fortress, as we passed along the north side, from one end to the other.*

The fort of Ummerapoora is an exact square: there are four principal gates, one in the centre of each face; there is also a smaller gate on each side of the great gate, equidistant between it and the angle of the fort, comprizing twelve gates in all. At each angle of the fort there is a large quadrangular bastion, that projects considerably. There are also eleven smaller bastions on each side, including those that are over the gateways. Between each of these bastions is extended a curtain about two hundred yards long. From this calculation, a side of the fort occupies two thousand four hundred yards; the Birmans, however, called it four thousand nine hundred royal cubits, which I conceive to be an exaggerated account. Every bastion and gateway is covered by a tiled roof, supported on four pillars of wood, to prevent injury from the lodgment of rain.

At each corner of the fort there is a gilded temple, nearly one hundred feet in height, but so insignificant, comparatively, with those we had just seen, as not to attract particular notice.

We could perceive, from our elephants, the roof of a range of buildings in the inside, parallel to the walls, and extending along one entire side of the fort, which our conductors said was the public granary and store-rooms.

* See a plan of the fort of Ummerapoora in the Map prefixed to this work.

We arrived at our grove half an hour after dark, wearied from the heat of the weather and the exercise of the day, but gratified to the highest degree, with the multiplicity and extraordinary splendour of the objects we had seen. Much as we had heard of the magnificence of their religious buildings, our expectations had been more than fulfilled. The unbounded expenditure of gilding which they bestow on the outside of the roofs, as well as within, must exhaust immense sums. I was informed that the gold leaf is exceedingly pure, and bears exposure to the air for a long time, without suffering injury. The size or glue used to make it adhere is called Seesee: it is the juice of the croton sebiferum, after undergoing a certain preparation. This is the only manner in which a people, naturally frugal and disinclined to luxury, seem to apply their superfluous wealth. It is to be lamented that their edifices are in general composed of such a perishable material as wood, which, though of the most durable kind perhaps in the world, cannot last for many generations, or leave to posterity a monumental proof, of the taste and magnificence of the national architecture.

CHAPTER XVII.

Reason to hope for a prosperous Termination of the Embassy—meet with strenuous Opposition—on what Grounds.—Vessel arrives at Rangoon from Mauritius—News from Europe unpleasant—industriously propagated.—Mr. Wood visits the Woongees—polite Reception—remarkable Circumstance—require to know his Majesty's Pleasure—Day appointed for the Delivery of Presents from the Birman King.—Conversation at the Lotoo—Arrogance of the Birman Court—resolve to remonstrate—uncivil Treatment.—Mr. Wood presents a written and solemn Declaration—Ferment caused by it—favourable Conclusion.—A Day appointed for our Reception by the King.—Liberal Return of Presents—different Articles.—Proceed to the Palace—Introduction—Hall of Audience—the King—his Dress—Person—Manner—Receive official Papers in the Rhoom.—Formality in conveying the King's Letter.—Return.

WHILST we were thus passing our time in amusement, and the indulgence of our curiosity, the more important interests of the mission were not forgotten. The council, I was informed, had held frequent deliberations on some general propositions, which I had submitted with a view to assist the mercantile interests of the two countries, and place commerce on a liberal and secure basis. I had reason given me to conclude, that my suggestions had met with a favourable reception, and I was likewise informed by an authority which I conceived to be competent, that it was intended to depute a Birman officer of distinction in an official capacity to Bengal, there to confirm, on the part of his Birman Majesty, the good understanding that was henceforth to subsist between the Court of Ummerapoora, and the Government General of India. Assurances of this nature, together with the attention paid to our private accommodation, induced me to hope for a ſavourable termination of the mission with which I was entrusted.

I however soon ſound, that the attainment of these objects, which were obviously calculated to be of reciprocal advantage to British India and the Birman empire, was opposed by the indirect artifices of individuals possessing weight, whose interests might eventually be affected by any innovation, and who on that account sedulously ſomented jealousy and distrust. I likewise learned that the pride of the court had been early awakened, by a representation that the government of Bengal being provincial, and the Governor-General, from whom I derived my commission, only the subject of a king, it would therefore be derogatory to the Birman monarch, to treat on terms of equality with an administration that was subordinate, or to correspond with any person beneath the dignity of a crowned head. It is however doubtful whether the Birman court would have manifested its sentiments so unequivocally, as to draw from me a formal explanation, had not circumstances subsequently occurred, which served to strengthen its arrogance, and which gave plausibility to the representations that had been fabricated to mislead.

Matters were in this state, when advice came of the arrival of a small vessel at Rangoon, from the isle of France, under Birman colours, which brought an unfavourable account of the situation of affairs in Europe; exaggerating the disappointment of the allies on the continent to a total defeat; and adding, that the Dutch and Spaniards having joined the republicans, the utter ruin of the English was not far distant. An obscure agent, maintained at Rangoon by the French, transmitted this information to a person of some official importance at the Birman capital, who immediately promulgated it with an addition, that a powerful fleet was on its voyage from France to India; and, that four French ships of war were triumphantly cruizing in the Indian seas.

This intelligence, which was asserted with confidence, was diligently improved by the Armenian and Mussulman merchants, who insinuated that, if our present overtures sprung not from treachery, they originated in fear; at the same time renewing a report, which has more than once been current, of a combination of all the powers of India to deprive Great Britain of her possessions in the East, and to expel all Europeans from those shores, which they were represented to have first visited as merchants, and afterwards invaded as usurpers. Although the Birmans probably did not give implicit credit to the last mentioned rumour, yet the news from Europe, co-operating with their own pride, determined them to persist in that arrogant assumption of superiority, which had hitherto been manifested, rather in their actions, than by their words.

On the 7th of September, Mr. Wood, in conformity with the instructions he received, waited on the two senior Woongees, accompanied by Doctor Buchanan, and attended by a proportion of the public servants. On his return, he addressed an official letter to me, (Appendix, No. I.) by which it appears, that in his reception, no part of the respect due to his public character was omitted; whilst in the solicitude expressed for our personal welfare, there was displayed the refined politeness of a polished court. The conversation that he held with the Woongees, was nevertheless marked by a circumstance, which served to indicate more pointedly the precise line that was intended to be drawn.

On the day of my public introduction at the Lotoo, it was an omission too remarkable to escape notice, that no enquiry whatever had been made respecting the Governor-General of India, nor in the conversations which I afterwards held with the several princes, was the name of the Governor-General once mentioned by them. Such however was not the case at the interview between Mr. Wood and the Woongees; these ministers enquired particularly concerning Sir John Shore, and the younger Woongee desired to be informed of the extent of the Governor-General's authority, which implied, on his part, either real or assumed ignorance. These questions also, as appears from Mr. Wood's report, did not arise from the casual suggestion of the moment, but were all preconcerted and methodically arranged; the inferences therefore to be deduced from them, were grounds on which I might form a judgment; they conveyed something more than a presumption, of the real sentiments entertained, respecting the delegating authority under which I acted.

There being no plausible pretext for any longer delay, I pressed the Woongees to inform me what his Majesty's pleasure was, regarding the several points which I had submitted to his council, and intimated the necessity I was under of obeying the orders of my own government, by returning as speedily, as was consistent with the objects for which I had been deputed. In reply to this application, I was apprized that the presents, which his Birman Majesty designed to send to Bengal in return for those he had received, would be prepared on the 19th of September, on which day, if I would come to the Lotoo, they should be delivered to me;

matters of business might be discussed, and I might fix on whatever day I thought proper to depart.

With this desire I willingly acquiesced, as affording me an opportunity of requiring to know his Majesty's real sentiments, as well as the motives that on their part gave rise to a conduct of so mysterious a nature.

Nothing passed in the interval, except that I received intimation through a private and respectable channel, that the court, although no objection would be formally stated, had come to a decided resolution of considering me as a person deputed from a provincial and subordinate power, and not as the representative of an equal and sovereign state; and that in pursuance of this estimation his Majesty did not intend to honour me with a personal audience of leave. Of the truth of this information I had no reason to doubt; but before I took any measures to undeceive the court in a public manner, I deemed it expedient to have an assumption so haughty and imperious, verified by the highest authority.

On the 19th of September, I proceeded to the Lotoo, where I arrived about twelve o'clock, and found the council of state already assembled; the ministers and the attendant officers being all dressed in their robes, and caps of ceremony. A few minutes after we had taken our seats, the presents were brought, consisting of three large boxes, covered with red cloth, and two elephant's teeth of considerable size. These I was desired to receive in the name of the Birman king, for the English government; at the same time, two large rings were presented to me; one a single ruby set in gold, the other a sapphire, which I was requested to accept as a personal token of his Majesty's favour: a ring was also given to Mr. Wood, and another to Doctor Buchanan. When this ceremony was ended, I addressed myself in the Birman language to the Woongees, and desired to know whether there were any reasons that applied to my situation, which had induced his Majesty to decline honouring me with a personal audience, which compliment, I understood, was usually paid by their court to the deputies of all sovereign states. To this interrogation I received an equivocal reply; and on repeating it, they persisted in returning an evasive answer. I then desired to be informed, whether or not it was his Majesty's intention to receive me in person, before my departure, as the representative of the Governor-General. This question they said they could not answer, not knowing his Majesty's pleasure. I afterwards asked whether the king preserved his intention of sending an authorized person from his court to Bengal, as had been intimated to me, by what I conceived to be competent authority, and whether the suggestions, which I had submitted for the advancement and protection of commerce, had been taken into consideration. These several points, they said, were then under discussion, and would be speedily determined; they acquainted me at the same time, that if I would fix on any precise period for my departure, the necessary papers and letters should be prepared, and delivered to me two days previous to my setting out. I mentioned the 3d of October; they replied that the letters should be in readiness by what I understood to be the 1st of October; but by some misapprehension was the 30th of September; adding their hope that I would come to town on the 28th of September, the anniversary of Sandaing-guite, a day on which all the nobility pay homage to his Majesty. To their invitation I answered, that my having that honour, must depend on circumstances not yet ascertained.

This interview left me little room to doubt of the estimation in which the Birman court held my public character, notwithstanding it was judged advisable, from motives of policy, to avoid making any direct avowal of such sentiments. Proceeding upon this plan, they concealed all their acts and determinations with a veil of ambiguity, which it sometimes was extremely difficult to penetrate.

Pride, the chief actuating principle of this arrogant court, was the source to which its conduct, in every transaction of a public nature, might ultimately be traced. The first object of their government is to impress on the minds of the people, the most reverential awe of their own sovereign, whose greatness they do not admit to be equalled by that of any monarch upon earth. Without attempting to diminish their veneration for their own prince, it became my duty, from the mode that was adopted in the display of his consequence, to acquaint the ministers in terms which could not be misconstrued, that there was another power, at no great distance, which would not readily subscribe to its own inferiority, or admit of any act in its negotiations with other states, which might either express or imply an assumption of superiority. It became necessary to inform them, that the Governor-General of India was not, in his relation to their court, or to that of any other eastern potentate, a subordinate provincial officer, but a personage in whom sovereign authority, over a widely extended empire was efficiently vested; that, as the representative of such authority, I held an indisputable claim to whatever consideration was granted to the ministers of other nations; and that the withholding it, would be accounted an incivility so great, as probably to prevent the English government from making any future advances, for the establishment of a friendly and confidential intercourse.

To convey a truth not less important for them to know, than incumbent on me to declare, I determined to address a letter to the principal Woongee and the council of state, expressing my dissatisfaction at the conduct which the Birman court had thought proper to observe in regard to my public character, to require an explanation of those points, which comprehended the objects of the embassy, and to demand that I should be received and acknowledged by the King in person, as the representative of an equal and sovereign state.

Had there even been room left for me to hesitate upon the adoption of this step, the following circumstances, which occurred immediately after my interview with the Woongees at the Lotoo, would have decided me, in making a public declaration of my sentiments on a mode of behaviour which exceeded even their usual extent of official arrogance, and fell little short of personal indignity.

The custom, which imposes an obligation on a foreign minister, to pay a mark of respect by a trifling present to each member of the royal family to whom he is introduced, has already been noticed: this compliment I offered in person to the several princes on the days of my presentation, and, in order to manifest that it was not my desire to withhold any attention, consistent with my situation to grant, soon after the visits of ceremony were ended, I had directed my Moonshee, or Persian secretary, to wait on each of the ministers and the principal officers of the court, and request in my name their acceptance of some rarity, the produce of Europe or of India. The gift to each individual was very trifling, a few yards of European broad cloth, an article of cut-glass, a piece of Bengal muslin or of silk, was received as a polite and handsome testimonial of a friendly disposition. These civilities, I was informed, were, by a special mandate, ordered to be returned by every person, to whom the attention had been shewn, in some production of the Birman country, and of value equal to what had been bestowed.

It being expected that I should wait on the royal princes to receive in person the remuneration they designed to make, for the presents they had obtained, I sent, on the 21st of September, a message to the Engy Teekien, to acquaint him that, if it suited his convenience, I would pay my respects to him the following day, or postpone my visit to any other, he might think proper to appoint: I likewise dispatched a messenger with a similar notification to the Prince of Prome. From the first I received a civil reply, excusing himself from seeing me on account of the indisposition of the princess, who had lately been brought to bed; but acquainting me, that if I chose to attend, the presents for the English government would be delivered to me in the Rhoom of his palace, or to any person whom I might appoint to receive them. I replied, that being debarred of the honour of seeing him, I would depute Mr. Wood to accept his presents in the name of the Governor-General of India: from the Prince of Prome I had not the honour of an answer.

On the 22d, Mr. Wood waited on the Engy Teekien, and was received with much civility at the Rhoom by his ministers; the presents were formally produced, and conveyed to our residence by the prince's servants. As the Prince of Prome had not returned an answer to my message, I imagined that some misapprehension had occurred. Being desirous of appearing to put the most favourable construction on every part of their conduct, I requested Mr. Wood to send a messenger, when he went to the house of the Engy Teekien, to apprize the Prince of Prome that he meant afterwards to pay his respects to him. To this intimation was returned, what Mr. Wood considered a satisfactory reply; and as soon as the first visit was ended, he proceeded to the Prince of Prome's palace, where the treatment he received, was extremely rude; after standing for some time at the outer gate, exposed to the sun, he was informed that the prince was not at home.

However deficient the members of the royal family might be in politeness to me, I determined not to suffer their example to influence my conduct towards them, or to neglect any mark of deference, that was due to their illustrious rank. Meedaw Praw, the mother of the Queen, being a personage venerable from her age, and dignified from her high connections; her behaviour also on our introduction having been distinguished by affability and politeness, I was, for these reasons, desirous of paying such a character particular respect; and with that view sent a complimentary message to her, similar to that which had been delivered to the two princes: she returned, in answer, that the next day would be perfectly convenient to her for my reception. I likewise intimated to the younger princes my intention of paying them a visit, to which they replied by a verbal compliment.

On the next day, the 23d, I proceeded in form to the house of Meedaw Praw at the appointed hour, and was received with sufficient politeness by her Woon, or principal officer: there were several persons of rank assembled in the hall when I entered. After we had been seated about a quarter of an hour, a person came forth from the inner apartment, and informed us that the princess had gone to the palace to see the Queen her daughter, but would return in a few minutes. This I thought rather an extraordinary step, as she herself had determined the precise time when I was to come. These minutes, however, were protracted to an hour; in the interval, pawn, fruit and sweetmeats were served up. At length, when her ministers perceived that my patience was exhausted, and I would wait no longer, a message was delivered to me from the princess, excusing her appearance, on a plea of indisposition; at the same time three gold rings, set with rubies and sapphires, and several boxes, handsomely japanned and painted, were laid before me, and my acceptance of them desired. A conduct marked by such deliberate impoliteness would have justified retaliation on my part, by a contemptuous rejection of her presents; I however refrained from any farther indication of displeasure, than withdrawing unceremoniously, without taking any notice of the boxes or rings, which were immediately conveyed to my residence by her servants. Having reason to apprehend that the junior princes meant to observe a similar line of conduct, I declined visiting them, but sent Mr. Wood to go through the ceremony of calling at their separate houses. As was expected, he saw not one of the princes, but was received by their Woons, who, though they carefully refrained from absolute rudeness, yet evinced in their conduct the utmost arrogance, under the cloak of supercilious civility.

Such strange and unwarrantable insolence could not be measured by any scale of true policy, and was hardly to be reconciled to reason or common sense; nor could any part of their conduct be laid to the account of ignorance; for no people on earth better understand, or more pointedly observe, the minute punctilios of official form. No candid and determinate reply could be extorted from them on any point in which their vanity was concerned: what their court intended to concede, I understood, was to be granted, not as an equivalent for reciprocal privileges on our part, but as a boon, as an act of gratuitous condescension to me, in the character of a petitioner, bearing the tribute of homage from an inferior state. Without the hardiness to avow these principles, which a sense of British power, and the proximity of the country, probably suppressed, they nevertheless acted upon them as an assumed fact, with a view to gratify their own pride, elude disagreeable explanations, and reap all the advantages derivable from an intercourse with British India, to which they certainly were far from being averse, provided the correspondence could be maintained upon their own terms.

In pursuance of my determination, I addressed the letter (Appendix, No. 2.) to the chief Woongee and council of state; and to give it all the publicity that such a declaration ought to have, I sent Mr. Wood to deliver it in person to the minister, directing him afterwards to wait on the two junior Woongees, and apprize them formally of my having written a letter of such a tenour.

Nor did I resolve on this measure without maturely considering the effect it was likely to produce, as well as the necessity in which it originated. The court had evidently been embarrassed in the first stages of the business, and was undetermined in what manner to act; to this irresolution I ascribe the petty artifice of misinforming me in matters of fact. The accounts from Europe certainly had great weight in influencing their conduct, and those could only be discredited by my holding higher language than before: to have acquiesced in silence would have been construed into at least a presumptive evidence of our weakness, whilst the slight that was attempted to be cast on the authority delegated to me, left no alternative but to endeavour to remove it by a temperate remonstrance, such as my letter was intended to convey, or to decline any further communication, and withdraw without ceremony. This latter step was not to be taken under any provocation short of personal injury, than which I believe nothing was farther from their intention. To enhance their own importance by the unworthy mode of lessening that of others, seemed to be the sole motive that actuated them, and which, as far as related to the government that I represented, it was clearly my duty to oppose.

My letter was written in the English and the Persian languages:* the intervention of holidays prevented the delivery of it before the 26th, when Mr. Wood waited on the principal Woongee, and presented it in form; he afterwards called upon the junior Woongees, and acquainted them of his having laid before the senior an address, which required their serious consideration.

I imagine that if this explicit avowal of my sentiments, had been made previously to our last-mentioned visits to the members of the royal family, we should have had less cause to complain of incivility. Such language I believe was not expected; the court had assured itself that the state of our affairs in Europe and in India was so critical, that we would tolerate yet greater arrogance of manner, rather than hazard the interruption of intercourse, and give our enemies the advantage of an alliance, which the native vanity of the Birmans, rendered them not unwilling to over-rate.

* It afforded me particular satisfaction to know, that the full purport and expression of my letter could not fail to be conveyed, through the channel of either of these languages, to the Birman court. The Armenian interpreter of English, who had spent the greater part of his life in the Birman country, was a man eminently qualified for the task: he spoke, read, and wrote English, superior to any person I ever knew, who had not been in Great Britain. It is a singular fact, that the first version of the late Sir William Jones's Translation of the Institutes of Hindoo Law, should be made in the Birman language. When I arrived at Ummerapoora, the Armenian had just completed the work, by command of his Birman Majesty. This circumstance offers no mean proof of the liberal and enlightened policy of a prince, who, superior to general prejudice, was willing to seek for information through a medium, by which few other nations of the East will condescend to accept of knowledge, however beneficial the attainment might prove to themselves.

Information was conveyed to me, from a respectable quarter, that the fermentation which my remonstrance excited in the council of the Lotoo, was by no means moderate; the Woongees, I was told, were divided in their opinions; the discussion continued till twelve o'clock on the night of the 27th, when the result of their deliberations was laid before the king.

Whatever might have been their separate sentiments, the ultimate decision was temperate and wise. I was apprized, late on the evening of the 28th, by a verbal communication from the Maywoon of Pegue, that on the day appointed for the delivery of the reply to the Governor-General's letter, I should be formally received at the palace of the King, who would grant me a personal audience in the character to which I laid claim, and that the propositions which I had suggested, for the regulation and encouragement of commerce, had for the most part received his Majesty's approbation.

I expressed in answer, the satisfaction I felt from hearing a resolution so creditable to themselves, but added, that as the letter I had written, was a public and solemn declaration, I should require more than a verbal assurance, before I could consistently subject myself, to a repetition of former disappointments, and requested that he would take the trouble to reduce his obliging message to writing; with this he readily complied by a short note written in the Birman language.

The form of receiving the presents, which were brought to me as a return for those that had been given, occupied a considerable portion of the last days. One of the three boxes, that had been sent by the King, contained amber in large pieces, uncommonly pure; another, a mass of stone of considerable size, in appearance resembling the chrysoprase; and the third, a large and beautiful group of crystals, rising from a matrix of amethyst, in the form of prisms, mostly hexagonal or pentagonal, slightly striated on the surface, and terminated at one end by a pyramid composed of three rhomboidal planes. It was a very curious production of nature, and doubtless, coming from such a quarter, must have been accounted of great value. The present from the Engy Teekien, consisted of six ruby and sapphire rings, two elephants teeth, several japanned boxes, and three horses, small, like all those which the country produces, but extremely well formed: two were piebald, to match in a carriage, and the other was a bright bay. The principal queen also, whose title is Nandoh Praw, and the second Queen, called Myack Nandoh, sent their separate offerings, and added to several rings and specimens of japanned ware, some handsome articles of plate, two large beetle boxes, of embossed silver, two trays and two drinking cups of the same metal, the workmanship of which did not afford a favourable proof of the skill of their artists. Retributory donations were now brought in troublesome abundance, from every individual, to whom the smallest gratification had been given; and in some instances the return far exceeded in value what had been received: my house was encumbered with all sorts of Birman utensils in painted and japanned ware, several of which were by no means of a portable size. I was also presented with pieces of silk and cotton cloth, of different dimensions and quality, in number not less than eighty or a hundred; also elephants teeth, amber wrought into beads, fifty or sixty pieces of plate formed into beetle boxes, mugs, spitting pots and cups; precious stones too constituted a very general gift, chiefly rubies and sapphires in their native state, rudely set in gold. I received from various persons, nearly a hundred of these stones, few of which were valuable, though some of the sapphires, on being polished by a lapidary, proved to have a very fine water. I must not, however, omit mentioning a beautiful specimen of filagree, in a large silver beetle-box, which was presented to me by one of the Attawoons; the workmanship was minutely delicate, and exquisitely finished, and in order to enhance the value of the gift, the donor, with a politeness that could not be surpassed in any court, had his title engraven in English letters on the side of the box: a compliment so handsomely conveyed, demanded my best acknowledgments, and I regretted exceedingly, that the official character which I held, denied me the personal acquaintance of this minister, as well as of some others, whom I should have been happy, under any other circumstances, to have cultivated.

On the 30th of September, the day appointed by his Birman Majesty to receive the English gentlemen in the character of an imperial deputation, we crossed the lake at ten o'clock in the morning, attended by our customary suite, and accompanied by Baba-Sheen and several Birman officers. We entered the fort, as usual, by the western gate, when instead of passing, as on former occasions, along the north side of the enclosure of the palace, to reach the street leading down to the Lotoo, we now proceeded round by the south, and in this new direction observed many more houses of distinguished structure, than by the other route. In our way we passed through a short street, entirely composed of saddlers and harness makers shops. On alighting, we were conducted into the Rhoom, to wait there until the Engy Teekien should arrive, which he did precisely at the hour of twelve. Several Chobwas, who were to be introduced on this day, had taken their seats in the Rhoom before we entered; each of them held a piece of silk or cotton cloth in his lap, designed, according to the established etiquette, as a propitiatory offering to his Majesty; and on the cloth was placed a saucer, containing a small quantity of unboiled rice, which it seems is an indispensable part of the ceremony. The Birman custom differs in this particular from the usage of Hindostan: a person, on his presentation at the imperial court of Delhi, offers to the sovereign an odd number of the gold coin commonly called Mohurs,* an even number being considered as inauspicious; but the court of Ummerapoora, with a more delicate refinement, never permits an offering in money, but requires from a foreigner something of the produce of his country, and from a subject, some article of manufacture. The donation of rice is not, as in India, when presented by Brahmins to the incarnations of Vishnu, meant as an acknowledgment of divine attributes, but is merely designed as a recognition of the power of the monarch, and an acknowledgment of the property of the soil being vested in him; a truth which is expressively declared, by offering him its most useful production. During our continuance in the Rhoom, tea was served to us, and when we advanced to the outer gate, we were not obliged to put off our shoes, but were permitted to wear them, until we had reached the inner inclosure, that separates the court of the Lotoo from that of the royal palace, within which, not any nobleman of the court is allowed to go with his feet covered. There is a double partition wall, dividing the two courts, with an intervening space of ten or twelve feet, through which a gallery leads that is appropriated exclusively to the use of the King when he chuses to preside in person in the Lotoo.

On entering the gate, we perceived the royal saloon of ceremony in front of us, and the court assembled in all the parade of pomp and decoration. It was an open hall, supported by colonnades of pillars

* Mohur is a corrupt name given by Europeans to this coin. Ashurfi is its proper term; Pagoda likewise, as applied to a coin, is an illegitimate word, of which the natives know nothing, except on the authority of their conquerors.

twenty in length, and only four in depth: we were conducted into it by a flight of steps, and advancing, took our places next the space opposite to the throne, which is always left vacant, as being in full view of his Majesty. On our entrance, the basement of the throne, as at the Lotoo, was alone visible, which we judged to be about five feet high; folding doors screened the seat from our view. The throne, called Yazapalay, was richly gilded and carved; on each side a small gallery, inclosed by a gilt balustrade, extended a few feet to the right and left, containing four umbrellas of state; and on two tables, at the foot of the throne, were placed several large vessels of gold, of various forms and for different purposes: immediately over the throne, a splendid piasath rose in seven stages above the roofs of the building, crowned by a tee, or umbrella, from which a spiral rod was elevated above the whole.

We had been seated a little more than a quarter of an hour, when the folding doors that concealed the seat, opened with a loud noise, and discovered his Majesty ascending a flight of steps, that led up to the throne from the inner apartment; he advanced but slowly, and seemed not to possess a free use of his limbs, being obliged to support himself with his hands on the balustrade. I was informed, however, that this appearance of weakness, did not proceed from any bodily infirmity, but from the weight of the regal habiliments in which he was clad; and if what we were told was true, that he carried on his dress fifteen viss, upwards of fifty pounds avoirdupois of gold, his difficulty of ascent was not surprising. On reaching the top he stood for a minute, as though to take breath, and then sat down on an embroidered cushion with his legs inverted. His crown was a high conical cap, richly studded with precious stones; his fingers were covered with rings, and in his dress he bore the appearance of a man, cased in golden armour, whilst a gilded, or probably a golden, wing on each shoulder, did not add much lightness to his figure. His looks denoted him to be between fifty and sixty years old, of a strong make, in stature rather beneath a middle height, with hard features and of a dark complexion; yet the expression of his countenance was not unpleasing and seemed, I thought, to indicate an intelligent and inquiring mind.

On the first appearance of his Majesty, all the courtiers bent their bodies, and held their hands joined in an attitude of supplication. Nothing farther was required of us, than to lean a little forward, and to turn in our legs as much as we could; not any act being so unpolite, or contrary to etiquette, as to present the soles of the feet towards the face of a dignified person. Four Bramins dressed in white caps and gowns, chanted the usual prayer at the foot of the throne: a Nakhaan then advanced into the vacant space before the King, and recited in a musical cadence, the name of each person who was to be introduced on that day, and the present of which, in the character of a suppliant, he entreated his Majesty's acceptance. My offering consisted of two pieces of Benares gold brocade; Doctor Buchanan and Mr. Wood each presented one. When our names were mentioned, we were separately desired to take a few grains of rice in our hands, and joining them, to bow to the King as low as we conveniently could, with which we immediately complied. When this ceremony was finished, the King uttered a few indistinct words, to convey, as I was informed, an order for investing some persons present, with the insignia of a certain degree of nobility: the imperial mandate was instantly proclaimed aloud by heralds in the court. His Majesty remained only a few minutes longer, and during that time he looked at us attentively, but did not honour us with any verbal notice, or speak at all, except to give the order before mentioned.

Drawn by Singey Boy. Engraved by J. Holland.

View of the Imperial Court at Ummerapoora, and the Ceremony of Introduction.

London Published Nov.r 1, 1799 by G Nicol, Pall Mall & J Wright, Piccadilly

When he rose to depart he manifested the same signs of infirmity as on his entrance; after he had withdrawn, the folding doors were closed, and the court broke up.

In descending, we took notice of two pieces of cannon, apparently nine pounders, which were placed in the court, on either side of the stairs, to defend the entrance of the palace. Sheds protected them from the weather, and they were gilded all over: a royal carriage also was in waiting, of curious workmanship, and ornamented with a royal spire; there was a a pair of horses harnessed to it, whose trappings glistened in the sun.

We returned as usual to the Rhoom, where I understood that the letter from the King to the Governor General of India was to be presented to me, together with some other documents that comprehended the objects of the embassy. Soon after the members of the royal family had ascended their elephants, the expected letter was brought from the Lotoo on a tray, borne by a Nakhaan, inclosed in a case of wood japanned and covered with a scarlet cloth. The mode of offering it, was not, I conceived, quite so ceremonious as the occasion seemed to require, and the officer who was charged with the delivery, indicated a reluctance to say, that it was a letter from the King, to the Governor General of India. This circumstance produced some difficulty, as without being distinctly informed to whom the letter was directed, I declined accepting it. At length the interpreter, finding I would not receive it on other terms, delivered it in a suitable manner, with a declaration that it was a reply from his Birman Majesty to the letter of the British Governor General of India, and that a copy of a royal mandate was annexed to it, granting to the English nation, certain valuable immunities and privileges of trade.

Whilst we were in the outer court, or that in which the Lotoo is situated, we had an opportunity of viewing the immense piece of ordnance found in the fortress of Arracan, when captured by the Engy Teekien, which was afterwards conveyed by water to adorn the capital of the conqueror, where it is now preserved as a trophy, and is highly honoured, being gilded, and covered by a roof of a dignified order. It is formed of brass, rudely manufactured; the length is thirty feet, the diameter at the muzzle two and a half, and the calibre measured ten inches; it is mounted on a low truck carriage supported by six wheels; near it lay a long rammer and sponge staff, and we perceived several shot made of hewn stone fitted to the calibre. It is remarkable, that most of the spoils which had been brought from Arracan were made of brass; the image of Gaudma, the lions, the demons, and the gun, all transported from thence, are composed of that metal.

The discussion, on the ceremony of delivering the letter, being ended, we returned home, proceeded by a Miouseree, or inferior secretary, on horseback, bearing in due form the royal letter, and dressed in his cap and gown of office. When we had reached our residence, I immediately addressed the chief minister, to request an official translation of the letter in the Persian language, also of the paper annexed to it, observing that as public interpreters of that tongue, were appointed by the court, and it being well understood by several persons resident at Ummerapoora, a medium of intercourse could never be wanting, which would be equally intelligible and convenient to their government and to mine. Within two days I received a notification, that his Majesty had given orders to supply me with the translation I required.

CHAPTER XVIII.

Substance of official Papers.—Prepare to depart.—Chinese Deputies—take Leave preparatory to their Return.—Birman Books—sold clandestinely to Strangers.—A Man imprisoned.—Liberal Conduct of the Court—Siamese Painter.—Birman Festival—the Court of the Queen attended by all the Women of Rank—Illuminations.—Unceremonious Visit to the Engy Teekien.—Embark on board our Boats—delayed.—Letter from the principal Woongee to the Governor-General of India.—Ill Treatment suffered by one of our People—Insolence of the Followers of the Prince of Tongho.—Leave Ummerapoora.—Visit Chagaing—Description of the Fort.—Oderua, or Pot Village.—Kieock, the great Manufactory of Birman Idols.—Temple of Commodoo Praw.—Fireworks—Rockets of extraordinary Magnitude.—Chagaing—an Emporium of Cotton—ancient Ava.—Temple of Logatherpoo Praw—stupendous Idol.—Sandaht, or Elephant Town.—Keenduem River.—Nioundoh.—Pegahm—Civility of the Mioudogee, or Deputy Governor—ride to view the Ruins—curious Temple—Art of turning Arches—lost by the Birmans.—Reach the Town of Sillah Mew.

THE intervention of holidays, together with the unavoidable delays of office, protracted the delivery of the Persian translations until the 14th of October; on which day the papers, properly authenticated, were brought from the Lotoo, and delivered to me, by an officer of government. In translating these documents, I carefully collated the Persian version with the Birman original, which I was enabled to do by the assistance of persons on the spot, who understood both languages, and found the Persian to be as literal a translation, as the different idioms would admit.

The letter of his Birman Majesty to the Governor-General (Appendix, No. III.) is a curious specimen of the extravagant phraseology of oriental composition: a great part of it is the diction of the minister, which may be considered as the preamble of the letter. In this portion are enumerated the royal titles, the honours conferred on the British representative, and the presents that were delivered; it next details the heads of certain propositions, which I had made with a view to advance the commercial interests of both nations; his Majesty then speaks in his own person, and in the pompous style of an order, ratifies immunities of considerable importance to British merchants and mariners.

The paper which accompanied the letter (Appendix, No. IV.) is an order delivered by the principal Woongee, to carry into effect the imperial mandate, and is addressed to the Maywoon of Pegue in particular, as holding the jurisdiction of Rangoon, and to the governors of sea-port towns in general. It, however, became necessary, in order to give full operation to his Majesty's good intentions, to obtain several subsidiary papers, which, by expressing in clear detail, the regular dues of government, and specifying the authorized perquisites of office, might prevent in future any arbitrary exactions, and put an end to impositions, which had long been practised on British merchants trading to Birman ports, from whom, loud complaints had at different times reached the supreme government. These papers I found no difficulty in obtaining: it was determined by them, that all goods of Europe and British India manufacture, imported in British ships, should be subject to a duty of ten per cent. to the King; the price of anchorage and pilotage, for ships of every rate, was determined; the fees of the provincial and port officers, charges for warehouse room, for interpreters and clearance, the customs to be levied at each house of collection on goods conveying up the river, were accurately defined; and teak timber, to us by far the most valuable commodity which the country produces, was ordered to pay a duty of five per cent. ad valorem, at whatever port it might be shipped, and all further exactions on that article were prohibited. The several demands of the port and provincial officers on the masters of ships, which had heretofore been paid in rouni, or pure silver, were directed to be taken in the currency of the place, which, at Rangoon, is mowadzo, or silver depreciated twenty-five per cent.

These regulations, expressed in separate instruments with clearness and precision, were equally liberal and satisfactory; and, on the part of the Birman government, were voluntarily granted, from a conviction of the equity on which they were founded, and the reciprocal advantages they were likely to produce. From two propositions which I offered, the court thought proper to withhold its acquiescence; but it certainly was the intention of the King and his chief ministers, that the articles which were thus conceded, should be carried into complete effect. Intercourse, however, was not yet perfectly established; many obstacles still impeded the way; the road was only opened, and success depended on the discretion of those, who should first pursue the track that was now pointed out.

Having thus obtained the objects for which I had been deputed, to an extent that equalled my utmost expectation, I prepared to depart. The waters of the great river had been subsiding for some time, by which the lake became so much reduced, that boats of burthen were obliged to leave it.

and moor in the stream, the bar of sand at the entrance of the lake being almost dry in the fair season. The vast sheet of water, which, by taking a circuitous direction, had, on our first arrival, induced us to conclude that we were on an island, was now diminished to an inconsiderable surface, and left a large portion of land, which had recently been covered, in a state adapted for the cultivation of rice. We observed the peasants industriously employed in turning up the oozy soil, preparatory to the reception of seed; and it was now manifest, that the place of our residence, which, from the encroachment of the periodical waters, we had considered as low, was in fact an elevated and commanding situation.

Early in October, the Chinese deputies, having fulfilled their diplomatic mission, left the grove to return to their native country. They embarked on board commodious boats, in which I understood they were to travel for three weeks, and afterwards prosecute their route by land, until they got into the heart of the Chinese dominions, where water carriage is facilitated by numerous canals. They expected to find the cold intense before their arrival at Pekin; a journey which they stated would require three months to perform. I presented the senior, at his last visit to me, with a wrapper of English broad cloth, which he remarked would be more comfortable in his journey among the cold hills of China, in the month of December, than his own garments of silk quilted with cotton. He apologized for not having any thing better to give me in return than some pieces of silk and a few fans; but his son, a promising youth of seventeen, who attended his father in quality of page, and who had been on more familiar terms with us, than the natural gravity and public character of the seniors would allow to them, came to take leave of me just before his embarkation, and observing that he should probably never see me again, entreated my acceptance of his pillow and his purse, as memorials of the son of Keeloree.* When I hesitated in receiving what were conveniencies to him, but useless to me, he seemed so much hurt, that I could not wound the feelings of the ingenuous youth, by rejecting his artless token of good will. I had given him at different times a few trifling gratifications, and he could not reconcile himself to depart without making some return. His pillow was a light lacquered box, about eighteen inches long, circular at top, and covered with a case of silk, so thickly quilted with cotton as to render it soft. In a box of this sort, a Chinese, when he makes a journey, usually carries all his valuables; though unprovided with a lock, it is not easy to be opened, and the case is closely buttoned: thus a traveller secures all his property by sleeping on it. This box was not empty; it contained the purse† beforementioned, a steel and flint to light fire, and a bracelet and ring of agate, which the donor assured me were endued with certain cabalistic virtues, to protect the possessor from the perils of the road.

During the time that matters of business were under discussion, and the necessary papers preparing, Mr. Wood employed his leisure hours in digesting his survey of the river, and in making astronomical observations; whilst Doctor Buchanan, ever assiduous in the pursuit of knowledge, prosecuted botanical enquiries, and collected general information from every accessible source. Among other things, books in the Birman tongue were brought to him for sale, on which the owners put, what seemed to be, a

* This I conceive to be rather a title than his real name.

† This purse bore an exact resemblance to the representation in Sir George Staunton's work, of the purse which his imperial majesty of China presented to the embassador's page when the British embassy was formally introduced.

very exorbitant price; and either from real, or pretended apprehension, these venders of Birman literature always produced their wares in a clandestine manner; assigning as a reason, that if any person were discovered to have sold books to a foreigner without permission, he would be liable to a severe penalty. This assertion we were at first inclined to consider rather as a pretext for enhancing the demand, than as founded on fact; one day, however, we understood that a man had actually been imprisoned for an offence of this nature, and was likely to suffer punishment. I immediately sent a message to the chief Woongee, apprizing him of the circumstance, and desiring to know whether it was illegal to sell books to us; that if their law prohibited it, I should reject such as in future might be brought, and direct every person under my authority to do the same. The Woongee returned a civil message, and the man was set at liberty. His Majesty being made acquainted with the affair, summoned, on the following day, the principal Rhahaans to attend his council, and submitted to them, whether or not it was consistent with Birman tenets, to grant books that treated of their history and laws, to foreigners. The conclave, I was told, after solemn deliberation, determined in the affirmative; and added, that it was not only admissible, but laudable, for the dissemination of knowledge. His Majesty was thereupon pleased to order a handsome copy of the Razawayn, or History of their Kings, and of the Dhirmasath, or Code of Laws, to be delivered to me from the royal library: each was contained in one large volume, written in a beautiful manner, and handsomely adorned with painting and gilding.

My Bengal draftsmen, whose labours were principally directed by Dr. Buchanan in the delineation of plants, met at Ummerapoora with a brother artist in a Siamese painter, who was employed by the court. This man, though not so skilful as the person in my service, was nevertheless of much utility; he furnished me with several drawings descriptive of the costume of the country, which though executed with little taste, were finished with the most perfect fidelity; among other things he brought me a representation of the Shoepaundogee, or royal barge used by the King when he goes in state on the water; the painter reported that the length of the vessel was a hundred cubits (more than one hundred and fifty feet): I saw it through a glass, but at too great a distance to observe more than the elevated stern, the royal piasath in the centre, which occupied the place of a mast, and the splendour of the gilding, with which it was entirely covered. The King possesses a great variety of boats, some of them we had an opportunity of viewing, but the Shoepaundogee is by far the most magnificent.

The Birman month of Sandaingguite, which had just expired, is a season of universal festivity and rejoicing, and on the three terminating days, solemn homage is paid to the King, to the Engy Teekien, and to the principal Queen. At the court of the latter, all the wives and daughters of the nobles pay their respects, unaccompanied by their husbands or any male attendants; and in this assembly, as much state and ceremony are observed as at the court of his Majesty. The rank, which each lady bears in right of her husband, is expressed by her dress and ornaments; female priority being not less scrupulously maintained, than precedency amongst men. We regretted extremely, that their customs did not allow us to attend the Queen's court, in the same manner as at that of her illustrious mother. Age and widowhood, it seems, gave the latter a privilege of receiving visits from the other sex, without violating decorum, or incurring reproach.

During the fifteen days of this "decreasing moon," the city was illuminated every night; lanterns made of different coloured transparent paper were suspended from bamboo scaffolds, and disposed in various shapes, which produced a pleasing effect when seen from our residence on the opposite side of the lake. The superior brilliancy of the lights at the palace, was distinguishable above the rest. The Birmans are singularly expert in the display of fire-works of every description.

On the 13th of October, I received a verbal message from the Engy Teekien, that he should be glad to see me on the following day, when he meant to lay aside the parade of state, and honour me with an unceremonious reception. I embraced with pleasure an opportunity of an interview, unincumbered with the formalities of regal pomp, and accompanied by a few attendants, proceeded on horseback to his palace, at the appointed time. As soon as my arrival was announced, I was immediately introduced without the previous ceremony of waiting in the Rhoom. On this occasion he did not, as formerly, exhibit himself from a casement window like a pagod, but was seated at the upper end of the hall, upon a couch richly adorned with the customary ornaments. His dress was entirely simple; he wore a white vest of fine muslin, with a lower garment of silk, and his head was bound with an embroidered fillet. Several personages of rank were present, habited also in a plain manner, but distinguished by their gold tzaloe, or chain of nobility. The deportment of the prince at this interview was perfectly frank, and free from ostentation; I was disappointed, however, in his conversation; I expected that he would, by inquiring into the state of the British provinces, and the causes of their prosperity, have sought for information, that might hereafter prove beneficial to the country over which he is one day presumptively to reign. His discourse took a quite different turn; he asked only frivolous questions, and endeavoured to amuse

Drawn by Singey Bey.

Engraved by J. Medland

Shoepaundogee or Royal Golden Barge.

London, Published Nov.r 1 1796, by G. Nicol, Pall Mall & J. Wright, Piccadilly

me by the prattle of two sprightly children, his daughters. Half an hour having been spent in this trifling manner, I withdrew, and paid a visit to the Maywoon of Pegue, who told me that it was his intention to accompany us back to Rangoon, where he would order every necessary to be provided for our convenience and accommodation.

The distance to which our boats were obliged to remove, rendered the transportation of our baggage, a work of labour: after conveying it across the lake, it was to be laden on carts, and drawn for two miles over what was now a plain of sand, but at the time of our arrival had been a wide sheet of water, navigated by vessels of considerable burthen. The communication between the lake and the river, was now completely closed.

On the 23d of October we began to send off our heaviest articles. The commissary, or Kyewoon, had taken care to provide a carriage and labourers, the expence of which we were not suffered to defray; what I gave to the people, was considered as a private gratification.

Having embarked most of our baggage, Mr. Wood and Doctor Buchanan, with a proportion of the attendants, left me early on the 25th, to go on board the boats: I remained until evening, waiting for some papers which I expected from the city. Horses were in readiness for us to mount, on the opposite side of the lake.

On leaving Tounzemahn, as the boat pushed from the shore, I looked back with pleasure at the grove, under the shade of which we had resided, and bade a glad, but not unthankful adieu to an habitation, where I had experienced kind hospitality, and spent three months in a manner, that could not fail to impress me with a lasting recollection of the scene. To be placed in so singular and interesting a situation, cannot often occur; nor can the images created by it be easily obliterated from the mind.

Riding across the plain, over which I had lately sailed, I perceived that part of it, was already under tillage, but the largest portion was left for pasture. During the inundation, canoes navigated between the houses of the lower suburbs of the city, and all communication was maintained by water; but carts now plied in dusty lanes, and the foundations of the buildings, were at least fifteen feet above the level of the river. Our boats were at a creek called Sakyingua, where a number of trading vessels were also moored, some of them of considerable burthen. The noise of the boatmen on the bank, and the smoke from the fires which they made, rendered the situation by no means agreeable.

Various causes conspired to detain us at Sakyingua Creek, until the 29th. In the interval, I received a short letter from the principal Woongee, directed to the Governor-General of India, containing a desire of the King, to procure certain religious books written in the Shanscrit language; likewise that a Bramin, well versed in astronomy, might be sent from Bengal to his court, to instruct his own professors, of whose ignorance in that science, his Majesty was fully sensible. The letter, however, laid as much stress on the purity of the preceptor's cast, as on the extent of his knowledge, and comprehended a curious addition to the request, that a Bramin woman should accompany the sage, with a view, I imagine, of propagating a race of hereditary astronomers. I informed the Woongee, in reply, that Bramins of learning, have an invincible dislike to leave their native country, even for a limited period; but to emigrate with their families, I conceived, was an act, to which no temptation would induce them: I added, that the principles of the English government did not allow of force being used, to compel a subject into exile, who had not by any crime forfeited the protection of the law. This, I dare say, was not very intelligible doctrine to the despotic monarch of Ava, and at all events must have been perfectly novel.

Whilst we remained at this place, one of our people received ill treatment from the natives, which was remarkable, as being the first instance that had occurred. Doctor Buchanan, desirous of enriching his collection of plants, with every rare production of the country, used to employ a peasant boy of Bengal, to gather herbs for him, whom he every day sent for that purpose into the fields. The followers of the Prince of Tongho happened to reside in this quarter, a class of men, notorious among Birmans for their insolence and dishonesty: the lad unluckily chanced one day to meet a party of these ruffians, who took from him his knife, basket, and turban, and, threatening to put him to death, so frightened him that he botanized no more, till we were out of their reach. I had before heard much of the ferocity of these people, who were very numerous; report made their numbers ten thousand: they were always quarrelling with the followers of the other princes, particularly those of the Prince of Prome. It was said that the King, had on one occasion, whilst we were at Ummerapoora, sharply reprimanded his son, the Tongho Teekien, and confined his Woon, or minister, for not keeping his people in better subjection. I took no notice of their conduct; it was not expedient at my departure to make a public complaint of such a petty outrage.

The river, which three months before, had displayed an uninterrupted expanse of several miles, was now broken into separate streams, surrounding numerous islands, which had just emerged from the inundation. The principal branch of the river, even in its diminished state, was a mile wide. Doctor Buchanan and I crossed in a small boat to an island, where some fishermen and gardeners had begun to erect huts, in which they reside until returning floods in the ensuing year force them to abandon their habitations. They seemed to have the means of comfortable livelihood; their gardens were already sown with the sweet potatoe, convolvulus batatas, pulse, and Brenjals, solanum melongena; the latter are usually transplanted. The soil was extremely dry, notwithstanding it had so recently been covered with water, and the pasturage was luxuriant. The inhabitants possessed cattle and poultry in abundance, and doubtless were supplied with excellent fish.

Early on the 29th, the Maywoon of Pegue visited me, in a very handsome war-boat gilded to the water's edge, accompanied by several others that were plain; he invited me on board, and we took our seats on the prow, which, in Birman boats, is always the place of dignity. When we left the shore, the whole fleet pushed off and followed us; the morning was fine, and the water smooth, whilst the spires of Ummerapoora in our stern, the white temples and lofty hills of Chagaing opposite, and the fort of ancient Ava below, formed a very cheerful prospect. We rowed to Chagaing, where, soon after our arrival, the Maywoon took leave of me, to return to the capital, having business to detain him a few days longer; he however promised to overtake us on the way down, his boats being better adapted than ours, for expedition.

After dinner, Doctor Buchanan and I walked out to view the fort of Chagaing, which in the days of Namdoo Praw had been the seat of empire; we entered under a gateway, the arch of which was wide and well turned. This fort had nothing to distinguish it from others that have been already described; it was not nearly so large as Ummerapoora, or even equal in extent to the lines of ancient Ava; the defences were suffered to fall into ruins, and the houses were meanly built among weeds and rubbish.

Drawn by Singey Bey. *Engraved by T. Medland*

A Birman War Boat.

London, Published Nov. 1, 1799, by G. Nicol, Pall Mall & J. Wright, Piccadilly

We observed a well supplied herb market, which was attended wholly by women. Passing through the fort, we crossed a narrow fosse on a handsome wooden bridge, the length of which indicated, that during the monsoon the inundation extended to a considerable distance, and a little farther, we came to the great road leading to Meengoung. On our right, lay the low conical hills, whose summits, crowned with white temples, form such conspicuous objects from the river. Advancing about a mile, we arrived at a village called Oderua, or pot village, from its being a manufactory of earthen ware. The lateness of the evening prevented our further progress. We returned by a road that led to the left of the fort, passing in our way a neat village situated near the banks of the river.

By means of our horses, we now enjoyed a convenience which in coming up we did not possess. A platform had been constructed in a broad boat, capable of containing five horses: we brought three from the capital, and added two others on the way down: little trouble was occasioned by embarking or landing them; the Birman grooms were expert, and the beasts tractable. Early next morning we mounted, and pursued the route of the preceding evening. Numerous temples lined the road on either side, but one only of the number attracted particular notice; it was surrounded by a high brick wall, from which elephants heads, formed of masonry, were protruded in such a manner, as to give the wall an appearance of being supported on the backs of those animals; the temple was a pyramid of brick, about one hundred feet high, ornamented wih a gilded umbrella. Passing through Pot Village, we came to a town called Kyeock Zeit, remarkable for being the great manufactory of marble idols, the inhabitants of which were statuaries by trade. I saw thirty or forty large yards crowded with artists, at work on images of various sizes, but all of the same personage,

Gaudma, sitting cross legged on a pedestal. The quarries, whence the materials are procured, are only a few miles distant; the marble is brought hither in shapeless blocks, and after being fashioned, the images are publicly sold to those who have grace enough to purchase them. The largest that I observed, a little exceeded the human size, the price of which, they said, was one hundred tackals, twelve or thirteen pounds, but some diminutive Gaudmas were to be disposed of, as low as two or three tackals. The Leedegee, or steersman of my boat, bought one to protect us on the way down. The workmen were extremely civil and communicative; they would not part with their sacred commodity, I was told, to any except Birmans, but they answered our questions with good humour, and our curiosity neither excited surprise, nor gave umbrage. Their tools are simple; they shape the image, with a chisel and mallet, and afterwards smooth it, by freestone and water. Many of the idols were beautifully polished, which, I understood, was effected by rubbing the marble with three different sorts of stone; the first rough, the second finer, and the third such as hones are made of, the workmen afterwards use the palms of their hands. This operation gives it a transparent clearness, far surpassing the brightest polish of which European marble is susceptible. Such images as were designed for gilding, did not receive so high a finishing.

Half a league further we came to where the temple of Kommodoo rears its massive and antique pile. This venerable and curious edifice stands on an eminence, which renders it a conspicuous object, at the distance of many miles. It is composed of solid masonry without cavity of any sort, and in shape resembles a bell; there is a high railing of wood encircling it, twelve feet distant from the base; the circumference on the outside of the railing, by my measurement, was four hundred paces, perhaps three hundred and fifty yards, and the height did not appear less than three hundred feet; it ended in a clumsy cone, unadorned by a spire or the customary umbrella, and exhibited a striking contrast to the elegant and still larger temple of Shoemadoo: indeed the stile of its structure indicated, that it was built either by a people possessing totally different notions of architecture, or at a far more remote period; it was much the most inelegant and heavy building, we had seen in the country. The roof had once been richly gilded, and the remains of wooden galleries, from which the paint and gilding were not quite obliterated, lay scattered around; these ornaments had probably been often renewed since the first erection of the temple. Kommodoo was once celebrated for its sanctity, and is still held in great reverence; many devotees were sauntering round the hill, whilst others were prostrate at their devotions. The Birmans boast of the antiquity of this building; they ascribe its rise to supernatural agency, and fix its date further back than the Mosaic æra: these, however, were the tales of ignorance to conceal the want of knowledge, but the traces of long duration were certainly evident, and from its size and form, Kommodoo Praw seems likely to resist the effects of time, for many ages.

From the site of Kommodoo, we had an extended view of the river winding through a rich and level country. A considerable lake lay to the southward; the plains were now cultivating, whilst numerous villages and herds of cattle denoted population and plenty. At a short distance from the foot of the hill, was a long avenue formed by a double row of tamarind trees of uncommon stateliness and beauty, under the shade of which a line of shops was erected on either side, where, besides provisions and cloth, utensils in brass ware, and fireworks, were sold. On a green, a little way retired from the road, we observed a number of people employed in making rockets, the tubes of which were the solid trunks of trees bored after the manner of a pump; in some, the cavity of the cylinder was nine or ten inches in diameter, and the wood about two inches thick; the length of these tubes varied from twelve to twenty feet; they were filled with a composition of charcoal, saltpetre, and gunpowder, rammed in very hard. The enormous size of Birman rockets, has already been noticed, in the account given of the fireworks of Pegue, but several that we saw here, far exceeded those in magnitude. The large ones are fired from a high scaffold erected for the purpose; bamboos fastened together, of a length adapted to preserve the poise, form the tail of the rocket; in this branch of pyrotechny the Birmans take particular delight, and are extremely skilful.

The day was now far advanced, and the sun become powerful. Having satisfied our curiosity, we galloped back to our boats, a distance of about seven miles. I took notice in my way, of frequent sheds, built at the side of the road, in which pots of water were placed, for the refreshment of travellers.

Chagaing is the principal emporium, to which cotton is brought from all parts of the country, and where, after being cleaned, it is embarked for the China market: females perform the labour of clearing it from the seeds; this is effected by double cylinders turned by a lathe, which the woman works with her foot, whilst she supplies the cotton with her hands. I was told, that the most opulent merchant in the empire, resides at Chagaing, who deals solely in this article. In the afternoon we loosed our boats and dropped down to Ava on the opposite side.

Early on the following morning, I walked out to examine the ruins of this deserted capital. The disposition of its streets and buildings nearly resembled that of Ummerapoora at the present day. We could trace the separate divisions of the palace, amidst heaps of rubbish overgrown by weeds and thorns: on the spot where but a few years since, the Lotoo stood, and justice was administered to a mighty empire, pulse and Indian corn were now growing. Passing to the westward, among ruinous walls and fallen temples, we came upon a good road, and a miserable old woman, "the sad historian" and living emblem of the place, pointed out the way to Logatherpoo Praw, formerly the residence of the Seredaw, or high priest of the empire, where the colossal image of Gaudma was still to be viewed.

The area on which the temple stands, is a square surrounded by an arcade of masonry; on each side, nine cubical towers are erected, and several buildings are comprehended within the space inclosed by the arcade. The temple in which the stupendous idol is placed, differs from the other pyramidical buildings, by having an arched excavation that contains the image. On entering this dome, our surprise was greatly excited at beholding such a monstrous representation of the divinity. It was a Gaudma of marble seated on a pedestal, in its customary position. The height of the idol, from the top of the head to the pedestal on which it sat, was nearly twenty-four feet; the head was eight feet in diameter, and across the breast it measured ten; the hands were from five to six feet long; the pedestal, which was also of marble, was raised eight feet from the ground. The neck and the left side of the image were gilded, but the right arm and shoulder remained uncovered. The Birmans asserted, that this, like every other Gaudma which I had seen of the same material, was composed of one entire block of marble; nor could we on the closest inspection, observe any junction of parts. If what they said was true, it remains a matter of much curiosity, to discover how such a ponderous mass could be transported from its native bed, and raised in this place. The building had evidently been erected over the idol, as the entrance would scarcely admit the introduction of the head. No intelligent Birman happening to be with us, all that I could learn in answer to my inquiries, was, that the image had been placed there an hundred years ago, by a King named Podoo Sembuan. Whatever may be its real history, it is an extraordinary specimen of idolatrous extravagance.

On our return, we perceived a man driving a cart drawn by a pair of oxen, which was filled with rubbish from the ruined buildings. I learnt that he was carrying the load to a neighbouring brook, to wash it, expecting to discover gold, silver, or some article of value, which not unfrequently happened. Old Ava is said to be the resort of numerous thieves, who find shelter and places of concealment, among the decayed religious edifices.

Our researches being ended, we re-embarked and immediately got under way, the boatmen using their oars with just sufficient force to accelerate in a slight degree, our motion down a gently gliding current. The river, except in those places where islands divided its stream, was above a mile wide. A little before sun set, we brought to for the night on the left hand, under a high bank near the town of Sandaht, and in the evening we took our customary walk, which at this place was among lanes, separated by hedge rows, inclosing fields planted with pulse, sesamum, and Indian corn.

We left Sandaht betimes the next morning, and continued to float down the stream, with little exertion or labour to our people. The river having fallen at least fifteen feet since the time we came up, we could not, as before, observe the towns and villages on each side, nor indeed could any object be seen that was not immediately on the edge of the banks, which hung perpendicularly over the river, in many places to a considerable height; but we knew when a town or a collection of houses was nigh, by the steps that were cut in the bank, for the convenience of fetching water. About four o'clock we passed the place where the Keenduem unites with the Irrawaddy. The mouth of the former did not seem to be much diminished by the change of season. We brought to in the evening, on the east side in the neighbourhood of a poor village, a short way below Tirroup Mew, where the country presented a cheerful aspect; grass was growing and cattle feeding in every direction.

On the following day, November 2d, we continued to travel in the same tranquil manner, the current of the river flowing two or three miles an hour with an unruffled surface. The weather was serene, and the temperature of the air moderate. Abundance of water fowl, collected on the sands which had recently emerged from the inundation, afforded us good shooting. As we approached the city of Nioundoh, I made inquiry concerning the excavations in the banks, which formerly had been the retreats of hermits, and was told that no person would now venture to explore them, as they had become the habitation of innumerable snakes and other noxious reptiles. We brought to in the evening among a fleet of at least two hundred large trading boats, which were moored at the bank, waiting to deliver or receive a lading. Nioundoh is a place of much commerce, having usurped all the trade that formerly was carried on at Pagahm: cotton, japanned ware, and oil extracted from sesamum, are the principal articles of exportation. The land adjacent to the town, did not wear a more fertile aspect, than when we passed it four months before; no change of season could effect an alteration in its barren soil, but on the opposite bank of the river, rich crops were waving, and cattle grazing in luxuriant pasture.

Early on the following day, we left Nioundoh and reached Pagahm by breakfast time. Although the distance by land is so short, that Nioundoh may be called the modern appendage to ancient Pagahm, yet we were above two hours between them, owing to the circuitous course of the river, which lengthens the way to eight or nine miles.

Mention of Pegahm has often occurred in this narrative, a city celebrated for its numerous temples, and the traces which it bears of former magnificence. To examine its extensive and various ruins with the accuracy of a speculative traveller, would have occupied more time than we had to spare. Shortly after the fleet had brought to, I was visited by the Mioudogee, or the person who governed the town and district in the absence of the prince; he informed me, that his royal master was expected on the following day from Ummerapoora. In the afternoon we walked out to view a very curious and ancient temple, which was repairing at the expence of the Engy Teekien, or prince royal. It was built of masonry, and comprehended several arches forming separate domes, into which four arched porches led, that faced the four cardinal points; on each side of the doors, in recesses in the wall, were seated gigantic human figures made of stucco, with large staring eyes, and the head protruded forward, as if to look at those who approached the threshold. These, I was told, were the supernatural porters of the doors, whose power of perception was such, that they could penetrate the recesses of the human breast, and discover the sincerity of devotion. The Mioudogee observed, that it was the prince's intention to gild this temple; and that four viss of gold, about the value of six hundred pounds, were already prepared for that purpose; he added that a considerable sum of silver had been expended on the repairs.

We were on this occasion, informed of a circumstance, that shews how easily an art once well known, may be lost to a country from disuse and the capriciousness of fashion; notwithstanding that well formed arches of brick are still to be seen in many of the ancient temples, yet Birman workmen can no longer turn them. Masonry has not in latter ages been much practised; wooden buildings have superseded the more solid structures of brick and mortar.

On our return, the Mioudogee politely invited us to stop and rest ourselves at his house. We accepted the invitation, and were ushered into a commodious dwelling inclosed by a railing; where we found several persons seated in a spacious hall. Soon after our entrance, the Mioudogee's wife came forth from an inner apartment, and sat down by her husband; she was attended by two female servants, and held by the hand her daughter, a pretty delicate child about eight years of age, who was not at all alarmed at the sight of strangers, but came and examined my hat and epaulette, with much engaging familiarity. Her father was extremely civil; not knowing that we had horses, he kindly offered us the use of his, if we chose to remain another day, and amuse ourselves by riding through the ancient city, which was too extensive to be traversed in so short a time on foot. Doctor Buchanan having expressed a wish to examine the Launzan, a rare species of plant, he promised to send one of his people on the following day some distance off, to procure it for him, which he punctually performed. Such instances of genuine hospitality are amongst the highest gratifications that a traveller can experience.

Next morning we mounted our horses at an early hour, pursuing an eastward direction on a road that led to hills, called Torroendong, about ten miles distant; beyond which, and more southerly, we perceived Poupa, a conical mountain mentioned in our former journey. On each side of the road, innumerable religious buildings appeared, in every stage of dilapidation. At the distance of two or three miles from the river, the soil became less barren. A few inconsiderable gardens were inclosed by the inhabitants, sown chiefly with Indian corn and pulse, and in some places the cotton plant was growing. We continued our ride five or six miles, as far as a small village, named Minangdoo, where the ruins seem to end in that direction. There I saw for the first time a Kioum, or monastery, built of masonry. We got back about twelve o'clock, and found crowds of people assembled at the water side, waiting for the arrival of the prince of Pagahm, who was hourly expected: all the men of distinction belonging to the city, had gone up the river to meet him. In order to make more room near the spot where he was to land, we loosed our boats, and removed to a situation lower down. Shortly after the fleet came in sight. We were at too great a distance to distinguish the prince's barge, the decorations of which were said to be very handsome; but we saw an immense number of boats, and heard the shouts of the people, who welcomed their royal governor with every demonstration of joy.

Being unacquainted with the etiquette proper to be observed on such an occasion, I consulted the Mioudogee, whether a visit from me was expected, or would be agreeable to the prince. He replied, that my paying a visit, would lay the prince under the necessity of desiring our stay for two or three days, to partake of an entertainment. As such a ceremony could not be convenient to him, and had no inducement for me, I sent Baba-Sheen to apologize in my name, pleading haste and the lateness of the season, as my excuse for not having the honour to wait on him.

At sun rise next morning, the prince of Prome passed by, with a very numerous and noisy retinue; from the number of boats there could not be fewer than three or four thousand persons: all the boatmen were singing in unison with the strokes of their oars. The Maywoon of Pegue who was in his suite, sent me a complimentary message, saying that he meant to attend the prince as far as Meeaday, his own Jaghire, or estate, where he should wait our arrival.

We were delayed at Pegahm by our boat people, till near ten o'clock, when we pushed off. The river, during the early part of this day, where islands of sand did not intervene, was not less than two miles wide: at one place, however, the channel contracted, and the current rushed round a projecting rock, with excessive rapidity. We saw several ranges of hills, some of which approached near the river, but these were of no considerable magnitude. The Arracan mountains, fifty or sixty miles distant, which were visible at intervals, towered high above the rest. In the evening we reached Sillamew, an ancient city which had once been a place of considerable note. A little way to the northward, we perceived the ruins of a brick fort erected in a very judicious situation; the ditch and wall were still to be traced. We had been so much engaged, when we were here before, with the silk and cotton merchants who brought their goods to sell, that we entirely overlooked the site of this fortress, an oversight that might easily happen, as its ramparts and towers are nearly level with the dust.

CHAPTER XIX.

Arrive at Sembewghewn.—Politeness of the Maywoon of Arracan.—Yaynangheoum.—Wells of Petroleum.—Patanago.—Meeaday—friendly Attention of the Maywoon of Pegue.—Kayn, or Mountaineers.—Strange Custom.—Notions of Religion.—Pulloo.—Prome.—Visit the Site of an Ancient City.—Peeinghee.—Mayahoun.—Prejudice of Birman Boatmen.—Disagreeable Circumstance.—Western River.—Denoobew.—Enter the Rangoon Branch of the Irrawaddy.—Mosquetoes.—Meet Captain Thomas.—Arrive at Rangoon.

WE departed from Sillahmew at the customary hour, and by nine o'clock in the morning reached Sembewgewn on the east bank of the river. The town is a league inland, but there is a village at the place where boats usually stop. We perceived a temporary house at some distance, such as is built for the accommodation of a man of rank when he travels, surrounded by small huts; and were informed that it was the encampment of the governor of Arracan. This officer had been newly appointed, and was on his way to take possession of his vice-royalty, which confers the title of Maywoon on the possessor, and is accounted one of the most important governments of the empire. I sent a message to him with compliments, and a request that he would forward a dispatch for me to Chittagong; the frontier British province that borders on Arracan. He obligingly undertook the commission, and punctually fulfilled his promise. I had afterwards the satisfaction to know, that the first advice which the Governor-General received of my proceedings at Ummerapoora, was by this conveyance.

We continued at Sembewghewn only a short time. I did not land; but the Doctor went on shore, he saw nothing however that merited particular notice. Mr. Wood remained till the afternoon, to observe the distance between the sun and moon; the latter being at this time visible, and the sky unclouded. We rowed till two o'clock, at which hour we reached Yaynangheoum, or Petroleum creek; a place already noticed in our journey up the river.

Doctor Buchanan partook of an early dinner with me; and when the sun had descended so low as to be no longer inconvenient, we mounted our horses to visit the celebrated wells that produce the oil, an article of universal use throughout the Birman empire. The face of the country was cheerless and sterile; the road, which wound among rocky eminences, was barely wide enough to admit the passage of a single cart, and in many places the track, in which the wheels must run, was a foot and a half lower on one side than the other: there were several of these lanes, some more circuitous than others, according to the situation of the small hills among which they led. Vehicles, going and returning, were thus enabled to pursue different routes, except at particular places where the nature of the ground would only admit of one road: when a cart came to the entrance of such a defile, the driver hallooed out to stop any that might interfere with him from the opposite side, no part being sufficiently wide for two carts to pass. The hills, or rather hillocks, were covered with gravel, and yielded no other vegetation than a few stunted bushes. The wheels had worn ruts deep into the rock, which seemed to be rather a mass of concreted gravel, than hard stone, and many pieces of petrified wood lay strewed about. It is remarkable, that wherever these petrefactions were found, the soil was unproductive, and the ground destitute of verdure. The evening being far advanced, we met but few carts; those we did observe were drawn each by a pair of oxen, and of a length disproportionate to the breadth to allow space for the earthen pots that contained the oil. It was a matter of surprise to us, how they could convey such brittle ware, with any degree of safety, over so rugged a road: each pot was packed in a separate basket, and laid on straw, nothwithstanding which precaution, the ground all the way was strewed with the fragments of the vessels, and wet with oil; for no care can prevent the fracture of some in every journey. As we approached the pits, which were more distant than we had imagined, the country became less uneven, and the soil produced herbage; it was nearly dark when we reached them, and the labourers had retired from work. There seemed to be a great many pits within a small compass: walking to the nearest, we found the aperture about four feet square, and the sides, as far as we could see down, were lined with timber; the oil is drawn up in an iron pot, fastened to a rope passed over a wooden cylinder, which revolves on an axis supported by two upright posts. When the pot is filled, two men take the rope by the end, and run down a declivity, which is cut in the ground, to a distance equivalent to the depth of the well; thus when they reach the end of their track, the pot is raised to its proper elevation, the contents, water and oil together, are then discharged into a cistern, and the water is afterwards drawn off through a hole at the bottom. Our guide, an active intelligent fellow, went to a neighbouring house and procured a well rope, by means of which we were enabled to measure the depth, and ascertained it to be thirty-seven fathom, but of the quantity of oil at the bottom we could not judge: the owner of the rope, who followed our guide, affirmed, that when a pit yielded as much as came up to the waist of a man, it was deemed tolerably productive; if it reached to his neck, it was abundant; but that which rose no higher than the knee, was accounted indifferent. When a well is exhausted, they restore the spring by cutting deeper into the rock, which is extremely hard in those places where the oil is produced. Government farm out the ground that supplies this useful commodity; and it is again let to adventurers who dig wells at their own hazard, by which they sometimes gain, and often lose, as the labour and expence of digging are considerable. The oil is sold on the spot for a mere trifle; I think two or three hundred pots for a tackal, or half-a-crown. The principal charge is incurred by the transportation and purchase of vessels. We had but half gratified our curiosity when it grew dark, and our guide urged us not to remain any longer, as the road was said to be infested by tigers, that prowled at night among the rocky uninhabited ways, through which we had to pass. We followed his advice, and returned with greater risk, as I thought, of breaking our necks from the badness of the road, than of being devoured by wild beasts. At ten o'clock we reached our boats without any misadventure.

We left Yaynangheoum before sunrise, and, committing ourselves to the current, glided almost imperceptibly down the stream, the boatmen lying in idle ease, some on the roof, and others on the lateral platforms of the vessel; whilst their only occupation was singing, praying, and sleeping by turns. The present manner of passing their time, was a contrast to what they experienced on the former journey, during which their labour had been excessive and without intermission; they all appeared pleased to return to Rangoon, where the necessaries of life are much cheaper than at the capital. We lay this night near the town of Patanago, a place already noticed. Walking out in the afternoon, I started several hares: the country abounds in game, and is beautifully diversified with hanging woods and rising grounds.

The fleet parted from Patanago very early, Doctor Buchanan's boat going ahead of the rest; he reached Loonghee half an hour before his companions, and, profiting by his celerity, went on shore at this romantic spot, where we had passed several days on our journey upwards. He walked to some distance, in the hope of finding fruit on a tree, which about four months before he had left in the earliest stage of blossom; but the fruit had since that time ripened and decayed, and the tree was now putting forth fresh flowers. Between this place and Meeaday, there are several ridges of low hills, clothed with wood and destitute of cultivation, which my people said were the haunts of numerous tigers and elephants. At sunset we got to Meeaday and perceived a number of boats fastened to the bank below the town, and among others we distinguished that of the Maywoon of Pegue: I immediately sent a message to his house, notifying our arrival, and in return received a civil reply, expressing a desire to see me.

On the following morning about nine o'clock, a nephew of the Maywoon came down to welcome us: after conversing sometime, I walked with him to visit his relation, by whom I was received with every demonstration of friendship: he politely asked me to remain at Meeaday for a day or two, and visit his garden and country house; but as the season was advanced, I felt solicitous to avoid unnecessary delay, and therefore excused myself: in fact, our stay would have put him to an inconvenience, having business, he said, to adjust on his estate, which would employ him for several days, but he expected to arrive at Rangoon as soon as ourselves. On my expressing a desire to see some of the mountaineers called Kayn, he obligingly offered to send one of his attendants to a village a few miles off, inhabited by these people, with directions to bring some of them for our inspection, dressed in the proper garb of their country. I understood from him that, since our departure from Ummerapoora, not less than 50,000 persons had left that city in the train of the several princes and men of rank, who, after paying homage at the golden feet, had returned to their respective governments. When I took leave, he ordered a pair of horses to be brought from his stable, and requested my acceptance of them; they were very handsome, and one was of an uncommon colour, having a number of circular black spots, on a milk white skin. In return, I presented him with a marquee made of European canvass, lined with English broad cloth, and my rifle-barrelled gun, which I more highly valued.

In the evening I walked over grounds which I had often trod before. Every thing in this district seemed to be flourishing; the peasants and farmers acknowledge in the Maywoon, a mild and beneficent landlord; if they were not so opulent as some, they were not so poor as many others: content, I thought, shone in every countenance, and comfort appeared to be an inmate of every dwelling. In my walks I saw a good deal of game, and shot a henza, or Braminy goose. The natives, although it is the symbol of their nation, hold the bird in no estimation; it is somewhat larger than a barnacle; the plumage is beautiful, but the flesh indifferent.

Next morning on my return from a long ride, I found a number of people collected on the banks opposite to our boats; these I learned were the Kayn, or mountaineers, with their conductors, for whom the Maywoon had sent on the preceding day. I desired that the principal man and woman should be brought on board. This curious couple were dressed in their best attire, consisting of an ill shaped sleeved coat made of coarse black cotton cloth; that of the man was much shorter than the woman's; both were bordered with stripes of white, red, and yellow; the man had a belt over his right shoulder, from which was suspended a pouch, ornamented with strings and small shells; on their heads they wore fillets nearly in the Birman manner; to the woman's were fastened tassels, composed of the Calyptra of the Buprestis ignita; she had also decorated her neck and arms with many strings of beads and cowries; but the most remarkable part was her face, which was tattowed all over in lines mostly describing segments of circles. This ceremony, which in some other countries is performed on the parts of women not publicly exposed, among the Kayn is confined wholly to the visage of their females, to which, in the eye of an unaccustomed beholder, it gives a most extraordinary appearance; the aspect of the woman, though she was not old, nor in other respects ugly, from the effect of the operation was truly hideous. I asked the origin of the custom; this they did not know, but said it had existed from time immemorial, and that it was invariably performed on every female, at a certain age. I immediately employed my painter to make a drawing of these singular figures, in the attitude in which they stood before me: a task which he performed in two hours, with great exactness, and drew striking resemblances. There was some difficulty in taking a likeness of the man, who was alarmed and restless, from a supposition that we were imposing magical spells upon him; but the woman stood still with her hands crossed, apparently in perfect good humour and

Drawn by Singey Roy

Engraved by T. Holland.

A Man & a Woman of the Tribe of Mountaineers, called Kayn

London, Publish'd Nov.r 1, 1799 by G. Nicol Pall Mall & J. Wright, Piccadilly

content; they spoke the Birman language indifferently, and, in order to engage their attention, we asked the man several questions, where he expected to go when he died? He replied, that he should again become a child. Who will make you a child? "The Mounzing." Who are the Mounzing? "The father and mother of the world, who grow on the earth as two trees in a field, one ever green, the other dry." What he meant by this metaphor we could not tell, unless it was a type of successive and eternal renovation and decay. He added, that the Mounzing resided on the great mountain Gnowa, where the images of the dead are deposited. They had no idea of a place of future rewards and punishments, and deny the existence of sin in their country; they do not pray whilst living, because they cannot, in this life, see the Mounzing, but they think that their images pray to them after mortal decease. They burn their dead, and afterwards collect their ashes in an urn, which they convey to a house, where, if the urn contain the relics of a man, they keep it six days, if of a woman, five; after which it is carried to the place of interment, and deposited in a grave, and on the sod that covers it, is laid a wooden image of the deceased, to pray to the Mounzing and protect the bones and ashes.

These are the rude notions of religion entertained by the harmless untaught race, that inhabit the lofty mountains which divide Arracan from Ava, and who, as children of nature, delighting in their wild and native freedom, are for the most part insuperably averse to hold any commerce with the people of the plains. The Birmans, since the conquest of Arracan, have compelled many, and allured a few, to settle in villages at the foot of the hills, where they are treated with a humanity that tends to conciliate them, to their new and more civilized state. A large proportion of

Kayn are, however, still independent. The Birmans have not yet carried sacrilegious invasion to their holy mountain, which probably is not worth acquiring. When a Kayn dies within the jurisdiction of the Birmans, the relations of the deceased always convey the urn, and the image of the departed person, to Gnowa, there to deposit them in hallowed earth. These people have no letters, nor any law, except custom; to this the Birmans prudently leave them, never interfering in their municipal and social economy.

Our curiosity being satisfied, we left Meeaday as soon as the painter had finished the drawings. The country through which we sailed this day had a pleasing appearance; spots of cultivation and frequent towns skirted the river, while small hills clothed with trees rose behind them. We passed in our way through a flock of thirty or forty elephants, who were swimming across the river, carrying their riders on their necks; these were all females, and had been employed in hunting their own species; males are seldom used by the Birmans for that purpose. Late in the evening we brought to, at a small town called Pulloo, where there is a custom house, having now entered the government of the Prince of Prome.

We got under way early the ensuing morning, and about two o'clock stopped at the lower suburbs of Prome, in the midst of a great concourse of boats. Landing our horses, we rode in the evening to view the site of a very ancient city, which ages ago was the residence of a dynasty of Pegue kings, before their country had submitted to the Birman yoke. On our right, we left a large temple named Shoe Sanda Praw, situated on an eminence, round the foot of which were several kioums, or monasteries; pursuing a southerly direction, we came on a level road leading through well cultivated fields, interspersed with groves of tall palmyra trees. We observed the channels of two rivers at this time almost dry; but which in the rainy season roll down an impetuous current from the mountains, and empty their waters into the Irrawaddy; by these streams, teak timber is floated from the forests during the monsoon, and is sold here very cheap. A plank three inches thick, and from sixteen to twenty feet long, may be purchased for a tackal, or half a crown. The soil in the neighbourhood of Prome, is remarkably well adapted for gardens, and we met several persons carrying loads of fruit on their heads to market. The evening was far advanced before we reached Yættee, on entering which we passed through an old gateway, that appeared to be narrower, but of greater depth, than any we had yet seen; indeed the ruinous state both of the gateway and the wall, rendered it difficult to judge accurately of their dimensions; within we could distinguish nothing but houses and fields, and it was now too late to explore the antiquities of the place. Two intelligent men, whom we overtook riding along the road, informed us that it had once been a great fortified city of a square form, each side measuring a space equal to two miles and a half; that it had flourished for several centuries, before the fall of the Pegue monarchy, and that the vestiges of the imperial palace and a large temple were still remaining.

During our ride, we observed two caravans of waggons drawn up in a circular form, in the same manner as those we had remarked at Meeaday, on our journey to the capital: here, however, the number of carts was much greater; one of the caravans containing not less than a hundred, which were disposed in two circles, one within the other, presenting a very formidable barrier against the assaults either of men, or of wild beasts. They were chiefly loaden with gnapee and salt fish, and had come from a town called Omow, situated on the banks of a lake where fish is caught in such abundance, as to constitute an article of commercial exportation. The road in this direction seemed to be well made, and much frequented. The Ledegee, or steersman, of Doctor Buchanan's boat, who had travelled by land from Prome to Rangoon, a journey of six days, said, that it was equally good the whole way. Timber and stone flags are the principal articles of export trade at Prome.

When the day broke we resumed our journey; the temperature of the air was now extremely pleasant, and the mornings and evenings cool: at sunrise, the quicksilver in the thermometer stood at 67 degrees. In the earlier part of this day, the villages, particularly those on the east bank, had a very inviting appearance, from the orchards of plantain, mango, and other fruit trees, with which they were surrounded. After passing Peinghee, the country assumed a rougher aspect; the river, at the narrow strait where our boat had been wrecked on the way up, did not now run with such rapid violence as before. Just above Tirroupmiou, we passed a large island covered with reeds and brushwood, which the boat people said was much infested by tigers. The handsome town of Kainggain was situated below it: we continued our course till after dark, and passing the lights of the long and populous city of Mayahoun, formerly Loonzay, brought to at the west bank, a little to the southward of the town; but it was too late to think of landing.

Next morning (Nov. 13th) we put off, at an early hour. In the middle of the preceding night, I had been alarmed by a scene of discord, between the boatmen and my people, which had nearly produced serious consequences. The Birmans have a superstitious abhorrence of any person's passing over them, when they are asleep; it is deemed a great indignity, as well as injurious from the apprehended effects of supernatural agency. The boatmen usually slept either on the roof of the boat, or on the platform projecting from the sides, whilst my people occupied the inner part. It happened that in the night, one of the soldiers went out on the platform, and, regardless of the Birmans who were taking their rest, stepped over them without ceremony, most likely ignorant of their prejudice, and perhaps half asleep himself: one of the Birmans, however, chanced unluckily to be awake, who, jumping up, instantly attacked the offender with his fists; a scuffle ensued, attended with no small outcry; the other Birmans rose, and armed themselves with the bamboos, that were kept for oar handles; the soldiers flew to their bayonets, and my servants were preparing to take their part. In this state of hostility I came among them, just time enough to prevent mischief. The Seree of Rangoon and the Ledegee at length pacified the enraged crew, and I ordered my own people to return to their births. This accident produced no future enmity, and it was the only disagreement that occurred. The Birmans, though sometimes irascible, were in general extremely good tempered, and seldom refused to accommodate the colars (strangers), even at the expence of their own convenience.

We rowed all this day through a country, not so well cultivated or so thickly inhabited, as that we had passed on the preceding: a little below Spainwah, a considerable branch of the river takes a southwesterly course, leading, we were informed, to Bassien; it is called Keidowa, and sometimes Anou Kioup, or the Western River: the Arracan mountains were visible in the north-west quarter. We brought to after dark, a little above Henzadah, under a reedy bank, from which we were invaded by myriads of troublesome insects.

The following day brought us without any remarkable incident to Denoobew. The high bank and beautiful situation of Terriato or Mango village, on the west side, tempted me to go on shore. It is a charming spot; the town is inconsiderable, but the houses are neat and commodious. Denoobew, where we arrived after sunset, is distinguished by a fine temple, and is also celebrated for its manufactory of mats, which are made here in beautiful variety, and superior in quality to what are fabricated in any other part of the empire; long reeds and grass skirted the banks during the greatest part of this day's journey.

From Denoobew to Yangain Chaingah, the river preserves nearly a direct course. About ten o'clock in the morning of the 15th, we got to the entrance of the Panlang river, where it separates from the great stream, in the same manner as the Hoogly does from the Ganges; the principal branch pursuing a southerly course, divides as it approaches the sea into a number of channels, which are filled by the tide, and are for the most part navigable. The river we now entered, is called by various names, Ashay Kioup, or the Eastern River, Panlang river, and Rangoon river, the width of which did not exceed four hundred yards. The eastern bank is within the jurisdiction of Pegue; but the opposite country is included in the province of Dalla, and is governed by a person of a much less dignified title than Maywoon. Through the high reeds, which on each side overhung the water, several pathways were made leading to Carrian villages. As we passed, I perceived a watercourse, which my people said came from a lake called Mallatoo. We had now reached the place, where in going up, we had been so severely teized by mosquitos, and again felt their venomous influence; they even assailed us in the daytime, and in such numbers, that we were obliged to fortify our legs with boots, and put on thick gloves, whilst by continually flapping with an handkerchief, we endeavoured to defend our faces. But no sooner had darkness commenced, than these troublesome insects redoubled their attacks, in such multitudes, of such a size, and so poisonous, that I am persuaded if an European with a delicate skin were to be exposed uncovered to their ravages for one night, it would nearly prove fatal; even the Birman boatmen, whose skins are not easily penetrated, cannot repose within their action; and my Bengal servants actually cried out in torment. I lay in boots with my cloaths on, and a double napkin over my face, and even thus could procure no rest. About nine o'clock we anchored below the town of Panlang, being unable to stem the tide; and at eleven my people hailed a strange boat coming with the flood, that rowed towards us. Instantly I heard an European voice, to which I had not of late been accustomed, and soon recognized that of Captain Thomas, of the Sea-Horse. I had sent an express when we were at Meeaday, to apprize him of our approach, and desire him to get ready for sea; he had learned from a small vessel that we were at hand, and came thus far to meet us. It being impossible to sleep, we passed the night in conversation; the account he gave of his treatment by the municipal government of Rangoon during my absence, and of the conduct of the Birmans in general towards his crew, was perfectly satisfactory. He had unrigged his ship during the monsoon, and covered the decks with an awning of mats, as a protection against the weather. Being in possession of a tolerably commodious house near the quay, he obligingly offered me a room in it; of this I availed myself, having no intention to remain at Rangoon longer than absolutely necessary, and hoped to limit my stay to a very few days. At midnight we got under way, and brought to again at six in the morning: the banks on each side of the river do not indicate much cultivation in its neighbourhood; but of the state of the interior country we could not judge, being prevented by the bushes and tall reeds from seeing any distant objects. At ten o'clock the boatmen resumed their labour, and we passed on the left a very miserable village named Teet-heet. We were again obliged to anchor on account of the tide; and early on the morning of the 17th of November, landed at Rangoon.

CHAPTER XX.

Imperial Order registered at the Rhoom.—Reflections on our Commerce and Connection with the Birman Empire.—Receive a Visit from the Maywoon.—Account of a Carrian Village.—Birman Game of Chess.—Instance of a Trial by Ordeal.—Letter from the Maywoon to the Governor General.—Take leave.—Embark on board the Sea-Horse—Voyage to Bengal.—Conclusion.

The Maywoon of Pegue arrived at Rangoon a few hours after we had landed. I paid him a visit on the following morning, and apprized him of my intention to sail for Bengal in a few days, when he politely said that he would continue at Rangoon until we departed. He informed me that the orders for carrying into effect the late regulations, would be publicly read and registered at the Rhoom on the following day; and he invited me to send a confidential person to be present at the ceremony; adding that the records were always open to public inspection, and that whoever chose, might at any time procure a copy, by paying a trifling fee to the officer of the court.

It may not be improper in this stage of my narrative to offer a few observations on the relative connection that subsists between the British possessions in India, and the Birman empire; to point out the commercial objects that render the intercourse desirable, and the political necessity there is for our preserving such a degree of national influence with that government, as may enable us hereafter to counteract any attempts to diminish our weight, or to erect an alien power that might eventually injure our interests, and even one day rival our authority. The propriety of discussing a subject of so much moment, naturally suggests itself; but a moment's reflection serves to convince that it ought not to be passed over in silence. It is too true, that the importance of the objects is hidden only from ourselves. Those against whom it is most incumbent on us to guard, are well apprised of their extent and magnitude; but even were it otherwise, the security which is to arise from the suppression of points of general knowledge, is fallacious and without dignity. Prudence requires that the transactions of a cabinet should not be divulged, but that policy must be very short sighted which attempts to conceal from the world what every person may discover; the bounties of providence, the products, resources, and local advantages of a great empire.

British India is more deeply concerned in her commerce and connection with that part of the Birman empire, called Pegue, than many persons, in other respects intimately versed in the affairs of India, seem to be aware. This interest points to three distinct objects; first, to secure from that quarter regular supplies of timber for ship building, without which the British marine of India could exist but on a very contracted scale; secondly, to introduce into that country, as much of our manufactures as its consumption may require, and to endeavour to find a mart in the south-west dominions of China, by means of the great river of Ava; thirdly, to guard with vigilance against every encroachment or advance, which may be made by foreign nations to divert the trade into other channels, and obtain a permanent settlement in a country so contiguous to the capital of our possessions. This last consideration supersedes all others in the magnitude of the consequences that might ultimately result from it.

It is impossible to impress my reader by any stronger proof with the vast importance of the Pegue trade than briefly to state, that a durable vessel* of burthen cannot be built in the river of Bengal, except by the aid of teak plank, which is procurable from Pegue alone; and that if the timber trade with that country should by any act of power be wrested from us, if it should be lost by misfortune, or forfeited through misconduct, the marine of Calcutta, which of late years has proved a source of unexampled prosperity to our principal settlement †, essentially benefited the parent country, and given honourable affluence to individuals,

* Ships have been constructed of saul wood, and of other indigenous timber of Bengal, but on trial they were not found to be serviceable.

† The following remarkable instance of public spirit, will evince the advantages that have already been derived by the parent country from the marine of India, and the benefit that may in future be expected.

In the year 1794, when the horrors of impending famine aggravated the miseries of war, the Secret Committee of the Court of Directors, at the recommendation of his Majesty's ministers, transmitted by express to Lord Teignmouth, then Governor General of India, intelligence of the calamity that threatened Great Britain, and desiring whatever aid the Government of India could supply. On receipt of the dispatch, the Governor General, with that promptitude and energy, which distinguished his administration, exerted the influence of government with such effect, that 14000 tons of shipping, almost entirely India built, were freighted to carry rice to England; and were loaden and cleared from the port of Calcutta in less than five months from the date of the arrival of the letter. This supply, with the exception of the casualties of the sea, arrived most opportunely for the relief of the poor of London, and reduced the price of that excellent article of food to three halfpence a pound. So extraordinary an exertion is neither so widely known, nor so justly appreciated, as it merits. It is a circumstance which reflects the highest credit on all the parties concerned, and deserves to be recorded in order to declare to posterity the vast resources of Great Britain, which was enabled to draw seasonable supplies of provision for the relief of the metropolis, from colonies situated at the distance of nearly two thirds of the equatorial circumference of the globe.

must be reduced nearly to annihilation, without the possibility of our being able to find any adequate substitute for the material of which we should be deprived. Within the last six years, some of the finest merchant ships, ever seen in the river Thames, have arrived from Calcutta*, where they were built of teak timber; and, after delivering valuable cargoes in London, were usefully employed in the service of the state: nor would the destruction of the Pegue trade be confined solely, in its effects, to Bengal: the other settlements would sensibly share in the loss. Madras is supplied from Rangoon, with timber for all the common purposes of domestic use; and even Bombay, although the coast of Malabar is its principal storehouse, finds it worth while, annually to import a large quantity of planks from Pegue.

But whilst it is advantageous to us, to promote the exportation of timber from the maritime towns of Pegue, it is as manifestly our interest to discourage the building of ships in the Rangoon river, where the construction is facilitated by local advantages, equal to those of any port in the world, and superior to most. The progress made in this art†, by the Birmans, has of late years been rapid, and increases in proportion as foreigners can place confidence in the Birman government. When merchants find that they can build, with security in the Rangoon river, for one-third less cost than in the Ganges, and for nearly half of what they can at Bombay,

* The Cuvera and the Gabriel, built at Calcutta of Pegue timber, are now in the river, and exhibit no contemptible specimens of the naval architecture of India. The port of Calcutta can furnish 40,000 tons of shipping.

† The Superb, a very fine ship, which was on the stocks when I was at Rangoon, has lately delivered a valuable cargo in the river Thames; the Laurestone also, a vessel of considerable force, which, I believe, was taken into the French line during the last war, was constructed at the same port.

few will hesitate in their choice of a place. It is said, that the ships of Pegue are not so firmly constructed, as those built in our ports, and in general this assertion is true; but the defect does not arise from the want of materials, but because the owners were speculative adventurers, without sufficient funds to defray the charges of labour and of iron, in which material, Pegue ships have, by fatal experience, been found deficient. The shipwrights, however, are as expert as any workmen of the East, and their models, which are all from France, are excellent; the detriment, therefore, that arises to us, from the construction of ships at Rangoon, is not less evident than the benefit that we derive, from importing the unmanufactured material. The Birmans, sagaciously knowing their own interest, set us an example of policy, by remitting all duty on cordage, canvas, and wrought iron, provided these articles are, *bona fide*, brought for the equipment of a new vessel; the port charges also are not exacted from a new ship, on leaving the river to proceed on her first voyage. A conduct on their part so wise, suggests to us the expediency of adopting some measures for our own interest; an alien duty, or a modified disqualification, would probably, like the acts of parliament in aid of British navigation, prove the most effectual remedy. Trade cannot be prosecuted in the Indian seas to any extent, except with British ports; many objections, it is true, may be made to such a proposition, but the good resulting to us, would be immediate and certain, whilst the ill consequences, if any there be, are equivocal and remote.

But if we are called upon by our interest in a commercial point of view, to check the growth of ship building at Rangoon, how much more important is the subject when seen in a political light? It is a fact, which appears to merit some consideration, and is perhaps not generally adverted to, that in a very few years, and at a small comparative expence, a formidable navy may rise on the banks of the Irrawaddy, from the forests of Pegue. It is probably not known, that artificers* are educating by our enemies for that express purpose, whilst we encourage their progress in the science, by enabling them to derive benefit, and acquire experience at the same time. National security, therefore, as well as mercantile advantage, strongly urge a vigilant attention to a quarter, whence the means of injury to ourselves, may so abundantly be drawn.

The imports into Rangoon from the British settlements, in the year 1794-5, amounted, I was informed, to more than twelve lacks of rupees, about £.135,000 sterling; these consisted chiefly of coarse piece goods, glass, hardware, and broad cloth. The demand for the last article, in the year 1795, was considerable; returns were made almost wholly in timber. A few unimportant commodities are annually carried from Pegue to the coast of Pedier and the Prince of Wales's Island, for the China market. The timber trade, though attended with a certain advantage to the carrier, yet not producing such large profits, as a more hazardous venture to the eastern straits, to China, and the Malay coast, is seldom prosecuted by merchants of the highest commercial credit, who aim at making a fortune by the success of a single voyage, for which the ship is usually freighted with that valuable and alluring drug opium, so eagerly sought after by the Chinese, yet so strictly prohibited by their government. Owing to this enterprizing spirit among merchants in India, a ship is seldom sent to carry wood, except when the owners have not funds to provide a more valuable cargo; and this inability frequently extends even to the means of

* The French have long maintained an agent at Rangoon, and are thoroughly acquainted with the advantages which the country of Pegue offers.

defraying the expence of a lading of timber: hence the master of a vessel often finds himself embarrassed when on the eve of departure, and the vessel is sometimes detained by legal demands which he cannot discharge. Difficulty produces contention, and provokes bitter and generally groundless invectives against the laws of the country, which, though oppressive to the subject, are certainly lenient to foreigners.

Timber for maritime purposes is the only article the Birman empire produces, of which we stand in indispensable need, and to promote or encourage the culture and exportation of those commodities, which form the valuable staples of British India, almost all of which the kingdom of Ava is capable of yielding, would operate to the manifest injury of our own provinces. We require and should seek for nothing more than a mart for our manufactured goods, and, in return, to bring back their unwrought materials; interference in any other shape appears to be impolitic, and likely, in the end, to prove prejudicial to ourselves.

The maritime ports of this great empire are commodious for shipping, and better situated for Indian commerce, than those of any other power. Great Britain possesses the western side of what is called the Bay of Bengal; the government of Ava, the eastern; which is far superior to the former in the facilities it affords to navigation. From the mouth of the Ganges to cape Comorin, the whole range of our continental territory, there is not a single harbour capable of affording shelter to a vessel of five hundred tons burthen; it is an unbroken line of exposed shore where ships must ride in open roads: but Ava comprehends within her extent of coast, three excellent ports; Negrais, the most secure harbour in the bay; Rangoon and Mergui, each of these is equally convenient and much more accessible than the river of Bengal, which is the only port within the bay, in our possession.

The entrance into the river of Bengal, presents as intricate and dangerous a channel, as any that is known; and during three months of the year, a ship, in leaving the Ganges, incurs considerable hazard from being obliged to beat against a foul wind, in shoal water, among surrounding sands; but from the harbour of Negrais, a ship launches at once into the open bay, and may work to the southward without any other impediment, than what the monsoon opposes. Rangoon, at that particular season, is more perilous than Negrais, especially to vessels bound from the straits of Malacca, Pulo Penang, and other eastern ports; these, if not well acquainted with the violent current setting at that period to the eastward, are liable to be deceived in their reckoning, and, imagining themselves to be farther west than they really are, sometimes stand too much to the northward, till they get entangled among the shoals of what is called the bay of Martaban, whence a retreat is very difficult, and where the tide flows with such impetuosity, and rises so high, that anchors are useless, and retard, but for a very short period, the impending fate. Ships sailing from the westward, by making cape Negrais, and keeping within sight of the coast, until they come near the bar of Rangoon, avoid those dangers; at every other season Rangoon may be approached, and left with perfect security; the bar is narrow, and contains depth of water, at three-quarters flood, sufficient for vessels of any burthen. The channel of the river is unimpeded, carrying from six to eight fathoms, as high as the town of Rangoon.

Blessed with so extraordinary a coincidence of advantages, arising from situation, extent, produce, and climate, the kingdom of Ava, or more properly the Birman empire, is among eastern nations, second in importance to China alone, whilst, from its contiguity to British India, it becomes to us, of much greater consequence. We can have no reason, in the present prosperous state of our affairs, to dread the hostilities of all the native powers of India combined. Our hereditary foe is destroyed, and there remains no other, who bears towards us any fixed or rooted enmity: the Birmans certainly do not, but however favourable their natural disposition may be, that characteristic pride and unbounded arrogance, which govern their conduct towards other states, may lead them to offer indignity, which we cannot avoid resenting, and to commit acts of aggression, as in the affair at Chittagong, which we shall be obliged to repel. Such necessity is sincerely to be deprecated: steadiness and temper in our negociations, and a reasonable allowance for their mistaken principles, will go far, to avert the ill consequences that might arise from their haughty and weak assumption. We cannot expect from a proud and victorious people, impressed with an extravagant opinion of their own power, that reverence, which the states of India have been taught to feel for our established character. The principal nations to the east of Bengal are to be considered by themselves as a kind of body politic, wholly distinct from all others; and, in fact, China, Ava, and the countries south of them, compose a body, in extent and number of inhabitants, more than equal to all Europe. These nations are connected by a striking similarity of manners and political maxims, to which, as they cannot be suddenly changed, we ought to assimilate, in our intercourse with their governments, as far as the dignity of our own will permit. To preserve a correspondence and a good understanding with the court of Ava, is essentially expedient for our own prosperity; but, for the reasons already stated, that connection should not be too intimate. A limited trade and a preponderating influence, sufficient to counteract the machinations of our enemies, are the utmost lengths that we should go; by not interfering farther, the Birmans will be convinced of the moderation and justice of our principles, and learn from them to repel the insidious advances of any other power, made with a latent view to undermine their dominion, and ultimately to wrest their country from them. It is our interest to maintain their independence, and to guard it from foreign encroachment, whilst a knowledge of this truth cannot fail, in the end, to unite the Birman government to ours, in bonds of reciprocal amity and confidence.

During the few days that we continued at Rangoon, I had the pleasure to interchange many reciprocal marks of civility with the Maywoon, who paid me a visit on board the Sea Horse; after which we rowed in his war-boat to a very fine ship belonging to him, which had recently been built, and, he assured me, was entirely the workmanship of native artificers.

Whilst we remained here, Doctor Buchanan, accompanied by one of the officers of the Sea Horse, made an excursion on horseback a few miles off, to view a village inhabited by Carianers, the simple rural race of people, of whom mention has already been made*. Passing by the great temple of Shoedagoung, they proceeded along an indifferent road, about three miles, till they arrived at one of the villages which they sought: it contained not more than ten or a dozen houses raised on posts, and disposed in such a manner as to inclose a square yard, in which were a number of buffaloes. The head man was gone to a distant village, but one of the inhabitants invited the strangers to enter his dwelling, and hospitably offered what his house afforded. The visitants ascended a

* See page 207.

narrow ladder about twelve feet high into a sort of barn, divided into two by a mat partition; the floor was of rough boards, the sides of mats, and a roof, composed of bamboos, was covered with thatch; at night they draw up the ladder, and, closing the door, sleep secure from the assaults of wild beasts, or the depredations of thieves. Seven or eight men, as many women, and several children, constituted a numerous family; they seemed a healthy and vigorous race of people, and were of a fairer complexion than the generality of southern Birmans; some of the women wore rich strings of coral round their necks, and were even adorned with ornaments of gold and silver; they speak a dialect peculiar to themselves, but their language is radically the same as the Birman. There are both Pegue and Birman Carianers, who differ in the same degree as the nations to which they are attached; they complain of being oppressed by the Birmans, but their appearance did not indicate severe oppression, and they have a certain sale for whatever their industry can raise. Doctor Buchanan saw several Birmans on the road, carrying baskets; some going for the produce of their gardens, others returning with burthens of fruit and vegetables. The life these people lead, is truly pastoral; they have no other business or object except that of cultivating the soil, and tending their flocks; their religion is the worship of Gaudma, but in these rites they do not join with the same fervour that animates the Birmans; they rather seem to acquiesce in the doctrines of their conquerors, which they do not even profess to understand.

Dr. Buchanan interrogated one of the men, who admitted their want of knowledge, and assigned as the reason, that God once wrote his laws and commands on the skin of a buffalo, and called upon all nations of the earth to come and take a copy; a summons which all obeyed, except the Carianers, who had not leisure, being occupied in the business of husbandry; and that in consequence of this neglect, they remained ever since in a state of ignorance, without any other cares, than those which related to their pastoral employment. On going away, Dr. Buchanan offered them a few pieces of silver, which so excited their surprise, being quite unaccustomed to such acts of liberality, that they hesitated to receive the money, and seemed at a loss to what motive, to ascribe his bounty. After looking at one another, and talking for a minute or two, with much earnestness, the women, on a sudden, as if his design had just been discovered, all ran away laughing, whilst the men sullenly declined the gift; in fact, they concluded that the Doctor wanted to purchase the favours of one of their females, having no notion of a disinterested donation. The ladies however did not wait to ascertain for whom the golden apple was designed, and it was in vain he tried to convince the men that their suspicions were ill founded. These poor people entertain a delicacy in regard to women, which their more enlightened conquerors do not feel. To prove, however, the purity of his intentions, the Doctor left the money on the floor when he departed. The gentlemen returned by the same road, and in their way, examined a mineral spring, in the neighbourhood of the great Pagoda.

I had an opportunity at Rangoon, of observing that the Birmans of distinction played at chess, a circumstance which, from our secluded situation at the capital, had escaped my notice. This game is held in high estimation among the superior ranks: the board they use is exactly similar to ours, containing 64 squares, and their number of troops the same, 16 on each side; but the names, the power and disposal of them differ essentially: the king and his minister (a queen is never introduced by the Orientals) are mounted on elephants; these are defended by two castles or yettay, two knights on horseback, Mene, two officers on foot, one called Meem, the other Chekéy, and eight Maundelay or foot soldiers: the forces of each party are arranged on three lines, by which eight squares remain unoccupied; none of the pieces possess equal force with our queen; and this restricted operation, renders the Birman mode of playing more complex and difficult than ours. The Birmans affirm that it is a game of high antiquity, and that it is acknowledged and authorized by their sacred writings, although every play of chance is prohibited. This testimony confirms* the opinion of the late Sir William Jones, that chess was invented in India, and is not, as generally imagined, of Persian origin: the Birmans call it Chedreen, a word that bears some resemblance to the name which is given to the game, in most other parts of the world.

During the time that the English deputation was at Ummerapoora, Captain Thomas witnessed at Rangoon, a remarkable instance of a trial by the ordeal of water, the circumstances of which he thus related to me: Two women of the middling class litigated a small property before the court of justice, and as the judges found great difficulty in deciding the question of right, it was at length agreed, by mutual consent, to put the matter to the issue of an ordeal. The parties, attended by the officers of the court, several Rhahaans, or priests, and a vast concourse of people, repaired to a tank or pond, in the vicinity of the town. After praying to the Rhahaans for some time, and performing certain purificatory ceremonials, the litigants entered the pond, and waded in it, till the water reached their breasts; they were accompanied by two or three men, one of whom placing the women close to each other, and putting a board on their heads,

* See a paper on the Indian game of Chess by the President of the Asiatic Society, in the 2d vol. of Asiatic Researches.

at a signal given, pressed upon the board till he immersed them both at the same instant. They remained out of sight about a minute and a half, when one of them, nearly suffocated, raised her head, whilst the other continued to sit upon her hams at the bottom, but was immediately lifted up by the men; after which an officer of the court solemnly pronounced judgment in her favour, and of the justice of this decision none of the bye-standers appeared to entertain the smallest doubt, from the infallibility of the proof which had been given.

The trial by ordeal, in all countries where the Hindoo religion prevails, is as ancient as their records. The late Ali Ibrahim Khan, native chief magistrate of Benares, has communicated, in a very curious paper*, the modes by which this appeal to the Deity is made, as they are described in the Metaschera, or comment on the Dherma Sastra, in the chapter on oaths: the Birmans being governed by the same authority, observe nearly similar forms; but as knowledge increases, and mankind become more enlightened, these absurd practices lose ground, and have of late years been discountenanced, by the judicial courts both of India and of Ava.

Previous to our departure, the Maywoon of Pegue delivered to my care a letter addressed to the Governor General of India, couched in very friendly terms, but dictated in the usual style of turgid extravagance; he enumerated in it the concessions granted in favour of English commerce, and expressed a determination to execute his part with punctuality and attention. His Birman Majesty has long entertained a desire to procure an English carriage, with the distinctions of Birman royalty attached to it:

* This paper was presented to the Asiatic Society by Warren Hastings, Esq. See "On the trial by ordeal among the Hindoos," Asiatic Researches, vol. I.

in this letter the Maywoon made a request that such a one might be sent; and in order to direct the artist, I was furnished with a very intelligible and well executed drawing*, performed at Ummerapoora, by the King's painter. It displayed the carriage and body of an English crane-necked chariot, gilded all over: from the top of the body, there rose a regal spire, or piasath, in separate stages, bearing a miniature resemblance to those which ornamented the palace and royal barge; four lions in a crouching attitude, guarded the carriage, two on the fore part, and two behind, and a bird, designed, I imagine, to represent the Henza, or tutelary goose, was placed in front with expanded wings. The Maywoon's letter, however, contained a requisition of yet greater importance, that was, to obtain materials for the establishment of a mint, a design which, if carried into effect†, must considerably promote the prosperity of the country, as the necessity of weighing lumps of lead and silver, and ascertaining the purity, operate as a sensible impediment to commerce.

On the 26th of November, the day preceding that of our embarkation, I waited on the Maywoon, accompanied by the gentlemen of the deputation and Captain Thomas, to take our final leave. I had occasion to feel

* The European part of this drawing was made from an old carriage, which had been introduced into the Ava country, several years before. The Governor General complied with both the requests contained in the Maywoon's letter, and in the following year, sent a very superb chariot to his Birman Majesty, constructed according to the representation: the top of the spire, notwithstanding the body hung very low, was 18 feet from the ground; it was extremely rich and well executed.

† It is surprising that the Chinese have no national coin; at the port of Canton, dollars in some measure supply the deficiency, but in the interior of the kingdom, the inconvenience must be generally felt.

myself individually obliged to him for his personal attentions, whilst his mild administration and pleasing manners had acquired my esteem: he is universally acknowledged to be a good man, and seems highly to deserve that reputation. I had opportunities of witnessing several instances of his benevolence and humanity, and, although his authority within his own jurisdiction is absolute, I never heard him accused of an abuse of his power, or of a single act of oppression or injustice. Such a character in a country, where the most rigorous and often barbarous despotism prevails, is entitled to particular encomium. We parted with mutual, and, I am inclined to believe, not insincere, professions of permanent good will.

On the morning of the 27th, we breakfasted on board the Sea Horse; most of the attendants with our heavy baggage had embarked on the preceding day, and at ten o'clock we weighed anchor. It had previously been agreed that the Company's ship should salute the Birman flag with eleven guns, which were to be answered by an equal number from the battery on shore: Captain Thomas performed his part of the agreement, but the battery, which was very slow in acknowledging the compliment, returned only seven. This apparent mark of disrespect, which could not be attributed to ignorance, I conceived rather to originate in the person who had charge of the battery, and who might think to recommend himself by it, than from any higher authority; it was, however, such an ostensible and public slight to the Company's colours, that I judged it expedient to write a note to the Maywoon, to acquaint him of the fact.

We dropped down with the ebb as far as the Chokey, or watch station, from whence the custom-house officer had visited the Sea Horse, on her first arrival. In passing the mouth of the Pegue river we observed, that at the entrance, it was nearly as wide as the great river; but that breadth soon diminishes to a very contracted space: several large creeks branched off both to the right and the left, which the pilot said were navigable to a considerable distance by boats of heavy burthen. In the evening we again weighed, and crossed the bar at midnight; early next morning we saw the landmark called the Elephant, and favoured by the ebb, passed the China Bakir river. The wind not being strong enough, when the tide turned, to enable us to stem the flood, we again came to anchor, being in company with a ship named the Hope, bound also to Calcutta. On the following morning, we stood to the southward on the first of the ebb, which bore us along with it against an unfavourable breeze. On the 30th, we made Diamond Island and Cape Negrais, and next day at an early hour passed a ship standing towards Rangoon, which appeared to have suffered severely from a recent storm, having lost her main-top and fore-top-gallant masts; the wind was at this time north-north-west, and a heavy swell from the same quarter, indicated that there had lately been a hard gale, a very unusual circumstance at that season of the year.

Keeping within a few leagues of the coast, we continued to beat against a foul wind, until the 9th of December, when we made Cheduba, a fertile island belonging to the Birman government: the channel between this island and the main, is annually navigated by large trading boats, but it does not afford a safe passage for shipping. The length of the island we judged to be about 45 miles; it yields abundance of rice, and is governed by a Chekey or Lieutenant, who is subject to the Maywoon of Arracan. Having now the benefit of regular land and sea breezes, we were enabled to make some progress to the northward. On the morning of the 11th, we saw what are called the Broken Islands, on the coast of Arracan, which are for the most part a barren assemblage of rocky eminences, affording shelter only to pirates and thieves. On the 12th and 13th, we experienced much inconvenience, the wind, which was directly against us, blowing with such violence that the ship laboured greatly, and our fore-top-sail was torn from the yard. On the 14th, the weather moderated, and the wind veering a little to the eastward, we had the good fortune on the 16th to discover a pilot schooner at anchor, between the eastern and western reefs near the mouth of the Ganges: neap tides prevailing, our passage up the river was tedious, and the wind coming invariably from the northern quarter, rendered it hazardous to proceed by night. On the 22d, we reached Budge Budge, where I found a pulwar* waiting, which my friend, Captain Sandys, as soon as he heard of the arrival of the Sea Horse, had dispatched to meet me; at this place I quitted the ship, and in two hours reached Calcutta, after an eventful absence of ten months.

* A commodious kind of boat used in the river Ganges.

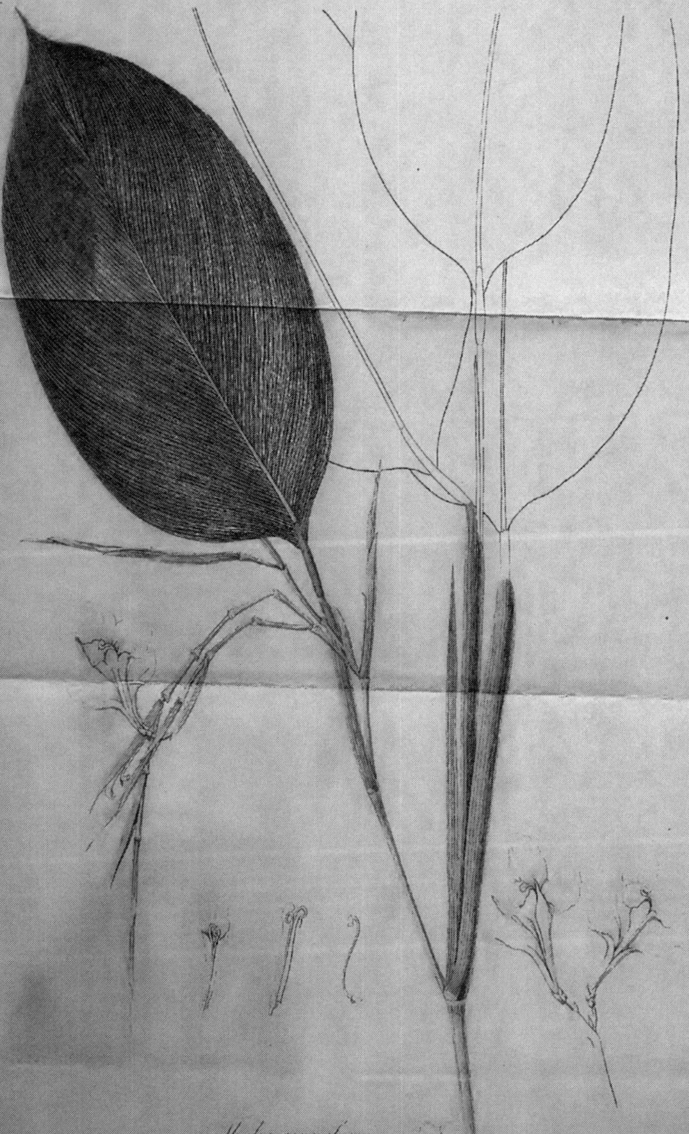

Thalia cannaformis

The Plants, of which the following descriptions and figures are given, have been selected by the President *of the* Royal Society, *as the most rare and curious among a copious and valuable collection made by* Doctor Buchanan, *who transmitted to the* Court *of* Directors *an* hortus siccus *in excellent preservation, together with delineations of each plant, executed on the spot.*

THALIA CANNÆFORMIS.

Forst. prodr. n. 3. *Linn. spec. plant. edit. Willdenow,* 1. *p.* 16.

Thayng payng *Birm.*

Habitat in sylvis, præsertim humidioribus, in Insulis Andamannicis, Rangoon; III. IV.

Culmus solidus, teres, glaber, ramosus. *Rami* geniculati, divaricati.

Folia caulina, alterna, patentia, petiolata, ovalia, integerrima, glabra: nervis plurimis lateralibus, adscendentibus, parallelis.

Petiolus geniculo instructus, superne teres, inferne membranaceus, vaginalis, amplexicaulis, ramulo oppositus. *Stipula* solitaria, petiolo opposita, sæpe vaginarum longitudine, subulata, dorso canaliculata; interdum etiam adsunt stipulæ sparsæ, infrafoliaceæ.

Panicula pendula, oppositifolia. *Rachis* flexuosa, articulata, compressa: articulis apice glumiferis. *Glumæ* bivalves, bifloræ, persistentes, pedunculum involventes: valvula inferiore longitudine pedunculi, duriore, superiorem tenuiorem, coloratam amplexa. *Pedunculus* coloratus, clavatus, bifidus, carnosus. *Flores* albi, solitarii, apicibus pedicelli insidentes; singuli rudimentum alterius ad basin habent.

Perianthium proprium tripartitum, superum, brevissimum, coloratum: laciniis erectis, acuminatis.

Corolla monopetala, irregularis. *Tubus* trigonus. *Limbus* duplex: Laciniæ tres exteriores æquales, lanceolatæ, patentes, acuminatæ, undulatæ; Laciniarum interiorum duæ latiores, patentes; tertia brevis, cucullata, genitalia tegens.

Filamentum petaloideum, bipartitum: laciniis falcatis. *Anthera* unica, clavata, margini laciniæ dextræ filamenti adnata.

Germen inferum, parvum. *Stylus* cylindraceus, longitudine filamenti, tubo corollæ ad basin adnatus, apice incurvus, liber. *Stigma* concavum.

GARDENIA CORONARIA.

Yæng-gap *Birm.*

Habitat in vicis et hortis: Rangoon. ♄. III—V.

Rami sparsi, foliati, læves, annulati, internodiis superne incrassatis.

Folia ramulorum opposita, approximata patentia, petiolata, ovalia, apicem versus plerumque latiora, integerrima, acuminata, utrinque nitida; juniora gummoso-viscida. *Petiolus* brevissimus, semiteres, supra convexus, erectus, scabriusculus.

Stipulæ intrafoliaceæ, vaginantes, erectæ, longitudine petiolorum, apicibus scariosis.

Flores axillares, sessiles, solitarii, folio longiores, flavi, patentes.

Calyx monophyllus, erectus, pentagonus, hinc dehiscens, apice obtusus.

Corolla hypocrateriformis. *Tubus* cylindraceus, calyce multo longior, gummoso-viscidus. *Faux* nuda. *Limbus* quinque-seu sex-partitus: laciniis ovalibus, obtusis, supra venosis, obliquis, margine exteriore rectiore.

Filamenta nulla. *Antheræ* quinque, lineares, apici tubi adnatæ.

Germen turbinatum, inferum, pentagonum, biloculare, polyspermum.

Stylus cylindraceus, longitudine tubi, apice dilatatus, compressus. *Stigma* margini apicis styli adnatum, sulco longitudinati contorto gummifero exaratum.

Drupa oblonga, umbilicata, quinque-carinata.

Nux ovalis, sub-bilocularis, pulpa repleta: *Semina* plura, ovata, plana, nidulantia.

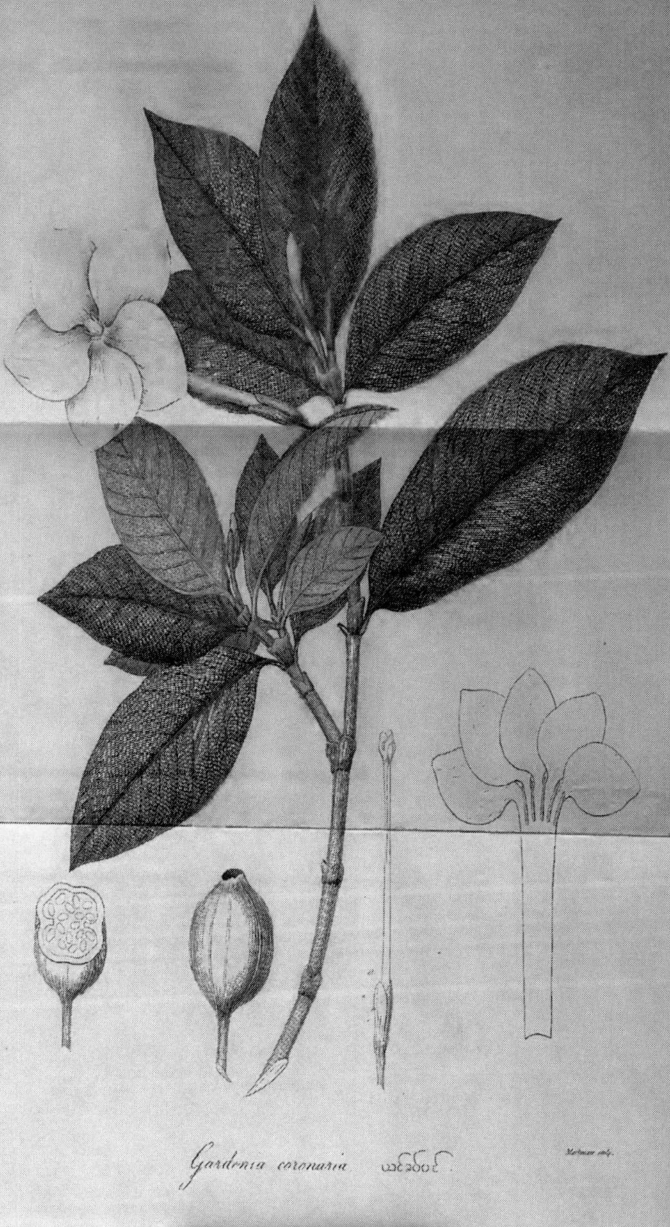

Gardenia coronaria

Pontederia dilatata

PONTEDERIA DILATATA.

Ka-dauk kyee *Birm.*

Habitat in aquosis: Rangoon. V.

Structura *Pontederiæ vaginali* L. simillima, sed multoties major.

Folia ovata, profunde cordata, angulis posteriorioribus oblongis, obtusis, minime divergentibus. *Petioli* dehiscentia spathæformis, ovata, magnitudine ovi gallinacei.

Flores coerulei, corymbosi, quibus præcipue differt a Pontederia hastata L.

Spatha multiflora, oblonga, monophylla, latere interiore dehiscens, petioli dehiscentiæ opposita.

Petala sex, sessilia, carinata, duplici serie posita: tria interiora, obovata, obtusa, supremo erecto; inferioribus patulis; tria exteriora lanceolata, acuta, patentia.

Filamenta sex, subulata, petalis inserta, iisque dimidio breviora: quinque superiora adscendentia; sextum erectum, ad latus dextrum deflexum. *Antheræ* lineares, bisulcæ, quinque declinatæ fertiles ad apicem dehiscentes; sexta inferior major, sterilis, diversi coloris.

Germen superum, ovatum, trigonum. *Stylus* cylindraceus, longitudine staminum, incurvus, ad latus sinistrum deflexus. *Stigma* obtusum, compressum.

Capsula ovata, acuminata, trilocularis, trivalvis, tecta carinis petalorum persistentibus, contortis.

Semina plurima, receptaculo communi affixa.

BAUHINIA DIPHYLLA.

Pa-lam *Birm.*

Habitat in sylvis. Mæaday. ♄. VI.

Caulis fruticosus, scandens, ramosus, glaber. *Rami* fructiferi crassi, teretes, foliosi; steriles tetragoni, quadrisulci.

Folia alterna, petiolata, conjugata. *Foliola* subreniformia, obtusa, integerrima, glabra. *Petiolus* longitudine fere foliorum, teres, utrinque incrassatus, apice subtus mucronatus.

Stipulæ nullæ, nisi tuberculum ad basin petioli utrinque.

Cirrhus lateralis, simplex, compressus, acuminatus, revolutus, folio brevior.

Aculeus reflexus, apici petioli inter folia insidens.

Racemus terminalis, simplex, erectus, subangulatus. *Flores* magni ante florescentiam recurvi; puberes erecti, sparsi, solitarii, pedicellati. *Pedicelli* compressi, longitudine fere floris, crassi, basi squamula acuminata, versus apicem cirrhulo notati. Petala albida, viscida. Pistillum castaneum.

Calyx persistens, monophyllus, quinque-fidus, crassus, basi turbinatus: laciniis longis, lanceolatis, revolutis, post florescentiam contortis.

Petala quinque, æqualia, longitudine calycis, lanceolata, erectiuscula, unguiculata, apici tubi calycis inserta.

Filamenta decem, erecta, subulata, longitudine fere corollæ, apici tubi corollæ inserta. *Antheræ* lineares, incumbentes, biloculares, supra sulcatæ.

Germen superum, pedicellatum, compressum, lineare, utrinque acuminatum. *Stylus* brevis, teres, longitudine staminum. *Stigma* obtusum.

Legumen maturum non vidi.

Bauhinia diphylla. ఆడౌ

Sonneratia apetala.

SONNERATIA APETALA.

Kam-ba-la *Birm.*

Habitat in ripis humidis, inundatis, maritimis. Rangoon. ♄. V.

Arbor pulcherrima, facie Salicis babylonicæ, sed élatior. *Rami* sparsi, penduli, teretes, glabri. *Ramuli* oppositi, divaricati, subbrachiati, glabri, filiformes.

Folia ramulorum pauca, opposita, petiolata, ovato-lanceolata, margine altero magis gibbo, integerrima, sæpius obtusa, enervia, avenia, plana, subcarnosa. *Petiolus* linearis, depressus, margine utrinque acutus, brevis, obliquus, glaber.

Flores pedunculati, cernui, virescentes, glabri, magnitudine nucis moschatæ, axillares subsolitarii; terminales subterni. Stamina alba. *Pedunculi* foliis dimidio breviores, penduli, uniflori, glabri, albidi, apicem versus incrassati, articulati, angulati.

Calyx monophyllus, coriaceus, crassus, campànulatus, ultra medium quadrifidus: laciniis ovatis, patulis, acutis.

Corolla nulla.

Nectarium: membrana crassa, fundo calycis adnata, margine integro, staminifero, ultra calycis divisuram producto.

Filamenta plurima, linearia, ad basin erecta, superius incurva, longitudine calycis, apici nectarii multiplici serie insidentia. *Antheræ* parvæ, erectæ, cordatæ.

Germen superum, turbinatum. *Stylus* teres, staminibus longior, flexuosus. *Stigma* maximum, supra convexum, subtus concavum, pileiforme.

Pomum orbiculatum, depressum, ad basin calyce patente cinctum, octo-loculare, stylo persistente mucronatum.

Semina plurima angulata, in pulpa nidulantia.

EPIDENDRUM MOSCHATUM.

Thee-kua nee *Birm.*

Habitat in arboribus. Rangoon. V.

Caulis fruticosus, crassitie digiti minoris, radicans, scandens, octo-sulcatus, vaginatus, articulatus, ramosus. *Rami* structura caulis, foliati, erectiusculi, orgyales.

Folia ramea plura, alterna, bifaria, patentia, vaginantia, lanceolata, integerrima, obtusa, nitida, subtus fusco maculata, enervia, venis longitudinalibus parallelis striata, plana, carnosa, internodiis multo longiora. *Vaginæ* adpressæ, ri atæ, ore integerrimo.

Racemi oppositifolii, simplices, ramis foliosis breviores. *Flores* odoratissimi, flavi, macula purpurea in nectario utrinque. *Bractea* striata ad basin singuli germinis.

Petala quinque, patula, venosa: tria exteriora lanceolata, obtusa, duobus inferioribus basi gibbis, coalitis; duo interiora latiora, longiora, ovata. *Nectarium* apice bicorne, ad basin acuminatum, carinatum, desinens in laminam assurgentem, cucullatam, intus pilosam.

Filamentum brevissimum, subulatum, ex parte summa nectarii postice inter cornua enatum, umbraculum supra gibbum, subtus bifoveatum gerens. *Antheræ* binæ, parvæ, in foveis umbraculi nidulantes, cavitati in suprema parte nectarii insidentes.

Germen inferum, longissimum, teres. *Stylus* nullus. *Stigma:* fovea subrotunda, mellifera, antice inter cornua superiora nectarii exarata, desinens in canalem ad germen penetrantem, a cavitate antherifera valvula obtusa separatum.

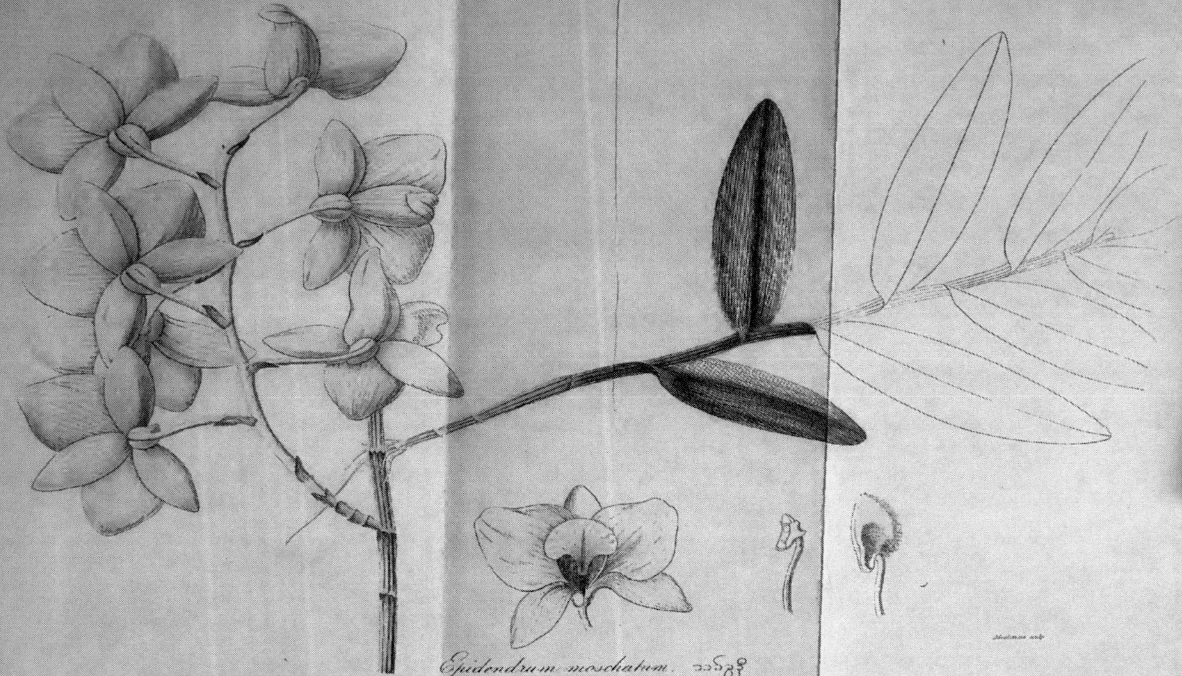

Epidendrum moschatum.

Agyneja coccinea.

AGYNEJA COCCINEA.

Ta-hmayng-tsoop kyee *Birm.*

Habitat in sylvis. Pegu. ♄. IV.

Folia esculenta.

Arbuscula ramulis rectis, teretibus, carinatis, e basi petiolorum utrinque decurrente; patulis, nitidis; tenellis pubescentibus.

Folia ramea plura, alterna, horizontalia, petiolata, lanceolata, integerrima, obtusa, nitida, internodiis multo longiora. *Petiolus* teres, gibbus, brevissimus, assurgens, glaber.

Stipulæ laterales, geminæ, caducæ, sessiles, subulatæ, erectæ.

Flores axillares, parvi, masculi decem seu duodecim, pedunculati, flavi, nutantes, mixti femineis totidem, sessilibus, erectis, viridibus. *Pedunculus* filiformis, petiolo longior, pubescens.

MASCULI FLORES.

Calyx sexpartitus, externe pubescens: laciniis oblongis, obtusis: tribus exterioribus reflexis, interioribus patentibus.

Corolla nulla.

Antheræ plures, lineares, adnatæ rudimento pistilli oblongo, acuminato.

FEMINEI FLORES.

Calyx sexpartitus: laciniis subulatis, persistentibus, germen arcte amplexis.

Corolla nulla.

Germen magnum, orbiculatum, depressum. *Stylus* crassus, brevis. *Stigma* cavum, margine vix sexdentato.

Capsula magna, orbiculata, depressa, umbilicata, novem-ad duodecim-sulcata, novem-ad duodecim-locularis: loculis medio dehiscentibus.

Semina in singulo loculo duo seu tria, verticalia, angulata, subovata, apice receptaculo centrali affixa.

HERITIERA FOMES.

Kanatso *Birm.*

Habitat in ripis æstu inundatis. Rangoon. ♄. IV.

Lignum fomes optimus; bona quoque materies naupegis et fabris lignariis.

Arbor ramis erectis, rigidis. *Ramuli* teretes, sulco obsoleto, ex latere utroque petiolorum decurrente, cinerei, fusco minutissime punctati.

Folia sparsa, petiolata, lanceolato-oblonga, obtusa, integerrima, venis minutissime reticulata; supra nitida, viridia; subtus incana, punctis fuscis adspersa. *Petiolus* brevis, teres, cinereus, glanduloso-punctatus.

Panicula axillaris, folio brevior, patens, nuda, supra decomposita. *Pedunculi* filiformes, pubescentes. *Flores* erecti, parvi, externe cinerei, intus rubicundi.

MASCULI FLORES.

Calyx cylindricus, monophyllus, quadrifidus: laciniis patulis, ovatis, acutis.

Corolla nulla.

Receptaculum orbiculatum, depressum, in fundo calycis, cui insidet *Filamentum* subulatum, erectum, calyce brevius. *Anthera* coadunatæ in unam, ovatam, acuminatam, parvam.

HERMAPHRODITI FLORES, in eadem panicula, pauciores.

Calyx ut in masculis.

Corolla nulla.

Filamenta nulla. *Antheræ* quatuor, bilobæ, germinis basin ambientes, minimæ (sine dubio effoetæ *Edit.*)

Germen ovatum, quadrisulcatum, superum, receptaculo magno insidens, acuminatum. *Styli* quatuor, brevissimi, coadunati. *Stigma* obtusum, quadri-lobum.

Capsulæ quatuor, pedicellatæ, orbiculatæ, marginatæ, basi exterius gibbæ, dorso carinatæ, lignosæ.

Semina solitaria, maxima, ovata, compressa, intus cava, apice corculifera. Fructificatio sæpe demit, aliquando addit quartam partem.

Heritiera fomes. ကနစိုဝ်

APPENDIX.

No. I.

To Captain Michael Symes, Agent to the Court of Ava.

SIR,

AGREEABLY to your desire, I proceeded this forenoon to the opposite side, to visit the two principal Woongees.

Some time after my arrival at the house of the first in rank, he made his appearance without any display of grandeur or parade, further than being in his court dress. His reception was polite, as was his behaviour during the time I remained; and, so far as I recollect, the following is the purport of our conversation, which was carried on through the medium of Baba-Sheen: he first asked me what kind of a passage we had from Bengal to Rangoon; whether since our arrival we had been comfortably situated, or otherwise? To these I replied, that our passage had been pleasant, and that we had experienced since our arrival every attention and comfort we could desire. His next question was, what period had elapsed since we left Bengal? which having answered, he then inquired how the King and Queen were when the last accounts left England? On receiving my answer to this, he asked how the Governor General was when we left Bengal, and what was his age?

These, I believe, are the only questions proposed: he then desired Baba-Sheen to inform me, that he would use his best endeavours with the King to promote the objects for which we had come; likewise that he was very anxious for our welfare on hearing of the sickness and mortality that prevailed amongst the Chinese, and on that account would recommend to his Majesty to allow us to depart as soon as the season was favourable; adding, that we should carry with us his good wishes for our safe return to Bengal. I desired Baba-Sheen to intimate the high sense we entertained of his solicitude for, and good intention towards, us; but requested he might not give himself any uneasiness on our account, as we had every comfort we could possibly desire, and during the time of our residence here, had found the climate to be a very healthy one. Having inquired who the

Moonshee, &c. were, he desired Baba-Sheen to request our acceptance of some sweetmeats, &c. which he had provided for us, and then withdrew.

From his house I went to that of the second Woongee, where, after I had been seated for a little while, he made his appearance, dressed, as I was told, in the proper war dress of the Birmans. His reception was polite, but more ostentatious than that of the first minister, having assembled a great number of people (in their various dresses used on occasions of ceremony) in the hall into which we were conducted; at each end of which were several racks full of muskets, spears, and swords; the different insignia of his office, were likewise displayed to the best advantage.

A little after he came in, a Nakhaan desired Baba-Sheen to inquire, whether our passage from Bengal had been favourable, and how we had been, with respect to convenience, since our arrival? These I answered in the same terms I had done before. I was then asked, what time a ship comm nly took to perform the voyage from Bengal to England; to which having replied, I was again asked how the King and Queen were, likewise whether the Governor General was in good health when we left Bengal? Having received my answers to these, they next inquired whether the Governor General's authority extended over all our possessions in India? This I answered in the affirmative, and here ended our conversation.

These several questions were put by the Nakhaan, no doubt by the Woongee's desire; but he did not speak a word himself till towards the conclu ion, when he gave orders, I believe, to bring tea, sweetmeats, &c. which being placed before us, he soon after retired. I remained in his house till I was told by the Shawbunder and Baba-Sheen, that it was not necessary to stay any longer.

Soon after we had set out on our return, I was informed that the King's eldest son was approaching on his way to the palace, and I was desired at the same time to withdraw into a bye street, which I complied with; but as not one of the public officers, who were with me, paid any compliment to the Prince, or desired me to do so, I remained where I was conducted without saluting him, concluding it was not customary, or that if it had, they would have informed me.

I am, &c.

T. Wood.

7th September 1795.

No. II.

To the Chief Woongee and Council of State.

The day being fixed for my departure, it becomes a duty incumbent on me freely to declare to you, as his Majesty's chief Minister, my sentiments on the conduct which the court of Ummerapoora has thought fit to observe towards me in my official character, that nothing may hereafter be attributed to misapprehension, or the want of a clear representation on my part, on subjects which may, at some future period, eventually involve the general interest and happiness.

There appears to have existed, from the time of my arrival, although not an avowed yet a real inclination, to consider me in the capacity of an agent, from a subordinate and commercial settlement, rather than the delegate of a great and sovereign state; as a person come in the character of a petitioner to solicit a favour, instead of the representative of a nation, which offers at least as much as it desires, and in the proposal can be actuated by no view, except what must tend to the mutual advantage of both countries.

Of the purity of the intentions of the English government, if any doubts ever did exist, those doubts must long since have been obliterated; you have had, in every transaction, the most unequivocal proofs of the conciliatory disposition of the Governor General; and latterly such an* instance, as is not often paralleled. Violence on one part, was repressed by moderation on the other; menaces were combated by reason, and that which was denied to intemperate demands, was afterwards granted as an act of cool and deliberate justice.

I have already clearly stated to his Majesty, in the memorial I had the honour to present shortly after my arrival, that the Governor General's principal view, in deputing me, was to promote confidence, and give to his Majesty authorized assurances of the Governor General's personal regard; and, I now repeat, that these were his motives, rather than the expectation of any great national benefit to arise to the English, from such an alliance. The individuals who prosecute trade to this country, are far from being merchants of the highest commercial consideration.

* The surrender of the delinquent refugees. See page 121.

Of the power and resources of the British in India, you cannot be so misinformed as to suppose, that they are under the necessity of soliciting the friendship of any nation on earth, out of a prudential regard to their own security, or from an inability to maintain a cause of justice and their national honour, in opposition to all the force that could combine against them. It is not from a petty island*, which may send out two or three piratical privateers, that a government, whose dominions extend from Ceylon to the mountains of Tibet, from the gulf of Bengal to the Western Sea, can have any thing to dread: apprehension, therefore, had no share in the present mission; and, I desire to have it clearly understood, that I come not to seek a favour, but to cement friendship; not to supplicate, but to propose.

It is, however, but too evident, that his Majesty has not been pleased to consider me in the light of an agent from a sovereign state; and from his total silence with regard to the Governor General of India, and his not honouring me with a personal audience, it is reasonable to conclude, that very erroneous estimations have been attempted to be held out, both of the importance of the Governor General individually, and of the nation at large. Permit me, therefore, now to acquaint you, that the authority of the Governor General is supreme over all the territories of the Company in the East; and the limits of the British possessions best explain their national consequence.

I was at one time taught to believe, by those with whom I officially communicated, that the non-appearance of his Majesty, when I made my first visit to the palace, was a circumstance merely accidental, and that, on the day of my dismission, I should be honoured with a formal interview; also, that the arrangement which I submitted to his Majesty's ministers, would be acceded to, and that a deputation would be sent to Bengal, to obtain a counterpart of the articles, ratified in due form. How far it may be intended to fulfil these assurances, the tenor of the language, held by his Majesty's ministers yesterday at the Lotoo, gives me sufficient room to doubt, and they best can tell what his Majesty's resolutions are on that head; but if it should not be meant to perform, what I had such grounds given me to expect, I shall certainly have just cause to complain of being egregiously misled.

He who undeceives has the best title to confidence, and I have, in this address,

* Mauritius.

the fairest pretensions to yours; were I to depart from Ummerapoora, dissembling the dissatisfaction I feel at the manner of my reception, and professing myself contented when I really was the reverse, I might, perhaps, be justified by prudent policy, but I should swerve from that candour which I have been instructed by the Governor General to observe, in all my communications with this court.

In conformity with the spirit of those instructions, I can, with great certainty, assure you, that unless I am honoured with an audience of his Majesty, in the capacity of agent from the Governor General, it will be the last time an agent from the Governor General, will ever be subjected to a similar mortification. The Governor General of India is actuated by far different principles, than to make a matter of incivility, in a point of form, grounds for a serious dispute, or suffer it to affect his general line of conduct; but should any cause of umbrage arise in future between the nations, it cannot be expected that advances will be again made, on the part of the English government, for an amicable explanation, however desirous it might be, unless the proposals originate here, and are couched in a style different from the language which is commonly held: it will otherwise be totally impossible to discuss any points that may occur, which, like the late business at Chittagong, would probably only require communication to end satisfactorily. To whom then can the blame be imputed? surely not to the English government, which has gone every honourable length to establish concord and confidence. They alone who are the advisers must be responsible for the consequences.

It is from the presumption, that his Majesty has no design to honour me with a personal interview, in the character of agent from the Governor General of India, that I write thus, a conclusion fairly drawn from the equivocal replies which you, and your coadjutors, gave to my questions yesterday at the Lotoo. Whilst the matter is yet undetermined, it is right you should know my opinion, as being apprized of the light in which it will be taken, you will have the means of forming a right judgment, and regulating your conduct accordingly. I will, with great pleasure, accept of an invitation to attend on the day of your festival, and join with the nobility in compliments to the throne, provided I receive assurances that on the 1st of October, when a reply is to be given to the Governor General's letter, I shall be received by his Majesty in person, as agent from the Governor General, and be honoured with a formal interview. Without such an assurance, specified in writing, it will be impossible for me to have the honour of joining in the general festivity.

Having thus delivered my sentiments with explicit freedom, I now close my correspondence, earnestly exhorting you, as a friend to your country and your king, to advise his Majesty with prudence and moderation, as many events to come may depend on the resolution of the present day, and an act which is to determine, whether or not any intercourse is in future to be held with a neighbouring and powerful state, is a matter of sufficient magnitude, at least to demand your most serious consideration.

MICHAEL SYMES,
Agent to the Court of Ava.

Ummerapoora. 20th Sept. 1795.

No. III.

Translation of a Letter from the King of Ava to Sir John Shore, Governor General, &c. &c.

THE Lord of Earth and Air, the Monarch of extensive Countries, the Sovereign of the kingdoms of *Sonahparinda, Tombadeva, Seawuttena, Zanieugnia, Soonaboomy*, in the district of *Hurry Mounza*, in the country of *Zemee, Hamaratta, Dzodinagara*, Sovereign of all these wide extended regions, Lord of the great cities of *Poucka Yama, Sirykettera, Sygnie, Leboo, Bamoo, Magone, Momeik, Momien, Neoum, Shoe Mona, Mobree, Quantong*, of all which countries and cities the governors and potentates send presents of respect and submission to the Royal Presence; also *Henzawuddy*, commonly called *Pegue*, the port of *Rangoou*, the port of *Bassien, Arracan*, the port of *Deniawuddy, Sandoway*, the port of *Dwarawuddy, Maoung*, the port of *Mickawuddy, Ramriè*, the port of *Ramawuddy, Moudema*, or *Martaban, Tavoy, Brieck*, or *Mergui*, and *Tenasserem*; ports belonging to his Majesty, where merchants trade and the inhabitants are protected; Proprietor of all kinds of precious stones, of the mines of Rubies, Agate, Lasni,* Sapphires, Opal; also the mines of Gold, Silver, Amber, Lead, Tin, Iron, and Petroleum; whence every thing desirable that the earth yields can be extracted, as the Trees, Leaves, and Fruit of excellence are produced in Paradise; Possessor of Elephants, Horses, Carriages, Fire Arms, Bows, Spears, Shields, and all manner of warlike weapons; Sovereign of valiant Generals and victorious Armies, invulnerable as the rock *Mahakonda*. *Mahanuggera, Ummerapoora*, the great and flourishing Golden City, illumined and illuminating, as the Habitation of Angels, lasting as the firmament, and embellished with Gold, Silver, Pearls, Agate, and the nine original† Stones; the Golden Throne, the seat of splendour, whence the royal mandate issues and protects mankind; the King who performs the ten duties, incumbent on all kings, called *Mangianterra*, all of which this great King duly performeth; whose understanding, by divine aid, is enlightened to guide his people in the right way, and preserve them

* I could not discover to what class of precious stones Lasni belonged.

† What these were I could not learn.

in pious obedience and the road of true religion; the ease and happiness of whom daily increase, under the auspices of such a Monarch; Master of the white, red, and mottled Elephants; may his praise be repeated, far as the influence of the sun and moon, of him whose servants place the fortunate foot of favour and confidence, like the blooming Lotos, on their obedient heads:—Such are the high Ministers, the Guardians of the State, from among whom the principal Woongee thus announceth.

The illustrious Governor General, the Representative of the King of England, the Governor of the Company at Calcutta in Bengal, having deputed Captain Michael Symes, with letters and presents to the Golden Feet, who happily arrived at the port of Rangoon on the eleventh of the month of Tagoo, in the Birman year one thousand one hundred and fifty-seven, and the Mohammedan year one thousand two hundred and nine, on the twenty-eighth of the month of Shabaan, of which the Governor of Henzawuddy transmitted regular information to the Golden Feet, together with a list of presents, as follows: two pieces of gold muslin, two pieces of silver muslin, four pieces of white flowered muslin, four pieces of silk, ten pieces of variegated silk, six pieces of plain satin, two pieces of flowered satin, two pieces of velvet, six corabahs* of rose water, one fine crystal stand with appendages, six crystal water cups bordered, two pair of candle shades, two crystal cups with silver feet, two large crystal bowls, two large mirrors, one double-barrel, one rifle-barrel, and one plain gun, one pair of pistols, six pair of golden slippers, twenty-five pieces of broad cloth, an electric machine, and the Bagwaat Geeta.† When this intelligence reached the Presence, orders were sent to the before-mentioned Governor, to expedite the journey of Captain Symes, with his attendants and baggage, also to provide suitable boats, and every thing requisite for his conveyance, and conformably to these orders, the Governor acted. When the deputation arrived near the great city of Pegham, officers of rank were sent from the Presence to meet Captain Symes, also a boat, such as is used by nobility, with two war-boats to tow it, likewise guards and attendants to do him honour, as is consistent with the duties of friendship. After his arrival, all necessaries and a suitable house, in an eligible place, were provided for his accommodation.

* A jar in which rose water is usually kept.

† A Shanscreet poem of high celebrity. See Mr. Wilkins's elegant translation.

From the east, from the city of *Oudeherit,** in the empire of Gondala Sirry Taing, comprehending Tartary, all the Nobles and Potentates whereof are dependant on the Sovereignty of China, the sublime Oudeboa, or Emperor, has sent to his Majesty three virtuous daughters;† intercourse and confidence subsist with his kingdom, presents are exchanged, and ambassadors pass between the monarchs. This year, according to custom, the illustrious messengers Intaloree, Kelloree, and Inloree, arrived at the Golden City with presents and rarities; near to the habitation of these a house was erected for the members of the English Deputation, neither far distant, nor very close, every thing they stood in need of was provided, and guards were stationed to protect them.

In the Birman year one thousand one hundred and fifty-seven, or year of the Higera one thousand two hundred and ten, and the sixteenth of the Birman month Toozalien, or fourteenth of the Mussulman month, Suffir, the Chinese Deputies and the Minister from Calcutta, Captain Michael Symes, bearing letters and presents, were attended to the Presence by officers of rank and dignity; and as on the mountain Meru, in the lofty Soudma, the *Deutas* resort to make obeisance to the divine Saggiami, so in the Golden Lotoo, where were seated the Engy Mien, or heir apparent, Meedaw, Lord of Chagaing, the eldest son of the Engy Mien,‡ Pie Mien, Lord of Prome, Bassein Mien, Lord of Bassein, and all the Royal Family, Ministers and Nobility, the English Gentlemen, together with the Deputies from China, were received with ceremonious attention, and the letters and the presents were there presented. In that splendid assembly they were honourably feasted, and at the same time was opened the friendly letter, which was read by the Reader of Government, and the contents, expressive of a desire to cement friendship, open a free intercourse, and encourage trade, were explained, and they gave to his Majesty the highest satisfaction. It was likewise mentioned that further particulars would be communicated by Captain Michael Symes, who accordingly addressed a Memorial to his Majesty, at which his Majesty was exceedingly pleased.

* I apprehend Oudeherit to be Jehol, the Tartarian residence of the Emperor of China.

† The King of Ava boasts of having three Chinese ladies, who, his courtiers say, were sent to him by the Emperor of China. Of the truth of this there seems room to doubt.

‡ The Prince Royal is called by various titles, Engy Praw, Engy Mien, Engy Tee Kien.

Captain Michael Symes in his Memorial states, that in the Birman year one thousand one hundred and fifty-six, and the Mohammedan year one thousand two hundred and nine, certain murderers and robbers of merchants and travellers having fled from Arracan into the district of Chittagong, the troops of this Government, and their leaders, entered the territories of the Company in quest of the offenders; but the English Government, being at that time unacquainted with the circumstances of the case, and uninformed what were the designs of those troops, did not think proper to deliver up the fugitives; and that, after a deliberate inquiry into the facts alledged against them, and a thorough knowledge of the matter, the criminals were apprehended and delivered up; and that, hereafter, upon application, (by letter) delinquents of this description will be surrendered, which will promote the welfare of both countries, and contribute to the satisfaction of their respective Sovereigns.

Captain Symes also desires, that from the English merchants and traders who come to the ports of this kingdom, only such duties, customs, and charges be exacted as are duly authorized, and established by ancient usage; and that merchants be allowed to carry their merchandize wheresoever they may think proper, and not be molested or prevented by any officer or subject under this Government; and after having disposed of their goods, they may be permitted to purchase, either personally or by agent, the produce of the country; and that no person at Rangoon be suffered to exact from merchants more than what is authorized; and that if the Government of Bengal should think fit hereafter to appoint a person to reside at Rangoon, on the part of the Company, to superintend mercantile concerns, and forward letters and presents to the Golden Feet, a right of residence be granted to such person; and that merchants or traders who think themselves aggrieved, shall have liberty to prefer their complaints at the Golden Feet, in any manner they may think most eligible; and that English merchants unacquainted with the Birman language, be permitted to employ whatever interpreters they choose, in the management of their affairs; and that English ships, when dismasted, and obliged to put into Birman ports by stress of weather, in want of repair and assistance, be aided by the officers of Government, and provided with necessaries to refit at the current prices of the country; and that on the frontiers of Arracan, on the borders of the river Naaf, a Chokey, or guard-house, and a village be established. Moreover, Captain Michael Symes notifies, that whatever Birman merchants shall resort to English ports, they shall be allowed, on paying the established duties, to buy and sell, and none shall molest or hinder them, and they shall have liberty to go and come, and barter at their pleasure; and that if any person oppress or act unjustly towards them, the law will take cognizance thereof, and punish the offender; and that if his Birman Majesty shall think fit to send any person to Calcutta or Bengal, or to any other English port, there to reside, for the purpose of superintending mercantile concerns, all representations made by such person to the English Government will be duly attended to, and justice done according to law; and that if any Birman ships put into English ports, through stress of weather, dismasted, and in want of repair, every assistance shall be given to such ships, on paying the equitable and accustomed rates; and that the enemies of the Birman nation shall not be assisted by the English with guns and weapons, powder, ball, or warlike stores; and in like manner, that the enemies of the English, as well European as Indian, shall not be aided by the Birmans, with stores, provisions, or timber, in any manner; and that if his Birman Majesty shall think fit to send any person to ratify these proposals, such person will be received with due regard, and meet with adequate attention.

These desires of Captain Michael Symes, and the contents of his Memorial, the tenor of which has been detailed, were conveyed to the golden ears of the Sovereign of Nobles and Potentates: therefore, seeing that the illustrious Governor General, the Representative of the King of England, has thus manifested his desire to cement friendship and amity, *I, the King Immortal, whose philanthropy is universal, whose anxiety for the benefit and welfare of all mankind never ceases,*

I DIRECT,

That all merchants of the English nation, who resort to Birman ports, shall pay customs, duties, charges, warehouse hire, searchers, &c. agreeably to former established usage.

English merchants are to be permitted to go to whatever part of the Birman dominions they think proper, either to buy or to sell, and they are on no account to be stopped, molested, or oppressed, and they shall have liberty to go to whatever town, village, or city they choose, for the purpose of buying, selling, or bartering; and whatsoever articles of the produce of this country they may be desirous of purchasing, they shall be allowed to do so, either in person, or by their agents: and English merchants having been long accustomed to trade to Birman ports without molestation, IT IS COMMANDED, that they continue their trade in future without molestation; and should the English Company think proper to depute a person to reside at Rangoon, to superintend mercantile affairs, maintain a friendly intercourse, and forward letters to the Presence, it is ordered, that such person shall have a right of residence; and should any English merchant be desirous of sending a representation, the officers of Government, in any port, district, and town, shall forward such representation; or if a merchant should be inclined to present in person, a petition at the Golden Feet, he shall be allowed to come to the Golden Presence for that purpose:—This is peremptory.—And as English merchants are unacquainted with the Birman language, they are to be allowed to employ whatever interpreters they think proper; and as, in the stormy season, English ships are often dismasted, and driven into Birman ports by stress of weather, ships in this unfortunate predicament shall be supplied with all necessary wood, workmen, &c. at the current rates of the country; and the arrangement that Captain Michael Symes has in friendship proposed, relative to commercial concerns, for the encouragement of merchants and traders, the Ministers of the Palace have received the Royal Command to signify to the Governors and Killedars of the several ports and districts, that such arrangement is to be observed and carried into effect: and respecting the establishment of a Chokey and village on the frontiers of Arracan, on the banks of the river Naaf, as there is strict and confidential friendship with the King of England, there can in future be no difference or distinction between the countries; and with respect to the desire, that aid should not be given by this state to the enemies of England, as well European as Indian, and that such enemies should not be assisted at our ports with warlike implements, timber, or provisions, it is to be observed, that, to purchase warlike weapons, lead, and powder, is forbidden to all nations; but when merchants come to trade, they will be allowed to carry away their commodities, agreeably to the usage of merchants. All the requisitions made by Captain Symes respecting customs, timber, searchers, and commercial matters, are notified to Killedars,* Governors, Guards of the Gauts,† and persons in authority, and observance of the orders issued thereupon strictly enjoined. And to Captain

* Commanders of forts. † Passes.

Michael Symes has been presented, as a mark of favour, one ruby and one sapphire ring; and to Mr. Wood, and Dr. Buchanan, each, one ruby ring; also to Captain Symes, a precious stone, called *Mobee*, weighing three viss and forty tackall, and a stone of jasper, weighing eight viss, also two elephant's teeth, weighing thirty-four viss: these have been delivered to the care of Captain Symes. The Queen, likewise, has presented him with a ruby ring of nine stones, a silver box weighing ninety tackall, * and a silver cup of eleven tackall and three quarters weight; also, another silver box, weighing forty-four tackall, and another cup weighing six tackall, and two silver trays, one weighing sixty-six tackall, the other seventy-seven, and two gilt trays of a different shape, and two large boxes; and from the second Queen, called Myack Nandoh, one ruby ring, and three sapphire rings, and a chest with a lock, and two gilt trays, and three painted cups. These several articles are sent to the illustrious Governor General, who is intrusted in confidence by the King of England, with the administration of India, and who, ever anxious for the welfare and prosperity of his country, encourages and assists Birmans that trade to English ports. In like manner, friendship is happily maintained with the Chinese Government, and a constant intercourse is preserved. It will therefore be right that the illustrious Governor General do acquaint the King of England, of the friendship that is, on this occasion, established, and which it is hoped will be permanent.

* A tackall weighs a little more than half an ounce.

Note.—The following were explained to me as the ten duties incumbent on all kings, which are alluded to in the foregoing letter:—*Dhanaan*, universal beneficence; *Seelaan*, daily prayer; *Owerodaan*, to shew mercy; *Dhasameda*, to exact only a tenth; *Dherma*, justice; *Yamatza*, to punish without anger; *Boumee*, to support mankind as the earth sustains the weight of all creation: *Abeedziet*, to employ prudent commanders; *Mantha*, to listen to counsel; *Deige Kunna*, to avoid pride.

No. IV.

Translation of the Royal Mandate, accompanying the Letter to the Governor General.

To all Commanders of Garrisons and Governors of Sea Ports, in like Virtue as to the Maywoon of Henzawuddy (Pegue).

THE Source of Greatness and Dignity Celestial, whose threshold is as the firmaments, and whose suppliants, when he places the Golden Foot of Majesty on their fortunate heads, like the blooming lotos, expand with confidence unbounded: —such are the Ministers of exalted rank, the Guardians of the Empire, from among whom the high and transcendant Woongee proclaims these orders.

Governor of Henzawuddy, whose title is Mein, Lla, Noo, Retha; Governor of the Waters, whose title is Raywoon; Collector of the King's revenues, whose title is Ackawoon; Commander of the Troops, whose title is Chekey:

Whereas English merchants resort to the port of Rangoon to carry on trade in friendship, good faith, and confidence in the Royal protection, therefore, when merchants come to the port of Rangoon, duties for Godown (warehouse), *Rabeat* (searchers or appraisers), and other charges, shall be regulated according to the former established rates, and no more on any pretence shall be taken.

English merchants who have paid the port duties, shall be allowed to go to whatever part of the country they think fit, having obtained a certificate and order from the Maywoon, or Governor of the province; and whatever goods English merchants wish to purchase in return, they shall not be impeded, or molested, or prevented in their barter, bargain, or purchase; and if it should be judged expedient to establish any person, on the part of the English Company* at Rangoon, for the purpose of trade, and to forward letters or presents to the King, to such person a right of residence is granted.

If any English merchant be aggrieved, or think that he suffers oppression, he may complain either through the governor of the province, by petition to the Throne, or prefer his complaint in person; and as Englishmen are, for the most

* The word Company is omitted in the Persian, but inserted in the original Birman.

part, unacquainted with the Birman tongue, they may employ whatever interpreters they think proper, previously acquainting the King's principal interpreter, what person they mean to employ.

English ships driven into Birman ports by stress of weather, and in want of repairs, on due notice of their distress being given to the officers of Government, such vessels shall be expeditiously supplied with workmen, timber, iron, and every requisite, and the work shall be done, and the supplies granted, at the current rates of the country.

As the English have long had commercial connections with the Birman nation, and are desirous of extending it, they are to be allowed to come and depart at their pleasure without hindrance; and seeing that the illustrious Governor of Calcutta in Bengal, on the part of the King of England, has sent tokens of friendship to the Golden Feet; these orders are therefore issued for the benefit, welfare, and protection of the English people.

" The original in Birman authenticated by the Great Seal."

No. V.

CAMMUAZA, *or the* CEREMONY *used at the Induction of a Birman into the Order of Priesthood, called* PHONGHI, *or* RHAHAAN.

PREVIOUS to ordination the Sabiet* and the yellow garment of priesthood shall be delivered to the Candidate; he shall then be enjoined to repeat thrice, with a distinct voice, the following sentence to the *Upizeé*† that presides:

"Venerable father, I acknowledge you to be my *Upizeé*, my preceptor, and ghostly guide." Having spoken these words he shall approach the *Cammuazara*, or him who reads the sacred Cammua, who shall say as follows:

"O Candidate, dost thou acknowledge this to be thy *Sabiet*, and these thy sacred vestments?" to which the Candidate shall audibly answer "Yea." The Cammuazara shall then command him to recede to the distance of twelve cubits, and turning towards the audience shall address them as follows.

"Let this sacred assembly of the professors of our holy religion attend to what I now impart. The Candidate who stands in your presence, humbly, and with due submission, implores of the Upizee to invest him with our holy function; and as the present time seemeth good for the purpose, and convenient unto this assembly, I will forthwith duly admonish the Candidate.

"O thou who seekest admission into our sacred order, be attentive unto my words, and beware lest on this occasion you utter an untruth, or criminally attempt to conceal aught from our knowledge: learn that there are certain incapacities and defects, which render a person unfit to receive the holy induction; moreover, when in this reverend assembly you shall be interrogated respecting such defects, you are to answer truly, and declare whatever incapacities you may labour under, of what nature soever they may be, and how they originated; nor ought you to stand silent, or decline your head when you are interrogated, through shame or fear. Now, even at this time, in the presence of this assembly, may any one of the brotherhood interrogate you at his pleasure.

* A blue lackered box borne by the priests when they perambulate to collect eleemosynary provisions. See page 210.

† The chief or principal of the monastery.

"O Candidate, art thou affected with the leprosy, or any impure disease?" To which the Candidate shall reply, "From such complaints I am free."

"Hast thou the scrofula, St. Anthony's fire, any schirrous affection, cancer, or itch? Hast thou an asthma or oppression of the lungs? Hast thou any hereditary complaint arising from a tainted source of blood? Art thou sprung from dwarfs or giants, or art thou under the influence of sorcerers, evil genii or the *Natt** of the woods and the mountains?"

"From all these disqualifications I am free."

"O Candidate, art thou a man perfect in thy virility, and all thy members?" "I am perfect."—"Art thou legitimate?" "I am legitimate."—"Art thou the bounden vassal of any lord, or the slave of any man in power?" "I am not." "Art thou free from debt?" "I am."—"Have thy parents granted thee permission, and hast thou attained the complete age of twenty years?" "My parents have consented, and I have attained the age of twenty years."—"Are thy vestments and Sabiet ready?" "They are ready."

"O Candidate, by what appellation wilt thou be known?" "By that of *Naca* (sinner)."—"What is the title of thy Upizeê?" "Assentriit (perfection)."

The Cammuazara shall thus proceed:

"Reverend Divines, I beseech you attend unto my words. The Candidate humbly intreats of his Upizeê admission into our holy order, and him have I duly admonished. Doth the present appear unto this assembly a meet and proper time that he should come forward?" The Priests reply "Come forward." The Candidate having advanced twelve cubits shall then say, "Venerable and holy men, I, a lowly suppliant, with humility implore your aid. Oh! if pity dwell within your breasts, snatch me from the walk of death, from the ways of sinners, and place me in the holy habitation, the seat of virtue and divine perfection." This intreaty shall be repeated three times, after which the reader of the Cammua thus proceeds:

"Reverend Fathers here convened, the Candidate in your presence, solicits holy orders from the venerable Upizeê. It appears that he is free from all defects, corporeal infirmities, and mental incapacities: he has likewise received the Sabiet; and the sacred vestments, and in the name, and with the sanction of the venerable Upizeê, intreats induction. Let those who assent to his admission keep silence,

* Aerial spirits.

but let such as object, and deem the Candidate a person unworthy to be received, speak out and declare their motives in presence of this assembly." These words shall be thrice repeated, and if no person dissent, and all are silent, the reception of the Candidate is determined on; when relinquishing his state of imperfection, he shall be translated into that of purity, and thenceforward be considered as one of the elect.

The Cammuazara shall then proceed:—" Let the Reverend Fathers present note with precision, under what shade of the foot, what hour, day, and season this ordination has been completed. Let the Candidate attend to the four following duties which it is incumbent on him to observe; and to the faults hereafter enumerated under four heads, which he must carefully avoid.

" First, a principal duty of our holy function consists in procuring maintenance by perambulation; by laborious and incessant motion* of the muscles of the legs. You must seek gratuitous sustenance by continual motion, and whatever superfluities you collect, shall be daily bestowed by you on those who are in want. Victuals that are offered to you in particular, given to the society in general, sent with letters desiring your prayers, or presented on the hebdomadal festivals of the increasing and decreasing moon, all such gifts may be accepted and distributed."

To which the Candidate shall reply, " As I am instructed so will I perform."

The reader of the Cammua thus proceeds:—" Secondly, It is part of the duty of a priest through humility to soil his garments with dust, and wear sepulchral vestments. But should the liberality of good men munificently reward your pious labours, it shall be allowed thee to wear cloth called *choma*; also silk or cotton yellow cloth; yellow woollen cloth; cloth made of the bark of certain trees, or the feathers of certain birds. Such vestments thou mayest use."

To which the Candidate shall reply, " As I am instructed," &c.

The reader of the Cammua continues:—" Thou shalt dwell as becometh our order, in houses built beneath the shade of the trees of the forest; in houses built of wood, or of masonry; houses having a pyramidical roof, of a triangular or quadrangular form, adorned with flowers and figures; houses raised on posts, or built on arches. Such dwellings mayest thou inhabit."

* See page 211.

Candidate :—" As I am instructed," &c.

The reader of the Cammua :—" Fourthly, Thou shalt turn to use such things as men cast away; and thou shalt search for healing qualities in simples, in which no virtue is supposed to exist. The following articles may be used medicinally; sweet and sour milk, oil, honey, sugar and syrups."

Candidate :—" As I am instructed," &c.

Cammuazara :—" Being now admitted an associate of the virtuous and immaculate, thou shalt not indulge thyself in any gratification either social or solitary, after the manner of seculars; nor shalt thou frequent the company of laymen, or of women. He who acts thus can no longer be numbered among the elect: sooner shall the severed head be joined again to the neck, and life restored to the breathless body, than a Rhahaan, who committeth fornication, recover his lost purity, and be received again within the sacred pale. Beware therefore lest thou pollute thyself with the knowledge of woman.

" Again, It is forbidden thee to steal, or by any unjust means possess thyself of the property of another, even though the amount should not exceed the fourth part of a tackall; for whatsoever Phongi or Rhahaan sinneth even to that small amount, he shall be divested of his sacred character, and be expelled the brotherhood. He who is guilty of such a crime can no more be restored to his pristine state of purity, than the blasted tree can bud anew, and bear fresh flowers and fruit. Remember therefore, O Candidate, and through thy mortal journey beware of theft.

" Again, Thou shalt not deprive any animal of life; such deeds are unlawful and profane. Thou shalt not take away life even from the smallest insect, or the vilest reptile. Sooner shall the cleft rock unite its severed fragments, and become whole, than he who destroys the vital principle in any animal be readmitted into our sacred institution. Avoid with caution this heinous transgression.

" Again, The holy professors of our religion are strictly forbidden to arrogate to themselves aught on account of the sanctity of their profession, or pretend to be endowed with any supernatural gift or power, such as *Meipo*, or endeavour to obtain the offering usually given to persons so endowed. Whosoever is actuated by such culpable pride shall fall like the lofty mountain palm beneath the stroke of the wood-cutter. Through life therefore, O my brother, observe these precepts; and act as thou art now commanded."

To which the Candidate shall with humility reply, "As I am instructed, so will I perform."—He shall then withdraw.

GLOSSARY.

AMEENDOZAAN, a Birman lawyer.
Assaywoon, Paymaster-General.
Attawoon, a Privy Counsellor.

Boomien, a General.

Carianer, a Pastoral race of People.
Chaingeewoon, Master of the Elephants.
Chekey, a Lieutenant.
Chobwa, a tributary Prince.
Colar, a Stranger, Foreigner.

Daywoon, Armourer-bearer to the King.

Engy Teekien, the Prince Royal.

Gaudma, the name of the Birman Idol.
Gnapee, a species of Sprat which the Birmans pickle.

Henza, a Goose, the symbol of the Birman nation.

Kayn, a race of Mountaineers.
Kioum, a Monastery, or residence of Rhahaans or Priests.
Kioup, a small river.

Leedegee, Chief or Steersman of a boat.
Lotoo, the Hall where the Grand Council of the Nation assemble.

Manchegee, the Birman name for the province of Yunan in China.

Maywoon, Viceroy of a Province.
Mioup, a River.
Miou, a City, a Town, a District.
Miou Gee, Chief of a District or Town.
Moonshee, a Mussulman Professor of Letters.

Nakhaan, a Register.

Phonghi, an inferior Order of Priesthood.
Piasath, the regal Spire that distinguishes the dwelling of the Monarch, and the Temples of the Divinity.
Pillaw, an Indian Dish, esteemed a great delicacy.
Praw, a Temple, a Lord, also a title given by an inferior to a superior.
Pundit, a learned Hindoo.
Pymon, a Banker, an Assayer of Metal.

Raywoon, an Officer of distinction, Governor of a Town.
Rhahaan, a Priest.
Rhoom, a public Hall, the Court of Justice.
Rua, a Village.

Sandohgaan, Master of the Ceremonies.
Sandozien, an Officer whose business is to read public documents.
Seree Dogee, a principal Secretary.
Seree Miou, a provincial Secretary.
Seree, a Clerk.
Shawbunder, an Intendant of the Port.
Siredaw, High Priest.

Tackall, a piece of Silver of about *2s. 6d.* value.
Talien, a Native of Pegue.
Tallepoin, a Preceptor, a name by which the Rhahaans or Priests were known to Europeans.
Tee, the Umbrella of a Pagoda, or Temples of the Divinity.

Teekien, a Prince.

Teelee, a War-boat.

Terrezogee, an Officer of an inferior dignity.

Tsaloe, the distinguishing chain of Nobility.

Woongee, First Counsellor of State.

Woondock, Second Counsellor of State.

THE END.

DIRECTIONS TO THE BINDER.

BOTANICAL PLATES.